from Mom and Dad

Christmas 1966

The
SEVENTEEN COOKBOOK

The SEVENTEEN COOKBOOK

BY
THE EDITORS OF
SEVENTEEN
MAGAZINE

ILLUSTRATED BY Alice Golden

THE MACMILLAN COMPANY, NEW YORK

COLLIER-MACMILLAN LIMITED, LONDON

Second Printing 1964

THE MACMILLAN COMPANY, NEW YORK

COLLIER-MACMILLAN CANADA, LTD., TORONTO, ONTARIO

Library of Congress catalog card number: 63–17089

Printed in the United States of America

DESIGNED BY ANDREW P. ZUTIS

Foreword

$\mathcal{C}$ooking is a convivial art. A painting can be admired in private, a poem cherished secretly, but a delicious snack, a mouth-watering dessert, a glorious meal are all meant to be enjoyed with a family, a host of friends —or one very special friend. Perhaps that is why it is wise to learn how to cook early, for friendship and its expression are especially important during the teen years.

Admiration is important, too, and cooking leads to that rainbow as well. To many men (and *most* teen-age boys) cooking is one of the feminine mysteries, one they can heartily appreciate. With an ever-hungry young man, few things enhance a girl's stock *as a girl* as swiftly, as surely, as something really good to eat that she made herself.

In planning this cookbook, we have tried to meet the needs of *all* types of teen-age girls—the girl who is engaged and wants (so rightly) to develop the skills that will make her a fine homemaker; the girl who likes to entertain her friends at home and experiment with different and exciting party foods; the girl who is acting home manager, filling in as grocery shopper and dinner chef for a busy mother—now and then, or as often as five times a week.

Why do these girls need a cookbook all their own? Because they are learning to cook in a way their mother never could—as active participants in today's food world, a world of boxed mixes, convenience foods, and zip-open packages.

For the neophyte, who may never have entered the kitchen except to raid the refrigerator, there are step-by-step recipes and menus in this cookbook to help her feel confident and at ease. For the more experienced cook, there is a collection of favorite recipes ranging from appetizers to desserts, sandwiches to sukiyaki. The hostess of the biggest record hops in town will find recipes in crowd-sized proportions. And every menu is planned with the knowledge that teens, like everyone else, eat with their eyes before they eat with their forks. Attractiveness counts.

With the aid of *The Seventeen Cookbook*, the teen-age girl can learn to cook completely on her own, she can develop into an expert, she can serve her dishes with flair, she can be the best hostess in her crowd. For she will learn the two basic truths of the culinary world:

Cooking is more than a means to an end: in its most exciting, satisfying form it becomes an end in itself—an expression of one's personality.

And the secret ingredient in any good meal is a good cook.

Enid A. Haupt

Contents

THE PARTY COOKBOOK

THE BEGINNER'S COOKBOOK

You Can Be
a *Wonderful* Cook

*D*o you know how to boil water?

If not, don't worry. We tell you just how to do it on page 14. In fact, this book has been planned to hold just the information a teen-ager is apt to need about how to cook—for herself, her family and for the crowd. If you *are* a beginner, take the time to read through the definitions in this first chapter. Even if you don't remember them all, you'll remember that they are *there* and you can find each one by consulting the index. Then go chapter by chapter through the Beginner's Cookbook—trying dishes and meals as you go along. Everything in this section is especially slanted to new cooks. Once you feel confident of your own competence, jump ahead. There are dinner dishes and party foods galore. In fact, we hope there's everything you want.

Oh, you *can* boil water?

Fine!—this book is for you, too. It includes the recipes that teens have been reading and trying from recent issues of *Seventeen*. It doesn't tell you how to press a duck or make your own mincemeat. But it is a practical collection of the recipes you'll find most useful through your teen years —recipes for your lunch box, the meals you cook on Mom's night out, the record hop you're giving for twenty and the dinner for eighty which is being given by the church young people's club.

Happy cooking!

BRASS TACKS DEPARTMENT

If the kitchen seems like a scary area, this chapter is for you. Here are the most important do's and don'ts for using the kitchen and, equally important, some explanations of what the kitchen contains.

KITCHEN DO'S AND DON'TS

Leave the kitchen at least as neat as you found it. Wash, dry and put away all the equipment you've used. Be sure the sink is left spotless and dry. Mop up all spills, and sweep the floor if necessary.

Cook with proper heat at all times. High heat on surface units is needed only to bring water or fat up to the right temperature—turn it to medium or low as soon as possible, so you maintain proper heat. (Too high heat encourages boil-overs and boil-dries, both of which are, at the least, very inconvenient.) If you are stirring or tasting frequently, provide yourself with a spoon rest (a saucer or a fold of paper towel), and you'll avoid another hard-to-clean-up spot. Use sudsy water, baking soda or non-abrasive cleaners on the range; also nylon or plastic scouring pads.

Bake neatly, too. If you're making something which might boil over (cherry pie, for example) place a cookie sheet or piece of aluminum foil on the shelf below it (not on the oven bottom) to catch any spills. Use the heat called for in the recipe; burning or smoking foods can discolor the oven's interior. If you should stain the oven, wait until it cools; then clean it. Solutions of ammonia or baking soda (one-fourth cup of either to a pint of water) are effective; so is commercial oven cleaner, used according to label directions.

Broil the smart way. Always preheat the broiler. To save cleaning-up time, line the broiling pan with foil. You may cover the rack, too, but you *must* puncture the foil frequently to permit drainage. If food is especially high in fat (like pork sausage), it's wise to drain off some fat midway in the broiling period. Let the broiling pan cool before you try to clean it.

Refrigerate foods promptly when necessary. If you've taken a quart of milk out of the refrigerator to measure a cupful, put the rest back at once. An hour at room temperature might cause the milk to sour. It's old-fashioned to wait until hot foods cool completely before refrigerating them—just wait until they stop steaming, then cover and chill. When in doubt—cover! Even the aroma of an uncut cantaloupe can permeate butter!

Protect the kitchen drain. *Nothing* should go down it except water and similar liquids. Keep the sink strainer in place to filter out small bits of food. Place waste grease in cans, cover well and put in the trash. Wrap coffee grounds in foil and ditto.

Take pride in working neatly as well as in being a good cook.

THE THINGS YOU'LL USE

The guides which follow are designed to help you understand the many objects you'll find in the cupboards and drawers of your kitchen. (Of

course, if your mother is a real gadget collector she'll have a hundred things
we haven't listed, but these are the basics.)

Baking Pan Primer

For pies, use glass or dull-finished aluminum pans, eight or nine inches
across the top. The standard plain-edge pan lets you make a pretty trimming on the crust edge. Pans with high fluted edges are good for fruit
pies since they prevent boil-overs.

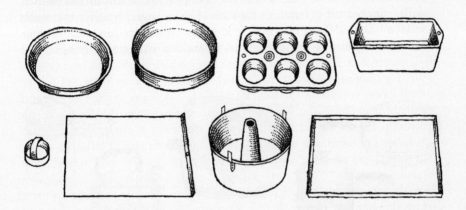

For cakes, use shiny aluminum or glass pans. Most recipes call for deep
eight- or nine-inch layer pans or eight-inch square pans. Use wire racks
for cooling cakes.

Breads can be baked in many shapes. For cupcakes and muffins, you'll need
muffin pans; a common size has six cups measuring two and one-fourth
inches across the top. For bread and loaf cakes, use loaf pans, about nine
by five by three inches (these can serve as casserole dishes, too). Use
round cutters to shape cookies and biscuits, and for baking them, use
a cookie sheet—a flat, rectangular pan, often with only one rim.

Angel cakes and spongecakes are usually baked in a high-sided tube pan,
preferably with a removable bottom. A long loaf pan may also be used.
Angel cake pans should have tiny "legs" on the top rim—these keep the
cake's surface off the counter as the cake cools upside down. Jelly rolls
are baked in baking trays with shallow sides. The usual size is fifteen by
ten inches—it can double as a cookie sheet.

Size is important—always use the one called for in the recipe.

Glass or aluminum? Aluminum is light and unbreakable with a surface that
heats evenly. It can be scoured easily with steel-wool soap pads or fine
cleansing powder. Ovenproof glass is very sturdy. Because it cooks food

quickly, your heat setting should be twenty-five degrees lower than the recipe calls for. To loosen stains on glass, use three tablespoons of baking soda in the "soak water." Glass is especially attractive for cakes or pies served warm from the oven.

PANS FOR RANGE-TOP COOKING

Skillets, for good results, should be suited in size for the job they do. Don't overcrowd. To cook four chops, for example, use a ten- or twelve-inch skillet. On the other hand, to cook two eggs, a large pan gives too much surface heat. (Which is why a little bacon in a large pan overbrowns.) When you clean a frying pan, avoid sudden changes in temperature

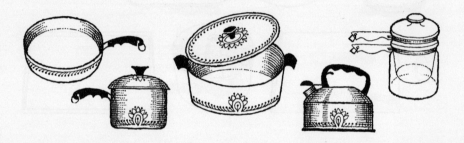

—like putting a hot pan under cold running water. Soak it in hot water instead.

Saucepans, too, follow the "right size" rule. For best taste and maximum nutrition, use the smallest saucepan possible (and the least water) to cook vegetables. For bulky vegetables like spinach or cabbage, use a two- or three-quart saucepan. Cook the more compact vegetables like peas or carrots in a one-quart size. For puddings or sauces, a three-cup pan is convenient.

A large kettle or Dutch oven is useful for long-simmering pot roasts, stews, etc. It should have thick sides to hold heat properly and keep the food from drying out or sticking. It's handy, too, for party-size cooking of spaghetti, corn.

A teakettle is the best utensil for boiling water quickly because it's especially designed for maximum heat retention. Use it not only to boil the water for tea or coffee, but to save time in cooking frozen vegetables. (Pour the boiling water over them.)

A double boiler is necessary to melt chocolate, make cream fillings and custards. The water in the bottom acts as insurance against overheating and prevents scorching or curdling. Check the bottom part occasionally to make sure it doesn't boil dry.

Good Knives and How To Use Them

The French cook's knife is a large knife with a blade which looks like an elongated triangle. It's ideal for chopping and dicing as well as for slicing large fruits and vegetables. To chop: hold knife tip on cutting board and move the handle up and down, sliding food under the blade.

The short-bladed paring knife is handy for a variety of little jobs such as paring potatoes and removing the eyes from them, trimming and peeling small fruits and vegetables. The blade should have a well-tapered, well-pointed tip.

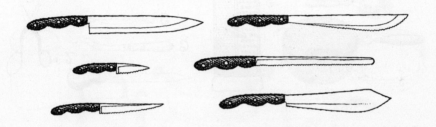

The trimmer (or long paring knife) is useful for peeling and trimming large fruits and vegetables. Use it also to slice small foods (potatoes, lemons) or to halve rolls or buns.

The carving knife has a long pointed blade. With an accompanying fork, it is well suited to slicing any meat. It also doubles as an excellent bread and cake knife.

The slicer with its blunt-tipped blade is used primarily to carve boneless roasts or to slice the white meat from turkey or chicken. It may also be used for shredding (cabbage, lettuce) and as a bread knife.

The butcher knife has a strong, thick blade tailored for heavy work. Use it to open squash or pumpkin, to disjoint a chicken, to cut up raw meat for stews or casseroles or to divide a block of frozen vegetables.

Buying guide: Look for rustproof, high-carbon steel blades which are riveted to handles. Check balance of knife: hold it in your hand as if you were going to use it. Is it comfortable?

Safety tips: If washing by hand, separate knives from other utensils and tableware, rinse, dry and put them away at once. Store knives separately in a divided drawer or on a wall rack. Be sure that the storage place is well out of reach of children.

Care: To keep knives sharp, cut *only* on a wooden surface. Avoid hitting blade against bone or any hard surface. To give it long life, use each knife only for the purpose for which it was designed. Follow the manufacturer's directions for sharpening.

Kitchen Helpers

The kitchen drawer may contain gadgets galore—but here are the items you're most likely to need and use:

1. A vegetable brush scrubs baking potatoes and beets clean for in-the-skin cooking.

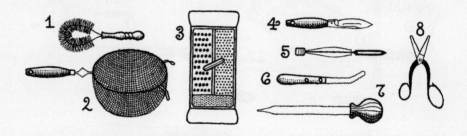

2. A large strainer drains vegetables, canned foods and may also be used to strain or purée foods. A small strainer catches tea leaves, tiny seeds and the pulp in fruit juices.
3. Graters may have several sizes put together on one handle or each size may be a single tool. Small-holed graters are for orange or lemon peel, hard cheese like Parmesan. Large holes are for softer cheese. Some graters also have a slicing blade for cheese, cucumbers.
4. An apple corer has a pointed tip, rounded cutting edge. With it, you can pierce the top of the fruit and neatly remove the core with one corkscrew motion.
5. A vegetable parer pares potatoes, apples, carrots, cucumbers and turnips.
6. A grapefruit knife separates fruit wedges from the peel and membrane for easy eating. Its curved serrated blade slips around and under each wedge.
7. A baster (glass or plastic) is used to baste or glaze roasting meat and scoops up makings of gravy from the bottom of the roasting pan.
8. Kitchen shears snip marshmallows, dates, cut up chives, cut out cake-pan liners, etc. Since the blades are serrated and strong, the scissors may also be used to disjoint poultry.
9. Tongs are useful to lift or arrange food too hot to handle.

10. A pastry brush is used to spread melted butter, egg yolk or frosting glaze on hot breads, rolls, pies. The best ones have natural bristles.
11. A rotary grater is used to make powder of dry bread cubes, nuts or dry cheese and to grate chocolate fine.
12. A wire whisk aerates cream sauce, beats eggs.
13. A rubber spatula is an excellent tool for folding foods together; also for scraping bowls whistling-clean.
14. A narrow metal spatula is used to frost cake, lift small cookies from baking sheet, level off solids in measuring cup or spoon.

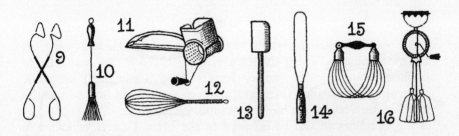

15. A pastry blender made of wire semicircles attached to a handle speeds the "cutting in" step in pastry making. It also makes quick work of chopping hard-cooked eggs.
16. A rotary beater whips cream and beats eggs. The handle should be comfortable and the beaters should run almost noiselessly. Tip: oil working parts occasionally with salad oil.

CANS, JARS AND OPENERS

Canned foods are great timesavers, but even these have their secrets. Read the label when you buy canned foods. It will tell you the ingredients and weight and may also give the number of servings, suggestions for heating or recipes for using contents. By experimenting, you'll find the particular brands you like best. Rust or light dents which have not caused leakage won't hurt the food inside, but there should be no bulging at either end of the can. Don't waste liquid from canned foods—use it in soups, sauces. Warm canned vegetables in their own liquid, over low heat to avoid sticking or overcooking. Then drain, season, add butter or margarine. Since the inside of the can has been sterilized, it will store leftovers safely —cover, refrigerate and use within three days. You might prefer to store fruit juices in decanters.

Can openers should leave a clean, smooth edge on can. Clean the blades after each use, following manufacturer's directions. If only an ancient spear-type can opener is available, punch point into lid at the rim and seesaw the blade around can's edge. Open evaporated milk with a beverage can opener. Make a large hole at one side, a small one opposite. Some openers will do both at once.

Jar openers are of several kinds to suit different types of lids. A vacuum lid with a lip can be lifted with a hook opener, but a device with a pointed end and squeeze-together handles does it better. If twist-off lids give trouble, there are openers which clamp over the lid, make turning easier. Other steps to loosen stubborn lids: run hot water over lid or tap edge of top gently on hard surface.

SMALL APPLIANCES

Always read the manufacturer's instructions carefully before using an electric appliance. They will tell you how to use it best and how to clean it. Many booklets provide recipes. Even if you don't use those particular ones, reading them will help you understand how to put the appliance to work for the food you want to prepare.

Heating directions should be followed to the letter. Correct temperature setting is especially important to keep the timing right and the food from sticking or burning.

A waffle baker, besides making waffles, may also have interchangeable grills for toasting sandwiches.

An electric fry pan offers carefully controlled heat for frying eggs or bacon, making skillet casseroles, browning meats, etc.

A blender will make frothy milk shakes, reduce nuts and bread crumbs to powder, chop or purée fruits or vegetables. Be careful not to overload the container and always begin blending with your hand on the cover, in case the mixture foams high at first.

A toaster is almost a necessity. Most important rule: never use a metal tool to pry loose half of an English muffin or any other food caught inside. Instead, disconnect toaster (to avoid a shock) and use a wooden spoon to gently ease out whatever is caught.

A deep-fat fryer offers the constantly controlled, even temperature so important for deep-fat cooking.

A griddle offers a nonstick surface for frying or pan-broiling and, usually, a drain to carry away excess grease. Handy for pancakes, bacon, grilled sandwiches, hamburgers, franks.

HOW TO MEASURE

Your basic set of measuring tools should contain:

A liquid-measuring cup, marked to show thirds, quarters and halves, and sometimes ounces, too. The one-cup line must be below the rim of the cup. Two-cup and one-quart sizes are also available.

A nest of dry measures. Each fits within the other: one-fourth cup, one-third cup, one-half cup and one cup.

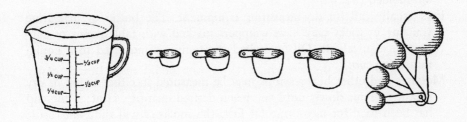

A set of measuring spoons. These come marked: one tablespoon, one teaspoon, one-half teaspoon and one-fourth teaspoon.

The essential facts of measuring are:

1 quart = 4 cups	⅓ cup = 5 tablespoons plus
1 pint = 2 cups	1 teaspoon
1 cup = 8 fluid ounces	1 fluid ounce = 2 tablespoons
1 cup = 16 tablespoons	3 teaspoons = 1 tablespoon

Liquids—milk, water, syrup—are measured like this: Set liquid measure on an even surface, eyes level with measure mark wanted (1). Fill to that line. If the surface is uneven or if you look from an angle, the measurement may be inaccurate. In using measuring spoons, pour liquid to barely full.

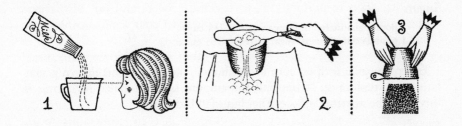

Solids—sugar, shortening, baking soda—are measured like this: Fill the container (cup or spoon) to overflowing (2), then skim off the top with edge of a straight spatula. For one-eighth teaspoon, fill a one-fourth teaspoon measure and level off as above. With knife tip, divide down the center; push half of contents off the side.

Flour must be sifted before measuring. Sift it onto waxed paper, then gently pour or spoon it into cup. *Don't* pack down. Level off with edge of spatula. (Some brands of flour do not require sifting; follow manufacturer's directions.)

Confectioners' sugar is sifted and measured like flour.

Brown sugar may be lumpy; if so, roll it with a rolling pin or sift it before measuring. Then pack it firmly into a dry-measuring cup—it should come out molded (3).

Fats usually call for dry-measuring equipment. The butter or margarine you buy in sticks may have wrappers marked with tablespoons or cup-fraction equivalents. Oil or melted shortening is measured in a liquid-measuring cup.

Molasses and other heavy syrups may be measured in either liquid or dry measures. Pour slowly until you reach desired quantity. Hint: if the cup has been used for measuring fat first, the molasses will slide out easily; otherwise, scrape with rubber spatula.

EQUIVALENTS AND SUBSTITUTES

Use these tips when you're trying to decide how much to buy or when, in an emergency, you must substitute.

Fats

1 ounce butter (or any fat) = 2 tablespoons
¼ pound (1 stick) butter = 8 tablespoons (½ cup)

Butter or margarine may be used in place of vegetable shortening *except* in quick-mix cakes or piecrust. You may always substitute vegetable shortening for butter or margarine unless the butter taste is important. Cooking oil may be substituted for melted fat.

Sugars

1 pound granulated or brown sugar = 2¼ cups
1 pound confectioners' sugar, sifted = 3½ cups

Except in cake recipes, corn syrup, honey, molasses or maple syrup may be used to replace up to one-half the amount of sugar called for. NOTE: if this thins the mixture, reduce other liquid in the recipe.

Flour

1 pound all-purpose flour, sifted = 4 cups

Substitutes

For thickening: 2 tablespoons flour = 1 tablespoon cornstarch
1 cup sifted all-purpose flour = 1 cup plus 2 tablespoons sifted cake flour

Dairy Products

1 pound American cheese, grated = 4 cups
½ pint heavy cream (1 cup) = 2 cups whipped cream

Substitutes

1 cup whole milk = ½ cup evaporated milk plus ½ cup water
1 cup sour milk = 1 cup fresh milk plus 1 tablespoon vinegar
In baking: 1 cup light cream = ⅞ cup milk plus 3 tablespoons butter or margarine

Other Ingredients

4-ounce can of shelled walnuts = 1 cup
1 box (15 ounces) seedless raisins = 2½ cups
1 pound apples (3 medium) = 3 cups, sliced
1 can (3½ ounces) flaked coconut = 1⅓ cups
Juice of 1 lemon = 3 tablespoons
¼ pound marshmallows = 16 marshmallows (2 cups miniatures)

Substitute

1 square (1 ounce) unsweetened chocolate = 3½ tablespoons cocoa plus 1½ tablespoons butter or margarine

How Much Do Cans Contain?

With the aid of the chart below, you'll be a smarter shopper for the most common canned foods. It shows you, for instance, that a No. 303 can is the same as a one-pound can, and that it will contain about two cups. Keep in mind that "contents" include any syrup or cooking liquid in the can. Therefore, if the recipe calls for "one cup drained crushed pineapple," better choose a can which holds more than one cup total contents.

Size	Usual Weight	Contents in Cups	Examples of Uses
6 oz.	6 oz.	¾ cup	Full-strength juices, frozen concentrates
8 oz.	8 oz.	1 cup	Fruits, vegetables, two-serving portions of main dishes
Picnic or No. 1	10½ to 12 oz.	1¼ cups	Condensed soups, gravies, fruits, vegetables
No. 300	14 oz. to 1 lb.	1¾ cups	Baked beans, main dishes, cranberry sauce
No. 303	1 lb. to 17 oz.	2 cups	Fruits, vegetables, some main dishes
No. 2	1 lb. 4 oz. or 1 pint 2 fl. oz.	2½ cups	Fruits, vegetables, juices
No. 2½	1 lb. 13 oz.	3½ cups	Fruits, vegetables
No. 3 cylinder or 46 oz.	3 lbs. 3 oz. or 1 quart 14 oz.	5¾ cups	Economy-size for fruit and vegetable juices; institutional size for condensed soups
No. 10	6½ lbs. to 7 lbs. 5 oz.	12 to 13 cups	Institutional size for fruits, vegetables

THE LANGUAGE OF COOKING

Every art and science has its terminology, and cooking is no different. You'll find that the terms which follow are like shorthand—they let us tell you quickly, and let you know quickly, just what you must do.

COOKING WITH LIQUIDS

Boil: To cook in liquid that is constantly bubbling gently. To boil vegetables, lower heat after bubbles appear so liquid doesn't churn up into a "rolling boil" (1).

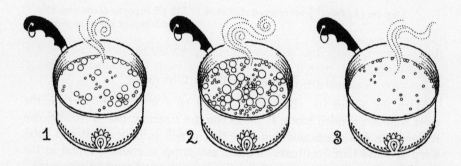

Full rolling boil: The rapid motion which occurs in liquid when its temperature is high enough. Cook cereal, macaroni products at this heat—it keeps food separated. Also used to make jams (2).

Poach or simmer: To cook in liquid below the boiling point. Bubbles form at bottom of pan but liquid barely moves. Eggs, fish are "poached," meat "simmered" (3).

Parboil: To boil food in a liquid until partially done. Cooking is then often completed in a different way. Cabbage, for example, may be parboiled, then stuffed and baked.

Steep: To let a dry food stand in liquid below the boiling point for the purpose of extracting its flavor, color or other qualities, as in steeping tea and coffee.

Blanch: To heat briefly in boiling water. Do it to loosen skins from nuts, fruits, vegetables. Also a first step in canning and freezing some fruits and vegetables.

Scald: To heat milk or cream to just below the boiling point. Bubbles form around edge; top of liquid appears glazed. Custard and yeast bread recipes call for scalding.

Steam: To cook by steam in a covered pot. Molded puddings or vegetables can rest on a rack above the water's surface. Dumplings may steam as they perch on stew. Fast version: pressure cooking.

OVEN AND BROILER COOKERY

The oven-temperature chart below should be used to guide you in setting the oven dial when the recipe reads simply "bake in moderate oven" or "slow oven," etc.

Very slow . . . . 250° or 275°F.
Slow . . . . 300° or 325°F.
Moderate . . . . 350° or 375°F.
Hot . . . . 400° or 425°F.
Very hot . . . . 450° or 475°F.
Extremely hot . . . . 500° or 525°F.

Roast: Usually applied to meat and poultry, to roast means to cook by dry heat—usually uncovered, in the oven. Use a meat thermometer to gauge doneness, or follow recipe time guide.

Bake: To cook in the oven. (The term roast, as explained above, is generally used for meats; ham is an exception.) For best results, preheat oven twenty minutes. The center of the oven is usually the best place to bake since foods brown evenly here.

Broil: To cook by direct heat—under open flame or electric unit of broiler or over charcoal. Always preheat the broiler. To check whether broiled meat is done all the way through, slit meat near the bone or in the thickest part.

Barbecue: Like broiling, to barbecue means to cook by direct heat—the difference being that in barbecuing you baste (moisten) the food with some seasoning sauce. Test for doneness as in broiling.

SOME GOURMET COOKING TERMS

Purée: To reduce to a smooth consistency by rubbing through a sieve. Many foods may be puréed quickly in an electric blender or a special food mill. Some soups are thickened by adding a purée of cooked vegetables.

Clarify: To make sparkling clear. For soup, skim off all fat, removing small particles by straining through cheesecloth. Then add a broken eggshell and a slightly beaten egg white. Slowly bring liquid to a boil, stirring constantly. Cool slightly; strain again.

Sauté: To brown and cook in a small amount of fat. Use a pan just big enough for food so the unused surface won't overheat. Meat may be covered to complete cooking but cook fish without a cover. Vegetables need no cover, just a gentle stirring.

Braise: To cook, covered, in a small amount of liquid or steam over low heat, ideally in a heavy pot that heats evenly. Foods are usually browned in fat before braising. Economy cuts of meat like pot roast are often braised. Carrots and celery taste good braised.

Marinate: To soak in a liquid. Meats are marinated in seasoned oil-vinegar mixtures for added flavor. Fruit may be marinated in syrups or bottled sodas. Important: use enough liquid to *cover*, or turn frequently. A bowl in which the meat just fits is best.

Flute: To make grooves or channels. Pastries are fluted with finger pressure, mushrooms with a sharp knife.

CUTTING FOODS TO SIZE

Chop: To cut food into small pieces. Do vegetables or nuts in a wooden bowl with a chopping blade, or on a cutting board with a sharp knife. Use wet scissors for soft foods like marshmallows, dates, raisins.

Mince: To cut into *very* small pieces. Just cut and cut—and cut. Mince garlic, scallions and clams on a board with a sharp knife. Use scissors for snipping hard-to-handle foods like parsley and chives—it's easier and much faster.

Cube: To cut foods into inch-square cubes. Tools are a sharp knife and a cutting board. Cube beef or lamb for kabobs. For snacks, cube cheese and spear on toothpicks.

Dice: Same as cube, but food is cut even smaller. Dice beets, carrots.

Julienne: Food cut into matchstick strips or slices—like tongue, ham or cheese in a chef's salad.

Sliver: To cut foods like almonds, garlic cloves into thin slices or strips.

Shred: To cut food into long, narrow lengths. Use a hand or mechanical shredder or a sharp knife. Many food grinders have blades for shredding, too. Shred crisp vegetables like cabbage and carrots for coleslaw. Shred cheese.

BEING A GOOD MIXER

Mix: A general term meaning simply to work two or more ingredients together until evenly combined.

Stir: To agitate gently by a round-the-bowl circular motion.

Stir in: To add gradually some ingredient to a mixture while stirring at same time.

Blend: To combine ingredients of different colors or textures so *thoroughly* that they attain a uniform one-color or one-texture consistency. Or the term may mean to agitate in an electric blender.

Beat: To make smooth and light. To beat a batter, work from bottom of
bowl, using a wooden spoon with a *brisk* up-and-over scooping motion.
Beat cream or egg white with a rotary beater. An electric mixer may be
used for all.

MATTERS OF TASTE

Even though we eat because we're hungry and our bodies need nourish-
ment, we enjoy food because it *tastes good*. That's why one of the first steps
in learning to be a wonderful cook is learning how to taste—with curiosity,
with discrimination, with inspiration.

Have you ever watched an expert tending a stew? She'll taste frequently,
savoring the natural flavors, then season as her palate dictates. It's the
touch of salt, the dash of sugar, the hint of garlic that heightens the flavors
and often adds a delicious excitement which wasn't there before. It takes
practice to develop sensitive taste buds that know when all the flavors are
properly balanced.

Start by really appreciating the natural flavor of foods. Your tongue
can distinguish only four flavors—sour, salt, sweet and bitter. But you also
"taste" through your nose—it tells you when the food tastes spicy or pun-
gent—or even burnt! Your other senses can be tempted, too. They tell you
how a food feels in your mouth, how it looks, how hot or cold it is.

For an advanced course in flavor, taste a stew, casserole or sauced food.
Certainly it contains many flavors. But if it's skillfully prepared, it presents
one blended flavor and no single seasoning stands out. Here are the flavorings most commonly used in main dishes:

Salt: The saying "a touch of salt makes sugar sweeter" is true. Salt brings
up the intensity of other flavors, adds a pleasant note of its own. (See
Seasoning with Salt, page 18.)

Pepper: Most of us have learned to expect the hot, spicy effect of pepper
on many foods, and they taste flat without it. But use it sparingly—it's
easy for your guests to add more. You'll find several grinds and types on
the market; best of all is the kind freshly ground by you.

Sugar: Many vegetables contain natural sugar, but this sweetness dis-
appears quickly if the vegetable is not eaten as soon as it's picked. You
can restore this natural sweetness by adding a bit of sugar to the cooking
water, particularly when you're cooking tomatoes, corn, peas and squash.
Try it too in pork dishes, stews and casseroles. With only a tiny amount
added (a teaspoonful for six servings is about right), the food won't taste
sweeter, just better.

Monosodium glutamate: This flavor blender belongs with the good cook's
basic seasonings. It's a vegetable substance in crystalline form, one of

the amino acids which occur naturally in food. Use it with vegetables to enhance natural flavor. Notice how it makes meats, poultry and fish richer in natural taste. Try it in stews and casseroles to blend and harmonize the flavors.

Spices and herbs: Like the accessories which perk up your favorite costume, spices and herbs accessorize an ordinary flavor. The range of tastes and aromas which these seasonings provide is boundless. What the good cook does is to use spices and herbs with a subtle hand and utmost discretion to achieve taste harmony. They're fun! (See *Spices and Herbs*, page 19.)

Seasoning with Salt

Use this salt seasoning chart to help you add salt at the right time and in the right amount.

When you make	Add salt to the liquid
Boiled shellfish	2 tablespoons to 1 quart water
Poached fish	1 teaspoon to 1 quart water
Stewed chicken	½ teaspoon for each pound of ready-to-cook weight
Gravy	1 teaspoon to 2 cups water
White sauce	1 teaspoon to 1 cup milk
Macaroni or spaghetti	1 tablespoon to 2 quarts water
Rice	1 teaspoon for each cup of rice
Potatoes	1 teaspoon to 2 cups water
Vegetables, fresh or frozen	¼ teaspoon to each ½ cup water
Yeast bread	1 teaspoon for each 3 cups flour

Did you know salt helps yeast bread to rise steadily? Without it, bread would be full of large, uneven bubbles.

When you make	Add salt to the egg whites
Meringues	⅓ teaspoon per egg white
Spongecake	Follow recipe for amount

Did you know salt helps to whip egg whites fluffier—faster?

When you make	Mix and sift salt with the flour
Quick breads like biscuits, muffins	1 teaspoon to 2 cups flour
Piecrust, other pastries	1 teaspoon to 2 cups flour
Butter cakes	Follow recipe for amount
Seasoned flour	1 teaspoon to ½ cup flour

Be sure to add salt to sweet dishes. Use just a bit—you won't taste the salt, but if you forget it, you'll miss its flavor.

About meats: when you make meat balls, stews, casseroles, add salt right at the start—one teaspoon to one pound of meat. (When figuring weight, discount for bone.) Salt a roast *before* you cook it. Even if salt doesn't penetrate deeply, it makes the outside surface taste delicious. Salt chops and steaks *after browning.* Don't salt dishes made with corned beef, smoked dried beef or ham until you've tasted the dish when it's ready to serve. These meats already contain salt and often don't need more.

SPICES AND HERBS

Is it a spice or an herb? Spices come from plant flowers, berries, bark, roots or seeds. Examples are: pepper, cinnamon, ginger, cloves, allspice, mustard, mace (which comes from the shell of nutmeg), nutmeg, dill seed, cardamom seed and caraway seed.

Herbs are almost always leaves: basil, marjoram, thyme, savory, parsley, and sage.

Spices and herbs may be bought in blends, too. Common mixtures are chili powder, curry, poultry seasoning and pie spices. Herbs are also blended into flavored salts (like garlic, onion, celery and seasoning salt), barbecue and salad mixtures.

Protect flavor of seasonings by closing containers tightly. Do not expose spices to air, heat, dampness or light. Replace yearly to keep them at peak flavor.

You can predict the flavor effect of a spice or herb: rub it between your palms and sniff. Your sense of smell and taste are so closely related you can almost "taste" the fragrance.

Sometimes a recipe will call for a *bouquet garni* or spice bag. To make it, tie spices and herbs in a square of cheesecloth, and drop into pot. Flavor will come through, but no loose leaves or peppercorns. Remove the bag after cooking. The basic *bouquet garni* mixture: one bay leaf, one-half teaspoon thyme, one teaspoon each parsley flakes and peppercorns.

Experiment with flavors—like mint with lamb chops—and taste the difference! But don't mix more than two herbs (an eighth-teaspoon of each in a dish for four) till you're experienced. Add flavor to meat before broiling or during last hour of roasting. Add flavor to salad, juice or dips thirty minutes before serving.

Solo Flights

*I*F YOU'VE NEVER COOKED BEFORE, start here. Even with the best recipe in the world, you may not have completely successful results without the magic ingredient *confidence*.

The three recipes in this chapter are designed to give you that essential ingredient. The first set of directions is for a packaged cake mix. Of course the manufacturer tells you how to use it. But just what do you do when the directions say "preheat the oven" or "grease the pans?" How in the world do you get those cake layers out of the pan onto cake racks right side up without breaking them into pieces? You'll find the answers below.

After your fledgling flight, proceed to a reputation-making dish—a real French omelet. Start with a plain one, just for yourself. Next time, try it filled. Then for Saturday lunch or Sunday supper, make a filled omelet big enough for the family. Once you have the knack, you'll add your own creative touches.

To graduate from this three-part course in freshman cooking, make *Seventeen*'s Sky-High Lemon Pie. Although the recipe is more involved than the others, its rewards are great. By preparing it, you'll learn several basic techniques. And once you've mastered them, you'll feel like a real cooking professional. Not only is the pie ideal date bait, but it will also convince your mother and father—and Aunt Matilda, too—that you're going to be a wonderful cook.

Here we go!

MIX A MASTER PIECE OF CAKE

Start with a cake mix—whatever flavor you like best. Check the package for extra ingredients you might need, suggested fillings and frostings.

Begin by preheating the oven. To do this, turn the thermostat to the baking temperature (see package) and heat twenty minutes.

For a homework date, Ham and Egg Boats (page 28) ▶

Now assemble equipment: the electric mixer and a rubber scraper *or a* mixing bowl and wooden spoon; pans, of the sizes called for; glass measuring cup and, if needed, measuring spoons.

Prepare the pans next. To grease a pan: dab a piece of waxed paper in shortening or oil and evenly coat inside surfaces. To flour a pan: sprinkle the greased pan lightly with flour, then tilt pan back and forth, tapping sides with hand. Shake out excess flour. To line the pan: set it on waxed or plain paper and trace around it with the point of kitchen scissors. Cut out tracing and insert. When pans are ready, start the cake.

If you use an electric mixer, blend dry ingredients with liquid at a slow speed (or flour will fly), then beat at high speed. Stop the mixer occasionally and scrape off the beaters and the bowl with a rubber spatula to ensure even mixing. Follow timing directions accurately.

If you mix by hand, use an up-and-over scooping motion and work vigorously. Occasionally, scrape sides and bottom of bowl. For each minute of mixing called for on package, use 150 vigorous strokes by hand.

When the batter is ready, pour it into prepared pans. Place the pans on the center shelf of a preheated oven. A kitchen timer will remind you when to check the cake. If the top of the cake springs back when you touch it

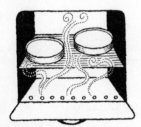 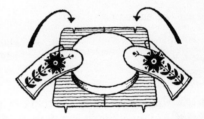

lightly and if its sides have shrunk a bit away from the sides of the pan, it's ready. Remove it from the oven and set it on a cooling rack for ten minutes.

Then run a sharp knife around sides of pan to loosen the cake. And here's how to turn it out: set a cooling rack over the cake; invert both together. Remove pan from cake, put a second rack over the cake and invert both again—so cake is top side up. Cool. Brush off crumbs lightly with your hand. Then frost, using suggestions on the package or one of the recipes on pages 226 and 227.

NOTE: Chiffon, angel and sponge cakes are treated a little differently. Follow label directions.

◀ *It's ten inches round and serves eight with ease: Giant Party Burger (page 58).*

HOW TO MAKE PERFECT FRENCH OMELETS

A perfect omelet pan is a big help. Though you can use a regular skillet, the ideal pan has rounded sides, a long handle and is made of heavy cast iron, aluminum or copper. Size is important. If the pan is too small for the number of eggs used, the omelet will be runny. If the pan is too big, the omelet will be thin and overbrowned. Follow the chart below to choose the right-size pan.

Number of eggs	Pan diameter
One	Six inches
Two	Seven and one-half inches
Four	Nine inches
Six	Eleven inches

How many will an omelet serve? That depends not only on your guests' appetites, but also on when and how you plan to serve the omelet. For dessert or a light lunch, count on one egg per person. As a main dish, two eggs. If you need to serve a crowd, plan to make several omelets rather than one tremendous one—it's difficult to handle more than six eggs at once.

Here are the basic proportions:

1 egg	Dash of pepper
1 teaspoon water	1 teaspoon butter
⅛ teaspoon salt	

Multiply this recipe by the number of eggs you're using. For a four-egg omelet, for instance, you'll use four teaspoons each of water and butter, one-half teaspoon salt. Add a pinch of herbs if you like. For dessert omelets, omit the pepper, add one teaspoon sugar for four eggs.

First, put the eggs, water, salt and pepper in a bowl. Beat thirty seconds with a wire whisk, fork or other hand beater (not a rotary beater) just to blend whites and yolks. Heat the butter until it is bubbling and just beginning to brown.

Pour the egg mixture into the pan and begin at once to shake the pan gently. The bottom of the omelet will begin to set immediately. Gently lift its edge with a spatula and tip the pan so liquid egg on top will slide over to bottom of pan (1). Continue—lifting the pan occasionally from the heat so the omelet won't burn—until the top looks shiny, creamy and set. Add a filling (below), then fold.

To fold: lift right side of pan up a bit; use a spatula to turn one-third of the omelet over the filling (2). Change hands and hold pan over serving dish (3). Tilt pan just enough to slide unfolded side onto dish, then flip folded part neatly over it (4). Garnish.

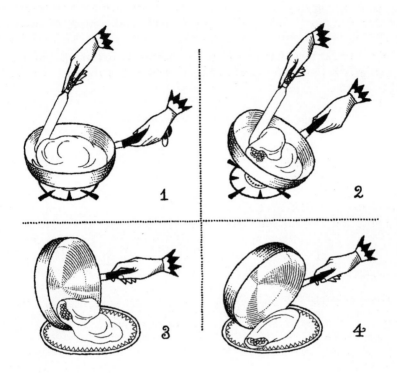

OMELET FILLINGS

Each is for a four-egg omelet—a main dish for two or dessert for four.

Cheese omelet: Fill with one-fourth cup grated American or Swiss cheese.

Crunchy omelet: Fill with one-half cup tiny bread cubes, fried in butter until toasty.

Spanish omelet: Fill with one-half cup canned stewed tomatoes, heated and seasoned to taste.

Party omelet: Sauté one-fourth pound sliced mushrooms and one-fourth pound cooked diced ham in two tablespoons butter. When lightly browned, add two tablespoons sour cream and one-fourth teaspoon crumbled tarragon. Use to fill omelet.

Dessert omelet: Use one-third cup thawed frozen strawberries to fill omelet, and a few more to garnish top; dust with confectioners' sugar.

HOW TO MAKE SKY-HIGH LEMON PIE

The first requirement is a perfect eight- or nine-inch baked pastry shell. You can make it from:

½ package piecrust mix

But if you've never made a piecrust before, turn to page 188 for the illustrated directions. While the crust is cooling, start the pie.

First assemble the equipment you'll need:

measuring spoons	grater
nest of dry-measuring cups	rotary beater or electric
liquid-measuring cup	mixer
wooden spoon	double boiler
two bowls	spatula

The Lemon Filling

4 to 5 tablespoons cornstarch	4 egg yolks
¼ teaspoon salt	⅓ cup lemon juice
1 cup sugar, divided	1 teaspoon grated lemon peel
½ cup cold water	2 tablespoons butter
1 cup milk	

If you use four tablespoons of cornstarch, the filling will be soft and creamy. Five tablespoons yield a pie which cuts very dependably—choose the type of pie you like best. Mix cornstarch with the salt and one-half cup of the sugar in the top of the double boiler. Stir in the water a little at a time. Then stir in the milk. Fill the bottom of the double boiler with about two inches of water and start it heating. Place the top of the double boiler over low heat and stir the milk mixture constantly until the mixture comes to a boil. Then place it over boiling water, cover and cook for ten minutes, stirring occasionally.

Next, place the second half-cup of sugar in a mixing bowl along with the egg yolks. With a rotary beater, beat together. Stir one-third of the hot mixture rapidly into the beaten yolk-sugar mixture. (This step keeps yolks from scrambling.) Return mixture to the top of the double boiler and blend well. Stirring removes any lumpy look. Cook two minutes more. Remove from heat. Gradually stir in lemon juice, peel and butter, mixing just enough to combine. Let cool thirty minutes without stirring.

Fluffy Meringue

6 egg whites (see note)	¾ cup sugar

Place the egg whites in a large mixing bowl and, with mixer at high speed or with a rotary beater, beat until soft peaks form when you withdraw beater. (Turn off electric mixer before withdrawing beaters.) Then add the sugar while you beat, two tablespoons at a time. Be sure to beat in each addition thoroughly before adding the next. Continue to beat until the mixture is shiny, glossy and stands in really stiff peaks when you lift out the beater. The sugar must be thoroughly dissolved. To test, taste: you should feel no graininess on your tongue.

Preheat the oven to 400°F. (hot). Pour the cooled filling into the pie shell. Pile on the meringue, starting at the edges and anchoring it firmly to the crust, then building high peaks in the center. Place in 400°F. oven and bake until delicately brown (six to eight minutes). Let cool to room temperature before cutting gently with a hot, wet knife or a sharp-edged pie server. Keep leftover pie cool, but not refrigerated. *Makes eight servings.*

NOTE: Two of the egg whites called for are purely for extra glamour. You can make a very nice meringue with four egg whites and one-half cup of sugar. Or for everyday serving, use only three egg yolks in the filling and make the meringue of three egg whites and six tablespoons of sugar.

For the Boy
Who Carries Your Books

*O*NCE you've mastered a few recipes, you'll probably begin thinking of asking a boy home after school to sample the results of your culinary skill. Or perhaps a girl you know will drop in for a chat. This chapter is planned for precisely such occasions. At the outset are some goodies to be made in advance, so they can be proudly presented, moments after your guest's arrival, with a steaming mug of cocoa or a refreshing soft drink. This group offers the best bets for beginning cooks since you'll know before the crucial moment just how delicious they are.

After those come the let's-do-it-togethers—fun during the making and fun to eat the minute they're complete. Use these recipes after you've acquired confidence, or for someone you know very well.

In addition there's a guide on how to pack up sweet somethings for the boy who is far away. (And there's nothing lost if you use these same tips for your big brother or your Aunt Gladys.)

Here are the recipes to make mostly or entirely in advance—foolproof, and favorites of boys.

If you have a package of date-bar mix on hand, and seven minutes, you're on your way! These fruit bars are quick to make and stay fresh for quite a while—*if* you can resist them.

SEVEN–MINUTE FRUIT BARS

2 packages (14 oz. each) date-bar mix   2 tablespoons water
1 can (1 lb.) applesauce

Empty both packages of date-bar mix into bowl. Remove filling packets and empty these into another bowl. Pour applesauce into a saucepan and heat until bubbling. Stir hot applesauce into date filling. Stir until well combined. Add water to crumb mixture; stir to blend (mix will still be crumbly). Pat half the crumb mixture evenly and firmly over bottom of nine-by-thirteen-inch baking pan. Spread filling evenly over crumbs, then sprinkle remaining crumbs over top. Bake at 375°F. (moderate) thirty-five to forty minutes or until crumb top is lightly browned. Cut into forty-eight small, easy-to-handle squares. They'll keep fresh at room temperature (covered, of course) for three or four days—even longer in the refrigerator. *Makes forty-eight.*

No baking for this sweet treat. Make it ahead, or let him watch—it's fun.

SNACK BARS

4 small packages (1 lb.)
  marshmallows
½ cup butter or margarine
1 package (6 oz.) butterscotch pieces

1 teaspoon vanilla
¼ teaspoon salt
1 package (4½ oz.) puffed rice cereal

Place marshmallows, butter and butterscotch pieces in a large saucepan or kettle. Melt over low heat, stirring constantly. Stir in vanilla and salt. Next add cereal, tossing to combine well. Turn mixture into a well-greased nine-by-thirteen-inch pan and press down gently with palm of hand to even the surface. Let cool thoroughly. Cut into one-by-two-inch pieces. *Makes forty-eight bars.*

Since concentration is required to read a candy thermometer, you may prefer to make this recipe when you're alone, serve anytime.

PEANUT BUTTER MUNCH

⅔ cup water
1 tablespoon vinegar
½ teaspoon salt
2 cups sugar
1¾ cups molasses

7 quarts salted, freshly popped corn
1 cup peanut butter (crunchy
  preferred)
½ teaspoon baking soda

Combine water, vinegar, salt, sugar and molasses in a very large kettle. Cook till a small amount forms a firm ball when dropped in cold water (or until candy thermometer registers 244°F.). While syrup cooks, place popcorn in two large bowls. Scatter peanut butter evenly over surface. Remove cooked syrup from heat. Add baking soda and stir. At once, pour over popcorn and mix with a large spoon until all popcorn is coated. *Press lightly with hands into twenty-five flat cakes or balls, or break apart into nibblers.*

The recipes which follow are meant to be fixed *after* the boy arrives. Invite him into the kitchen to watch!

THE VERY UNSQUARE ROLL

6 slices bacon
4 slices white bread, crusts trimmed

2 rectangular slices Swiss cheese

Put the bacon in a shallow pan and bake for five minutes at 400°F. (hot). Drain bacon on paper towel and discard the drippings, but save the pan. Place three slices of bacon on a breadboard, cover with two slices of white bread, edges touching. Top with one slice of Swiss cheese. Roll up (bacon outside) and secure with toothpicks. Repeat for second roll. Return to pan and bake ten minutes more at 400°F. until golden. *Makes two rolls.*

HAM AND EGG BOATS

2 hard club rolls
1 small can deviled ham

2 eggs
2 slices process American cheese

Cut off tops of club rolls and hollow out, leaving a half-inch shell. Spread inside bottom and sides of shells with deviled ham. Break each egg into a custard cup first, then pour into hollow. Cut cheese into strips and arrange over eggs; make sure yolks are covered. Bake at 350°F. (moderate) twenty minutes or until egg white is firm. *Serve with forks to two.*

PLAID PIZZA

2 English muffins
2 slices mozzarella (pizza) cheese
Garlic salt
Italian seasoning

2 tablespoons chopped black olives
2 tablespoons chili sauce
1 egg, beaten

Preheat a waffle iron, oiling it generously. Split muffins. Place a slice of mozzarella on crust side of each of two muffin halves. Sprinkle with garlic salt, Italian seasoning and, for each, one tablespoon each of olives and chili sauce. Top with second muffin half, cut side up. Dip both sides in beaten egg and place in waffle iron. Toast two minutes or until cheese barely begins to melt. *Makes two.*

Make this one for a boy who cares about how things look.

HOT KABOB

¼ lb. chopped beef
1 frankfurter
4 thick half-slices tomato
2 fresh mushrooms, halved
4 squares green pepper

2 small canned onions
Hot barbecue sauce for meat
2 frankfurter rolls, buttered and
    toasted
Lettuce

Shape the beef into four small meat balls. Cut the frank into four chunks. Lace two skewers like this: meat ball, tomato, mushroom, frank, pepper, onion—then in reverse order: pepper, frank, etc. Broil slowly six minutes, basting with barbecue sauce and turning often. Slide from skewer onto hot rolls lined with lettuce, and top with more barbecue sauce. *Makes two kabobs.*

Here's a hero or a grinder or a submarine in the best tradition.

VERY HEROIC SANDWICH

8 Italian green peppers, cored and
    quartered
¼ cup olive oil
1 loaf French or Italian bread, twelve
    inches long
Butter

¼ lb. sliced salami
¼ lb. sliced boiled ham
Salt and pepper
1 large tomato, sliced thin
Anchovy fillets to taste

Cook peppers in olive oil, turning occasionally, until soft. Split the French bread and butter cut sides. On one half place salami and ham alternately to cover bread in thick layer. Add a layer of peppers. Season with salt and pepper. Cover with tomato slices, then anchovy fillets. Top with the other half of the bread. *Serve to one boy with a gargantuan appetite, or cut to serve three girls.*

Some people like this even better than pizza!

GRILLED CHEESE ITALIANO

2 teaspoons butter or margarine
1 teaspoon olive oil
¼ teaspoon minced garlic
2 slices white bread
2 slices mozzarella (pizza) cheese
¼ cup shredded natural Cheddar
    cheese

3 thin slices tomato
3 slices bacon, fried crisp and drained
Freshly ground black pepper
Crumbled sweet basil

Combine butter, olive oil and garlic. Spread on bread. On one slice, arrange mozzarella, top with Cheddar, then two slices each tomato and bacon. Dust heavily with pepper and lightly with basil. Top with the second slice of bread. Preheat a skillet containing a little butter. When butter sizzles, add sandwich and cook, pressing down firmly with pancake turner, until brown on both sides. Top with tomato slice and bacon, cut in quarters and enjoy. *Makes one sandwich.*

Here's a particularly good blend of "everything nice" in a quick and easy unbaked cereal cookie.

SHAGGY DATE COOKIES

2 tablespoons butter or margarine
1 cup chopped pitted dates
1 cup sugar
1 egg

1 teaspoon vanilla
½ cup chopped pecans
2 cups crisp rice cereal
1 can (3½ oz.) flaked coconut

In a saucepan, combine butter, dates, sugar and egg. Cook over low heat ten minutes, stirring constantly. Remove from heat. Add vanilla, pecans and cereal and stir well. Let cool enough to handle easily. Shape into one-inch balls. Roll in coconut. *Makes forty-eight.*

If the boy has a sweet tooth, he'll love this recipe. Better if he helps you make it—because it's so good while still warm.

CHECKERS

¼ cup butter or margarine
1 tablespoon light molasses

1 cup light brown sugar, firmly packed
4 cups bite-size shredded rice cereal

Heat the butter with molasses in a big, heavy skillet over low heat until the butter melts. Stir in brown sugar. Heat very slowly without stirring until mixture is all foam and doubles in volume. Then begin timing and cook for two minutes more. Add cereal all at once and stir to coat each bite-size piece. Spread out over a greased cookie sheet. Cool and break into small pieces. *Makes five cups or light snacking for ten.*

TRAVELING TREATS

When that special someone is away from home, you may still want to remember him or her with something from your kitchen. Here's a directory of what to send and how to send it.

Candy: Fudge or penuche makes an ideal shipping sweet. Pour it hot into a foil pan, let harden, then mark into squares. (Don't cut through or candy may crumble.) Wrap pan in foil or plastic film, decorate and place in a sturdy box. Stuff the box with enough filler (crushed or shredded paper) to make it "tight." For candy other than fudge types, pieces should be individually wrapped and packed between layers of filler. Cover coffee or shortening cans with gift paper for containers.

Cake: Fruitcakes and applesauce cakes stay moist, mail easily. Bake them in foil pans or coffee cans and mail right in their gift-wrapped baking containers. Frosted poundcakes or chiffon cakes mail well in any temperate zone. To ship, cut out a cardboard pattern slightly larger than the cake; cover it with foil. Frost the cake on it—a butter cream frosting travels best. When the frosting hardens, put the cardboard "plate" with cake into a corrugated box. Tape to the bottom of the box. Set cardboard wedges (as tall as box) in corners so cake won't slip. Lay waxed paper over top; pad empty spaces with filler.

Cookies: Drop or cutout cookies should be wrapped individually—or back to back in pairs. To pack: put filler under bottom layer and in between layers. Put enough filler on top so you have to press the lid down. Bar cookies may be baked in foil pans, scored and mailed like fudge.

Mailing tips: Use a sturdy box, wrapping paper and cord. Address clearly; don't forget your return address. Use permanent ink. To "waterproof" address, use cellophane tape or colorless nail polish.

Here's an ideal sweet to mail—firm enough not to crumble, rich enough to stay moist as the package wends its way.

OATMEAL RAISIN BARS

½ cup butter or margarine, melted
2 cups rolled oats (quick or
   old-fashioned)
½ cup brown sugar
¼ cup dark corn syrup
½ teaspoon salt
1 teaspoon cinnamon

½ teaspoon nutmeg
½ teaspoon allspice
½ teaspoon ginger
1 teaspoon vanilla
1 tablespoon lemon juice
1 cup seedless raisins

Pour melted butter over oats and mix well. Add remaining ingredients and blend well. Spread out in a greased nine-inch square baking pan. Bake at 450°F. (hot) twelve minutes or until golden brown. Cool partially on a rack; chill. Spread with Tangy Glaze (below). *Cut into twenty bars.*

Tangy Glaze

1 cup sifted confectioners' sugar
½ teaspoon grated lemon peel

1½ tablespoons lemon juice

Blend ingredients together, use as indicated above.

Breakfasts—Just for You

*H*AVE you ever thought how practical it would be to fix your own breakfast? Your mother will applaud—she may be rushed in the morning. And if your appetite is temperamental early in the day, you can suit it exactly. The recipes follow many different tastes, yet all are quick *and* nutritious.

Did we hear you say, "Why eat breakfast at all? Who needs it?" The answer is, you do. Breakfast gives you glow power (to smile at the boys on your way to school). It makes you feel snug inside and all go-go-go! Besides, the foods that are usually associated with breakfast—like eggs and cereals and citrus fruits—are among the ones which make you pretty. Bonus: if you're dieting, breakfast helps you last till lunch—without snacking.

Any breakfast is better than none, and anything from peanut butter to beefsteak can star as the starting point for a bright, beautiful day. The classic breakfasts have this pattern:

Orange juice, or other fruit high in Vitamin C
An egg or a bowl of cereal
Toast or other bread
Milk

But what really counts is what the foods supply. You can get Vitamin C from melon or even sliced tomato. Protein can come from cheese, meat or the aforesaid peanut butter. Your milk might be in the form of cheese or even ice cream.

So choose what *you* like to eat. Then be sure to leave enough time for breakfast. Organize yourself the night before—clothes, books, lunch money. Next morning, ten minutes (cooking *and* eating!) will see you off with a spring in your step on the way to a marvelous day.

Our compliments to you if you enjoy beginning the day with eggs—one egg a day is a giant step forward to beauty. Read how to cook eggs exactly right in five popular ways—you may pick up some tips that will surprise you.

EGGS FOR BREAKFAST

Store eggs in the refrigerator to guard freshness, but for easiest cooking and best taste, let them come to room temperature before you cook them. Or warm them before cooking in hot water. *Always* cook eggs with moderate heat.

Soft-cooked eggs: Never boil—even "soft-boil"—an egg. Boiling tends to make it tough and unevenly cooked. To soft-cook: put eggs in glass or stainless steel saucepan and cover with water. When water boils, remove pan from heat, cover it and time eggs—three minutes for a soft, jellied white; four minutes for a firm white and runny yolk. When time's up, rinse eggs instantly in cold water. To open: hold egg over dish and strike sharply at "waist" with a table knife. Let yolk run into dish, scoop out white with spoon. Add butter, salt and pepper to taste.

Hard-cooked eggs: For breakfast? Just try them! Put a rack on the bottom of the pan to help prevent a ring around the yolk when eggs are cooked. Place eggs on rack, cover with water. When water boils, remove pan from heat, cover and time eggs ten minutes. Cool eggs instantly with cold water. Tap the shell all over and peel it off like a skin; rinse off any shell bits. To chop hard-cooked eggs in a hurry, use a wire pastry blender.

Poached eggs: If you use an egg poacher, butter all the cups. Then break each egg into a small bowl first and slide it into poacher. Cook over simmering water three minutes or less, until white is set and yolk congealed. Remove cup from poacher; turn egg out with a table knife. To poach in a skillet, put two inches of water in the pan. Add one teaspoon each salt and vinegar. When water is simmering, break egg into bowl or saucer, slide into pan. Cook three minutes; remove with a slotted spoon.

Fried eggs: Melt two tablespoons butter or bacon fat in skillet until hot but not brown. Break egg into saucer, slip into pan. When edges of egg become white, begin basting occasionally until yolk has a film over it. Season, then remove with slotted turner. If you like your egg "over," turn it just before you remove it and cook thirty seconds on other side.

Scrambled eggs: Combine with a fork two eggs, one-fourth teaspoon salt, dash of pepper and one tablespoon milk. Melt two tablespoons butter in a skillet. Add the eggs, let cook one minute, then "scramble" in pan with spatula or wooden spoon. Eggs are done when set but still shiny.

If you have an electric blender, you can have the quickest breakfast of all—the kind you drink. Two examples follow:

ALL-SHOOK-UP

1 cup milk	2 graham crackers, broken
1 teaspoon sugar	1 egg
½ cup orange juice	

Measure ingredients into blender, cover and run on high speed thirty seconds or until graham crackers are blended. Pour into one tall glass.

QUICK EGGS-IT

¾ cup milk	3 tablespoons orange juice
1 egg	concentrate
½ cup puffed rice cereal	3 ice cubes
2 tablespoons quick strawberry drink mix	

Measure into blender, cover and blend thirty seconds. Makes one tall glassful.

Here's a gay way to have your egg a day!

EGG LEMONADE

Cracked ice	1 tablespoon lemon juice
2 teaspoons maraschino cherry syrup	1 egg

Fill a one-pint jar three-fourths full of cracked ice. Add syrup, juice and egg. Shake vigorously and strain into a fruit juice glass. To your health!

Here's a complete double-quick breakfast, oddball but good.

LICKETY-SPLIT

Spread four double graham crackers with a pat of butter, two tablespoons peanut butter, one tablespoon of grape jelly. Eat these with a tall glass of milk. Add—as a tart starter or a finishing touch—a half grapefruit sprinkled with sugar. (If you like, brown it under the broiler for a minute.)

Love hot cereal? It's extra delicious this way:

INSTANT PARFAIT

Make up your favorite hot cereal—whole-wheat or oatmeal, regular or instant. Arrange in a glass, layering with your favorite jam (or jams!) and top with brown sugar and half-and-half (not quite so rich as cream). Enjoy with a tangerine to nibble section by section and a cup of hot cocoa.

If regular "breakfast foods" bore you, you'll be especially fond of the next three suggestions.

HUSTLE BUSTLE

The day before, buy some of the flat corn muffins that fit the toaster. Next morning, preheat the broiler. Split a corncake and spread it thickly with Old English or bacon-cheese spread from a jar. Place under broiler four inches from heat about two minutes or until browned and bubbly. Particularly good with honeydew melon splashed with lime juice. And for a beverage, try instant *café au lait* which is quickly made and instantly drinkable! Place one teaspoon instant coffee in a cup. Fill one-third full with boiling water and stir. Then fill with milk and sugar to taste.

SOUP–ER DELICIOUS

The night before, hard-cook an egg. In the morning, while you drink a glass of chilled pineapple-grapefruit juice, gradually add one cup of milk to two-thirds cup of canned, condensed tomato soup. Heat gently; don't boil, but let the soup simmer a minute before you ladle it into your soup plate. Garnish with slices of hard-cooked egg and accompany with crisp buttered saltines.

SUNDAY SPECIAL

Heat a frying pan with one tablespoon of butter until the butter sizzles. Add two frozen sandwich steaks and two thick tomato slices. Turn sandwich steaks when well browned (about a minute) and begin toasting two slices of bread. By the time meat is done and toast pops up, tomatoes will be grilled on both sides too. That breakfast sandwich is ready to go with a mug of cold milk.

BREAKFAST À LA MODE

Before you go to bed, put a package of frozen peaches in the refrigerator to thaw overnight. When you get up in the morning, fill a bowl half full of your favorite breakfast cereal—we like the crisp rice kind. Add a half-cup scoop of vanilla ice cream, and over the top ladle two-thirds cup of peaches. Add milk, flavored or plain, and it's breakfast for one!

If you have a sweet tooth, breakfast is a lovely time to pamper it, and here are four just-for-you ways to do it:

WAFFLY NICE

Preheat a waffle iron, following manufacurer's directions. Butter two slices of bread lightly on both sides. With a fork, beat an egg in a flat bowl. Add bread and turn it on both sides to soak thoroughly. Place in waffle iron to bake brown (about five minutes). Nice with maple-blended syrup or honey. And extra nice if the first course is a half cantaloupe, zesty with a squeeze of lemon juice. Add a glass of milk, and your breakfast is complete.

STRIKE–ME–PINK

Two recipes to this breakfast, but together, they're a perfect harmony. The night before, start a package of frozen strawberries thawing. In the morning, preheat the griddle and make Solo Special Pancakes. In a shaker or jar, measure one-fourth cup of milk, one-fourth cup pancake mix, one egg and one tablespoon cooking oil. Shake until smooth. Pour about one-fourth cup on lightly greased hot griddle and brown both sides. Repeat to make four large pancakes. Meanwhile, open a can of deviled ham and spread a little on each of three pancakes. Arrange in layers like a cake and top with fourth pancake. Top *that* with currant jelly. Put the thawed strawberries in a bowl and with an electric hand mixer or wire whisk, beat in two tablespoons of quick strawberry drink mix and one cup of cold milk. Yummy!

CANDY BALLS

The night before, melt twelve caramels in the top of a double boiler with one tablespoon water. Stir in three cups puffed wheat or O-shaped oat cereal. Form into two-inch balls. Eat three for breakfast with a glass of orange-grapefruit juice and another of milk. Store remaining Candy Balls in a metal tin—they're delicious after school.

SUNDAY MORNING SPECIAL

Place a big scoop of cottage cheese in a bowl. Top with citrus fruit sections (buy them already prepared and refrigerated in jars). Top with preserved lingonberries or cherries. With buttery, sugary cinnamon toast, very good indeed.

And even cinnamon toast can be made surprising and different!

CINNAMON TOAST

2 slices bread	4 teaspoons sugar
Soft butter	½ teaspoon cinnamon

Place bread on rack of broiler pan. Toast on one side until golden. Remove, turn and butter untoasted side. Combine sugar and cinnamon and sprinkle over butter. Return to broiler for about thirty seconds or until sugar mixture melts and bubbles. Cut in halves or quarters and serve at once.

Quick Cocoa Toast: Omit cinnamon; use just two teaspoons sugar mixed with two teaspoons quick chocolate drink mix. Broil as above.

Candied Cinnamon Toast: Use raisin bread. Toast one side and butter as above. Sprinkle with a mixture of two teaspoons instant orange-flavored breakfast drink, two teaspoons sugar and one-fourth teaspoon cinnamon.

You and Your Lunch Box

$\mathcal{M}$AKING your own lunch is fun and satisfying. Even if it takes some of the surprise out of noontime eating, the combinations are sure to be your favorites, and you can plan the meal to suit your appetite.

Just be sure to make your "sack lunch" as nutritious as it ought to be. That paper bag (but why not make it a pretty tote or a charming basket or a bright gift box?) should contain a big helping of beauty which, translated, means the right foods. To name them:

A protein: meat, cheese, fish, poultry or egg.
A vegetable: a salad or some crisp nibbles.
Bread, according to need; less if you're watching your figure.
Milk: bring it in a thermos or buy it at school.
Fruit: preferably uncooked.

Here are the basic rules for *how* to pack, and some ideas for *what* to pack, to make your lunch a real picnic. You'll find more conventional suggestions for sandwich fillings on pages 316 through 320.

TIPS FOR BETTER-PACKED LUNCH BOX SNACKS

Most of the foods you pack in your lunch box will be safer—and better tasting—if kept as cold as possible. For best results, use an insulated lunch bag to tote food. Or use an insulated ice cream bag, tucked in a basket.

Whenever possible, fix your lunch the night before and refrigerate. It will stay colder next morning.

Use a drugstore fold when you wrap sandwiches in foil, waxed paper or plastic film. Here's how: For a regular-size sandwich, use a twelve-inch square of wrap. Lay sandwich in center. Bring two opposite edges of wrap together. Fold them (together) over and over in one-inch folds until the fold rests flat against sandwich. Fold up other two ends until they rest against sandwich, too.

Or freeze part of your lunch, and turn your tote into a portable icebox. For instance, tuck a one-serving can of fruit or vegetable juice in the freezer at bedtime. When you get up in the morning, wrap it in a strong paper napkin, then in a plastic bag and add it to your lunch. It will keep the foods around it chilly cool, and should be thawed and ready to sip by lunchtime. Don't forget an opener! (If the freezer compartment is set at 0°F., count on about five hours for the juice to defrost. It will take about two hours to defrost if placed in an 18°F. ice cube compartment.)

A frozen sandwich or a piece of cake straight from the freezer will also add cold comfort to box lunches.

Freeze-Ahead Instant Lunches

Once in a while, when you're fixing lunch, instead of making just one sandwich, make one or two extra. Pop these into the freezer for sleepy-head mornings. You can freeze up to a month's supply! Not every kind of sandwich will freeze well, of course.

Don't freeze any sandwich which contains egg, jelly, sea food, mayonnaise, salad dressing or uncooked vegetables.

Do choose plain meats, cheeses, canned meat spreads like deviled ham, liver pâté—or any of the instant specials below. Try pineapple, orange or lemon juice in place of dressing; use commercial sour cream or applesauce, not mayonnaise. Butter bread well before adding filling. Wrap each sandwich snugly in plastic wrap; seal with freezer tape.

Instant Sandwich Specials

Turkey with jellied cranberry sauce on Parker House rolls.
Tuna or salmon with sour cream on rye.
Cream cheese, dates, walnuts on banana bread.
Chopped ham and piccalilli on onion rolls.
Cream cheese and crushed pineapple on whole-wheat.

Note to the Chef

Since you can't count on refrigeration during mornings at school, don't pack mayonnaise mixtures. (It is safe, however, to put plain mayonnaise in a paper jigger cup, protect the top with plastic wrap.) One more don't: don't pack desserts that have custard or cream fillings.

FAVORITE SANDWICHES

Peanut butter and jelly

Tuna or salmon with chopped celery

Cheeses in jars and sliced packaged
   cheeses

Cream cheese with nuts, chopped
   olives or jam

Sliced canned meats

Tongue

Dry sausage meats, like salami

Home-cooked meats
   (keep extra cold)

FAVORITE DESSERTS

Cookies

Fruit pies

Turnovers

Canned or fresh fruits

Cake (without custard or cream
   filling)

OTHER SWEETS

Marshmallows

Raisins

Candy bars

Nuts

Popcorn

Hard candies

Crackers, sandwiched with jelly

HOT TIPS

If you have a vacuum jug with a wide mouth, you can include baked beans, chili or other at-home favorites on your box lunch menus—and, of course, soups. Scald the vacuum jug first with hot water, then fill with *steaming* hot food.

UNDER WRAPS

Foil or plastic wrap (including plastic bags) helps seal in the flavors of your lunch box foods and keeps them just-made fresh. Waxed paper also makes a good cold-food wrap-up.

SALAD TOTES

Use plastic-coated paper cereal bowls; add a lid of plastic wrap for neat, easy going.

FRUIT CUPS

Carry squashables like grapes and juicy fruits like canned peaches in moistureproof paper cups or freezer containers.

With the recipe that follows, you have all the taste surprise of a sandwich, but none of the bread!

TINY TOMS

Cut tops from very small tomatoes; scoop out inside pulp (reserve it for a salad). Fill tomatoes with diced cheese, lunch meat, canned liver pâté, tuna or deviled ham mixed with chopped green pepper. Replace the tops; decorate with a sprig of fresh parsley. Pack in plastic wrap or paper freezer containers. Chill well before carrying to school.

How to take an apple salad to school? In an apple, of course.

APPLE DANDY

Lay an apple on its side and cut in half from stem to base. Remove center core with a melon-baller or measuring spoon. To keep apple from turning brown, brush it with a little lemon juice. Now scoop out almost all the meat, dice and place in a bowl with about a tablespoon of lemon juice. Add two tablespoons chopped celery, one tablespoon chopped nuts and one tablespoon School Belle Dressing (below). Fill apple halves and fit back together again. Wrap in foil or plastic wrap. Chill well.

School Belle Dressing

¼ cup sugar	1 teaspoon dry mustard
½ cup vinegar	1 teaspoon salt
½ cup cooking oil	¼ teaspoon pepper
¼ cup water	

Combine all ingredients in a tightly covered jar. Shake well. Refrigerate.

Lunchtime spectacular—and fabulous feasting, too.

COCONUT CURRY

First, make a tuna rice salad:

1 cup cooled, fluffy rice	½ cup diced green pepper
¼ cup minced chutney	½ cup chopped onion
2 cans (7 oz. each) chunk tuna, drained	½ teaspoon curry powder
	Salt and pepper to taste
½ cup sliced celery	Curry cups and coconuts (page 42)

To rice, add chutney, tuna, celery, green pepper, onion and curry, and season to taste with salt and pepper. Toss, then pack into moistureproof paper cups or into coconut containers. Refrigerate. Wrap well in plastic film and keep as cold as possible until lunchtime. Have a party—the recipe *serves six.*

Curry cups: In moistureproof tiny paper cups, pack the curry extras— the condiments that usually accompany curry. Your friends can sprinkle their choice over their salad at school. Pick at least three: chopped peanuts, slivered, toasted almonds, grated coconut, raisins, crumbled bacon, finely diced orange rind, minced olives.

To scoop out a coconut: First punch out one of the "monkey's eyes" in the coconut and drain out all the milk. Have a handy man in the family cut a third of the top from the coconut, using a hack saw or heavy-bladed electric band saw. Smooth off cut rims with a vegetable peeler. Scoop out most of the coconut meat. (Treat your handy man with it!) Cover with plastic wrap and refrigerate until ready to fill with salad for one.

Stuffed eggs can look and taste very special. See below.

HICKETY–PICKETY EGGS

First, hard-cook as many eggs as you'll want (see page 33). When cool, remove shells and make a picket-edge cut: About halfway down the egg, make a tiny slanting cut with the tip of the paring knife. (Cut through *only* to center of yolk.) Next to first cut, add a tiny slanting cut in other direction to make a point—like the top of a picket fence. Repeat till you reach starting point, then carefully lift off top of egg. Scoop out yolk and mix with mustard sauce or hot-dog relish. Stuff eggs gently; fit tops back on.

Great fun for a lunchtime party.

GIANT HERO FOR FOUR

1 foot-long hero loaf
Sliced cold pork with Bermuda onion
  rings and appleberry sauce
Boiled ham and Swiss cheese with
  coleslaw

Little shrimps with crumbled blue
  cheese, salad pickles
Sliced white meat of turkey or chicken
  with cranberry sauce and lettuce
Mayonnaise

Slice the loaf of French bread in half lengthwise. Place the fillings side by side across the sandwich—not one on top of the other. Wrap and take to school with a sharp knife. Slice so that each girl can have a taste of each filling. Pack the mayonnaise separately in a paper cup and let each girl add as desired. *Serves four.*

NOTE: For coleslaw, use three cups shredded raw cabbage and toss with one-half cup School Belle Dressing (page 41).

Here's a pretty schoolday treat.

AMBROSIA IN A C-SHELL

Cut the top from an orange. With a grapefruit knife and spoon, remove the fruit sections. In a bowl, cut them into small pieces; add shredded coconut and fresh or canned cherries. With a sharp knife "pink" the top edge of the orange shell (Vitamin C-shell!), then fill with fruit.

Save up everybody's birthday and celebrate together at lunchtime. For fun, exchange dime-store gifts.

COMMUNITY BIRTHDAY CAKE

1 package (16 oz.) brownie mix	½ cup chopped walnuts
½ cup water, divided	1 package creamy frosting mix
2 eggs, unbeaten	Tubes of decorator frosting to trim
2 teaspoons instant coffee	top

Preheat the oven to 350°F. (moderate). Grease a seven-by-eleven-inch pan. Empty brownie mix into bowl; blend in one-fourth cup of the water and the eggs. Beat one minute in electric mixer at medium speed or 180 strokes by hand. Dissolve instant coffee in remaining one-fourth cup water and add to mix. Beat again for one minute. Fold in walnuts. Turn into prepared pan. Bake thirty minutes or until cake begins to shrink from sides of pan. Cool in pan. Frost with creamy frosting, preparing it according to package directions. Use the same frosting, tinted into different colors, or frosting in tubes to trim. With these, make lines on the cake to form a rectangular piece for each birthday girl. Inside her square, write her name. Wrap in plastic film or foil. At school, add candles (everybody blow!) and cut. *Serves up to twelve.*

A chef's salad lets you get your protein and vegetables in a low-calorie and high-appeal way.

CHEF'S FANCY

Use the standard ingredients if you like: salad greens plus thin strips of Swiss cheese, ham, chicken and tongue. Or use your own favorites: strips of cold cuts or turkey, perhaps; hard-cooked eggs, small, pitted ripe olives, quartered tomatoes or radishes. Arrange them all on a variety of greens in a plastic-coated paper bowl; cover with plastic wrap. Pack about one-fourth cup School Belle Dressing (page 41) separately in a jar and add it just before eating. Don't forget a plastic fork.

For really serious dieters or as a first course for the girl who has no weight worries, this crisp idea:

NIBBLER'S NOSEGAY

Wash and trim your favorite raw vegetables: cucumber sticks, carrot sticks, celery fans, water cress, raw turnip strips, scallions (green onions), radish roses. Lay them on a wet-strength paper napkin, then in a paper doily, last in foil. Twist to form a cone. Now wrap it all (cone and vegetables) in foil or plastic. Vegetables will stay crispy-fresh. At school eat them with a cheese dip or thinned cheese-in-a-jar.

Here's an ice cream soda you can make right at school!

FIZZ WHIZZ

Pack a tall paper cup and a fizzing drink tablet (cherry, strawberry or root beer flavors go best with milk). At school, dissolve the tablet in two tablespoons water in the cup and let it bubble. Add a scoop of ice cream and a small (8-ounce) carton of milk.

Three Beginner Dinners

*P*ARTICULARLY if you've done your homework in previous chapters, you're ready now to graduate. The examination? A dinner meal, of course.

The nicest part of fixing a dinner for the family is that it establishes you in their minds as being a real cook—someone who is worthy of real responsibility.

The trickiest part of cooking a dinner for the first time is getting everything ready to serve at the same time. And for that reason, the dinners which follow are carefully planned so you will do things in the right order.

As you become practiced, you'll learn to spot which parts of a meal can be done in advance and which must be done at the last possible moment. When you choose a menu, you'll automatically eliminate combinations which require, for instance, more burners than your range has to offer. Then you'll be quite safe in plunging forward into the next section, where creative menu making is very much in order.

In the meantime, try these. The resulting dinners are noteworthy, but the step-by-step directions make them a cinch.

BEGINNER DINNER ONE: TURKEY!

Not a whole roast turkey, of course—but almost as special. This menu is party-pretty, and since everything is frozen, canned or boxed, it's a snap.

THE MENU

Turkey Slices with Giblet Gravy
Almond Rice
Italian Beans with Mushrooms
Cranberry Butterflies
Hot Biscuits   Butter
Hot Mincemeat Sundaes
Milk   Coffee

4 5

SHOPPING GUIDE FOR FOUR

5 boxes (5 oz. each) frozen turkey
   slices with gravy
1 package (9 oz.) frozen Italian green
   beans
1 can (8 oz.) refrigerated buttermilk
   biscuits

1 pint vanilla ice cream
1 box precooked rice
1 can (5 oz.) chopped almonds
1 can (4 oz.) sliced mushrooms
1 can (1 lb.) cranberry jelly
1 small jar moist mincemeat

Check your supply of: honey, salt, rum extract, butter.

TIME PLAN

Combine the ingredients for the mincemeat topping (recipe follows on page 47).

Open can of cranberry jelly and slide out contents. Cut off four inch-thick slices. Cut each in half. Put rounded edges together, then trim straight edges a bit to look more like butterfly wings. Arrange on plate; chill.

Open mushrooms; drain slices.

Open chopped almonds; measure out one-half cup.

Read the rice package directions and measure out needed amount.

Set the table with mats or cloth, silver, glasses. Keep the plates warm in the kitchen. You will serve directly onto plates.

About twenty minutes before dinner, preheat the oven to 425°F. (hot).

Fill a large saucepan with water and begin to heat it to boiling for the packets of turkey slices.

Cook rice as package directs.

Bake the biscuits in preheated oven.

Cook beans as package directs.

Measure ground coffee into pot. Use six ounces of water and two tablespoons coffee (one standard coffee measure) for each cup to be made. For four cups, this means four coffee measures of coffee and three eight-ounce cups of water.

Finish setting the table with butter, glasses of water and milk.

Drop packets of turkey slices into boiling water to heat, following label directions.

Just before serving, add mushroom slices to beans for last two minutes of cooking.

When rice is ready, add chopped almonds and two tablespoons butter; toss together and keep warm.

Arrange each plate like this: First, a serving of almond rice. Next, the turkey slices and gravy. Garnish with the two wings of a cranberry butterfly. Last, add the drained Italian beans and mushrooms. Call your guests. Carry plates to the table. Take biscuits from oven, place in basket and serve them. Before you sit down, start the coffee.

At dessert time, begin warming mincemeat honey sauce (below) while you clear the table. Scoop ice cream into four dessert dishes and top each with sauce. Take to table with coffee, cups, cream and sugar.

MINCEMEAT TOPPING

½ cup mincemeat   1 tablespoon honey
½ teaspoon rum extract

Combine in small saucepan over medium heat. Stir until mixture is bubbly. Spoon hot over ice cream. *Serves four.*

BEGINNER DINNER TWO: LAMB CHOPS!

This menu calls for some real cooking, but proceed with confidence. Every step is spelled out.

THE MENU

Broiler Meal: Saratoga Lamb Chops with Barbecued
Potatoes and Onions
Garden Salad
Butterflake Rolls
Cantaloupe and Ice Cream
Milk Coffee Tea

SHOPPING GUIDE FOR FOUR

1 bunch fresh parsley
1 can (1 lb.) potatoes
1 can (1 lb.) onions
1 package (10 oz.) frozen peas
1 small tomato
1 cucumber
1 sweet Bermuda onion

1 head lettuce or other salad greens
1 cantaloupe
1 can (8 oz.) refrigerated butterflake rolls
1 pint vanilla ice cream
5 shoulder lamb chops (1¼ to 1½ lbs.)*

*NOTE: The finest shoulder lamb chop is the Saratoga chop, a boneless, tender cut. You can also use blade or round-bone shoulder chops.

Check your supply of: dry mustard, chili sauce, salt, pepper, vinegar, sugar, lemons, mayonnaise or salad dressing, milk, coffee or tea for a beverage.

TIME PLAN

When you get home from shopping, wash the parsley and lettuce. Drain and pat the greens dry in a paper or linen towel.

Prepare the garden salad (see recipe, page 49) and put it in refrigerator to chill.

Open the cans of onions and potatoes and drain them. Mix up the barbecue sauce as described in the Broiler Meal recipe below.

Cut the melon into four sections and scoop out the seeds with a tablespoon. Sprinkle the wedges with lemon juice and set them on a platter, covered with plastic film or foil, in the refrigerator.

Set the table with all the nonperishables. (The rest of the meal will take only thirty minutes, so you probably have time now for a homework or telephone break.)

Half an hour before dinnertime, heat the broiler, setting the rack so meat will be five inches from heat source. Meantime, bake the butterflake rolls, following directions on can. Finish the salad.

Fifteen minutes before dinner, begin broiling the lamb chops. Then add glasses of water or milk to the table; also the salad, and butter.

As you complete the broiler dinner, make coffee or tea if it is part of your menu.

The moment of truth! Set the hot rolls in a napkin-lined basket, place the meat and vegetables on a platter, garnish with a few sprigs of parsley and take to the table. It's dinnertime!

Afterglow! At dessert time, scoop ice cream onto the melon wedges and serve, along with coffee, to your pleased and proud family. The blue ribbon is all yours!

THE BROILER MEAL

⅓ cup chili sauce
⅓ cup vinegar
2 tablespoons sugar
¼ cup chopped parsley
2 teaspoons salt

¼ teaspoon pepper
5 shoulder lamb chops (1¼ to 1½ lbs.)
1 can (1 lb.) potatoes, drained
1 can (1 lb.) onions, drained

Combine chili sauce, vinegar, sugar, parsley, salt and pepper; mix well. Preheat broiler. Arrange chops on broiler rack. Broil five inches from heat source for five minutes. Turn lamb with cooking fork; add potatoes and onions to pan. Brush all with half the chili sauce mixture. Broil five minutes more. Turn lamb and vegetables (kitchen tongs are handy, if you have them); brush with remaining sauce. Broil five minutes more or until the lamb chops are well browned and tender. *Serves four.*

GARDEN SALAD

1 package (10 oz.) frozen peas	½ teaspoon salt
1 small tomato	⅛ teaspoon pepper
1 cucumber	⅓ cup vinegar
½ sweet onion	½ cup mayonnaise, if desired
⅛ teaspoon dry mustard	Lettuce or other salad greens

Bring one-half cup of water and one-half teaspoon salt to boil. Add peas and bring back to boil. Cook just two minutes more. Turn into strainer to drain off cooking liquid. Rinse for about a minute in running cold water to quick-chill peas. Core the tomato and chop it. Lift pieces into strainer with peas to drain. Peel and chop cucumber into big dice. Peel the half onion and slice it. Separate enough small rings to garnish your salad and chop the rest. Combine mustard, salt, pepper and vinegar. Mix with all vegetables (except onion rings). Chill. Near serving time, drain off the liquid from the salad; taste. If you like, fold in the mayonnaise for a creamy dressing. Place in lettuce-lined bowl; garnish with onion rings. *Serves six.*

BEGINNER DINNER THREE: STEAK FOR COMPANY!

This dinner is planned for eight, but if you want to serve only four, follow the time plan and simply reduce the amounts.

THE MENU

Tomato Juice
Assorted Crackers   Onion Dip
London Broil
Green Peas   Tossed Green Salad
Garlic French Bread
Do-It-Yourself Sundaes

Shopping Guide for Eight

2 flank steaks, 2 lbs. each
4 loaves brown-and-serve French
   bread
¾ lb. butter
1 package onion-soup mix
1 pint commercial sour cream
Crackers and/or chips (follow the
   crowd's preference)
2 quarts tomato juice
2 packages frozen peas
1 head Simpson lettuce

1 head Boston lettuce
1 bunch celery
2 tomatoes
1 package frozen strawberries
1 small can crushed pineapple
1 small can chocolate syrup
1 package chopped pecans
1 jar maraschino cherries
1 can pressure-packed whipped cream
2 quarts ice cream
2 quarts milk

And check supplies of: bottled salad dressing, garlic.

Time Plan

In advance, shop.

Get out linens, silver, glassware, china.

Trim and wash lettuce, celery and tomatoes. Break up lettuce and pat dry. Arrange in salad bowl. Slice enough celery to make two cups, and spread over lettuce. Cover with damp toweling and place, with tomato, in refrigerator.

About three hours before the party, begin thawing strawberries.

Make onion dip, place in serving dish and refrigerate.

An hour before the party, set the table.

Prepare steak and bread for cooking.

Arrange a lazy Suzan full of sundae trimmings: cherries, nuts, pineapple, chocolate syrup and thawed strawberries. Refrigerate.

Arrange a tray of crackers, chips and glasses for tomato juice.

When guests arrive, serve tomato juice, chips and dip.

Preheat broiler and start bread baking.

Add last-minute items to table.

Cook the peas.

Begin broiling steak.

Cut up tomatoes, add to salad and place this on the table with dressing.

At dessert time, scoop ice cream into individual dessert dishes and present, with the lazy Susan of toppings, to your guests.

Then: get help with the dishes!

ONION DIP

1 package onion soup mix   1 pint commercial sour cream

Blend; chill one hour. *Serves eight.*

GARLIC FRENCH BREAD

2 loaves brown-and-serve French   ½ pound butter
   bread   2 cloves garlic, peeled and cut in half

Before baking the bread, slash it diagonally, but not through the bottom of the loaf, into one-inch slices. Melt the butter, add garlic and simmer over very low heat thirty minutes. With a pastry brush, slather hot butter in the cuts and over top and sides of loaf. (Use remaining garlic butter on steak, below.) Bake as package directs. *Serves four boys, four girls.*

LONDON BROIL

Remove excess fat from the two flank steaks. Preheat the broiler and sharpen carving knife. Coat the steak on both sides with garlic butter (above). Set steak on rack of broiler pan so top of steak is two inches from heat. Broil five minutes per side or until brown. Place on cutting board and slice *very* thin, diagonally and across grain. Serve on a warm platter.

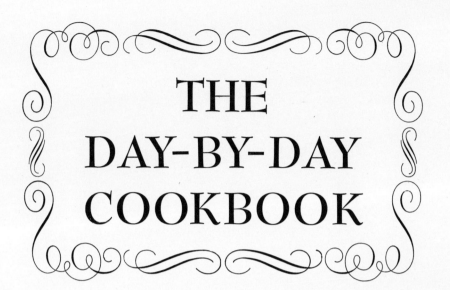

THE
DAY-BY-DAY
COOKBOOK

Main Dishes

BEEF

*A*LPHABETICALLY, beef comes first—which is just as well because it comes first with most men too! Here's a collection of beef recipes—from hamburger to roast beef à la Bordelaise—to make your meat-cooking reputation. But first, to help you at the market:

Ways To Cook Popular Cuts of Beef

Broil these steaks: sirloin, porterhouse, T-bone, club, strip, filet, flank, rib.
Roast: standing ribs, rolled ribs, top sirloin and tenderloin.
Pot-roast: rump, chuck, heel or eye of round and brisket.
Stew: the pot-roast cuts listed above (cut into cubes), plus neck, plate, flank, foreshanks, hind shanks and short ribs.
Braise these steaks: round, rump, chuck (arm or blade steak).

NOTE: At your meat market, you may find cuts with names different from those above. If so, consult the department manager. He'll identify the cut and suggest a cooking method.

Try a Little Tenderness

The wonders of this modern world include—yes!—modern meats. Packers are experimenting with methods of treating meats which increase the tenderness of what were formerly considered the tougher cuts. You may find them in the meat cases under different names, with recommendations to oven-roast what once had to be pot-roasted, and to broil the steak which used to require simmering. Follow the packer's directions for cooking—these cuts are money-saving and often have surprisingly good flavor.

You can alter the tenderness of many cuts yourself by using meat tenderizer, which is on the market in both an unseasoned and seasoned form.

Here again, the label tells you how. Tenderizer is harmless (it is made from *papain*, which comes from the papaya) and serves several purposes besides making meat easier to chew. It tends to reduce shrinkage, reduce cooking time and keep meat juicier.

Everybody's Favorite—Hamburger

When you are learning to cook—for your friends or for your family— you'll find that ground beef is the answer to a beginner's prayer. It's easy to buy, easy to cook, easy to portion out and it can take on a new shape or flavor at the drop of a mixing spoon.

How To Buy Ground Beef

You will find several types at your food market. Choose according to your taste and pocketbook.

Hamburger or Ground Beef—Most meat bearing one of these labels is all ground beef with no more than 30 per cent fat included. Fat keeps beef juicy, so you will find this a flavorful and inexpensive cut, even though you should expect to lose part of the weight in "drippings." (Your local butcher may prepare a special chopped meat for meat loaf. He will tell you if it is all beef or whether veal and pork have been added.)

Ground Chuck—Relatively inexpensive. Good flavor and in general a good choice when chopped beef is called for.

Ground Round—Slightly higher in price. Not so richly flavored but lower in fat. A good choice for the diet-conscious.

Ground Sirloin—Excellent flavor but higher in price.

Any chopped beef you buy should be freshly ground and bright red in color. (If you have an electric meat grinder, you might even grind it yourself!) One pound serves three to four persons, maybe more, if other ingredients are added. Unless it is frozen, chopped meat should be wrapped loosely in waxed paper, kept in the coldest part of the refrigerator and used within two days. If it is already cooked, it should be refrigerated promptly (with a cover) and used within three days.

How To Make Good Hamburgers

Use beef chuck, allowing one-fourth pound per person. Divide meat (use clean hands or a kitchen fork) into as many portions as you want patties. Shape them thick (up to one inch) or thin (one-fourth inch), making sure they are symmetrical and flat.

Seasoning: For a rich brown crust, spread both sides of patties with prepared mustard, steak or Worcestershire sauce, or even gravy coloring.
Sprinkle with monosodium glutamate and, according to taste, with
salt, pepper, onion or garlic salt.

To pan-broil: Heat a skillet or griddle until a drop of water dances on its
surface. Grease lightly. Add patties; brown on both sides. Reduce heat
and cook to desired doneness. For thick patties: four to eight minutes.
For thin patties: one to five minutes.

Serve with catchup, chili sauce, pickle relish or sliced pickles, sweet onion
rings, bits of crumbled blue cheese, steak sauce, grated Cheddar cheese.
Or top each patty with a slice of process American cheese and return
to the broiler for a minute—cheeseburgers!

Hamburger buns are best when they have been buttered in advance and
warmed for ten minutes in a moderate oven or opened and broiled for
thirty seconds or so. By putting special seasonings (curry, garlic salt,
minced chives) in the butter, you can add an exciting taste.

Here's our very best meat loaf recipe, all prettied up for a party. Of
course, it's not strictly necessary to use the ring mold. You can pat the meat
mixture into a log shape and bake it in any rimmed pan. Or pack it
lightly into a bread loaf pan and turn it out for browning as the directions
below indicate.

RING–AROUND MEAT LOAF

2½ lbs. beef chuck	1½ cups corn flakes
½ lb. lean pork	⅓ cup tomato sauce
2 packages dehydrated onion-soup mix	1 teaspoon monosodium glutamate
3 eggs, lightly beaten	1 teaspoon gravy coloring
⅔ cup tomato sauce	¼ cup flour
3 cups water (about)	

Have your butcher grind beef and pork together. Place in bowl. Place
one whole envelope of onion-soup mix and two tablespoons of the second
into a smaller bowl. (Remaining soup mix is used in gravy.) Add eggs,
tomato sauce and one-half cup warm water. Mix well and add to meat,
working in with a fork. Now add corn flakes and mix lightly but thoroughly. Pack into a lightly greased six-and-one-half cup ring mold. Pat
down with back of spoon. Place mold on shallow baking pan; bake at
350°F. (moderate) for one hour. Carefully pour off drippings into a cup.
Invert meat loaf onto shallow baking pan. Brush entire surface of loaf with
two tablespoons of the drippings combined with a few drops of gravy
coloring. Brown at 350°F. five to ten minutes. When meat is brown, set

oven heating to 450°F. (hot) to brown potatoes. Using two spatulas (and help, if possible) gently transfer meat loaf to serving platter. To make gravy, place remaining soup mix in a bowl with two and two-thirds cups of water, the tomato sauce and monosodium glutamate. Measure six table-spoons drippings and one teaspoon gravy coloring into a saucepan. Place over very low heat; gradually stir in flour. Gradually add the tomato-onion mixture, stirring constantly until thickened. Pour the gravy into a boat. If desired, surround meat loaf with mashed potatoes and garnish with parsley. Fill center with cooked peas heated with slivered, canned water chestnuts. *Makes eight to ten servings.*

The fun in this recipe is its heroic size. You cut it like a pie—in wedges —at serving time.

GIANT PARTY BURGER FOR EIGHT

First, make the bun from a mix:

1 package (14 oz.) hot-roll mix	**1 teaspoon instant minced green**
1 cup warm (not hot) water	**onion**

Open box of hot-roll mix and remove yeast packet. Combine water and green onion in a mixing bowl. Sprinkle yeast over water. Stir until dis-solved. Add hot-roll mix, blending well. Cover and let rise in a warm place until almost double in bulk, about thirty minutes. Place dough on a floured board and roll out into a seven-inch round. Transfer to a cookie sheet, cover with a towel, and let rise for thirty minutes. For a crispy golden crust, brush surface with an egg yolk beaten with a little water. Bake at 375°F. (moder-ate) for twenty minutes or until golden brown. While it is cooling on a rack, cook the meat.

Make the skillet-size burger:

2 lbs. ground beef	**½ teaspoon garlic powder**
⅓ cup finely chopped onion	**¼ teaspoon poultry seasoning**
¾ cup dry bread crumbs	**2 teaspoons salt**
2 tablespoons minced parsley	**¼ teaspoon pepper**
½ cup milk	**¼ teaspoon Tabasco sauce**
1 egg	**½ teaspoon monosodium glutamate**
1 teaspoon celery salt	

With a fork, blend beef, onion, bread crumbs and parsley in a bowl. In another bowl beat together the remaining ingredients. Add milk-egg mix-ture to the meat, blending thoroughly with fork. To shape: use a flat ten-inch circle (like the bottom of a spring-form pan) as a guide and press meat onto it to form a flat ten-inch burger. Heat two tablespoons butter in an electric skillet set at 350°F. Add the meat to the skillet this way: flip the circle over into the pan; remove circle, which is now on top. Cook about twelve minutes, pressing down with spatula occasionally. To cook the other side: transfer meat with spatulas to the circle again, then flip into skillet; remove circle. Cook twelve minutes longer. (Burger may also be cooked in oven-proof skillet. Pan-fry on one side over moderate heat twelve minutes. Then place in broiler five inches from heat source for ten minutes more or until top is well browned.) Now split your giant bun in half and transfer meat to bottom half; garnish with catchup and/or onion rings and pickles. Add top of bun and serve. To help you slice the burger evenly into eight pie-shaped wedges, circle the top with flags—one per wedge. Make flags from wooden skewers or party picks, gold seals and colored paper. *Makes eight servings.*

Another partyfied meat loaf, this one features a baked-on cloak of gold!

GOLDEN IGLOO MEAT LOAF

First make a plump, round meat loaf as follows:

1½ cups fine soft bread crumbs	¼ teaspoon Tabasco sauce
1½ lbs. ground lean beef chuck	½ cup evaporated milk
4 egg yolks	3 tablespoons minced green pepper
1½ teaspoons salt	2 tablespoons instant minced onion
2 tablespoons prepared mustard	

Toss together the bread crumbs and meat, then in another bowl mix the remaining ingredients; or measure each ingredient into a blender (substitute one-fourth of a green pepper, seeded) and blend two seconds. Turn the egg mixture into the meat and toss lightly but thoroughly with hands or wooden spoon until blended. Pack lightly but evenly into a one-quart metal or ovenproof glass mixing bowl. Bake at 325°F. (slow) forty minutes. Remove from oven.

Now make the tangy topping:

4 egg whites	¼ teaspoon cream of tartar
Few drops of yellow food coloring	2 tablespoons prepared mustard

Beat egg whites with rotary beater until foamy. Add food color and cream of tartar. Continue beating until very stiff. Fold in mustard gently. Turn meat loaf out of bowl and place in shallow baking dish. Use the topping to coat loaf completely. To simulate the golden ice blocks:

With the sharp edge of a knife cut around and around the topping, about one-fourth inch deep. Then make up-and-down lines between the circular ones, staggering the lines like bricks in a wall. Continue baking the loaf twenty to twenty-five minutes until it is lightly browned. *Makes eight servings.*

A favorite at parties and at family dinners, this recipe goes by many names, though "Sloppy Joes" is perhaps the best known. You can vary its taste by varying the soup used. Examples: tomato, tomato-vegetable, minestrone, chili. When you serve this at parties, provide forks.

SLOPPY JOES

2 tablespoons butter or other fat	½ cup chili sauce
2 lbs. ground beef chuck	2 tablespoons prepared mustard
1 cup chopped onion	¼ teaspoon black pepper
2 cans cream of mushroom soup, undiluted	12 hamburger buns, toasted and buttered

Melt butter in a large skillet. Add beef and onion; cook, stirring until broken up and well browned. Add soup and seasonings; simmer for about ten minutes to blend, stirring occasionally. Serve by ladling mixture onto hot hamburger buns. *Makes twelve.*

Below we tell you how to serve chili in buns hollowed out to form bowls. If you would prefer to omit buns, add enough hot water to bring chili mixture to desired consistency, and serve topped with grated cheese, accompanied by rice or saltines.

RIO GRANDE CHILI BOWL

1 lb. ground beef chuck	1 can (8 oz.) tomato sauce
2 tablespoons flour	2 tablespoons chopped pimiento
1 teaspoon chili powder	8 unsliced hamburger buns or soft
1 teaspoon garlic salt	dinner rolls
1 small onion, chopped	1 can (1 lb.) red kidney beans,
2 tablespoons melted butter	drained
2 cups hot water	

Mix together ground beef, flour, chili powder and garlic salt. Sauté onion in melted butter until transparent. Add meat mixture and cook until well browned. Add hot water, tomato sauce and pimiento and cook twenty to thirty minutes more or until thickened. Meantime, prepare "bowls" from buns. Cut a circle in top of bun leaving a half-inch rim. Lift off circle and hollow out bun to form "bowl," reserving one-fourth cup of crumbs. Add the crumbs and kidney beans during last five minutes of cooking time. If you like, refrigerate chili mixture at this point. Reheat before serving, then fill bun-bowls with the chili mixture. *Eight servings.*

Here's a good flavor in a substantial dinner dish which will wait for late arrivals.

LIMA JOEY

1½ lbs. ground beef chuck
1 medium onion, chopped fine
1 medium green pepper, chopped fine
1 tablespoon chili powder
1 tablespoon prepared mustard
1 tablespoon Worcestershire sauce
1½ teaspoons salt

1 can condensed tomato soup
⅔ cup water
1½ cups cooked dried lima beans
1 can whole kernel corn
1 can (5 oz.) water chestnuts, thinly
   sliced

Cook ground chuck over medium heat until browned, turning frequently. Add onion and green pepper; cook until softened. Add chili powder, mustard, Worcestershire sauce, salt, soup and water. Cover; cook at slow heat twenty minutes. Add limas, corn and water chestnuts. Continue to heat ten minutes more. *Serves six.*

Almost a meal in itself, this oriental combination. Add a tossed salad and serve to discriminating diners.

CANTONESE BEEF BALLS

1 lb. ground beef
¼ cup chopped onion
1 teaspoon salt
1 teaspoon pepper
½ cup milk
¼ cup sugar
1½ tablespoons cornstarch
1 can (8 oz.) pineapple juice
¼ cup vinegar

2 tablespoons water
1 teaspoon soy sauce
3 tablespoons butter, divided
½ cup blanched almonds
1 cup precooked rice
1 cup sliced celery
½ cup sliced green onions
½ small green pepper, cut into strips

Preheat oven to 350°F. (moderate). Combine meat, onion, salt, pepper and milk; mix well and form into twenty balls. Turn into baking pan and bake thirty-five to forty minutes. Meanwhile, combine sugar and cornstarch in saucepan and slowly stir in pineapple juice, vinegar, water, soy sauce and one tablespoon of the butter. Cook over low heat until clear, stirring constantly. Fry almonds in remaining two tablespoons butter until golden; set aside. Cook rice, following package directions. Five minutes before serving time, add celery, onion and green pepper to pineapple soy-sauce mixture. Arrange on platter in layers the rice, meat, vegetable sauce; then top with crisp almonds. *Serves four.*

Here's a casserole just right for entertaining on a budget. It tastes different (but not too different), yet one pound of beef serves six to eight!

HAMBURGER NOODLE BAKE

2 tablespoons butter	2 cans (8 oz. each) tomato sauce
1 lb. chopped beef chuck	1 package (8 oz.) broad noodles
1 clove garlic, minced	6 medium green onions
1 teaspoon salt	1 package (3 oz.) cream cheese
Dash of pepper	½ pint commercial sour cream
1 teaspoon sugar	1 cup grated Cheddar cheese

Melt butter in a large frying pan. Break up and scramble meat in pan until well browned. Add garlic, salt, pepper, sugar and tomato sauce; stir. Cover and simmer for fifteen to twenty minutes. Meantime cook noodles, following package directions, and drain. Cut green onions into large pieces. Place in blender container with cream cheese and sour cream. Blend until green onions are chopped fine and mixture is smooth. (If you haven't a blender, hand-chop the green onions fine and blend with softened cream cheese and sour cream until smooth.) Place one-third of noodles in a two-quart casserole, top with one-third of cheese mixture, then add one-third of the meat mixture. Repeat layers, ending with meat. Sprinkle Cheddar cheese on top. At this point you may either cover and refrigerate overnight, which makes the dish better than ever, or you may bake it immediately. Bake at 350°F. (moderate) for twenty minutes. Let stand ten minutes and serve. *Serves six to eight.*

Here's a meal-in-one but it's *not* a casserole—a skillet does the blending and cooking. Zesty!

CHILI SKILLIE

⅓ cup butter or margarine	1 can (1 lb.) stewed tomatoes
3 cups (8 oz.) shell macaroni	½ cup chili sauce
1 large onion, peeled and chopped	½ cup water
1 lb. chopped beef round	

Melt butter in a large skillet. Add macaroni and onion; cook and stir over medium heat until browned. Push to one side. Add beef. Cook, stirring frequently until browned. Add tomatoes, chili sauce and water. Simmer, stirring often, fifteen minutes. Cover; cook until tender, about ten minutes more. *Serves four.*

Another meal-in-one recipe: add crisp vegetable relishes and dessert and dinner's done!

EASY STROGANOFF BAKE

First make the meat mixture:

1½ lbs. ground beef chuck	¼ teaspoon pepper
1 tablespoon shortening	⅔ cup (7 oz. can) drained mushroom
½ cup chopped onion	caps
2 tablespoons chopped parsley	1 can condensed vegetable soup
½ small clove garlic, minced	1 cup commercial sour cream
1 teaspoon salt	½ cup milk

Brown beef in shortening with onion, parsley and garlic. Stir in salt, pepper, mushrooms and soup; simmer fifteen minutes. Blend in sour cream and milk; heat thoroughly. Place in a nine-inch square baking dish or a two-and-one-half-quart ovenproof casserole dish.

And now, the biscuit topping:

1½ cups sifted flour	¼ teaspoon pepper
2 teaspoons baking powder	¼ cup shortening
1 teaspoon paprika	¾ cup milk
½ teaspoon salt	1 teaspoon poppy seeds
½ teaspoon celery seed	

Sift into a mixing bowl the flour, baking powder, paprika, salt, celery seed and pepper. Cut in shortening with pastry blender or two knives until particles are fine. Add milk; stir only until all dry particles are moistened. Drop by tablespoonfuls onto meat mixture. Sprinkle with poppy seed. Bake at 475°F. (hot) fifteen to twenty minutes until golden brown. *Serves six.*

Fun to taste, these meat balls. Fun to talk about, too, if you add a surprise feature like this: Make up the meat mixture below, but leave the olives and pitted prunes whole. Shape the meat into twenty little patties. Place an olive inside each prune, then press two patties around each stuffed prune to form flattened meat balls. Then proceed with the browning of meat balls and preparation of sauce as recipe directs. Your guests will be delighted.

HIDDEN TREASURES

1½ lbs. chopped beef chuck
½ cup finely chopped onion
⅔ cup fine dry bread crumbs
1 egg, slightly beaten
½ cup milk
½ teaspoon salt
¼ teaspoon pepper
2 teaspoons Worcestershire sauce
½ teaspooned seasoned meat
   tenderizer

10 stuffed green olives, chopped
10 plumped prunes, pitted and diced
2 tablespoons shortening
1 can condensed cream of mushroom
   soup
½ soup can of water
1 package (8 oz.) broad noodles
⅓ cup butter or margarine

In a large bowl, combine meat, onions, bread crumbs, egg, milk, salt, pepper, Worcestershire sauce, tenderizer, olives and prunes. Mix lightly but well. Shape into small (one-and-one-half-inch) balls. Heat fat in a large skillet. Add meat balls and brown on all sides. To soup, gradually add water. Pour over meat balls. Cover and simmer twenty minutes or until done. (If you make the meat balls the night before your party, refrigerate them at this point. Before serving, heat fifteen to twenty minutes—while the noodles are cooking.) Cook noodles in boiling salted water according to package directions, until tender. Drain and toss with butter. Place meat balls and gravy in a chafing dish and serve with noodles. *Serves eight.* (Recipe may be doubled for sixteen.)

When you want to dazzle company with something a little more sophisticated than spaghetti, yet a guaranteed crowd-pleaser, make it lasagne. It can be prepared a day ahead and baked near party time. Add a tossed green salad, a fresh fruit dessert and your sensational supper is complete.

LASAGNE

First make the meat sauce:

1 lb. chopped beef chuck
½ cup soft bread crumbs
⅓ cup grated Parmesan cheese
1 teaspoon minced parsley
½ teaspoon grated lemon peel
¼ teaspoon minced garlic

Dash of nutmeg
¼ teaspoon pepper
1 teaspoon salt
2 tablespoons olive or cooking oil
2 cans (15½ oz. each) mushroom
   spaghetti sauce

Combine beef in a mixing bowl with everything except oil and spaghetti sauce. Shape by half-teaspoonfuls into tiny meat balls. Heat the oil in a

Dutch oven or large deep skillet. Add meat balls and brown on all sides. Add the spaghetti sauce and stir lightly to combine; then simmer gently thirty minutes. Meanwhile, prepare the other ingredients.

To cook the noodles:

6 quarts boiling water	1 tablespoon oil
2 tablespoons salt	1 lb. lasagne noodles

When water comes to a full rolling boil, add salt and oil. Then add the noodles, one strip at a time, stirring often to keep them from sticking to the pan or to one another. Cook, following package directions, until just tender. Put into colander; rinse in cold water. Lay out noodles on paper toweling to prevent sticking.

To complete the dish:

1½ lbs. ricotta or cottage cheese	2 teaspoons minced parsley
2 eggs	½ lb. mozzarella cheese, sliced very
1 teaspoon salt	thin
¼ teaspoon pepper	¾ cup grated Parmesan cheese

Combine ricotta with eggs, salt, pepper and parsley and set aside. Grease a casserole thirteen-by-nine-by-two inches. On the bottom, spread one-fourth (about a cup) of the sauce mixture. For the first layer: add a third of the noodles, overlapping each. Distribute over this a third of the ricotta mixture, a third of the mozzarella and another fourth of the sauce, distributing meat balls. Sprinkle all with a third of the Parmesan. Repeat to make three layers. Bake half an hour at 350°F. (moderate). Or refrigerate until party time, then bake forty-five minutes. Cool ten minutes. *Cut into about ten squares; serve.*

ONE WAY TO A MAN'S HEART—STEAK

In times past, a young lady who wanted to choose a perfect steak would blush prettily, blink worriedly and explain her problem to a very good butcher. This still works—if there's a butcher in evidence! But if, instead, you are faced with tidy rows of labeled packages, follow the general guide for selection below:

Choose high-quality meat. The label of a reputable packer ensures a high standard. So does a grade stamped by the United States Department of Agriculture. For broiling, beef should be stamped U.S.D.A. Prime or Choice. Choice beef is marbled with streaks of white fat throughout the bright red, firm meat.

Buy the amount you will need. Most people eat between six and twelve ounces of bone-free steak. That means a three-pound steak will serve five to six people.

Select a good thickness. For broiling, steaks should be between one and two inches thick. Steaks thinner than one inch should be pan-broiled quickly.

Pick a broilable cut. Referring to the guide on page 55, you will find these are sirloin, porterhouse, T-bone, club, strip, filet, flank, rib. In addition, your meat market may offer special cuts with which you can experiment and perhaps achieve excellent results. Flank steak is delicious broiled, but needs a special slicing technique before serving. (See *London Broil*, page 51.)

How To Broil a Steak

Preheat the broiler. If desired, pretreat steak with tenderizer.

Trim extra fat from the steak, but leave at least a one-third inch margin of fat. Slash this fat edge with a sharp knife at one-inch intervals. This prevents curling while steak broils.

Season the surfaces of the steak as you like: Tabasco, Worcestershire, bottled steak sauce, a cut clove of garlic, salt, freshly ground pepper, prepared mustard or any of the seasoned salts may be used.

Adjust broiling pan so top of steak will be from four inches away from heat (when the steak is very thick) to two inches away (for one-inch-thick steak). Place steak on rack over broiling pan.

Time your broiling *and* test for doneness. The time will depend not only on how thick the steak is, but also how *you* like it. Steaks two inches thick will be broiled rare in about fifteen minutes per side—it takes twenty minutes per side to make them well done. Steaks one inch thick will be rare after only five minutes per side, and eight minutes for each side will make them well done. To be sure, test by cutting deeply into meat and looking at color.

To turn all-American steak into an international experience (a party in itself, really) try the recipe below. The inspiration came from *Fondue Bourguignonne*, a classic served in the chalets of the Swiss Alps. But in its journey across the Atlantic it has collected a new name!

DUNK–A–BOBS AND DIPS

Essential for the fun is a chafing dish (used without the water pan) or an electric skillet set at 210°F. or a special fondue cooker with an alcohol burner. Get everything ready some time before the party—your guests will do the cooking.

1 lb. boneless beef, cut into one-inch cubes (use filet, boneless sirloin or club steak, or round steak treated with meat tenderizer)

¼ lb. chicken livers, drained
1 package (8 oz.) brown-and-serve sausages
1 jar (6 oz.) cocktail franks

Arrange these meats in an attractive pattern on a serving platter, cover and refrigerate until cooking time.

Prepare the garnishes:

1 sweet onion, peeled and chopped
½ cup minced parsley
1 pint mayonnaise
1 can (3½ oz.) deviled ham

2 teaspoons prepared horse-radish
1 tablespoon minced onion
3 tablespoons sweet pickle relish

Select six pretty serving bowls. Place onion in one bowl, parsley in second. Divide mayonnaise into four bowls. Mix one-fourth with deviled ham, one-fourth with horse-radish, one-fourth with onion and one-fourth with pickle. Cover these and refrigerate until party time, too.

Set the table with a large plate and two forks (preferably fondue forks, which are very pointed) for each guest. The chafing dish or other cooker goes in the center of the table. Meat and sauces will be passed about by the guests.

Now to cook:

½ lb. butter   1 pint peanut oil

Heat enough butter and peanut oil to be one and one-half inches deep in cooker. Fat should be bubbling, but not smoking. Now guests proceed —one fork spears the meat of choice, dunks it in the bubbling butter to cook (about one minute), then dunks it into one of the savory dips before eating. Meanwhile, the other fork cooks the next piece. Informal, gay, delicious. *The amounts above will serve six generously.*

So inexpensive it can be a regular family dinner—so much fun you can serve it for company.

CHUCKABOBS

1 lb. beef chuck cut in 1½-inch cubes
Meat tenderizer
2 tablespoons bottled barbecue sauce

2 tablespoons cooking oil
2 tablespoons vinegar

Sprinkle beef chuck with tenderizer, and pierce it with a fork all over. Mix sauce, oil and vinegar and pour over chuck. Let stand at least thirty minutes, turning occasionally. Place on skewers, or in a wire-grill steak basket. Broil about two inches from heat, turning frequently until browned. *Serves three to four.*

For glamour: Alternate cubes of beef with canned tiny white onions, wedges of sweet green or red pepper, mushrooms, chunks of tomato. Brush vegetables with melted butter, sprinkle with salt and pepper, then proceed as above.

It's Polynesia which inspires the combination of pineapple and soy sauce for main-dish cooking. Try this at your next *luau!*

HAWAIIAN STEAK

1 round steak (about 2 lbs.), 1½ inches thick	⅛ teaspoon black pepper
Nonseasoned meat tenderizer	1 teaspoon dry mustard
2 teaspoons powdered ginger	1 tablespoon sugar
1 clove garlic, minced	¼ cup soy sauce
	¼ cup pineapple juice

Over the round steak, sprinkle meat tenderizer evenly. Prick deeply all over with fork; let stand at room temperature one hour. Meanwhile make the steak sauce by combining all remaining ingredients except pineapple juice. Preheat the broiler. Place steak on a rack in broiling pan. Pour pineapple juice over steak, then brush with half the soy mixture. Broil steak five inches from source of heat ten minutes. Turn; brush with remaining sauce. Broil ten minutes more. *Serves five.*

If you thought chuck steak was good *before,* try it à la Stroganoff!

RUSSIAN STEAK

1½ lbs. lean chuck steak	½ teaspoon salt
1 teaspoon meat tenderizer	¼ teaspoon pepper
6 slices bacon, diced	1 can condensed consommé
1 medium onion, minced	2 cans (3 oz. each) sliced mushrooms
1 clove garlic, minced	1 cup commercial sour cream
¼ cup flour	

Place steak on cutting board. Sprinkle both sides with meat tenderizer; pierce all over with a kitchen fork. Allow to stand at room temperature one hour, then cut into thin strips, about one-fourth inch thick and two inches in length. Fry diced bacon slowly in a large skillet, pouring off excess fat as it collects. Remove bacon and all but two tablespoons of fat; reserve bacon. Add onion and garlic to pan, sauté till golden. Combine flour, salt, pepper; coat meat with this mixture and add to pan. Brown on all sides; stir in consommé and mushrooms (with their liquid). Simmer, uncovered, twenty minutes or until mixture has thickened and meat is tender. Before serving stir in sour cream and bacon bits. Heat for a minute (but don't boil!). *Serve over buttered noodles to six.*

Sure way to fun is the Sukiyaki party. Most people enjoy sitting on cushions around a low table and watching their meal prepared before their eyes. You try it!

SUKIYAKI

Buy a steak two inches thick. Cut it into slices three inches wide and one-eighth inch thick. You'll need one and one-half pounds of beef. You can use club, rib, sirloin or less expensive round or chuck steak. After slicing it wafer thin, sprinkle all sides—one hour before eating time—with one and one-half teaspoons unseasoned meat tenderizer. Let stand at room temperature. Also prepare:

2 Bermuda onions, sliced
8 scallions, cut in 1½-inch pieces
4 stalks celery, sliced
1 cup sliced green cabbage
¼ cup sliced canned bamboo shoots

½ cup drained canned water chestnuts
1 cup drained canned bean sprouts
¾ cup sliced mushrooms
1 cup raw spinach, washed, drained and shredded

Arrange the vegetables in symmetrical rows on a serving tray, leaving room for the tenderized beef. Cover with foil and refrigerate until ready to cook. Then combine and have ready:

⅓ cup soy sauce
⅔ cup beef bouillon
2 tablespoons lemon juice

2 tablespoons sugar
2 teaspoons monosodium glutamate

At party time, heat in an electric skillet, preheated to 360°F.:

2 tablespoons cooking oil

At the table: Add the strips of beef to the skillet and, turning frequently, brown evenly. Add the soy sauce mixture. Turn heat to low (in electric skillet, 220°F.). Push the beef to one side. Add onions, scallions, celery and cabbage. Cook for four minutes, tossing vegetables as they soften. Then add the remaining vegetables and cook about five minutes more or until vegetables are crispy-tender. *Serve* on heapings of hot, fluffy rice, in separate bowls, *to eight newly oriented Americans.*

It is perfectly true that men like stew. And when the stew is really good, so does everyone else. Here's a really good one, with a special trick for serving it hot at parties.

HARVEST STEW

½ lb. bacon slices, diced
4 lbs. round steak, cut into 1-inch cubes
Salt and pepper
4 green onions, chopped
6 carrots, cut into 1-inch thick slices
1 clove garlic, minced
2 tablespoons flour

2 cans condensed beef consommé
1 can (1 lb.) boiled white onions with liquid
1 can (6 oz.) mushroom caps with liquid
2 teaspoons parsley flakes
1 teaspoon celery salt

In a large skillet, fry bacon till crisp, then set aside—leaving enough fat to cover bottom of pan. Season beef with salt and pepper; brown in bacon pan, adding more fat as needed. Add green onions, carrots and garlic; continue cooking till carrots take on color. Add flour, stir lightly, then transfer stew to Dutch oven. Add consommé, boiled onions, mushrooms (with liquids), parsley and celery salt. Add water if needed, to make liquid cover meat. Bring to boil, reduce heat, simmer for an hour and a quarter, until meat is tender. Season gravy to taste. Serve at once, or, if desired, refrigerate. To serve: fill individual foil pans with one cup each of stew; top with bacon. Wrap pans in foil, put remaining stew in casserole. Keep warm in slow oven; *serve in the foil pans to eight.*

RIB ROAST OF BEEF

How to buy: There are three styles of rib roast—a standing ten-inch rib roast which weighs from seven pounds (for two ribs) up. A standing seven-inch rib roast is similar, but the "short ribs" have been removed, to be sold separately. It is a little more expensive per pound, but it includes less waste. A rolled rib roast has no bone and little waste. Because of this, and because it involves more effort on the part of the butcher, it is more expensive, but it is a great joy to the carver.

How to store: Place the roast on a platter, loosely cover and keep refrigerated not longer than five days before cooking.

How to roast: Look up, on the timetable below, the time required to roast the cut you've chosen to the desired degree of doneness, and plan your preparations accordingly. The roast should be finished twenty minutes before dinner hour. This gives the meat time to "firm up" out of the oven, makes carving easier, and gives you time to make the gravy.

Preheat the oven to 325°F. (slow). If you like, rub the surface of the roast with salt and pepper. Place meat on a rack in a roasting pan, fat side up. Insert a roast meat thermometer into the thickest part of the meat. Be sure the point of the thermometer does not rest against bone, gristle or fat. Roast according to timetable. Basting should not be necessary. Remove to platter or cutting board while you make gravy. Carve after fifteen minutes.

See also Brown Gravy for Roast (page 120).

TIMETABLE FOR RIB ROAST

	Weight	For *Rare*—Meat Thermometer should read 140°F.	For *Medium*—Meat Thermometer should read 160°F.
Standing ribs	4 lbs.	1 hr. 45 min.	2 hrs.
	6 lbs.	2 hrs. 15 min.	2 hrs. 30 min.
	8 lbs.	3 hrs.	3 hrs. 30 min.
Rolled ribs	4 lbs.	2 hrs. 15 min.	2 hrs. 30 min.
	6 lbs.	3 hrs.	3 hrs. 20 min.

NOTE: If it's very important that meat be just right—very rare, for instance—you should know that internal temperature will continue to climb after meat is removed from oven. If you take out roast at 135° on meat thermometer, it will be 140° by carving time.

SMALL BEEF ROASTS FOR DINNERS FOR FOUR

Buying the roast: For four people, you need about three pounds of beef without bone. One good small cut for roasting is a sirloin tip, sometimes called silver tip. Have the butcher wrap it in suet and tie it in shape. (You can cut strings a half hour before serving and pull them off.) There are also several pre-tenderized beef cuts which might fit your plans. Among these tasty, thrifty cuts are boneless chuck roast, Savoy oven roast and Miami roll oven roast.

Cooking your roast: Follow the rules in the preceding directions for Rib Roast, using the same temperatures but the time guides below.

Sirloin tip: Cook it thirty-three minutes per pound if you want it rare; thirty-seven minutes per pound for medium. You may want to use a tenderizer. If you do, follow the directions on tenderizer label.

Pre-tenderized cuts: The meat thermometer is especially important with these meats, since thickness varies. Time guides which follow are approximate.

Pre-tenderized boneless chuck roast: A three-pound roast takes about two and a quarter hours for rare; two and three-quarter hours for medium.

Savoy oven roast: Three pounds will take about fifty minutes for rare; about one and a quarter hours for medium.

Miami-roll oven roast: A three-pound roast of this cut takes one and three-quarter hours for rare, two and a quarter hours for medium.

The French believe that nothing is so good it can't be better. Hence, they devised this way of making pot-roast-gone-to-heaven. It's savory and rich in herb flavor.

ROAST BEEF À LA BORDELAISE

1 piece (4 lbs.) boneless beef: sirloin
tip or rolled rump cut
2 teaspoons meat tenderizer
1 onion, peeled and sliced
4 scallions, peeled and chopped
1 bay leaf, crumbled

4 sprigs parsley
½ teaspoon dried thyme
2 teaspoons salt
⅛ teaspoon pepper
½ cup olive oil
¼ cup wine vinegar

Begin a day in advance. Remove the fat from outside the roast and save for following day. Sprinkle all over with meat tenderizer and pierce deeply with fork. In a bowl just big enough to hold meat, mix the remaining ingredients. Add the beef, cover and place in the refrigerator to marinate overnight. (Turn beef from time to time.) About three hours before beef is to be served, place a large piece of beef fat in the bottom of a roasting pan. Arrange the herbs and vegetables from the marinade over fat, then top with beef. Bake at 325°F. (slow) two and a half hours. Baste often with the marinade liquid. At serving time, skim off the fat from the juice in pan; serve the juice with the meat. *Enough for eight.*

VEAL

Veal, which is really very young beef, can be a good friend to a new cook. Veal roasts are delicious, and many people are fond of veal chops. Veal is low in fat, and just because of this, it often requires a slightly slower, longer cooking than beef. Our odds-on favorite among veal dishes follows. It's so good it can go to dinner parties as well as family meals.

VEAL SURPRISE

¾ lb. veal scallopine (very thin veal
cutlet)
4 thin slices boiled ham or prosciutto
(Italian ham)

4 thin slices Swiss cheese
1 egg, lightly beaten
⅔ cup crumbled blue-cheese crackers
¼ cup cooking oil or butter

On each thin slice of veal place a slice of Swiss cheese, top with a slice of ham. Roll up together, skewer with a toothpick. Dip meat in beaten egg. Then roll in cracker crumbs. Fry in gently bubbling fat, turning to brown all sides—about fifteen minutes. *Serves four.*

Here's a dish that has become a classic:

VEAL PARMIGIANA

2 tablespoons olive oil
2 tablespoons chopped onion
1 small clove garlic, slivered
1 can (8 oz.) tomato purée
2 tablespoons tomato paste
¼ cup water
¼ teaspoon salt
Dash of pepper

1 teaspoon minced fresh parsley
⅛ teaspoon orégano
½ cup butter or margarine
2 boxes (8 oz. each) frozen breaded
  veal cutlets
2 tablespoons grated Parmesan cheese
¾ cup shredded process American
  cheese

Heat olive oil in a small saucepan and in it brown lightly the onion and garlic. Add tomato purée and paste, water, salt, pepper, parsley and orégano. Simmer gently twenty minutes. Meanwhile, heat butter in a heavy skillet. Add the veal cutlets and brown well. Place in a single layer in a baking dish and spoon over the tomato sauce. Sprinkle with cheeses. Bake at 350°F. (moderate) for ten to fifteen minutes. *Serves four.*

LIVER

Also from the young beef animal comes calf's liver. And if there was ever a meat you should eat faithfully—once a week at least—it's liver. It's a first-class source of iron *and* vitamin A, both nutrients that teen-age girls are apt to be short of. Liver is delicious when floured and fried in bacon fat, about three minutes per side, or until brown. (Fried onions and crisp bacon enhance it further.) It's also a treat when broiled in lemon juice and butter—three to four inches from heat and about four minutes per side. And for a really marvelous European flavor, try:

THURSDAY DINNER

1 lb. calf's liver, sliced thin
½ cup (1 stick) butter
1 envelope (1½ oz.) dehydrated
  onion soup

½ cup water
2 teaspoons wine vinegar
⅛ teaspoon pepper

Cut across slices of liver to make thin strips. Melt butter in a large skillet over medium heat. Add strips of liver and sauté until just browned on all sides, about two minutes. Stir in remaining ingredients. Blend well. Cook for three minutes. Serve immediately with hot buttered rice. *Serves four.*

DRIED BEEF

Does the emergency shelf at your house include dried beef? (Some people call it chipped beef.) Its salty, smoky flavor can be especially welcome as a relief from rich foods. Many like it in cream sauce on toast. We like it best in the recipe below. Use a piecrust mix or your own pastry for the shell.

SUPER SUPPER PIE

1 can (1 lb.) baked beans with
    tomato sauce
⅓ cup catchup
2 tablespoons dark brown sugar
1 package (4 oz.) dried beef (rinse if
    desired)

¼ lb. soft process American cheese
½ lb. sliced bacon
1 nine-inch chilled, unbaked pastry
    shell with decorative stand-up edge

Combine beans, catchup and brown sugar. Tear dried beef into bits. Cut cheese into half-inch cubes. Fry the bacon until it is not quite crisp; drain. Now assemble: place bean mixture in pie shell, cover with dried beef, then cheese and last the bacon, arranged in a pretty pattern. Bake at 400°F. (hot) twenty-five to thirty minutes, long enough to melt cheese and brown other ingredients. *Serves six.*

CHICKEN

Chicken ranks right up with franks and hamburgers as tops for party fare. Its low price makes it ideal for family meals, too. Boys like fried chicken best, of course, but for dinner and supper parties, there are marvelous ways to vary its flavor to please the group you've invited.

CHOOSING, PREPARING AND SERVING CHICKEN

Rock Cornish
1–1½ lbs.

A special new breed of small, plump chicken. Best for roasting or baking whole, in sauce. Serve one to a person.

Broiler-Fryer
1½–3½ lbs.

Most versatile type—a young, meaty chicken which can be broiled, fried, simmered in sauce, sautéed, rotisseried, baked or roasted! Serves two to four. When cut up, good for frying or baking. Use wings, breast, second joints and legs but save neck, back and giblets for soups.

Roaster 3½–5 lbs.	A bit heavier, older than broiler-fryer. Best when roasted—with or without stuffing. Serves four to six.
Capon 4–7 lbs.	Lots of white meat; ideal for roast chicken dinner. Serves six to eight.
Stewing Chicken 4½–6 lbs.	Odd fact: larger stewing hens are more tender. Use for creamed or simmered dishes, stews, soups. Serves about six.
Chicken parts	For parties you can buy packaged legs, breasts to add to broiler-fryer. For special dishes, you may want to buy only legs or breasts.

To store chicken: Put in coldest part of the refrigerator, lightly wrapped, until ready to use—keep no more than four days. Wash and pat dry. If chicken is frozen, thaw in refrigerator overnight.

To make fried chicken extra crusty: Shake chicken pieces in a bag with seasoned flour. (For one-half cup flour, use one-half teaspoon salt, a dash of pepper, one teaspoon paprika.) Dip pieces quickly into one egg beaten with a little water, then roll in remaining seasoned flour mixed with fine, dry bread crumbs, crumbled potato chips or crisp cereal. Fry in a half-inch of fat, meaty pieces first. Use moderate heat, turn chicken with tongs (not fork). When browned, pour off excess fat, cover pan; cook slowly on top of range or in slow oven (325°F.) thirty to forty minutes, until leg feels tender when pressed. For crispness, cook uncovered last ten minutes.

Chicken *can* have a crisp crust even if it's not deep-fried. The following recipe trims a few calories from conventional fried chicken; it is one to keep in mind if Dad's on a low cholesterol diet. Easy, too.

NO–FRY FRIED CHICKEN

1 broiler-fryer chicken	1 tablespoon sesame seeds
1 cup packaged corn flake crumbs	½ teaspoon paprika
1 teaspoon salt	¼ teaspoon powdered thyme
⅛ teaspoon pepper	½ cup undiluted evaporated milk
1 teaspoon monosodium glutamate	

Cut chicken into serving pieces. Combine corn flake crumbs and seasonings in a pie plate. Dip chicken in milk, then roll in corn flake crumbs. Place in a shallow, foil-lined baking pan, skin side up. Bake, uncovered, in moderate oven (350°F.) for one hour or until tender. No need to turn during baking. *Serves four.*

Here's still another recipe which gives the fried chicken effect without really frying. Butter and bread crumbs are the secret.

SUCCULENT BAKED CHICKEN

1 small onion, minced	2 teaspoons salt
¼ cup minced parsley	⅛ teaspoon pepper
2 cups fine dry bread crumbs	1 broiler-fryer, cut in serving pieces
¾ cup grated Parmesan cheese	¾ cup (1½ sticks) butter, melted

Combine onion, parsley, crumbs, cheese, salt and pepper. Dip pieces of chicken in melted butter; roll in crumb mixture. Place chicken pieces in baking pan large enough to hold them with no overlapping. Sprinkle all the remaining bread-crumb mixture and melted butter over chicken. Bake at 350°F. (moderate) one hour. *Serves four.*

And here's another to serve right away or later, cold or heated up again on a picnic grill! It's highly spiced and different.

DIXIE–DEVILED CHICKEN

2 broiler-fryers (about 2½ lbs. each) cut up	1½ teaspoons monosodium glutamate
1 cup chili sauce	3 teaspoons salt
2 tablespoons cooking oil	½ teaspoon pepper
2 eggs	¼ teaspoon Tabasco sauce

A day in advance, prepare the chicken. It will absorb even more flavor if you skin it before it is marinated. The skin peels off like a tight stocking —cover your fingers with a paper towel to eliminate slipperiness. When it's ready, mix all the ingredients above in a large bowl, and place the chicken pieces in it. Cover and marinate at least three hours, preferably overnight.

Now to fry the chicken:

2 cups flour	2 teaspoons dry mustard
2 teaspoons salt	2 teaspoons garlic salt
4 teaspoons paprika	4 tablespoons grated Parmesan cheese
½ teaspoon cayenne pepper	Cooking oil for deep frying

Mix all these ingredients except the oil in a clean large paper or plastic bag. Place chicken pieces on a rack to drain briefly, then place a few at a time in flour bag and shake to coat thoroughly. Heat fat (you'll need a depth of about one and one-half inches) to 360°F. Lower chicken into fat and fry about eight minutes per side or until deep golden brown. Drain on paper towel. Serve at once. Or cool thoroughly, then seal carefully in foil, allowing two pieces of chicken per foil packet. Carry to picnic to eat cold or reheat in foil wrapping over barbecue fire—about eight minutes per side. *Serves six generously.*

This chicken tastes good hot or cold. Great for picnics, long car trips, even lunch at school.

BATTER–FRIED CHICKEN

2 broiler-fryer chickens, about 2 lbs. each
2 teaspoons monosodium glutamate
1 teaspoon garlic powder
Salt and pepper to taste

Fat for deep frying
1 cup pancake mix
¼ teaspoon salt
¾ cup water

Cut the broiler-fryers into serving-size pieces. Sprinkle cut sides with monosodium glutamate, garlic powder and salt and pepper. Heat the fat to 350°F. In a mixing bowl, combine pancake mix, salt and water and beat about two minutes. Dip the chicken, one piece at a time, into batter; drain well on wire rack. Fry in hot fat until brown. Drain on paper toweling. Place in greased skillet, cover and cook over low heat ten minutes more. Serve at once or cool thoroughly, wrap in aluminum foil and keep refrigerated until picnic time. *Serves five.*

Most of the "work" of roast chicken, we have discovered, is in stuffing it. Since we believe in "easy does it," we make this daring suggestion: don't stuff it! The chicken will still be delicious, especially when onion and celery are used in the baking. For your conventional moods, however, directions for stuffing a chicken appear below.

ROAST CHICKEN

1 roasting chicken (4 lbs.)
2 teaspoons meat tenderizer
1 onion, peeled

1 rib celery
4 tablespoons butter or margarine

Rinse chicken inside and out with cold water and pat dry. Sprinkle entire cavity with meat tenderizer. Holding the cavity open, use a fork to prick thigh area from the cavity side. Do not pierce skin. Cover chicken loosely with aluminum foil and allow to stand at room temperature for one hour before cooking or refrigerate overnight. Before roasting, place onion and celery stalk in cavity. Tie legs together and rub skin with butter. Place bird, breast side up, on a V-shaped rack in a shallow pan. Roast chicken at 300°F. (slow). During roasting, baste with drippings from pan. If surface browns in spots, cover spots with wet paper towel. Roast for two hours or until juice runs clear when fork is inserted in thigh. *Serves six.*

Stuffing the chicken: If stuffing is desired, try the prepared dry stuffing; follow package directions. Spoon a little into breast cavity through neck opening. Close neck opening by folding skin onto the back and fastening with a skewer. Stuff the main cavity, not too full; close the opening by placing skewers across it and lacing them with string. A stuffed four-pound chicken will take about two and one-half hours.

This recipe *tastes* like spring—lemony and scalliony—and it's the kind of springtime you can have all year 'round. Low in calories, too.

SPRING CHICKEN

1 broiler-fryer chicken cut into serving pieces	2 tablespoons melted butter
1 teaspoon monosodium glutamate	2 tablespoons lemon juice
1 teaspoon salt	½ cup chopped scallions
1 teaspoon paprika	2 tablespoons chopped parsley

Wash and pat chicken dry. Sprinkle with monosodium glutamate, salt and paprika. Place pieces skin side up in a shallow baking dish. Combine butter, lemon juice, scallions and parsley. Spoon over chicken. Bake at 375°F. (moderate) one hour or until golden. Baste occasionally with pan drippings. *Serves four.*

Mexican dish: the chicken is first sautéed, then gently simmered in many delicious ingredients.

CHICKEN SOUTH OF THE BORDER

2 frying chickens (2 lbs. each), cut into serving-size pieces	2 medium tomatoes, chopped
Seasoned flour	1 cup raisins
¼ cup shortening	½ cup sliced stuffed olives
1 medium onion, chopped	2 cups water
	1 stick cinnamon

Dip pieces of chicken into seasoned flour. Heat shortening in a large skillet. Add onion and chicken pieces and brown well over moderate heat.

Add tomatoes and cook five minutes. Add raisins, olives and water. Cover pan and reduce heat. Simmer one hour. Add cinnamon stick and stir five minutes. Remove cinnamon stick and serve with hot rice. *Serves six.*

Paella, made in Spain, is usually a time-consuming dish to prepare. But if you take advantage of convenience foods you can make it *pronto!* And from all who eat you'll hear *olé!*

PAELLA PRONTO

To begin, you'll need:

½ lb. hot Italian sausage
¼ cup flour
1 teaspoon salt
⅛ teaspoon pepper
2 broiler-fryers, cut into serving pieces
 (total weight, 4 lbs.)

2 tablespoons olive oil
1 can condensed chicken vegetable
 soup
½ soup-can water

Cut sausage into one-inch pieces and fry in large skillet. While sausage is browning, mix flour, salt and pepper in a dish and dip chicken pieces into it. (Use only breasts, legs, second joints, wings.) When sausage is done, transfer it to a Dutch oven, leaving sausage fat in the skillet. Add olive oil to skillet, then chicken, and brown pieces lightly all over. When done, put chicken in Dutch oven, add soup and water; simmer, tightly covered, about fifteen to twenty minutes.

To prepare the rice:

2 cans (1 lb. each) tomatoes
¼ teaspoon powdered saffron

2 boxes (6 oz. each) Spanish rice mix

While chicken is cooking, heat tomatoes to the boiling point. Remove from heat, then stir in the saffron and rice mix; cover and let stand about twenty minutes.

Now for the last touch:

1 package (10 oz.) frozen peas
1 package (9 oz.) frozen artichoke
 hearts
1 lb. frozen, cleaned, uncooked
 shrimp

1 can (7 oz.) pimiento, cut in strips
1 teaspoon garlic salt
1 quart cherrystone clams

Add all but the clams to the chicken, toss to mix and continue heating. Fifteen minutes before serving time arrange the scrubbed cherrystone clams —in the shell—on top of the chicken. (Or use canned clams, tossing them in with vegetables.) When clam shells open, you're ready to serve! Remove a few clams for garnishing, then mix the saffron rice in thoroughly with the chicken and turn everything into a big serving dish. Top with clams. This will stretch to serve ten guests. Or *serve it to six—with seconds.*

Something marvelous from South America—chicken stuffed with savory noodles and mushrooms. Fun for a fiesta dinner.

ROAST CHICKEN PARAGUAY

1 roasting chicken (5 lbs.)
Cooking oil
Salt and paprika to taste
1 tablespoon olive oil
1 small clove garlic, peeled
1 tablespoon minced onion
2 cups fresh sliced mushrooms (or 1 cup canned)
⅓ cup soft bread crumbs
½ lb. broad noodles

2 tablespoons chopped pimiento
Pinch of powdered thyme
Pinch of powdered basil
1¼ teaspoons salt
½ cup melted butter
1 can condensed bouillon
4 tablespoons flour
2 tablespoons lemon juice
1 cup light cream

Rub roasting chicken with oil, salt and paprika. To make the stuffing: Heat olive oil in frying pan. Add garlic; cook until yellow, then remove. Add onion and cook until soft. Add mushrooms; cook five minutes. Add bread crumbs and heat through. Now mix noodles, pimiento, thyme, basil and salt. Stuff into body and breast cavity of chicken (pack lightly) and sew or skewer to close opening. Bake at 375°F. (moderate) two hours, basting every half hour with melted butter and some of the condensed bouillon. Remove chicken to carving platter. Pour off one-fourth cup of pan drippings into a saucepan to make gravy: blend in flour, then add lemon juice and light cream. Thin to desired consistency with bouillon. *Serves six.*

When the crowd (or the family) is tired of eating "the same old thing," here's a surprise treat. The flavor is rich—a little like a Creole sauce, a little like a curry.

CHICKEN BOMBAY WITH WALNUT RICE

6 whole chicken breasts
4 tablespoons butter
1 large onion, thinly sliced
2 cans (No. 2) tomatoes
2 cans (4 oz. each) chopped
mushrooms
⅓ cup currants
1 green pepper, chopped

1 clove garlic, minced
1 teaspoon chopped parsley
3 teaspoons salt
1 teaspoon black pepper
¾ teaspoon curry powder
¼ teaspoon orégano
¼ teaspoon Tabasco sauce

Remove skin and bones from chicken. Cut into one-inch pieces and put into two large skillets with two tablespoons butter in each. Sauté over medium heat till light gold. Remove chicken and add onion to fat in one pan. Cook until tender, then add remaining ingredients, mashing tomatoes with a spoon. Now add all chicken pieces, cover and simmer fifteen minutes, stirring occasionally, until chicken is tender. If you are preparing this dish in advance, divide the cooking time: simmer only five minutes with the tomato mixture, then cool and refrigerate. At party time, simmer fifteen minutes. *Serve hot to eight.*

Walnut Rice

Follow the package directions to cook rice for eight. Before serving, stir in one-fourth cup butter, one-half cup sliced walnuts.

A close relative of Chicken Bombay, the following dish makes its appearance as a casserole. It has almost the same delicious seasoning, but it's an all-in-one dish.

COUNTRY CAPTAIN

1 broiler-fryer chicken (3 lbs.) cut
into serving-size pieces
Seasoned flour
Fat for frying
2 tablespoons butter
1 onion, thinly sliced
1 can (No. 2) tomatoes, mashed
1 cup canned mushroom sauce
1 can (4 oz.) blanched almonds
(sliver half; bake remainder until
golden brown)

¼ cup currants
1 green pepper, chopped
1 clove garlic, minced
1 teaspoon chopped parsley
1 teaspoon salt
1 teaspoon white pepper
1½ teaspoons curry powder
¼ teaspoon orégano
1 cup cooked rice
6 slices bacon

Shake chicken two or three pieces at a time in a bag containing flour seasoned with salt and pepper. In a large skillet, fry in hot fat ten to fifteen minutes or until well browned. Remove from skillet and drain on paper toweling. Preheat oven to 350°F. (moderate). Add butter to fat remaining in skillet; add onion and cook over low heat until soft. Then add all remaining ingredients except rice and bacon, and simmer fifteen minutes, stirring occasionally. Place fried chicken in a lightly greased casserole. Sprinkle cooked rice over chicken and cover all with sauce. Bake thirty-five to forty-five minutes. Top with bacon, fried until crisp. *Serves six.*

Another utterly elegant party dish: chicken breasts, ham, mushrooms and heavy cream. Every guest will love it.

CREAMED CHICKEN CASSEROLE

2 packages (10 oz. each) frozen peas	1 can (4 oz.) mushroom slices, drained
4 chicken breasts, halved	1 cup chicken broth
½ cup flour	½ pint heavy cream
½ teaspoon salt	Salt and pepper to taste
Dash of pepper	¼ teaspoon instant minced green onion
1 clove garlic	
Butter	
8 thin slices ham	

Place peas in a strainer and pour boiling water over them. Wipe the chicken with a damp cloth. Combine flour, salt and pepper in a paper bag; shake the chicken in seasoned flour mixture. Cut garlic clove in half and rub cut side over inside of a large casserole, then rub casserole with butter. Spread half the peas evenly over bottom of casserole, then mound two tablespoons of peas near rim of dish, put half a chicken breast on mound, top with slice of ham and mushrooms. Repeat. When chicken is all arranged, pour broth over casserole, then heavy cream. Sprinkle with salt, pepper and the onion. Cover and bake at 350°F. (moderate) for one hour, or until chicken is tender; then—if desired—brown under the broiler for a few minutes. *Serves six to eight.*

BONUS CHICKEN DISHES

When there's chicken left over, there are lots of delicious things to do with it. Let the chicken pieces cool thoroughly, then remove meat from bones. (Your fingers can do this job best and most sensitively.) Cut up and store, covered, in the refrigerator until ready to use.

Did you know that if you leave a little meat clinging to the bones, you can use them to make soup? Put them in a pot with the neck, wing tips, liver and heart of the chicken, add a rib or two of celery, a peeled onion and a clump of parsley. Cover with water, add a teaspoonful of salt, then simmer for an hour or so. Strain this broth, cool and refrigerate. Remove any fat which comes to the surface during chilling and discard. There—you have a delicious chicken broth, ready to use in a recipe or to add to packaged or canned soup for extra flavor.

Very rich, very good, very easy!

CHICKEN AND NOODLE DELIGHT

1 package (8 oz.) cream cheese
2 cups commercial sour cream
2 cups (2 cans, 6 oz. each) chopped cooked chicken
½ cup drained canned mushrooms
2 tablespoons chopped onion

2 tablespoons chopped parsley
1 teaspoon salt
1 teaspoon onion salt
1 package (8 oz.) fine noodles, cooked
1 cup buttered bread crumbs

Soften cream cheese and blend with one cup of the sour cream. Add chicken, mushrooms, onion, parsley, seasonings and cooked noodles. Mix with two forks until well blended. Place in a shallow baking dish; pour remaining sour cream over the top and sprinkle generously with buttered crumbs. Bake at 350°F. (moderate) thirty minutes or until browned and bubbly. *Serves four.*

This recipe is a little unbelievable to read, so you'll just have to try it! Nice for a Sunday supper or an all-girl luncheon, accompanied by crusty hot French bread.

HOT CHICKEN SALAD

2 cups diced cooked chicken
1 cup drained canned pineapple tidbits
⅔ cup mayonnaise
½ cup coarsely chopped salted, toasted almonds

½ green pepper, diced small
½ cup diced raw celery
½ green pepper, cut in thin rings

Heat the chicken and pineapple together in the top of a double boiler for twenty-five minutes. Mix in mayonnaise; heat five minutes more. Stir in two heaping tablespoonfuls of the chopped almonds, the diced pepper and celery. Garnish with remaining nuts and pepper rings. *Serves four.*

CHICKEN CURRIES

There's more than one way to curry a chicken! In India, the dish is made spicy hot, hot, hot! The typical American curry is no more than cream sauce with curry powder added. Polynesian curries tend to be as sweet as the island breezes. Try all these curry recipes and find the one exactly right for you.

Curry Accompaniments: No matter how hot the curry, half the fun of serving it is in adding a wide range of accompaniments. Guests help themselves to what they like the best, dip into each as desired. Select an assortment from:

Crisp crumbled bacon
Chopped peanuts
Chopped pickles
Chutney
Raisins
Sliced lemons
Chopped watermelon-rind pickle

Grated coconut
Grated American cheese
Chopped hard-cooked egg whites
Chopped hard-cooked egg yolks
Chopped fresh cranberries with
    orange peel

Here's the simplest and least expensive curry recipe we know. To cut costs even further, use half-and-half instead of heavy cream. Amounts given are party-size.

CURRIED CHICKEN

4½ cups water
3 broiler-fryers, cut up
3 teaspoons monosodium glutamate
3 teaspoons salt
1 stalk celery, with leaves
2 bay leaves
¼ teaspoon peppercorns

½ cup butter or margarine
1 cup diced onions
2 large apples, peeled and diced
¾ cup flour
6 teaspoons curry powder
1 teaspoon ginger
2 cups heavy cream

Bring water to a boil. Add chicken and seasonings. Simmer gently forty minutes. Remove chicken and cool. Remove meat from bones and cut into bite-size pieces. Strain the broth and put it aside. Melt butter in a three-quart saucepan. Add onions and apples and cook until onion is tender but not brown. Combine flour, curry powder and ginger and stir in. Cook one minute. Gradually add five cups of the reserved broth and cook, stirring

An elegant dish: Creamed Chicken Casserole (page 82) ▶

constantly until thickened. Stir in cream, then the chicken; heat to serving temperature. Serve with rice and curry accompaniments. *Serves twelve.*

This authentic island recipe features the fresh coconut and ginger root which are so easy to obtain there. But you can make it with mainland ingredients.

HAWAIIAN CURRY

2 cups grated fresh coconut or 1½ cups canned, flaked coconut
3 cups milk
2 cloves garlic, chopped
1 tablespoon chopped fresh ginger root or ¾ teaspoon powdered ginger
2 medium onions, chopped

2 apples, diced
2 tablespoons curry powder
½ cup butter or margarine, softened
½ cup flour
½ teaspoon salt
½ cup top milk or cream
2½ cups diced, cooked chicken, shrimp or meat

Combine coconut and milk; bring to simmer over low heat. Add garlic, ginger, onions and apples. Blend curry powder and two tablespoons of the butter; add to coconut mixture. Cook slowly for three hours, stirring frequently. Remove from heat; cool for several hours. Strain. Blend flour with remaining butter and add to strained mixture. Cook over medium heat, stirring constantly until thickened. Add salt, milk or cream, chicken, shrimp or meat and continue to cook over low heat for thirty minutes. Serve with rice and curry accompaniments. *Serves four.*

A glamorous curry, served in pineapple shells!

FESTIVAL CHICKEN IN PINEAPPLE BOATS

4 pineapples (optional)
⅓ cup butter or margarine
2 cups chopped onion
1½ cups diced cooked ham
2 teaspoons curry powder
2 tablespoons flour
6 cups sliced fresh mushrooms or 3 small cans, drained

2 cups clear chicken bouillon or stock
2 cups heavy cream
½ cup canned pineapple juice
3 tablespoons lemon juice
1 teaspoon salt
5 cups cooked chicken meat, cut up
4 cups cooked rice
Toasted flaked coconut (about 1 cup)

If you are planning to serve the chicken in pineapple boats, split each pineapple lengthwise, leaving some of the "plume" on each half. Cut out

◀ *Light and low-caloried: Soup-to-Nuts Salad (page 151).*

core and discard. Remove remaining meat and use as a dessert. Brush shells with lemon juice and keep refrigerated. To make the chicken mixture, melt butter in a Dutch oven or large saucepan. Add onion and ham and brown lightly. Stir in curry, flour, mushrooms, stock and cream. Simmer ten minutes. Add pineapple juice, lemon juice and salt. Taste and add more salt if you like. Stir in the chicken meat and heat together ten minutes. Now, place one-half cup of rice in each pineapple shell and portion the chicken into the eight shells. Place in 350°F. oven (moderate) and heat ten minutes. (If you don't use the pineapple shells, place everything in an attractive oven-to-table casserole to heat.) Serve garnished with toasted coconut. *Serves eight.*

See also "Three-Way Curry," especially designed for Friday night parties, on page 386.

Here's an echo recipe—it echoes all the goodness of holiday eating, but adds its own special touch, too.

CHICKEN AND HAM ON RICE WITH FRUIT SAUCE

1½ cups seedless green grapes, fresh or canned
¾ cup seedless raisins
¾ cup water
2 teaspoons cornstarch
1 tablespoon sugar
¼ teaspoon salt
1 tablespoon cold water

2 tablespoons lemon juice
4 cups cooked rice
1 lb. (about) sliced baked ham
1 lb. (about) sliced white meat of chicken or turkey
2 cups buttered cooked carrots, if desired

Place grapes, raisins and water in saucepan. Cook, covered, until grapes are white and raisins puffed. Combine cornstarch, sugar, salt and cold water and stir into boiling liquid. Cook over low heat, stirring constantly until thickened. Sauce may be refrigerated, covered, for reheating later, or kept warm for immediate use. Just before serving, stir in lemon juice. Arrange rice, ham, chicken and carrots on a heatproof platter. Cover with foil. If desired, refrigerate until just before serving time; then heat in 350°F. oven (moderate) about twenty minutes or until warm through. Spoon hot sauce over all. *Makes ten servings.*

Leftover turkey, of course, can be used in all the same ways that chicken can. Avoid the more dried-out portions of meat on legs and wing tips, but use all the rest—even the back meat.

Even though this recipe could be made with chicken, we dedicate it to turkey because the name fits it so well!

TURKEY–IN–THE–CORN CASSEROLE

1 box (14 oz.) corn-bread mix	¼ cup minced onion
½ teaspoon poultry seasoning	3 tablespoons minced parsley
1 teaspoon celery seeds	½ cup melted butter or margarine
⅛ teaspoon pepper	5 cups diced, cooked turkey or 8 cans
¾ teaspoon salt	(5 oz. each) canned turkey

Prepare and bake corn-bread mix according to package directions. Cool and crumble bread. Combine with all other ingredients except turkey and toss lightly with a fork. Spread in the bottom of a thirteen-by-nine-inch baking dish or pan. Over this arrange the turkey.

Now make the sauce:

¼ cup butter or margarine	2 cups clear chicken broth
¼ cup flour	2 eggs, well beaten
1½ teaspoons salt	1 quart milk

Melt butter in a Dutch oven or heavy saucepan. Stir in flour and salt. Gradually stir in broth and cook until thickened, stirring constantly. Mix eggs and milk and blend into sauce. Stir constantly over moderate heat until mixture thickens slightly. Pour over turkey. Bake at 375°F. (moderate) forty-five minutes. *Makes ten servings.*
NOTE: If desired, make in advance, refrigerate and bake at party time. Allow ten minutes extra baking time.

LAMB

To all of you who think that lamb is a difficult let-Mother-cook-it meat, we say below in a variety of ways—"Baa!" Chops, for example, with a salad, French bread and dessert, make one of the simplest hurry-up party dinners. Hurry up and learn how to cook them. (Chop-chop, as they say!) Choose one of the less expensive rib or shoulder cuts—good budget training, young homemaker-to-be! Then give it a gourmet touch of sauce or special seasoning. There are many delicious, little-known lamb cuts that are easy to cook.

To Broil Lamb

While you preheat the broiler for chops or steak, slash the edges of fat around the meat to prevent curling. If your butcher hasn't removed the paper-thin "fell" which outlines the fat, cut it off before slashing. Place meat on broiler rack—three inches from flame for one-inch cuts, four inches for thicker cuts. (For four chops or fewer, line a cake pan with foil—to make dishwashing easier—and set chops on a rack in the pan.) Brown meat on one side, then turn and brown on other side. When done, meat should be faintly pink inside, crisp outside. Timing will run as follows:

Cut and Thickness	Cooking Time per Side
one-inch rib chops	6 minutes
double lamb chops, two-inch	12 minutes
leg steaks, one-inch	6 minutes *
shoulder chops, one-inch	10 minutes *

Treat leg steaks and shoulder chops with tenderizer before broiling. Sprinkle both sides of meat evenly with tenderizer, allowing half a teaspoon per pound. Pierce meat surface with a fork. Let stand about a half-hour for one-inch cuts, an hour for thicker cuts. Broil.

Here's a nice do-ahead dish for company or family. Serve it with rice mixed with Italian pine nuts (pignolias) or almonds, a green salad and a hard-crusted bread.

ARMENIAN LAMB SHANKS

3 tablespoons flour	2 tablespoons olive oil or other fat
1 teaspoon salt	2 cups sliced fresh mushrooms or 2
⅛ teaspoon pepper	small cans sliced mushrooms
1 teaspoon garlic salt	2 cans (No. 2) whole tomatoes
1 teaspoon paprika	¼ teaspoon thyme
4 (1½ lbs. each) lamb shanks, cut up	2 teaspoons dried mint leaves, crushed

Combine flour, salt, pepper, garlic salt and paprika. Roll the lamb shanks in this mixture. Heat fat in a heavy ovenproof skillet or Dutch oven. Brown the meat on all sides (you will probably need several fryings to avoid overcrowding pan). Then add remaining ingredients to skillet with all the browned meat and cover tightly. Bake at 350°F. (moderate) about two hours or until meat is tender. *Makes four servings.*

GOURMET TOUCHES

Add flavor to lamb chops or steak by rubbing meat with a split, peeled clove of garlic before cooking. Or press dried, crumbled tarragon or dried chives into meat before broiling.

Lemon-garlic sauce perks up lamb's flavor too: mince one clove of garlic and add it to one-fourth cup cooking oil mixed with one tablespoon of

* This time applies when the cut has been treated with meat tenderizer.

lemon juice. Simmer gently five minutes, then brush on meat before and again after broiling.

Mint sauce—traditional with roast lamb—tastes delicious with chops. Here's how to make one: Save two tablespoons drippings from broiling pan, add one-fourth cup of water and heat to the boiling point. Then stir in one-fourth cup mint jelly and cook until the jelly melts, stirring frequently. Serve with chops.

There are almost as many recipes for shish-kabob as for hamburger. We find this one both delectable and inexpensive.

CHARCOAL–BROILED SHISH–KABOBS

2 lbs. lamb shanks or shoulder lamb chops
1 onion, peeled and chopped
1 clove garlic, minced
2 tablespoons olive oil
¼ cup tomato juice
Pinch of thyme
Pinch of orégano
½ teaspoon salt

⅛ teaspoon pepper
½ teaspoon nonseasoned meat tenderizer
1 teaspoon monosodium glutamate
1 green pepper, cored and cubed
8 small onions, peeled and cooked ten minutes
2 underripe tomatoes, cubed

Trim fat and bone from lamb and cut into two-inch cubes. Mix chopped onion and garlic with olive oil, tomato juice and seasonings. Add lamb, cover and refrigerate overnight. Now alternate cubes of lamb with peppers, onions and tomatoes on skewers. Brush the vegetables with butter. Charcoal-grill or broil fifteen minutes, turning often. *Serves four generously.*

Many a girl has started a permanent friendship with a simple dish like this one:

LAMB STEW

2 lbs. boned lamb shoulder
3 tablespoons cooking oil
¼ cup minced onion
2 cloves garlic, minced
½ cup flour, divided
2 teaspoons salt
⅛ teaspoon pepper
1 bay leaf

3 cups boiling water
8 medium-size carrots, peeled
12 small white onions, peeled
1 package frozen cut green beans
½ cup water
1 tablespoon Worcestershire sauce
1 teaspoon gravy coloring

Cut meat into serving-size pieces. Heat cooking oil in a large Dutch oven, add onion and garlic. Sauté until golden brown; set aside. Combine one-fourth cup flour, salt, pepper. Coat meat with this mixture. (Save left-over seasoned flour.) Brown meat on all sides in the Dutch oven. Add rest of seasoned flour, browned onion and garlic, bay leaf and boiling water. Cover; simmer one hour. Add carrots, cut lengthwise into quarters, and white onions. Cover; simmer for forty minutes more. Add frozen green beans, cook for ten minutes more. Transfer meat and vegetables to a warmed platter. Remove bay leaf. Combine remaining one-fourth cup flour and water. Stir into pan juices. Add Worcestershire sauce and gravy coloring. Return vegetables and meat to gravy, then heat briefly. *Makes eight servings.*

PORK

Commit to memory: "I will never serve rare pork." Pork is the only meat which must be served well done—not a trace of pink should remain. (Fortunately, it tastes very good this way!)

If your family likes fried pork chops or steaks, prepare them this way: Rub the fat side of the chop over a skillet to grease it. Heat pan and brown chops well over moderate heat on both sides. Reduce heat to low, cover and continue cooking, turning occasionally, for at least twenty-five minutes more.

When the recipe calls for baking, you should bake chops at 325°F. (slow) for one hour if they are no more than an inch thick, one and one-half hours if they are one-and-a-quarter inches thick.

Better yet, try pork in a new way. Suggestions follow.

The miracle combination of sour cream and onion soup you know as California Dip does something wonderful for pork.

BAKED PORK CHOPS

6 ribs or loin pork chops, cut one inch thick
Flour

1 package dehydrated onion soup mix
1½ cups boiling water
1 cup commercial sour cream

Grease a skillet with the fat edge of one pork chop. Then dust chops all over lightly with flour. Heat skillet and brown chops well. Arrange chops in a baking pan. Pour fat out of skillet, and in it put the onion-soup mix and the boiling water. Blend well. Pour over chops in baking pan. Cover with foil. Bake at 350°F. (moderate) thirty minutes. Uncover and bake thirty to forty minutes longer or until chops are tender and no longer pink inside. Remove from oven. Place chops on platter. Stir sour cream gently into liquid in pan and cook over very low heat until slightly thickened. Serve as gravy, over or along with chops. *Makes six servings.*

The big news here is for spaghetti fans—a switch to pork chops, plus the fact that the spaghetti is cooked in the sauce! Serve it with a tossed green salad and hard rolls.

PORK SPAGHETTI

4 lean loin pork chops	½ teaspoon seasoned salt
2 teaspoons salt	¼ teaspoon pepper
1 clove garlic, minced	1 tablespoon brown sugar
1 small onion, minced	1 tablespoon vinegar
½ green pepper, seeded and chopped	¼ lb. thin spaghetti, broken
1 can (No. 2½) tomatoes	

Trim some fat from pork chops. Heat this fat in a chicken fryer, large skillet or Dutch oven until bottom of pan has about one-eighth inch of drippings. Sprinkle chops with one-half teaspoon of the salt and brown them well on both sides. Add garlic, onion and green pepper; cook over moderate heat about five minutes, stirring from time to time. Then add tomatoes, seasoned salt, remainder of regular salt, pepper, sugar and vinegar. Cover; simmer for about forty-five minutes. Add broken spaghetti. Cover and simmer thirty minutes longer or until the spaghetti is tender. *Serves four.*

In some quarters, this would be known simply as "Barbecue."

SPICY PORK CREOLE

8 slices bacon	1 clove garlic, minced
3 lbs. boneless pork	1 cup chopped green pepper
½ cup flour	1 cup chopped onion
1 teaspoon salt	1 cup chili sauce
½ teaspoon pepper	2 cans (No. 2) tomatoes

Fry bacon slowly in a large skillet until crisp; crumble and reserve. Cut meat into one-inch cubes. Combine flour, salt and pepper in a paper bag. Shake meat in flour mixture until coated. Brown well on all sides in bacon fat. Remove from skillet; add garlic, green pepper and onion and cook until onion is transparent and tender. Return meat to skillet and stir in chili sauce and drained tomatoes. (Save liquid for use during cooking if sauce becomes too thick.) Cover and simmer for an hour and a half, or until meat is tender. Store in refrigerator until party time. *Serve with hot fluffy rice to eight or ten.*

Little pork birds have a different flavor. Try, and see!

PUDGY PORKIES

1½ lbs. pork steak, pounded to ¼-inch thickness	2 cups soft rye-bread crumbs
Seasoned flour	1 cup soft white-bread crumbs
4 tablespoons fat	1 can condensed consommé
1 medium onion, chopped fine	6 sprigs parsley, chopped fine
1 clove garlic, chopped fine	½ teaspoon caraway seeds
	½ teaspoon monosodium glutamate

Cut and arrange meat in eight pieces, each about four by six inches. Dust all sides with seasoned flour. Heat two tablespoons of the fat in a skillet. Add the onion and garlic. Cook over moderate heat until tender, not brown. Combine with bread crumbs, one-half cup of the consommé and remaining ingredients. Toss gently to mix. Divide stuffing, placing a heaping tablespoonful on each steak. Roll up and skewer with toothpicks. Place remaining fat in skillet and heat. Brown the porkies on all sides, turning frequently (in electric skillet, set at 400°F.). Pour remaining consommé over all. Cover and bring to a boil. Reduce heat to low (200°F.). Cook thirty to forty minutes. *Makes six servings.*

HAM AND OTHER SMOKED PORK PRODUCTS

Once pork has been smoked, not only its flavor, but its cooking characteristics change. You need no longer worry about cooking until well done for safety reasons. But you should cook it long enough to be both hot and tender. You'll find smoked ham—and ham steaks—available in several types. Labels will help you decide how to cook your choice.

CHOOSING AND USING HAM

Fully cooked hams may be eaten cold or heated before serving. Follow label directions to heat. Most packers suggest ten to fifteen minutes per pound in a 325°F. (slow) oven—or until the meat thermometer reaches 130°F.

Uncooked hams need a real baking. At 325°F. (slow) a whole ham will take about twenty minutes per pound to cook through; a half ham about twenty-five minutes per pound; a boneless ham thirty minutes per pound. When ham is done, meat thermometer should register 160°F.

Meal time-guide: Add a half-hour for scoring and "resting" (see below).

Country-style hams can be bought in some areas. These need an overnight soaking and precooking. Bake as label directs. Or ask the butcher.

How many pounds should you buy? Figure four servings per pound for boneless ham; two and a half servings per pound for bone-in ham.

For a large party one of the most economical buys is a *whole ham, bone-in*. It weighs twelve to twenty pounds. If label is marked shankless or short shank, this means the amount of bone has been reduced. *Whole bone-less hams* cost a bit more but are easier to carve. They are pressed into a roll or "ham" shape and run from eight to twelve pounds.

For a small party buy a *butt-end half ham*, a *shankless shank end* or a *boneless half ham*. These run from four to eight pounds.

For economy meals try a *shank-end half ham*. This is excellent for "boiled dinners."

To bake ham, place it on a rack in an open pan, fat side up. One hour before baking time is up—this may mean *before* baking for fully cooked hams—trim off any skin (1) and smoothly slice off all but about one-half inch of fat.

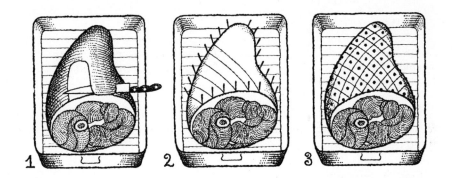

Score ham now. Use toothpicks and string, as shown, to guide your knife. Make long cuts in fat—one-fourth inch deep (2). For prettiness, make a second cut right beside each score line, slanting the knife so that you cut out a thin wedge-shaped ribbon. Make one-way diagonal cuts all across top; then cross these to form diamonds (3). Add whole cloves.

To glaze ham, use one of the glazes on page 94. Spoon half of it over ham; return to oven for a half-hour. Spoon on one third of remaining glaze every ten minutes.

Rest ham fifteen minutes to firm it before carving.

GOOD GLAZES FOR BAKED HAM

(All glazes should be applied for last hour of baking only.)

Country Kitchen: Combine one-half cup dark brown sugar with one-half cup honey. Use a rubber spatula to spread about two-thirds of glaze over ham. Bake twenty minutes, then add a little more glaze every ten minutes. Or use one cup of orange marmalade the same way.

Nicely Spicy: Use crab apple, plum, currant, apricot or apple jelly. Empty a small jar—about one cup—into a bowl and beat with a fork until fluffy. Beat in one teaspoon dry mustard, one-half teaspoon allspice, two tablespoons vinegar. Apply as directed above.

Lemon Glisten: Spread ham with mixture of equal parts of prepared mustard and honey. Pour over this about one-third of a seven-ounce bottle of lemon-lime carbonated beverage. Baste with remaining soda during remainder of cooking.

This is easy to serve buffet style at your next party. Prepare the makings of each part of the dish in advance and you can have it table-ready in less than fifteen minutes.

GOLDEN CRESCENT HAMBOREE

For the zesty rice:

2 cups water	1 teaspoon soy sauce
1 tablespoon butter	2 cups packaged precooked rice
1/8 teaspoon garlic powder	

Place water, butter, garlic powder and soy sauce in a saucepan. Place rice in a bowl. Bring water mixture to a boil. Pour over rice, stir and cover. Let stand five to ten minutes.

For the colorful fruit sauce:

1 flat can (8 oz.) pineapple slices	2 tablespoons cornstarch
1 small can (8 oz.) sliced peaches	1/2 teaspoon Angostura bitters
1 can (11 oz.) mandarin orange sections	1/4 teaspoon garlic powder
1 lemon	2 tablespoons vinegar
1/2 cup cold water	2 tablespoons dark brown sugar

Drain the pineapple, peaches and oranges, saving all syrup (about one and one-half cups) in a saucepan. Cut the lemon in two lengthwise, then slice crosswise (use only one half) to form paper-thin half circles. Remove seeds, place slices with other fruit. Gradually add water to cornstarch, stirring to form a smooth paste; now stir in bitters, garlic powder, vinegar and brown sugar. Add to mixed fruit syrup. Bring to a boil, stirring constantly; boil three minutes or until mixture thickens and clears. Reduce heat. Add fruit. Heat two minutes, stirring occasionally with care so fruit slices remain intact.

For the cashew-ham mixture:

1 lb. precooked ham, sliced ⅛ inch thick	¼ cup sweet butter 1 can (6 oz.) cashew nuts

Cut ham into strips one-half inch wide and two inches long. Near serving time, melt butter in skillet, add ham and cashews and fry five to ten minutes, stirring constantly until cashews are lightly browned.

To serve: On each plate, place a large serving-spoonful of rice. Top with a serving of cashew-ham mixture. Add two spoonfuls of fruit and sauce, dividing fruit as evenly as possible. *Serves six generously.*

Like the ham-and-cheese taste? Then try this—with the sauce, which adds just the right delicious note.

NEVER–FAIL HAM AND CHEESE DELIGHT

1 can (12 oz.) pressed chopped ham or luncheon meat	3 eggs, lightly beaten 1½ cups milk
1 package (13¼ oz.) natural Cheddar cheese	Sour Cream Sauce (below)
15 crisp soda crackers, rolled to fine crumbs	

Preheat oven to 350°F. (moderate). Coarsely chop ham and cheese (use coarse blade of food grinder) and mix in a large bowl, with cracker crumbs. Add the beaten eggs and milk and blend well. Turn into an ungreased two-quart baking dish or bread loaf pan. Set dish in shallow pan of hot water and bake for one hour. Top each portion with a spoonful of Sour Cream Sauce. *Makes ten servings.*

Sour Cream Sauce

1 cup commercial sour cream	1 tablespoon sugar
2 tablespoons vinegar	1 teaspoon salt
1 tablespoon lemon juice	¼ teaspoon pepper

Combine all ingredients in bowl. Mix thoroughly.

Extra Zesty Casserole: Follow preceding directions for Never-Fail Ham and Cheese Delight (page 95), but add to cracker mixture one can (1 lb. 1 oz.) peas with onions, drained, and one-eighth teaspoon Tabasco sauce. You may also add one-half cup tomato purée and reduce the milk to one cup.

A new company version of a family favorite:

BAKED HAM STEAK SANDWICH

2 precooked ham steaks, ½ inch thick (about 1½ lbs. each)
2 tablespoons prepared mustard
½ cup dry bread crumbs

¼ cup brown sugar, well packed
4 to 5 canned pineapple rings
2 teaspoons butter or margarine

Score edges of ham steaks to prevent curling. Spread all but one teaspoon prepared mustard on one side of each steak. Combine bread crumbs and brown sugar and coat sides spread with mustard. Place one steak, coated side down, in a shallow pan. Top with pineapple rings, then second steak, coated side up. With remaining mustard and bread-crumb mixture coat all edges. Dot top with butter and bake at 375°F. (moderate) about forty to fifty minutes or until tender, hot and lightly browned. Serve in pie-shaped wedges. *Makes ten servings.*

NOTE: For smaller families, halve recipe by using two thin steaks, about three-fourths of a pound each. Use same amounts of other ingredients.

CANADIAN BACON

Though you may be more familiar with sliced Canadian bacon (so delicious as a breakfast meat or in sandwiches) it is also available whole, packaged or canned. It gives you hamlike flavor in a small no-waste way.

"BRANDED" CANADIAN BACON

1 piece Canadian bacon (about 3 lbs.)
½ cup currant jelly

1 can (1 lb.) apricot halves
Maraschino cherries

Remove casing from Canadian bacon and place on rack in roasting pan, fat side up. To "brand," use a small cookie cutter or the removable center of a doughnut cutter and make a three-ring pattern. Deepen cuts slightly with knife if desired. Bake at 325°F. (slow) one and one-half to two hours or until meat thermometer inserted in center of meat registers 170°F. While bacon is cooking, put jelly in a small saucepan and melt over low heat. When meat is done, remove from oven and spoon jelly over surface. Bake at 400°F. (hot) fifteen minutes. Place on a platter and garnish with apricot halves topped with cherries. (Apricots may be heated in roasting pan for last fifteen minutes of cooking time.) *Serves eight—with seconds.*

Breakfast Bacon

For just you, you'll most often want to cook bacon a strip or two at a time as a breakfast treat. The simplest way: Let bacon warm long enough at room temperature so that slices can be separated. Place in a skillet or on a griddle and cook slowly over low heat until browned on both sides, turning once. Never let bacon fat smoke. When bacon is crisp, remove and drain on paper towels.

For a crowd, or when you want to serve a half pound or more, proceed in one of these easy ways: Place the bacon with slices overlapping slightly on a rack over a shallow pan. Then place pan in the broiler, three inches from source of heat. Broil three minutes per side or until crisp but not brittle. Or place similarly on rack over pan and preheat oven to 400°F. (hot). Bake without turning twelve to fifteen minutes or until crisp. For either way, drain on paper toweling.

To make curly bacon, useful for garnishing casseroles or sandwiches, partly fry or broil the bacon until it is lightly brown but still pliable. Shape with fork into an s-curve or corkscrew curl. Finish by frying till crisp or by browning in the oven.

Pork Sausage

Old-fashioned pork sausage comes in two principal types—links and loose sausage meat, sometimes formed into patties. Either type should be cooked with patience to develop its best flavor.

Sausage meat patties should be shaped no more than one-half inch thick. They may be pan-fried slowly over low heat about seven minutes per side or until meat is browned outside and uniformly gray inside. Or they may be baked on a rack over a pan twenty to thirty minutes.

Sausage links may also be baked: follow directions for patties but turn the links frequently, using tongs. There are two methods of frying. You may prick each link in several places with a fork, then brown slowly over low heat about fifteen minutes, turning frequently. But we recommend an even faster, surer way. Place the links in a skillet, then add enough water to stand one-eighth of an inch deep. Cover and boil slowly about five minutes or until most of the water has evaporated. Drain off the water, put pan back over moderate heat and fry, turning frequently, about eight minutes or until browned and crisp. Drain on paper towel before serving piping hot.

When you're dying to have friends in after the game and the piggy bank is dying of malnutrition, remember *this* recipe. It makes one pound of pork sausage stretch for eight—and the flavor is unique and unforgettable.

MOCK CHICKEN CASSEROLE

1 lb. loose pork sausage
1½ cups finely diced celery
¼ cup chopped green pepper
1 cup uncooked rice
½ cup chopped blanched almonds, toasted

2 packages dehydrated chicken-noodle soup
5 cups boiling water

In an electric saucepan set at 350°F. or a heavy skillet over direct heat, crumble and brown the sausage. Pour off (and save) most of the fat. Remove sausage and add celery and green pepper. Cook till barely tender, adding reserved sausage fat when needed. Return sausage to pan. Add uncooked rice and chopped almonds. Mix well. Dissolve chicken noodle soup in five cups of boiling water; add. Cook, covered, forty minutes in an electric saucepan at 250°F. or in the oven at 350°F. Remove cover; bake twenty minutes more or until liquid is almost absorbed. (May be made ahead, refrigerated and reheated at party time.) *Makes eight servings.*

This recipe gives pork sausage links a completely new flavor—smooth, yet deliciously spicy.

SAUSAGES À LA MEXICAN

1 lb. pork sausage links
3 large onions, thinly sliced
1 green pepper, cut into thin strips
1 can (No. 2) tomatoes
1 teaspoon salt
¼ teaspoon pepper

1 tablespoon sugar
1 teaspoon chili powder
1 bay leaf
½ cup elbow macaroni
½ cup commercial sour cream

Cut sausages in half and brown slowly in a large frying pan or Dutch oven. When thoroughly browned, remove from pan and pour off half the fat. Sauté onion slices and green pepper in remaining fat until onions are golden. Add tomatoes, salt, pepper, sugar, chili powder and bay leaf. Stir. Heat to boiling point, then add macaroni. Cook twenty minutes, stirring occasionally until macaroni is tender. Just before serving, stir in sour cream. Heat, but do not boil. *Serve to four hungry people.*

FRANKFURTERS

Otherwise known as wieners and hot dogs—and otherwise known as fun at parties and savory budget-stretchers at family meals. You can buy franks in many styles from the cocktail-size peanut franks to giant knockwurst. During the summer many meat departments feature extra-long franks or giant-size packages for parties. If kept in their original packages, they may be safely refrigerated for three or four days.

How To Cook Franks

Some frankfurters have a thin plastic casing around each sausage. Be sure this is removed before cooking.

Pan-fried: Preheat a skillet or electric griddle to moderate. Add a little butter or margarine and spread to coat surface. Add franks and pan-fry gently about four minutes, turning to brown all sides. (Franks may also be split lengthwise before browning. This is a particularly good way to reheat leftover franks.)

Broiled: Broil franks two to three inches from source of heat, turning several times, about eight minutes in all. If you like, coat the franks with oil or melted butter before broiling.

Stuffed: Split franks almost through lengthwise. Broil cut side down four minutes. Then turn and fill with a strip of cheese or dill pickle or seasoned bread stuffing. Complete the broiling.

Recipes for barbecuing frankfurters are on page 371.

When you read this recipe, you may think we got our ingredients mixed up, but proceed with faith. Certainly the recipe is different, but honestly, it's surprisingly good.

THE TERROR OF HIGHWAY 101

1 lb. ground beef	1 can (8 oz.) tomato sauce
1 tablespoon olive oil	1 teaspoon salt
1 large onion, minced	3 cups sauerkraut
1 clove garlic, minced	6 frankfurters
1 tablespoon chili powder	6 frankfurter rolls

Brown ground beef in olive oil until crumbly. Stir in minced onion, garlic, chili powder, tomato sauce and salt. Simmer over low heat about fifteen minutes or until flavors are well blended. Heat sauerkraut until limp but juicy. Meanwhile cook frankfurters in boiling water, split them in half lengthwise and keep hot. Lightly butter split frankfurter rolls and toast under broiler. Place each roll on a serving plate. Place a split frankfurter in center. Cover with a portion of sauerkraut, then top with meat sauce. *Serves six.*

Here's a twist on hot dogs which makes them entirely different.

FRENCH WRAP–AROUNDS

3 eggs
¾ cup milk
¼ teaspoon salt
⅛ teaspoon pepper
10 slices day-old white bread

3 teaspoons (about) prepared
  mustard
2 cups grated Cheddar cheese
10 frankfurters

Beat eggs, milk, salt and pepper together. Make French toast by dipping bread in the egg-milk mixture, then browning lightly on both sides on a hot, buttered griddle. Spread each slice lightly with mustard, and sprinkle with grated cheese, using about one and one-half tablespoons for each. Place a frank diagonally across center of each slice and fold over the corners, fastening with a toothpick. Place in a seven-by-twelve-inch oblong baking dish. Pour any remaining egg mixture over this, and sprinkle with remaining cheese. Bake at 350°F. (moderate) until cheese is melted and dish is heated through. *Makes five servings.*

Another tasteful penny-stretcher, this casserole has a Creole flavor.

FRANKFURTER–CORN BREAD CASSEROLE

First make the frankfurter filling. You will need:

1 cup chopped celery
1½ cups chopped onions
⅔ cup chopped green pepper
¼ cup butter

1 can (No. 2) tomatoes
1 teaspoon salt
2 lbs. frankfurters

Sauté celery, onions and green pepper in butter until golden. Remove from heat; stir in tomatoes and salt. Cut franks into pennies. Reserve about one dozen for garnish. Add remaining frankfurter pennies to vegetables and turn into a greased shallow three-quart casserole. (Refrigerate now if desired.)

For corn-bread topping you'll need:

1 cup flour	1 tablespoon butter
4 teaspoons baking powder	1 egg, well beaten
1¼ teaspoons salt	1 cup milk
1 cup corn meal	

Sift together flour, baking powder and salt. Stir in corn meal. Cut butter into mixture with a pastry blender. Combine egg and milk. If you are making the casserole in advance, refrigerate the egg-milk and flour mixtures (in separate bowls). Just before baking, stir egg and milk into dry ingredients—until the flour mixture is barely moistened; spread over vegetable-frankfurter mixture. Garnish top with reserved frankfurter pennies and some pepper slices. Bake at 375°F. (moderate) for forty to forty-five minutes, until a straw inserted into center comes out clean. *Serves eight.*

FISH AND OTHER SEA FOOD

You'll know you're really cooking when you learn to recognize fish (and its shelly friends) not as Friday night necessities but as welcome changes which inspire you to gourmet adventures.

Because of the sweet, mild flavor of most fish, small changes in seasoning can produce a completely new dish. Most sea food is low in fat, high in protein—a boon to the dieter.

We've found that boys are perfectly happy when the menu includes tuna or shrimp—you needn't hesitate to serve it at parties.

The rules for sea-food cookery are easy ones. Use fresh sea food as quickly as possible—within two days. Use frozen sea food as soon as—or even before—it's thawed. Never overcook sea food—that only toughens it. If high temperatures are used (as in broiling or frying) keep the time short.

You'll find fish available in several forms. The whole fish may be cut into *steaks*, from one to one and one-half inches thick. These usually contain a center bone and are surrounded by skin. You leave steaks intact for cooking, but the skin is not eaten. *Fillets* are thin, tender lengthwise slices of fish (usually white fish); they contain no bone. *Portions* are smaller, thicker patty-size cuts of fish, sold frozen, both uncooked and precooked.

Some kinds of frozen fish need only heating: fish sticks and tidbits, breaded, fried shrimp, scallops and clams need only the tender touch of the oven. These days, you can be landlocked on a mountain top and still have fresh-tasting fish.

Canned seafare occasionally tastes a little different from the fresh variety, but many people prefer it. There's tuna and salmon, of course, but also shrimp, clams, crab and lobster, herrings and sardines. Each makes a lovely start on a sandwich filling, an hors d'oeuvre or a casserole.

This casserole echoes your favorite spaghetti casserole, but the sea food makes it taste different—and makes it particularly adaptable for Friday night suppers.

TUNA SPAGHETTI CASSEROLE

2 lbs. spaghetti
½ cup (1 stick) butter
4 tablespoons flour
2 cups milk
1 onion, peeled and chopped
1 green pepper, washed, seeded and
  chopped
1 can condensed tomato soup or 1
  can (6 oz.) tomato paste

½ lb. processed Cheddar cheese,
  cubed or grated
2 teaspoons chopped parsley
Salt and pepper
½ teaspoon Tabasco sauce
2 cups chopped tuna fish or crab
  meat, cooked or canned

Cook spaghetti according to package directions in boiling salted water until tender. Melt one-fourth cup of the butter, stir in flour, then gradually stir in milk over low heat. Continue to stir over low heat until thickened and boiling. Keep warm. Melt remaining one-fourth cup of butter in skillet, add onion and pepper and cook until soft. Stir in the warm white sauce, tomato soup or paste, and cheese; cook over low heat until cheese is melted. Add parsley and season with salt, pepper and Tabasco. Drain spaghetti and place in large casserole. Fold in tuna or crab meat. Pour sauce over all. Bake at 350°F. (moderate) thirty minutes. *Makes twelve servings.*

The French make a hearty, well-flavored dish with tuna. Try this; it gives the fish a new personality.

TUNA PROVENÇAL

2 cans (about 7 oz. each) tuna
⅓ cup olive oil (about)
2 medium onions, thinly sliced
2 cloves garlic, minced
2 cans (1 lb. each) tomatoes, mashed
  slightly with fork
1 teaspoon salt
¼ teaspoon pepper

2 teaspoons parsley flakes
½ teaspoon sugar
Pinch of thyme
⅛ teaspoon Tabasco sauce
2 cans (3 oz. each) sliced mushrooms,
  drained
2⅔ cups packaged precooked rice
¼ cup butter or margarine

Open tuna and drain oil into measuring cup. Add enough olive oil to make one-half cup. Pour this into medium saucepan and heat gently. Add onions and garlic and sauté until onion is tender and transparent, but not browned. Add tomatoes and seasonings and simmer gently fifteen minutes. Now add the drained tuna and mushrooms and simmer, uncovered, fifteen minutes longer. Meanwhile, prepare the rice, following package directions, and add butter to the cooked rice. Turn buttered rice onto serving platter and spoon tuna-tomato mixture over it. *Serves eight.*

This recipe starts out like a conventional stuffed tomato salad, but the next thing you know, it's a delicious hot dish.

TUNA–TOMATO SURPRISE

3 large tomatoes, cut in half crosswise
2 cans tuna (about 7 oz. each) drained
½ cup mayonnaise

½ teaspoon onion salt
2 slices white bread, toasted
2 tablespoons grated cheese
2 tablespoons fine dry bread crumbs

Scoop out pulp from tomatoes. (Use in soups or with other vegetables.) If you like, notch a pretty edge on the cup. Mix drained tuna with mayonnaise and onion salt. Cut toast into tiny cubes and fold into tuna mixture. Spoon into the tomato cups. Broil about three minutes. Meantime mix grated cheese and bread crumbs. Sprinkle some of this mixture over each half-broiled tomato, and return to broil one or two minutes more or until browned. *Makes six servings.*

Because this dish contains an assortment of sea food *and* vegetables plus rice and sauce, it really is a meal-in-one dish.

SEA FOOD SCRAMBLE

3 tablespoons cooking oil
1 onion, peeled and minced
¼ cup diced green pepper
2 cans condensed Manhattan-style clam chowder
1 soup can of water
1 can (5 oz.) lobster, drained, picked over and flaked
1 can (7 oz.) tuna fish, drained and flaked
1 can (5 oz.) frozen cooked deveined shrimp, thawed

1 can (3 oz.) sliced mushrooms, drained
1 can (10½ oz.) peas, drained
1 teaspoon salt
1 crumbled bay leaf
Dash of garlic powder
Dash of cayenne pepper
1 cup packaged precooked rice
½ cup crumbled potato chips

Heat cooking oil in a saucepan, add onion and green pepper and cook gently until soft. Add soup, water, all sea food, vegetables and seasonings.

Bring to a boil, remove from heat and add the rice. Turn into a two-quart baking dish; sprinkle with potato chips. Bake at 375°F. (moderate) for fifteen minutes. *Makes eight servings.*

How to make fillets taste heavenly—get them friendly with a large amount of butter and judicious amounts of eggs, onions and seasonings.

ROLLED FISH FILLETS DE LUXE

8 fillets of sole or flounder (about 2 lbs.)
1 cup butter, divided
2 onions, peeled and chopped
1½ cups cracker meal
4 egg yolks, lightly beaten

2 tablespoons heavy cream
¼ cup lemon juice
1½ teaspoons salt
½ teaspoon pepper
¼ teaspoon nutmeg

Thaw the fish if frozen and separate so it can drain. Melt one-half cup of the butter in a skillet. Add onions and sauté until tender, stirring frequently. Add cracker meal and cook over low heat two minutes, stirring constantly. Remove from heat. Combine egg yolks and heavy cream and blend in. Next blend in lemon juice and seasonings. Spread the crumb mixture evenly on one side of each fillet. Then roll up each fillet, fastening with a toothpick. Melt remaining half-cup of butter in a large baking dish and arrange the rolled fillets in it. Bake at 400°F. (hot) for thirty minutes, basting frequently. *Makes eight servings.*

Though perhaps not so widely publicized, fish and almonds are as natural a pair of companions as ham and eggs. For example:

FILLETS OF SOLE AMANDINE

¼ cup blanched almonds, coarsely chopped
3 tablespoons softened butter or margarine
½ teaspoon salt

½ teaspoon paprika
⅛ teaspoon pepper
Grated peel of 1 lemon
1 package (1 lb.) frozen skinless fillets of sole or flounder, thawed

Combine almonds, butter, salt, paprika, pepper and lemon rind in a small bowl and mix with a wooden spoon or rubber spatula. Separate thawed fish and cut into serving-size pieces. Arrange in a baking dish and spread each piece with the almond butter. Bake at 350°F. (moderate) fifteen to twenty minutes or until the fish flakes easily when tested with fork. *Makes four servings.*

French-inspired but strictly American in interpretation. Pretty, too.

FLOUNDER FILLETS ON ASPARAGUS

1 package (10 oz.) frozen asparagus
1 package (1 lb.) thawed frozen
   flounder fillets or 1 lb. fresh fillets
Salt and pepper to taste
Butter

1 can condensed cream of mushroom
   soup
⅓ cup milk
¼ cup grated Cheddar cheese

Cook asparagus until just tender. Drain and set aside. Season fillets with salt and pepper. Brown lightly one and one-half minutes per side in hot butter. Remove from heat. Drain on paper toweling. Arrange cooked asparagus in a buttered baking pan. Sprinkle lightly with salt and pepper. Place fillets over asparagus. Combine soup and milk to make sauce; pour over fish. Sprinkle with the grated cheese. Place in broiler for three to four minutes until cheese is bubbly and lightly browned. *Makes four servings.*

If you would like to make a creamy tuna topping for toast or waffles, turn to page 286 for Tuna Velouté.

A famous sea-food combination which also includes chicken can be found on page 79—Paella Pronto.

SHRIMP

Learn how to buy, prepare and cook shrimp.

Buying: Shrimp varies in size from tiny to jumbo. You can buy shrimp raw (either fresh or frozen) or cooked (frozen or canned). The pre-cooked frozen variety is available in cocktail sauce or breaded (to be fried) or breaded and fried, ready to heat.

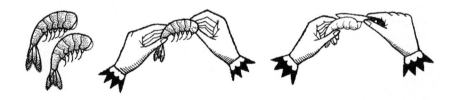

Shelling: Hold tail end of shrimp in left hand; slip right thumb under shell between feelers and gently lift several segments. Then pull out shrimp from remaining shell.

Deveining: Although the black sand vein is harmless, most people prefer to remove it. Hold shelled shrimp in one hand, knife in the other and cut along outside curvature directly over the vein. Under running water, lift out vein with point of knife or fingertips.

Boiling: This is the basic method of cooking shrimp for numerous hot dishes as well as cold. Boil in a stock made with boiling water, celery, onion, lemon juice and seasonings or in plain salted water—enough to cover—three to five minutes, until pink and firm.

Frying: Shrimp may be deep-fat or pan-fried. An attractive way to fix shrimp is the butterfly method: remove shell, leaving tail section. Slit center back with a knife, cutting almost through. Wash. Flatten, dip in egg and bread crumbs and fry in deep fat.

This recipe accents the sweetness of a versatile sea food.

BLUSHING SHRIMP

¼ cup butter or margarine
1 lb. fresh or frozen thawed shrimp, shelled and deveined
1 tablespoon flour
½ cup chili sauce
1 teaspoon Worcestershire sauce

⅛ teaspoon Tabasco sauce
½ teaspoon celery salt
¼ teaspoon salt
1 pint light cream or half-and-half
4 to 6 slices bread

Heat butter in a medium-size saucepan until bubbling. Add shrimp and cook over medium heat, stirring gently, until all are pink. Sprinkle with flour and stir. Add chili sauce and seasonings and cook, stirring constantly, until mixture is blended and slightly thickened. Blend in cream and cook just until heated. Meanwhile, toast the bread and cut diagonally into quarters. *Serve shrimp over these toast points to four.*

Here's a shrimp dish which blends the flavor of bacon and spices with that of the sweet crustacean. Good for parties, especially for buffet service.

DIXIE SHRIMP MULL

18 slices bacon, diced
½ cup butter (1 stick)
1½ cups chopped onion
5 cups water
2 cans (No. 2) tomatoes
1 can condensed tomato soup
1½ cups catchup
¾ cup chopped celery

1 lemon, sliced thin
2 cloves garlic, sliced
4 teaspoons Worcestershire sauce
1 teaspoon celery seed
½ teaspoon curry powder
¼ teaspoon allspice
5 lbs. fresh shrimp, cleaned
2 cups crushed soda crackers

In a Dutch oven or large heavy saucepan, brown the bacon. Add butter and melt over low heat. Add onions and sauté until golden, but not brown. Add remaining ingredients except shrimp and cracker crumbs. Simmer, covered, for two hours, stirring occasionally. Add shrimp and cook slowly for twenty minutes longer. Stir in cracker crumbs to thicken. Serve on fluffy rice. *Serves sixteen generously.*

Here is a Polynesian recipe for shrimp which turns out crisp and delicately sweet. Just right for a *luau.*

ISLANDER SHRIMP

1½ lbs. jumbo shrimp, fresh or frozen
   and thawed
¼ cup lime juice
½ teaspoon salt
1 teaspoon curry powder
⅛ teaspoon powdered ginger

1 cup flaked coconut
1 cup flour
⅔ cup milk
1 teaspoon baking powder
Fat for deep frying

Peel and devein shrimp. Mix lime juice, salt, curry and ginger. Let shrimp stand in this mixture about four hours, turning occasionally. Meanwhile, spread coconut in pie pan and heat in a very slow oven (200°F.) for ten minutes or just until dry, not toasted. Near party time, heat the fat to 375°F., combine flour, milk and baking powder. Lift shrimp out of marinade and add the marinade to the flour batter. Roll each shrimp in some additional flour, then in batter and finally in coconut. Fry until golden brown. Drain on paper toweling and serve hot. *Makes eight generous appetizer portions, or serves four as a main dish.*

Rock Lobster Tails

Shopping guide: You can buy frozen lobster tails in boxes (two to three to a box) or in plastic bags at supermarkets. Or singly packed at a fish store. Count on one five-ounce tail—or two smaller ones—per dinner serving. (See recipe on page 108.)

To boil lobster tails: Boil enough water just to cover tails; add one teaspoon of salt per quart of water. Add *unthawed* tails. Time by weight of largest tail (you can judge pretty well by weight on box); boil one minute per ounce, then three minutes more.

To serve whole boiled lobster tails: Cut away undershell immediately after boiling. Use sturdy kitchen scissors and snip around the undershell (see picture) close to the tough upper shell; pull undershell off. Serve in the shell with a bowl of hot melted butter. Garnish plates with lemon wedges, parsley sprigs.

For salads, lobster cocktail: Boil and remove undershell as above. Let cool a bit (for easy handling), then tuck fingers between shell and meat as shown (center) and lift the meat out of the shell. Cut up (not too small), blend with salad dressing or cocktail sauce; chill. If desired, leave shell-less tail whole, reheat by plunging into boiling water, and serve hot with mayonnaise or a sea food sauce.

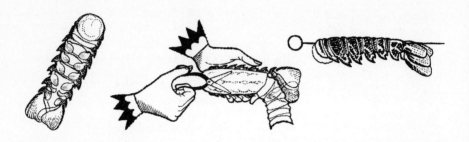

Party-broiled lobster: Unwrap the frozen tails; thaw at room temperature. Cut away undershell from uncooked, thawed tails. Then grasp tail at each end and bend outer shell till it cracks a few times. (This keeps it from curling during broiling.) Broil about five minutes per side. Serve with hot butter.

Extra-speedy broiling: This is quicker but not so pretty as party-broiled. Don't thaw tails or remove undershell. Instead, cut through outer shell with a butcher knife, spread tail apart like a butterfly. Broil four inches from heat for eight to ten minutes.

Barbecued lobster tails: Thaw tails, cut away undershell, and put tails on a spit or long metal skewer. (Insert skewer as shown: lengthwise, close to shell.) Brush with butter or barbecue sauce. Grill over coals about five minutes per side. Serve with sauce.

A colorful and delicious dish, this recipe can be made from on-hand ingredients in pantry and freezer.

ROCK LOBSTER BOATS

3 lobster tails, 5 oz. each	1 can condensed mushroom soup
2½ cups hot cooked rice	2 tablespoons lemon juice
¼ cup butter or margarine, about	Parsley for garnish
¼ cup chopped sweet onion	

Follow preceding directions to cook the lobster tails, lift the meat out of the shells and chop fine. Clean the shells and save. Toss hot rice with a tablespoon or two of butter, mound into the lobster shells, and place in a slow oven (250°F.) to keep warm. In a skillet, sizzle onion in two tablespoons butter until soft. Stir in soup, lemon juice and chopped lobster meat and heat through. To serve, place a boat of rice on each plate, spoon on lobster sauce generously and garnish with parsley. *Serves three.*

EGGS AND CHEESE

Most of the dishes in this section are skip-arounds—they might be served at any time of day. You'll find the basic information about cooking breakfast eggs included in Eggs for Breakfast (page 33) particularly helpful in working with these recipes.

Eggs are necessary to so many recipes that it's worth knowing the correct way to handle—as well as buy and store—them.

Separating egg yolk and white: Crack shell by tapping center sharply against rim of cup or small bowl. Press thumb tips into crack and pull shell apart, retaining yolk in one half, letting the white drain into cup. Slip yolk into the other half of the shell to complete draining, then drop yolk into a small bowl. If a speck of yolk has slipped into the white, remove it—or white will not beat stiff; then turn into beating bowl. For best results always let eggs stand at room temperature half an hour before use. Or put in warm water a minute.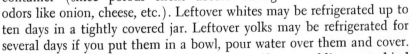

Storing: Remove eggs from carton, and refrigerate as soon as possible after buying to keep fresh. Store, unwashed, with broad ends up, in a closed container (since porous shells absorb strong odors like onion, cheese, etc.). Leftover whites may be refrigerated up to ten days in a tightly covered jar. Leftover yolks may be refrigerated for several days if you put them in a bowl, pour water over them and cover.

Beating: When recipe calls for a light beating (for scrambling or to bind other foods, etc.) use a fork or wire whisk and beat until yolk and white are just blended. When well-beaten eggs are called for (for cakes, cookies, etc.), use a rotary beater or electric mixer, and beat until volume increases and eggs are light and frothy. For "lightly beaten whites," beat till whites are just foamy. For whites beaten "stiff but not dry," beat till peaks form when beater is raised.

Sizing: Eggs are sorted into six classes, ranging from jumbo, extra large and large through peewee. The medium size is most accurate for use in recipes. Smaller eggs are often good buys in late summer, early fall. Color does *not* affect quality or taste of egg.

Grading: Eggs graded AA or A are freshest—best for table use. When these are hard-cooked, yolk is centered, white almost a perfect oval. In grades B and C—which are lower in quality but fine for use in cooking and baking—yolk is more off-center, and large air space may make white appear incomplete.

You know the perfect times for scrambled eggs. But find out just how pretty and delicious they can be with this dressed-up recipe for a crowd.

CONFETTI SCRAMBLED EGGS

1½ cups milk
1½ cups chopped onion
½ cup diced green pepper
1 can (4 oz.) pimiento, drained and
    chopped

12 eggs
1 teaspoon salt
⅛ teaspoon pepper
¼ cup butter or margarine

Combine milk and onion in a saucepan. Add green pepper and cook, covered, over low heat five minutes. Cool. Add chopped pimiento, then beat in the eggs with salt and pepper. Choose a large skillet. Melt the butter in it and when bubbling, stir in egg mixture and cook, scrambling with fork or spoon, over low heat until eggs are softly flaky and set. *Makes six generous servings.*

Another guise for scrambled eggs, good for lunch or brunch and good for you, too.

EGGS IN BASKETS

½ cup butter or margarine, about
6 slices white bread
6 slices Canadian bacon
6 eggs
1 jar pimiento-cheese spread

¼ cup light cream
½ teaspoon salt
⅛ teaspoon pepper
1 medium-size tomato, diced

Melt one-fourth cup of the butter in a small saucepan and remove from heat. Trim the crusts from the bread. Roll a rolling pin lightly over each slice and brush both sides of each with the melted butter. Press each slice into an individual muffin cup to form a basket shape. Bake at 375°F. (moderate) twelve minutes or until golden brown. Meanwhile, heat another tablespoon of butter in a skillet, add Canadian bacon and brown lightly on both sides; keep warm. Break eggs into mixing bowl. Add cheese spread, cream, salt and pepper and beat with a wire whisk or fork until just blended. Stir in diced tomato. Place two tablespoons butter in a large, heavy skillet and heat. When melted, pour in egg mixture and cook over low heat, scraping bottom and sides with spoon as mixture sets. Cook until eggs are set but still moist. Remove from heat. Remove hot toast baskets from muffin cups. Line each with browned bacon, then spoon in egg-cheese mixture, dividing equally. If desired, garnish with tomato wedges and crisp parsley. *Serves six.*

When there are two or three for company, it's fun to do something spectacular (but simple) and this dish is a breakfast example. Good go-alongs: crisp sausages, buttered toast and strawberry jam.

OMELET PUFF

4 eggs, separated
½ teaspoon salt
¼ cup water

⅛ teaspoon pepper
1 tablespoon butter or other fat

Place the egg whites, salt and water in a bowl and beat with a rotary beater until stiff but not dry. Using the same beater, beat the yolks with the pepper until they are thick and lemon colored. Fold yolks into whites. Heat fat in ten-inch skillet. Pour in eggs gently. Cook slowly, about five minutes or until puffy and lightly browned on bottom. Then bake at 325°F. (slow) fifteen minutes or until knife inserted in center comes out clean. *Serves two or three.*

If you're a gourmet, you'll like this for breakfast. But everybody likes it as a snack. Hearty, nutritious, delicious.

CHEESE AND EGG PANCAKES

2 eggs
2 tablespoons milk
2 tablespoons grated natural Cheddar
  cheese
1 tablespoon chopped green onion

1 tablespoon melted butter
Salt and pepper to taste
Parsley and additional butter for
  garnish

In a bowl, beat the eggs until light and foamy, then beat in milk, cheese, onion, butter, and salt and pepper. Drop by tablespoonfuls on hot greased skillet, turning to brown both sides. Serve topped with butter and garnished with parsley, *to two.*

As in a cheese soufflé, the flavor combination of eggs and cheese is surely a marriage made in heaven. Here it is again, in a different dish, with curly bacon toppers.

SWISS EGGS WITH BACON RINGS

4 to 8 slices bacon	4 eggs
1 package (8 oz.) process Swiss cheese slices	¼ teaspoon salt
	⅛ teaspoon pepper
1 cup heavy cream	Paprika

Before guests arrive for brunch: Fry bacon until almost done but still pliable. Drain on absorbent paper till cool enough to handle, then make bacon curls (stand curls close together so they don't unravel). Butter a nine-inch glass pie plate. Line bottom and sides with cheese; reserve two slices and cut them into four one-and-a-half-inch circles. Now pour half the cream into pie plate. Break eggs one at a time into a cup; slide into pie plate. Pour remaining cream over eggs; sprinkle with salt, pepper, paprika.

When guests arrive: Pop eggs into a hot oven (425°F.) After ten minutes, insert bacon curls into bubbling mixture and top each egg yolk with a circle of cheese. Bake five minutes longer or until mixture is set. *Serves four*.

NOTE: For eight servings, use eight eggs and two packages of cheese but keep the same amount of cream and seasoning. Bake in a long shallow dish.

This recipe is an easy version (and, we think, a better one) of Eggs Benedict. It's the ideal company breakfast or brunch dish, but equally good for informal dinners. You can make the sauce ahead.

EGGS À LA DUKE

4 English muffins	4 boneless ham steaks,
Butter	¼ inch thick
	8 eggs

Preheat the broiler, then split the English muffins and butter them lightly. Cut each ham steak into two pieces; put them on broiler pan, five inches from heat. Broil five minutes, then turn and broil about five minutes on the other side. Meantime, poach the eggs. While the eggs are poaching, put your muffins, cut side up, in the broiler with the ham. By the time they're toasted, the ham and eggs should be done too. Top each muffin half with an egg and arrange on a platter with the ham slices between. Serve immediately with Duke's sauce. *Serves four generously*.

Duke's Sauce

¼ cup butter
6 tablespoons flour
1 teaspoon instant minced onion
½ teaspoon dry mustard

2 teaspoons lemon juice
3 cups clear chicken broth
2 tablespoons mayonnaise

Melt the butter in a medium saucepan, then stir in the flour with a wooden spoon till you have a smooth paste. Remove from heat and stir in the onion, mustard and lemon juice. Gradually blend in one cup of the broth, stirring till smooth. Then stir in the rest of the broth and return to heat. Cook and stir the mixture until it comes to a boil and is smooth and thick. Cool the sauce, then cover it and put it in the refrigerator until the morning. Heat it in a double boiler at breakfast time. (Start heating it when you put the ham on to broil.) Give it a stir once in a while. Just before serving time stir in the mayonnaise until smooth.

To Hard-Cook Many Eggs

The rules are a little different for a dozen than for two or three, and it's wise to be especially careful when you have lots to do. Choose a big, broad-bottomed pot and find a rack which fits onto the bottom. (Crumpled aluminum foil may also be used—the object is to keep the eggs from coming into direct contact with pot bottom.) Place the eggs on the rack, about an inch apart, so they won't jostle together and crack in cooking. Add enough cold water just to cover the eggs. Bring it to a boil and immediately reduce heat to simmer. Cover and cook fifteen minutes. Drain off hot water, and fill pan to overflowing with cold water. When eggs have cooled, drain and dry. This method yields eggs with unbroken shells, and usually, no "green ring." Now they may be used for salads, casserole dishes or even for Easter eggs.

Even those hard-cooked Easter eggs may be used for the dish below. Follow the directions to make it party-pretty. But it is even more delicious if you layer the bottom of the baking dish with asparagus, cover with egg halves, pour the sauce over all and bake.

EGGS EDELWEISS

4 eggs
2 packages (10 oz. each) frozen
    asparagus spears

1 can condensed cheese soup
2 tablespoons flour
½ cup mayonnaise

Hard-cook two of the eggs. Shell and cut in half lengthwise. Cook asparagus according to package directions, until just tender. Separate one uncooked egg. (Store yolk for some other use.) With rotary beater beat egg white until it stands in peaks. In a separate bowl, use beater to combine soup, flour, remaining whole egg and mayonnaise, blending well. Fold in egg white. Divide the mixture into two shallow baking dishes. Arrange egg halves and asparagus spears in an attractive pattern over top. Bake at 350°F. (moderate), covered, for ten minutes. Remove cover and bake for an additional five minutes. *Serve piping hot to six.*

CHEESE

Any experienced teen hostess will tell you that a refrigerator stocked with several kinds of cheeses is an insurance policy: a guarantee that you can always rush out to the kitchen to whip up a little something—for a snack, for a surprise supper.

Storing: The best and simplest way to store cheese is in its original wrapping, which is specially designed to keep cheese at peak freshness. Many packages have dotted-line flaps so that you can reclose them neatly after opening. Other methods: store in a double thickness of moistureproof, odorproof wrapping and seal tightly, or store in a special cheese container. Keep in refrigerator.

Grating: Grate cheese according to its type. For soft cheese, use a coarse grater (or dice cheese with a knife). For "dry" or hard type, use a fine grater. You may grate cheese in advance and store it.

Melting: To melt cheese, first heat the liquid called for in recipe; add cheese, stir *only* until smooth. Overcooking toughens it. For snacks, serve a "rarebit" of cheese and tomato soup on toast.

Baking: To bake cheese, keep oven temperature at 350°F. (moderate). Try this: Make slits in brown-and-serve French bread. Butter and fill slits with Swiss or American cheese. Bake twenty minutes.

Broiling: When broiling cheese, watch it closely and remove as soon as melted. For Saturday lunch: Toast bread, spread with mustard and add cheese topped with olive, bacon or tomato. Broil.

We suspect that almost anything is better with a little sour cream added. The cheese puff below is an example.

ELEGANT CHEESE PUFF

1 cup sifted flour	1½ cups commercial sour cream
½ teaspoon salt	¼ cup grated Parmesan cheese
½ to 1 teaspoon pepper	5 eggs, separated

Sift flour with salt and pepper into mixing bowl. Blend in sour cream and cheese; beat until thick and creamy. Add egg yolks; beat until ivory yellow. Beat egg whites till stiff but not dry. Fold into the sour cream mixture gently but thoroughly. Turn into a one-and-one-half-quart casserole which has been well greased, then sprinkled with additional grated Parmesan cheese. Place casserole in a pan of hot water. Bake at 350°F. (moderate) for forty to fifty minutes until golden brown. Serve at once with melted butter and Parmesan cheese. *Serves four to six.*

Big, wide lasagne noodles are fun to eat rolled up instead of stacked as suggested in conventional recipes.

SPEEDY CHEESE AND LASAGNE ROLL-UPS

8 oz. lasagne noodles
1 can (8 oz.) tomato sauce
2 tablespoons chopped onion
¼ teaspoon basil
¼ teaspoon salt

⅛ teaspoon pepper
½ lb. mozzarella cheese, thinly sliced
3 tablespoons (about) grated
  Parmesan cheese

Cook the lasagne, following directions on package, and drain. Meanwhile combine tomato sauce with onion and seasonings. Lay cooked lasagne on cutting board, spread with tomato sauce and cover with cheese. Roll up each strip and place in a baking dish. Top with remaining sauce and sprinkle with Parmesan. Bake at 350°F. (moderate) twenty minutes or until bubbling and browned. *Makes four servings.*

When you hear people speak of Swiss fondue, what they mean is something like the recipe below. It's great fun around holiday time and after any winter sport. Play it like a game—anyone who drops his cube of bread into the fondue pays a forfeit (does the dishes, manages the hi-fi, or what have you).

SWISS FONDUE

1½ lbs. Swiss cheese, grated
⅓ cup flour
⅛ teaspoon nutmeg
2 loaves French bread, cut into cubes
  (or 4 loaves of brown-and-serve
  size)

4 cups canned chicken broth
1½ teaspoons vinegar
½ teaspoon Worcestershire sauce
1 teaspoon Angostura bitters

If you wish, you can fix part of this recipe in advance, to be ready for instant dramatics. Toss the grated cheese with flour and nutmeg, cover it and tuck it in the refrigerator. Cut up the bread, wrap it in airtight wrapping. Set the fondue table with a chafing dish or an electric skillet in the center, a fork and a napkin for each guest and perhaps a coffee service, too. Then go out sledding! When you come back, follow this procedure: In the chafing dish, or electric skillet set between "warm" and 220°F., bring the chicken broth to a gentle simmer. Add vinegar, Worcestershire and bitters. Add the prepared cheese gradually, stirring very well after each addition. Let the chafing dish or skillet slowly heat the cheese, while you stir every once in a while. When the cheese bubbles, it's ready. Each guest picks up a fork, spears a bread cube and swirls it into the bubbling mixture, then eats. *Plenty of snacking for eight.*

Here's a soufflé which stands up for its rights, but is airily light and well flavored. Special note to the weight-conscious: one serving which is about a fifth of the finished dish, contains only 270 calories and is almost *all* protein.

SWISS CHEESE SOUFFLÉ

1 cup water
⅓ cup instant nonfat dry milk
  powder
3 tablespoons flour
¾ teaspoon salt

½ lb. process Swiss cheese, shredded
¼ teaspoon Worcestershire sauce
¼ teaspoon nutmeg
4 eggs, separated

Place water in top of double boiler. Sprinkle with dry milk, flour and salt. Beat with rotary beater until just blended. Stir over boiling water until slightly thickened. Add shredded cheese, Worcestershire and nutmeg and stir until cheese melts; remove from heat. Beat egg yolks until thick. Stir a little cheese sauce into the yolks, then stir mixture back into cheese sauce. With a clean beater, beat the egg whites until stiff but not dry. Fold in the cheese sauce. Pour into ungreased one-quart casserole. Bake at 300°F. (slow) forty-five minutes. *Serve at once to four or five.*

Everything nice (including sugar and spice) is in this meatless main dish. Hearty for a party, lovely for dinner.

CHEESE AND NOODLE CASSEROLE

1 package (8 oz.) broad noodles
¼ cup butter or margarine
1 medium onion, minced
1 clove garlic, minced
2 teaspoons instant minced green
  onion
1 can (No. 2) tomatoes

1 can (8 oz.) tomato sauce
½ teaspoon sugar
½ teaspoon salt
⅛ teaspoon pepper
½ pint creamed cottage cheese
8 slices Cheddar cheese
⅓ cup grated Parmesan cheese

Cook noodles according to package directions. Drain. Set aside. Melt butter in a saucepan. Sauté onion and garlic in butter until transparent. Add minced green onion, drained tomatoes, tomato sauce and seasonings. Stir to blend. Simmer uncovered, stirring occasionally, for fifteen minutes. Combine noodles, tomato mixture and cottage cheese. Pour half of tomato-cheese mixture into a greased nine-inch-square baking pan. Top with four slices of Cheddar cheese; sprinkle with half the Parmesan cheese. Repeat layers. Bake at 350°F. (moderate) for about thirty minutes. Remove from oven and let stand five minutes before serving. *Makes six servings.*

For an impromptu Saturday lunch or a Sunday supper, this dish is made almost entirely from pantry-shelf ingredients.

LASAGNE PARTY RING

3 eggs	1 can (2 lb. 8 oz.) lasagne
½ teaspoon garlic salt	1 can (6 oz.) whole mushroom
1 can (15½ oz.) marinara sauce	crowns

Beat eggs in a large bowl with a fork. Beat in garlic salt and a half-cup of marinara sauce. Fold in lasagne. Grease a nine-inch ring mold; put mushrooms (drained) around bottom, add lasagne. Bake at 325°F. (slow) forty minutes or until firm. Invert on a large round platter. Before serving, heat remaining marinara sauce; serve in a bowl set in center of the ring mold. *Makes six servings.*

A delicious can't-fail dish for an at-home lunch or a light dinner. Crumbled crackers provide body and good flavor as well as energy; cheese and eggs provide good proteins. Fine Friday fare!

EASY CHEESE CASSEROLE

Preheat oven to 350° F. Place in a large bowl:

4 eggs, well beaten	1 tablespoon melted butter or
2 cups milk	margarine
2 cups crumbled saltines	½ teaspoon salt
2 cups grated pimiento-American	⅛ teaspoon paprika
cheese	

Combine lightly. Turn into a greased two-quart baking dish. Bake forty minutes or until golden and firm. *Makes six servings.*

Want to know a secret? Without the ham slices, this dish is called *Quiche Lorraine* (*keesh* is how you say it), and is proudly served in French and Swiss restaurants. It's delectable at brunch or at dinner.

HAM AND CHEESE PIE

12 oz. (about) sliced boiled ham	4 cups heavy cream
2 nine-inch pie shells, baked and cooled	1 teaspoon salt
	Dash of nutmeg
2 cups (½ lb.) grated Swiss cheese	Dash of cayenne pepper
8 eggs	

Cut ham into strips and reserve two dozen for garnish. Arrange the rest in pie shells. Sprinkle one cup of cheese into each shell. Beat eggs, cream, salt, nutmeg and cayenne and slowly pour mixture over the cheese in each shell. Bake at 425°F. (hot) fifteen minutes. Garnish pies with reserved ham, then bake at 300°F. (slow) forty minutes or till knife inserted in center comes out clean. *Serves eight generously.*

NOTE: For four to six guests, halve all ingredients and make one pie. For sixteen, double all, but make egg mixture in two batches for easy blending.

CHEESE FOR DESSERT

Cheese—served with fruit and crackers—makes a very simple, very Continental dessert. For variety: serve several kinds of cheese—blue or Roquefort, Cheddar and Camembert perhaps. For a sweet touch: serve cream cheese to be spread on crisp saltines with raspberry or currant jam. Let all cheeses stand at room temperature awhile before serving; it improves the taste.

SAUCES FOR MAIN DISHES

It's worthwhile learning and using a few sauces. How, for instance, could we get along without white sauce (which many people call cream sauce)? Where would any self-respecting barbecue chef be without a basting sauce? Here are a few—master the basics and you'll be on the way to inventing your own.

How much sauce should you make? For each serving of vegetables, you'll need at least two tablespoons of sauce. A cup of sauce should be ample for six servings of vegetables. For meat people tend to use more, unless it's a very spicy one. Allow one-fourth cup of meat sauces, like gravy, per person. If you have sauce left over (except Hollandaise, of course), it can be refrigerated and used in other ways—in a casserole, for example.

PERFECT WHITE SAUCE

Proportions for White Sauce

With Evaporated Milk (Protein-Rich)	Thin	Medium	Heavy
Butter or margarine	1 tablespoon	1 tablespoon	2 tablespoons
Flour	1 tablespoon	1 tablespoon	3 tablespoons
Undiluted evaporated milk	½ cup	1 cup	1 cup
Water	½ cup	none	none

With Whole or Nonfat Milk			
Butter or margarine	1 tablespoon	2 tablespoons	4 tablespoons
Flour	1 tablespoon	2 tablespoons	4 tablespoons
Whole or nonfat * milk	1 cup	1 cup	1 cup

What You Do—Step by Step

Get together everything you will need. See our chart above. Melt butter over very low heat. It should bubble but not brown.

Stir in flour and seasonings till blended and smooth. For one cup of white sauce use one-half teaspoon salt, a dash of pepper.

Add milk gradually to the flour-butter mixture, stirring constantly. (Use a wire whisk to make a smooth, velvety sauce.) While mixture cooks over low heat, continue to stir until thick.

Cook and stir until desired consistency is reached—about four minutes on low heat. Thin white sauce should be like light cream; heavy sauce should be like a pudding.

Wonderful Tricks with White Sauce

Amandine: After you've melted the butter for the sauce, add three table-spoons of finely chopped almonds and sauté until lightly browned. Then stir in flour, other ingredients.

Sesame: Substitute one tablespoon of sesame seeds for the almonds; sauté five minutes; add flour, etc.

Confetti: Make regular sauce, add a tablespoon of chopped parsley and two tablespoons of chopped pimiento just before serving.

Divan: Stir one-fourth cup of grated Parmesan cheese into the finished white sauce.

Pennsylvania Dutch: Use bacon drippings instead of butter to make sauce. Before serving, add three tablespoons crumbled cooked bacon.

* To make one cup of reliquefied nonfat dry milk, measure one-third cup of dry milk crystals in a glass measuring cup; add water to bring to the one-cup mark. Stir lightly. (Add an extra tablespoonful of dry milk to make the sauce richer in proteins.)

BROWN GRAVY FOR ROAST

When the roast has completed its baking time and is "resting" out of the oven before carving, you can make the gravy in the roasting pan. First pour off the liquid you'll find in the pan, leaving about one-fourth cup plus all the little brown baked-on bits in the pan. Place the roasting pan over low heat on the top of the stove. With a sturdy, long-handled spoon, loosen the brown bits. Then sprinkle two or three tablespoons of flour into the liquid. Cook and stir it over low heat until it bubbles. (The flour should cook slightly.) Next, gradually add water or bouillon to the mixture, stirring constantly. You will need about one and one-half cups in all, but add it slowly. Then cook and stir until mixture comes to a boil and thickens. Season with salt and pepper, perhaps a dash of Worcestershire sauce, and enough bottled gravy coloring to give the sauce just the color you like best. If there's a lump or two, simply force gravy through a strainer before pouring into gravy boat.

Though real Hollandaise sauce is not for freshman cooks, sophomores can make it. Just read and *heed* directions, then serve it forth—for example, with boiled artichoke hearts or broccoli spears.

HOLLANDAISE SAUCE

¾ cup butter	Dash of salt
1½ tablespoons lemon juice	Dash of cayenne pepper
3 egg yolks, well beaten	

In the top of a double boiler, place one-fourth cup of the butter, the lemon juice and the beaten egg yolks. Cook slowly over hot, *not boiling*, water, beating *constantly* with a wire whisk or beater until butter is melted. Still beating, add another quarter-cup of butter. Mixture should begin to thicken. Now add, stirring constantly, the remaining butter. Cook until well thickened. Remove immediately from water, add salt and cayenne and serve at once. (If the sauce shows signs of curdling, place the double boiler top on a bed of crushed ice and beat hard.) *Makes three-fourths of a cup.*

Try this on hot fish fillets or use as a spread for chicken sandwiches.

LEMON HERB BUTTER

½ cup butter or margarine	½ teaspoon dried basil
1 teaspoon grated lemon peel	½ teaspoon dried minced green onion
1 teaspoon dried parsley flakes	2 teaspoons prepared mustard

Cream butter, stir in remaining ingredients. Let stand three hours. *Makes one-half cup.*

Here's a good barbecue sauce—for basting hamburgers or franks, or just to serve, hot or cold, with them.

TOMATO BARBECUE SAUCE

¼ cup cooking oil
3 medium-size onions, chopped
½ cup chopped celery
½ cup chopped green pepper
1 bottle (14 oz.) catchup
¼ cup brown sugar, firmly packed

3 cans (8 oz. each) tomato sauce
½ teaspoon salt
¼ teaspoon black pepper
1 tablespoon prepared mustard
2 tablespoons Worcestershire sauce

Heat the cooking oil in a large heavy saucepan. Add the onions, celery and green pepper. Cook them slowly just until they're lightly browned and tender. Add all the remaining ingredients. Simmer this good-smelling red sauce until it's thick—about twenty minutes. Cool and refrigerate any remaining sauce. *Makes about five cups.*

This is one of those "little bit of this and that" recipes. The unusual combination of spices produces its pleasant flavor.

ITALIAN SPAGHETTI SAUCE

2 tablespoons cooking oil
1 clove garlic, minced
3 large onions, chopped
1 lb. ground beef chuck
6 cans (8 oz. each) tomato sauce
1 small can tomato paste
1 tablespoon brown sugar
¾ teaspoon chili powder
1 tablespoon Worcestershire sauce
½ teaspoon monosodium glutamate
¼ teaspoon turmeric
¼ teaspoon mace

1 teaspoon marjoram
½ teaspoon crushed cumin seed
¼ teaspoon powdered thyme
¼ teaspoon crumbled basil
1½ teaspoons crushed coriander seed
¼ teaspoon curry powder
¾ teaspoon dry mustard
½ teaspoon rosemary
1 teaspoon orégano
1 lb. spaghetti
Parmesan cheese

Heat oil in a large saucepan or Dutch oven. Add garlic, onions and chuck. Cook, breaking meat and stirring occasionally, over moderate heat until meat is browning and onion a little tender. Add all remaining ingredients except spaghetti and cheese. Bring to a boil, reduce heat and simmer, covered, one and one-half hours. Cook spaghetti in a large amount of boiling salted water until barely tender. Rinse with boiling water. Drain in colander. Place on serving platter and cover with sauce. Sprinkle with grated Parmesan cheese. *Makes six servings.*

Vegetables

$\mathcal{A}$LL YOUR LIFE probably you've been told that vegetables are good for you. We'd like to put the period after good! To prove our point, we've gathered together the vegetable dishes below. Some are cooked—with a dash of buttered nuts or a sprinkling of raisins to perk up the flavor; some are uncooked in salad form; some are sauced. *All* are delicious! Of course, if you "positively hate spinach!" you may not even want to try our new ways to cook it. But by avoiding it—or any other vegetable—you do miss a lot.

You need at least two or more vegetables every day—to put roses in your cheeks, as they used to say—and the more vegetables you learn to like, the more interesting your meals will be. And have you ever stopped to think that *maybe* you don't dislike a particular vegetable so much as the way it's prepared? Try a little "sugar-coating." Suggestions follow.

Consult the chapter after this one, too, for information on the salad vegetables—like lettuce and cucumbers.

ARTICHOKES

Select artichokes this way: Look for plump, firm globes with tightly closed leaves (petals). They may be any size but should always be bright green with very few dark spots. To prepare them for cooking, cut off stems with a sharp knife and pull off the tough or damaged outer leaves. Wash thoroughly in cold, running water or soak them in cold water about thirty minutes. Drain. Drop them into a large kettle of boiling salted water to cover. Add one tablespoonful of lemon juice or vinegar for each quart of water. Cook twenty to forty-five minutes (depending on size of artichokes) or until the hearts can be pierced easily with a fork. Drain upside down. Serve hot with melted butter, mayonnaise seasoned with prepared mustard, or Hollandaise sauce (page 120).

Eating artichokes is fun! Pull off one leaf and, holding it in your fingers, dip the fleshy part (the light-colored end) into the sauce. Eat only the tender part of the leaf. Set the remaining tip aside. Continue with all the leaves in this manner until you come to the prickly core or choke. Remove this choke with a knife and fork and discard it. With your fork cut the heart into bite-size pieces (one at a time), dip each piece in the sauce and eat it.

NOTE: Frozen artichoke hearts are available—and very good!

ARTICHOKE HEARTS VINAIGRETTE

Cook frozen artichoke hearts as package directs. Cool, then place in a bowl and add a simple French dressing to cover. Chill several hours or overnight, then serve on lettuce leaves, topped with a little of the marinade and garnished with thin lemon slices.

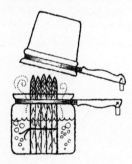

ASPARAGUS

Choose slim green stalks with compact tips. Snap off tough lower ends of stalks. Soak to clean. Under running water, cut off loose scales on stalks. Tie and place, as shown, in a double boiler with two inches of boiling salted water; cook fifteen minutes. Or make a two-inch slit in each stalk end (for even cooking) and cook flat in a covered skillet with one inch of boiling salted water.

ASPARAGUS ROMANO

Cook one package of frozen asparagus spears as package directs. Drain and place in a warmed serving dish. Melt one-fourth cup of butter or margarine and add two tablespoons of lemon juice. Pour this over the asparagus and garnish with halved lemon slices—stand the slices up between stalks to look like Roman arches. *Makes four servings.*

BETTER BAKED BEANS

The way to put the extra before the ordinary in canned beans is—season to taste! Just about everybody likes a little extra onion, for example. (Try instant minced onion; add it before heating beans.) Then why not add a few strips of bacon, fried only slightly, before you pop your beans in the oven? Or a can of cocktail franks or a small can of pineapple tidbits (drained). Fold in, heat in oven at 350°F. (moderate) for twenty minutes and serve with pride.

At a party or company dinner—or on just any day—this dish is always a huge success.

PARTY GREEN BEANS

1 can condensed mushroom soup
2 tablespoons soy sauce (or less, to taste)
Salt, pepper to taste
½ teaspoon monosodium glutamate

2 cans (1 lb. each) Blue Lake green beans, drained
1 can water chestnuts, drained and sliced thin
1 can French-fried onions

To condensed soup add soy sauce, salt, pepper and monosodium glutamate. Combine with beans and water chestnuts. Place in a greased casserole dish. Sprinkle with French-fried onions. Bake at 350° F. (moderate) forty minutes. *Makes six servings.*

BACON–Y BABY LIMAS

In a three-cup saucepan cook one package (10 oz.) frozen baby limas in boiling water as label directs. In a small skillet, fry four slices of bacon, diced, until crisp. Drain off all but two tablespoons of fat. Toss bacon with cooked limas, saving a little bacon to garnish top. *Makes four servings.*

BEETS

Select beets with crisp green tops, smooth skins. Cut off all but two inches of top. Wash but do not peel beets. Cook in boiling salted water, covered, forty minutes. Drain, cool, slip off skins.

Quicker method: Shred six peeled beets. Cook, covered, in one tablespoon water and two tablespoons butter, ten minutes.

BUTTERED BEETS AND GREENS

On the market in spring are tiny "new" beets complete with greens. Cook them whole (with skins and an inch of stem and root intact) twenty to thirty minutes, until tender; then peel. Wash the greens well (remove any tough stems) and cook these in boiling water about three minutes. Drain and chop coarsely. Mix with the baby beets and a generous amount of butter or margarine, freshly ground black pepper and a hint (maybe a teaspoon) of vinegar.

BROCCOLI

Select broccoli with all green tops, no opened flowers. Cut off leaves and knobs from stems. For even cooking, cut a cross in the bottom of each stalk. Cook in a little water, uncovered, three minutes. Cover; cook ten minutes more. Drain. Add butter.

BROCCOLI, CHINESE STYLE

Very Chinese, very sweet and tender if you keep flowerets whole, chop the stalks and cook five minutes, uncovered, in one cup of water. Drain, and, for one and one-half pounds, add one-fourth cup of butter to the pan; cover and reduce the heat. Steam for fifteen minutes or until tender. A sauce of whipped salad dressing blended with an equal amount of chili sauce and a tiny bit of sugar adds a pleasant last touch. *Makes four servings*.

BRUSSELS SPROUTS

These tiny cabbages are available frozen (use package directions) and fresh. When buying them at the vegetable counter, look for crisp, green, tight sprouts; avoid yellow spots. Trim off ragged leaves, and cut off a bit from the stem end. Wash thoroughly. Place in a small amount of boiling salted water. Cover and cook ten to twenty-five minutes, lifting cover occasionally during cooking. Delicious with butter or Hollandaise sauce (page 120). *One pound serves four.*

CAULIFLOWER

When you buy cauliflower, look for an unblemished white compact head surrounded with fresh green stalks. To prepare it, cut off a slice from the base, then strip off all outer leaves and stalks. If you like, leave the head whole; place base down in pan with two inches of boiling salted water. Cover and boil about thirty minutes until tender. Or break into cauliflowerets and score stem ends. Cook, covered, in boiling salted water ten to fifteen minutes. In either case, lift cover from time to time during cooking. A small head serves three, a large head serves six.

You'll be surprised at what good partners appear below.

CAULIFLOWER AND PEANUTS

1 package (10 oz.) frozen cauliflower ¼ cup chopped peanuts
¼ cup butter

Cook cauliflower as package directs. Meanwhile, melt butter in a small skillet. Add chopped peanuts. Sauté until lightly browned. Drain cauliflower. Add butter and peanuts. Toss lightly. Serve at once. *Makes three to four servings.*

CABBAGE

Select solid, heavy heads. Cut in wedges, core and wash. Shred if desired. Cook shredded cabbage eight minutes, wedges eighteen, but during first three minutes of cooking time, leave cover off. Wrap uncooked part in towel and refrigerate.

CARROTS

Choose firm, well-shaped carrots. Use peeler to remove skins. Cook, covered, in a small amount of water. Cook uncut carrots twenty minutes. Or cut carrots in dice, strips or "pennies" and cook for ten minutes.

You might even call these Carrots Celestial—something sweet and lovely happens to an old friend.

CARROTS HAWAIIAN

6 carrots, diced ½ cup crushed pineapple, drained
Pinch of salt 1 tablespoon butter
1 teaspoon sugar 2 teaspoons cornstarch
½ cup water

Peel and dice the carrots. Add with salt and sugar to the water and cook until slightly tender—about eight minutes. Add pineapple and butter.

Stir into cornstarch just enough water to make a smooth paste. Add to boiling carrots. Stir over medium heat until clear and thick. *Makes six servings*.

CORN

Though excellent canned corn is always available and though corn on the cob is found in some markets all year round, corn is remembered best when it's in season locally. Reason? The saying is, "Don't pick the corn until the water's boiling." In other words, corn is at its best when it's fresh from the field.

When you choose corn, be sure husks don't show worm damage. If possible, refrigerate corn in its husks until (as we said above) the water's boiling. Then strip off the husks, picking off every bit of silk. (Work on a large piece of newspaper—that silk may fly!) Drop corn into boiling water (salted and, if desired, containing a teaspoon of sugar) and cook three to five minutes. Serve with soft or melted butter and plenty of salt. Appetites for corn vary. *One ear is enough for many people, but some fans like three or four.*

Try this on a winter day. Homey-good.

MIXED VEGETABLES DE LUXE

1 cup water	1 package frozen mixed vegetables
1 package or can dehydrated chicken- noodle soup mix	

Bring water to a boil in a saucepan. Add soup mix and stir until dissolved. Add frozen vegetables, bring back to a boil, then cook, covered, over low heat ten minutes. *Makes four servings*.

A really different way to serve vegetables.

CRISP–FRIED MIXED VEGETABLES

1 cup pancake mix	4 small tomatoes
¼ teaspoon salt	2 medium onions, peeled
¾ cup water	½ cup milk
1 egg	Fat for deep frying
2 cups tender uncooked green beans	

Combine pancake mix with salt, water and egg and beat well. Wash beans, tomatoes and onions. Snip ends from beans. Cut the tomatoes in half. Slice the onions and separate them into rings, then soak the rings in milk for ten minutes. Meanwhile, heat fat to 375°F. Dip vegetables, a few at a time, into batter, lower into hot fat and fry for two or three minutes. *Serve hot as a side dish to four to six.*

MUSHROOMS

When fresh mushrooms are in season, they can add excitement to an ordinary menu for little cost. Large white mushrooms are a good bit more expensive than smaller varieties, so choose the kind best suited to your recipe. Fresh mushrooms rarely need peeling and require only the lightest washing. Just trim off the last quarter-inch of stem and any damaged portions.

For broiling, use large mushroom caps (remove stems and use in sauces or soups). Place rounded side down in broiling dish. Fill cavities with a teaspoon of butter, and season with salt, pepper and, if desired, lemon juice. Broil about six minutes. *Allow twelve to sixteen mushrooms for four people.*

For sautéing, use medium-size mushrooms, halved, or large mushrooms cut in slices from crown through stem. For four, buy a pound. In a skillet, melt one-fourth cup of butter or margarine. Add two or three tablespoons of chopped onion and cook over moderate heat until soft. Add sliced mushrooms and cook, stirring now and then, five to eight minutes. Cover and keep warm over lowest heat two minutes more or until some juices are absorbed. Season with salt, pepper, and, if desired, lemon juice.

Canned mushrooms are a speedy, all-season pantry shelf staple. Good in cream sauce and Italian dishes like pizza and spaghetti, mushrooms are also delicious with vegetables, in casseroles and stews. Available as caps or crowns, sliced, or as chopped stems and pieces.

THE ONION FAMILY

Second most popular vegetable in America, onions are a many-cousined clan with different tastes, different uses. Some are mild, some have a hearty flavor, some are sweet—try them all.

Globe onions (1) are yellow inside, have yellow, white or red skins, and are always in season. Use these when recipe calls simply for "onions." Average weight: three or four per pound.

Sweet onions (2) may be Bermudas or Spanish. Both are larger, milder than the globe type. Use in salads and sandwiches—or stuff with a meat-and-crumb mixture. They're most plentiful in the summertime.

Scallions (3) are young green onions of any variety. Small ones are good nibbling; larger ones may be boiled, cut into salad or used like any regular onion.

Boiling onions (4) are small and white, one to two inches in diameter. May be bought fresh or in cans. Delicious creamed.

Chives (5) come to market growing in a pot. Set them on a sunny kitchen window sill, snip as needed for recipes and garnishes.

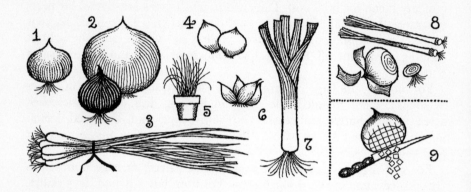

Shallots (6) are a purple-hued, mild little cousin to the onion. A fall and winter vegetable, shallots are used most in soups, stews.

Leeks (7) have a delicate onion flavor, are used in cream soups and stews. They are also boiled and served like asparagus, or cooked and served cold with a vinaigrette sauce, as a salad. Easiest to find in winter.

Instant onions: Included here are the canned or frozen whole onions, onion salt, onion powder, dehydrated minced green onions, instant minced onions (also dehydrated) and frozen minced green onions (scallions) or chives.

Remove skin from all onions before use. Start by cutting a small slice of skin from the root end, then peel outer skin off upward until intact underlayer is reached (8). Cut off tough greenery on scallions and leeks.

Peel without tears—by holding onions under cold running water as you peel.

To chop or mince onions: First cut off a slice (to get a flat surface), then make checkerboard cuts. Now slice just beneath cut surface (9); little pieces fall out easily.

Try this recipe. You'll find the flavor perfect, the appearance exciting, the appeal universal. In English, it's Green Onion Pie.

TARTE AUX POIREAUX

3 cups sliced green onions or scallions (include tender part of green tops)	2 eggs
	½ cup light cream
3 tablespoons butter or margarine	1 teaspoon salt
1 unbaked eight-inch pastry shell	Few grains of pepper

Cook green onions gently in butter, stirring frequently until tender. Arrange these in the pastry shell. Beat eggs just until blended and stir in cream, salt and pepper. Pour over onions. Bake at 425° F. (hot) about twenty minutes or until well browned and a knife inserted halfway between center and edge comes out clean. *Makes four servings as a main luncheon dish.*

Marvelous with steak or fried chicken:

BATTER–FRIED ONION RINGS

2 sweet Bermuda onions	1 teaspoon salt
1 egg	¾ cup sifted flour
½ cup milk	Fat for deep frying

Peel onions, slice and separate into rings. Beat egg with milk, then beat in salt and flour. Heat fat to 375° F. Dip the rings in egg batter. Separating carefully, lower into fat and fry until golden on both sides (about two minutes). Sprinkle with additional salt and keep warm until serving time. *As a garnish, makes eight servings.*

GREEN PEAS

Fresh peas are fun to fix! Choose pods with crisp, unblemished shells, small to medium peas inside. Buy three pounds in the shell to serve four. To open, hold pod in hand and press against seam with thumb until it cracks open. Run thumb down row of peas (like marble-shooting) to remove peas and shoot them into the cooking pot. Discard any peas which show shoots—they are overripe and will taste mealy. Cook peas, covered, in an inch of boiling water (add salt and a little bit of sugar) until peas are tender—ten to twenty-five minutes.

Frozen peas cook even more quickly. Turn a ten-ounce package into one-third cup of water with one-half teaspoon salt and two tablespoons butter. Cover and cook ten minutes or until tender. *Serve at once, with the buttery liquid, to three or four.*

SPINACH

Choose crisp, dark green leaves with small stems. Remove root ends. To clean, soak in a pan of water, lift out, drain. Repeat three times. Cook, covered, five minutes, in just the water that clings to the leaves.

In the recipe below, the fresh spinach taste is smoothed and sweetened.

SURPRISE SPINACH

1 bottle (7 oz.) lemon-lime
  carbonated beverage
2 packages (10 oz. each) frozen
  chopped spinach

1 teaspoon salt
½ cup raisins
1 tablespoon wine vinegar
1 tablespoon butter

Pour lemon-lime into a saucepan. Bring to a boil over medium heat. Add frozen spinach and salt. Bring to a boil again, breaking up large blocks with a kitchen fork. Reduce heat and simmer, covered, for three minutes. Add raisins and vinegar; cook three minutes more. Drain, add butter and toss to combine. *Makes eight servings.*

ACORN SQUASH

Acorn squash is easy to prepare as part of an oven meal. Select unblemished, firm squash. They may be solid dark green or mottled with orange. Count on half an acorn squash per person. Scrub outside well, then cut in half lengthwise. With a sturdy serving spoon, scoop out seeds and strings from center. Place cut side down on a baking sheet. Bake at 400°F. (hot) forty minutes. Turn cut side up. Brush each half with melted butter, and sprinkle with salt and pepper. If desired, brush with honey, brown sugar or corn syrup. Bake twenty to thirty minutes more or until squash is tender (test with a fork). *Two squashes serve four.*

If your family prefers mashed squash, try the frozen and canned varieties. They are excellent work savers.

SUMMER SQUASH AND ZUCCHINI

Both yellow summer squash and green-striped zucchini are best when small, young, firm and unbruised. For either, scrub well and cut off both ends. Some of the skin may be removed with a vegetable peeler if you like. Slice and cook in an inch of boiling salted water, covered— fifteen minutes for summer squash, five to ten for zucchini—until fork-tender. Or cook either vegetable this way: Slice very, very thin (the slicing blade on a grater is good). In a saucepan, heat one-fourth cup butter, olive oil or bacon fat. Add squash slices and, if desired, a little sliced onion or minced garlic. Add two tablespoons water, cover and boil gently ten minutes or until tender. *One pound serves three.*

SWEET POTATOES

Are sweet potatoes better if they're sweeter? Try this recipe and see.

SWEET POTATO BALLS

2 lbs. sweet potatoes
1 cup sifted flour
½ teaspoon salt
¾ cup flaked coconut, coarsely chopped

¾ cup firmly packed brown sugar
⅔ cup coarsely chopped salted almonds
Fat for deep frying

Cook unpeeled sweet potatoes in boiling water until they can be pierced easily with a fork (about thirty minutes). Drain, peel and mash. Mix flour and salt and sift into mashed potatoes; mix well. Form into balls on waxed paper, press rounds flat and place some chopped coconut on each patty. Fold in sides and edges of each and reroll into balls. Roll potato balls in brown sugar; then roll again in chopped almonds. Fry in deep hot fat (375°F.) five minutes to brown. Drain on paper towels. *Makes eight.*

An unusual snack with hot chocolate in the evening, or a delightful surprise at an all-out holiday dinner.

YAM APPLES

3 cups mashed canned yams
½ teaspoon cinnamon
½ teaspoon nutmeg
¼ teaspoon powdered cloves
⅓ cup light brown sugar

1 egg yolk
8 marshmallows
Paprika
8 whole cloves
Mint leaves

Beat yams until smooth; add spices and brown sugar and blend. Form this mixture into eight apple shapes with a marshmallow in the center of each. Beat egg yolk with a few drops of water and use to brush each "apple." Sprinkle lightly with paprika. Set each in a green paper baking cup in a muffin pan. Place a clove at the top of each to form stem. (If you like, Yam Apples may be covered and refrigerated at this point for later reheating.) Heat at 350°F. (moderate) twelve to fifteen minutes. Insert mint leaves beside each stem. *Makes eight.*

TOMATOES

To choose perfect, ripe tomatoes: Gently press them to see if they are firm (neither hard nor soft), then check the color, which should be red all over, with no discolored spots. Ripe tomatoes should be refrigerated and used within two or three days. If you buy tomatoes which are still greenish, store them in a cool place (about 70° F.) until they ripen to a rich red. It's best to store them away from light, in a paper bag or closed cupboard since daylight is apt to make the color splotchy.

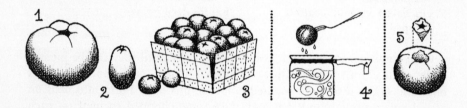

Kinds of tomatoes: Each has a distinctive size, shape and taste. Those pictured above are, beefsteak (1), plum (2) and cherry tomatoes (3). All are plentiful and good buys in July, August and September. Count on about four servings per pound.

To peel tomatoes: For one or two, use a vegetable parer. For large quantities: dip in boiling water till skin splits, slip skin off (4). While the water is boiling, poach a few medium-size tomatoes for a new vegetable treat. Cook them, covered, three or four minutes till done. Remove skin, salt and serve whole.

Tips on cutting up: Core the tomato, removing not only the green stem end but the tough cone-shaped portion just below (5). Then cut tomato crosswise into slices, or cut it in half, then into wedges.

To stuff tomatoes: Slice off the tops; scoop out the pulp into a strainer as shown. (Use pulp in sauces or mix with your stuffing.) Scallop edges of the tomato shells with a knife; drain well upside down.

To broil or bake tomatoes: Cut large tomatoes in half crosswise or cut a thin slice from the top of small tomatoes. Make slashes in cut surfaces with a knife; dot with butter, sprinkle with crumbs. Add salt, pepper and herbs as desired. Bake at 350°F. (moderate) a half-hour, or broil ten minutes.

TURNIPS

Turnips are of two kinds. White turnips make a crisp addition to salads and are often included in stews and soups. Yellow turnips, also called ruta-bagas, should be heavy for their size. Cut turnip in half so you have a steady base to help you work. With a vegetable parer, pare thinly. Wash and cut into two-inch pieces. Cover and cook in two inches of boiling salted water about forty minutes or until tender. Lift cover occasionally during cooking. Or cut into one-inch pieces and cook thirty minutes. Drain well, add butter to taste. Mash if desired. *Two pounds serves four to six.*

Ever tried potatoes and yellow turnips together?

TURNIPOTATOES

Peel, then cut turnips into bite-size pieces. Boil about twenty minutes in salted water to cover. At the same time, peel and cut up some potatoes (same amount as turnips); put on to boil. Meanwhile, frizzle a few slices of bacon, scissored coarsely. All cooked? Mash potatoes and turnips, mix together, blending with a little cream. Add some of the bacon drippings and the bacon. Serve hot.

POTATOES

New potatoes (1) stay firm and moist when cooked, are ideal for salads, creaming, boiling in the jackets. Harvested young in winter and spring, they are thin-skinned, will not keep too long.

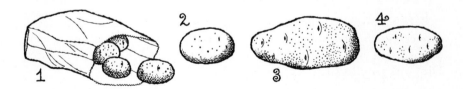

Boiling potatoes (2) are the year-round, everyday potatoes which are served boiled, mashed, fried or scalloped. They may be round or long. Kept in a cool, dark spot, they store well for months.

Baking potatoes (3), sold specially marked as "baking," are generally one-purpose potatoes though they may be mashed. When baked, they are mealy and fluffy, their thick skins crusty.

All-purpose potatoes (4), such as the Long White type shown here, are midway between bakers and boilers. When boiled, the potato is fluffy. When baked, it is moist, needs less butter than bakers.

To clean potatoes, scrub them well with a vegetable brush, then wash them in cold water. Remove the "eyes" with a potato peeler and cut away any bruised or greenish spots.

To boil: Leave jackets on if they are nice-looking. If not, peel *thinly.* New potatoes (usually left unpeeled) will cook faster if a belt of peel is removed from the middle. For even cooking, potatoes should be the same size; cut up large ones if necessary. Almost cover with boiling water, add a little salt, cover and cook fifteen to thirty minutes till fork-tender.

To bake: Wash, trim away bruised spots and rub skins with butter. Place potatoes in a baking pan and bake at 450°F. (very hot) fifty minutes or until they can be pierced easily with a fork. (Or bake at 350°F. for an hour and a half.) Then cut cross in top of potato and, protecting hands with a folded paper towel, squeeze potato until top puffs out. Add butter, paprika and serve *pronto.*

Delicious company-style baked potatoes—a mate for almost any meat.

STUFFED BAKED POTATOES

8 baking potatoes	2 teaspoons salt
1 cup commercial sour cream	2 teaspoons instant minced green
¼ cup butter or margarine	onion
¼ teaspoon pepper	Paprika

Bake potatoes as directed above. Cut a slice from the top of each. Scoop insides into bowl (don't break skins). Add remaining ingredients except paprika, and mix well. Restuff potatoes. Heat at 400°F. (hot) ten minutes. Dust with paprika and serve. *Makes eight.*

TO ROAST POTATOES WITH MEAT

Count on one large potato for each boy, a medium-size one for each girl. Peel and cut potatoes into uniform pieces about the size of small eggs. Cook, covered, in boiling salted water fifteen minutes or until you can pierce them (but not easily) with a fork. Drain; sprinkle with salt, pepper and paprika. Add to roast pan at least forty-five minutes before serving time and after some fat from roast has run into pan. About three times during cooking, loosen potatoes with spatula and turn. When you remove roast from oven (fifteen minutes before serving), return potatoes in pan to the oven to finish cooking.

PACKAGED POTATO PRODUCTS

Instant potatoes provide all kinds of welcome short cuts in preparation (no paring, cleaning, slicing). They will keep six months on the shelf.

Mashed potatoes can be made from flaked or granular products. For a quick party touch, try instant mashed potatoes (flaked or granular) either of these two ways:

Duchess potatoes. Prepare potatoes for four according to package directions, but use one-fourth cup less water. When potatoes are whipped, beat in two egg yolks. Force through a pastry tube or cookie press for piped borders or rosettes. Brown lightly in oven at 350°F (moderate).

Potato volcano. Spoon mashed potatoes into a mound and hollow out a hole in center. Brush mound with cream; sprinkle with cheese. Brown in oven at 400°F (hot); fill with creamed vegetables or meat. Make individual volcanoes if you like.

Sliced potatoes may be served plain, used in casseroles or salads.

Scalloped potatoes come with premeasured sauce ingredients.

Au gratin potatoes are similar to scalloped, with a cheese flavor.

Frozen potatoes are all precooked, ready to be heated, deep-fried, sauced or what have you. Stored in the freezer at 0°F., they will keep up to a year. Try them French-fried (below) or in a casserole.

French-fried potatoes come plain or crinkle-cut. They may be heated in the oven, but for rich crispiness sizzle them instead in one-fourth cup of hot fat in a skillet, stirring, for five minutes. Drain on paper towels; salt to taste.

Other frozen potato products are puffs, patties, mashed (to thaw in a double boiler) and diced.

Quick scalloped-potato casserole. In a shallow casserole dish mix two cans of condensed cream of celery soup, a one-pound package of frozen French fries and one and one-half cups tuna or cubed cheese or diced cooked ham. Season to taste and bake at 400°F. (hot) thirty minutes. *Makes six servings.*

Here a convenience product gets an extra flavor boost.

POTATO PUFF

2 envelopes (1 box) instant mashed
   potatoes
¼ cup butter
2 teaspoons parsley

Pepper to taste
2 eggs, separated
2 teaspoons instant minced green
   onion

First, make up the instant potatoes, following package directions and beating the mixture with a wire whisk until very smooth. Then beat in butter, parsley, pepper, egg yolks and one teaspoon of the instant green onion. Beat the egg whites stiff but not dry and fold them gently into the mashed potato mixture. Pile into a buttered casserole, sprinkling with remaining teaspoon of green onion. If desired, dish may now be covered and refrigerated. At dinnertime, remove cover and bake at 375°F. (moderate) forty-five minutes (or thirty-five minutes if dish was not refrigerated). Serve when well browned and hot. *Makes six servings.*

PARTY–PRETTY POTATO PEARS

Prepare a four-ounce package of instant mashed potatoes and shape into twelve tiny "pears." Brush each lightly with beaten egg yolk, dust with paprika to add rosy cheeks. Use cloves for stems. You can make all this ahead, bake at party time—in 350°F. (moderate) oven ten to fifteen minutes.

Don't overlook *Fancy French Fries* (page 341).

TIPS ON RICE

Rice tastes best when the grains are plump but fluffy and separate. It's sold in five varieties, but the general rule is *no rinsing!* (It's unnecessary before cooking, might destroy precious vitamins afterward.)

Long-grain regular rice is firm and translucent, fluffs and separates readily when cooked. This type is excellent to use for curries, stews, risottos and sauced dishes.

Short-grain regular rice cooks up softer and moister. Because grains tend to cling together more, this type is perfect for making puddings, croquettes and molds.

Brown rice is the whole unpolished kernel, rich in flavor and food value.

Cooking takes more time, more water, but the chewy texture and nutlike taste are worth it.

All three types: *one cup raw yields three cups cooked.*

Converted rice is a long-grain type specially treated by parboiling under steam pressure to retain its natural vitamins—thiamine and niacin. Cook as the package directs. One cup uncooked makes four cups cooked.

Precooked (quick) rice is readied in a jiffy—a joy for hurry-up meals, impromptu parties. Follow package directions. One cup from the box makes two cups to serve.

Quickest way to cook regular rice, either kind: measure into a saucepan two cups water, one cup uncooked rice, one teaspoon salt. Bring to a boil over high heat. Stir once, then cover tightly and turn heat low. Simmer fourteen minutes or until rice is tender, water absorbed.

Oven method (needs no watching): in a one-and-one-half-quart casserole place one cup uncooked rice, two tablespoons butter or margarine and one teaspoon salt. Stir in two cups boiling water. Cover. Bake at 350°F. (moderate) thirty minutes or until the rice is tender.

RICE AROUND

Rice can be as comfortable as breakfast, as exotic as a Japanese teahouse. It takes party shape when you set it in a ring mold and heap the center with some festive mixture (sky's the limit, from sauced fish to spiced fruit). For a five-cup ring mold cook enough rice (short-grain or precooked type is best) to make six cups. Stir in three tablespoons butter or margarine. Pack down gently but firmly into ring; let stand one minute. Turn out onto a large heated platter. *Makes eight to ten servings.*

For a *luau* or a sukiyaki party, you may want the rice made in the authentic Japanese manner. This is it:

ORIENTAL RICE

Use long-grain rice. Two cups of uncooked rice will make six cups of cooked rice, or more than enough for eight. In a bowl pour cold water over rice. Use hand to lift and wash grains. Drain off the starchy water. Pour fresh cold water onto the rice and continue washing and draining as described until the water remains clear. Drain off final washing water. Turn rice into an aluminum pot or electric saucepan. Pour in enough cold water to cover rice (about one inch). Cover tightly. Bring to a boil over high heat (212°F. on electric saucepan). As soon as steam escapes, let the rice cook for three minutes, then turn heat to moderate (keep electric saucepan at same setting). Cook two minutes longer, then turn heat as low as possible (175°F. on electric saucepan) and let stand fifteen minutes over this very low heat. The rice is then ready to be served. *Serves eight generously.*

Special rice for special meals—why not?

CHILI BEAN RICE

2 cans condensed chili soup
2 cups boiling water
2⅔ cups precooked rice

4 teaspoons butter
1 teaspoon salt

Combine chili soup and water in a large saucepan. Bring to a boil over moderate heat. Stir in rice, butter and salt. Remove from heat, cover, let stand five minutes. *Makes eight servings.*

PINEAPPLE RAISIN RICE

Drain one small can of water chestnuts and chop fine. Follow directions for Chili Bean Rice, using two and two-thirds cups of pineapple juice instead of water and soup. Stir in water chestnuts and one cup golden raisins before removing from the heat. *Makes eight servings.*

ALMOND MUSHROOM RICE

Follow directions for Chili Bean Rice, using two and two-thirds cup of chicken broth as the only liquid. Before removing from heat, stir in one cup of slivered almonds and two three-ounce cans of sliced mushrooms, well drained.

MACARONI, NOODLES AND SPAGHETTI

Cooking: Cook macaroni products in rapidly boiling salted water. For one-half pound, use three quarts of boiling water, one tablespoon of salt. Add macaroni a little at a time to keep water at a full rolling boil. Cook uncovered, stirring often.

Test for tenderness by pressing macaroni against the side of the pan with a spoon or by tasting or squeezing with the fingers. It should be fairly firm—*al dente* (ahl dehn′ teh) as they say in Italy. Overcooking makes macaroni pasty. Properly cooked, it retains its shape.

For salad: Drain cooked macaroni and rinse with cold water to hasten cooling. Chill in refrigerator; serve with dressing.

For hot dishes: Drain but don't rinse. Add butter, margarine or sauce. Top with grated cheese. Serve immediately, piping hot.

For snacks: Bake or fry fine egg noodles and season with poppy or caraway seeds and salt. To bake: melt one-fourth cup butter in a shallow pan and stir in two cups of noodles; bake ten minutes, stirring twice, at 400°F. (hot). To fry: cook in deep fat at 385°F. till golden.

You'll find a good spaghetti sauce on page 121.

Twelve types of macaroni products (American term for *pasta*) are shown:

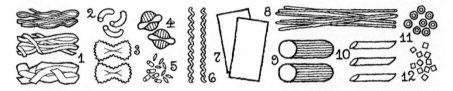

1. egg noodles, which come fine, medium and wide
2. elbow macaroni
3. egg bows
4. shells
5. tiny soup specialties
6. wavy *fusilli* (foo zeel' lee)
7. wide lasagne (la zah' nya)
8. spaghetti
9. *rigatoni* (ree gah toh' nee)
10. tubular *mostaccioli* (moh stah cho' lee)
11. small egg rings
12. egg flakes

The small types are used in soups. Others are used in salads and casseroles or served with a variety of sauces.

Salads

$\mathcal{W}$E DON'T NEED TO TELL YOU that salad is delicious—everybody knows *that*—but getting the daily salad habit has unexpected health bonuses, too. Vegetables and fruits keep more of their vitamins when they are served raw. Many of the vegetables we use uncooked in salads—tomatoes, water cress, green pepper—are unusually worthwhile nutritionally.

To the hostess, a salad for a party lunch, dinner or supper has even more of an advantage. Often, it adds the contrast of something cold, something crisp. Usually parts of it can be prepared in advance so that little last-minute attention will be needed. Always it allows more freedom in choosing other vegetables for the menu since "everybody likes salad!"

Be a dressing connoisseur. Try several bottled and packaged types—you may find one that is exactly right for you. Make your own, and see how you can vary it by adding more or less garlic, pepper, mustard. Try adding herbs, onion, sugar, paprika. Vary the dressing to suit the salad and the meal with which it will be served.

And be a perfectionist about salad greens: thorough draining and drying is almost as important as thorough rinsing. A selection of delectable salads and dressings is presented here—but there's always a new one around the corner, and you may invent it!

PERFECT GREEN SALAD

Select fresh unblemished salad greens, heavy for their size. Choose several of the ones shown here, keeping in mind color and texture contrast for your salad bowl:

1. Escarole, a broad-leaf green, sometimes mild, sometimes quite sharp.
2. Water cress, tart and peppery, rich in Vitamin A.

3. Romaine, a crisp, full-flavored long-leafed lettuce.
4. Belgian endive, deliciously bitter but expensive.
5. Boston lettuce, tender and sweet.
6. Chicory or curly endive, the most ruffly of the greens.
7. Iceberg lettuce, compact, crisp and adaptable.

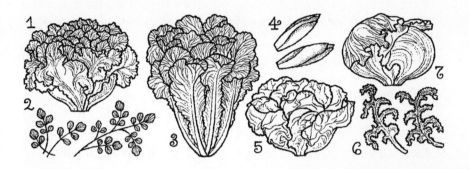

Wash greens well before storing. To get single leaves of lettuce, cut out core and run water into cavity. Leaves may then be removed unbroken. Shake excess moisture from washed greens, using a lettuce basket if possible. Pat dry with a towel; place in a hydrator pan, or wrap in a paper towel, then in waxed paper. Refrigerate.

Make the dressing. How much should you use? Count on one-fourth to one-third cup of French dressing for about eight cups of salad greens and expect this amount to make four to six servings. You will know if you have added the correct amount by this test: the salad vegetables or fruits will be lightly but evenly coated with dressing, yet there will be no excess dressing in the bottom of the bowl. Since creamy dressings such as those made with mayonnaise do not "go as far," you will need a little more of them. Use one-half cup for four servings.

To make salad in advance, tear the washed and dried greens into bite-size pieces. Add any other vegetables you wish. Cover and chill. At serving time, add dressing and toss thoroughly.

Accent your salad with these: Tomatoes—sliced or cut into half wedges (since they "weep," add them at the last minute); radishes—sliced or cut into rose garnishes; cucumbers—sliced (after removing some or all of the skin and scoring the surface lengthwise with a fork). Try adding a little sliced celery, celery cabbage or fennel (*finocchio*) with its licorice-like flavor.

Mix salad with dressing (recipes follow) at the table, unless otherwise specified.

CLASSIC FRENCH DRESSING

¾ cup olive or cooking oil
¼ cup vinegar (cider, wine or
   tarragon)
1 teaspoon salt

¼ teaspoon sugar
½ teaspoon paprika
¼ teaspoon dry mustard
Dash of pepper

Place all the ingredients above in a jar with a tight-fitting lid. Cover and shake until well blended. Refrigerate. Shake well before adding to salad. *Makes one cup.*

Roquefort dressing: At serving time, shake the mixture above and measure out one-half cup. Stir in two tablespoons of crumbled Roquefort or blue cheese.

Garlic dressing: Before storing, add one clove of garlic, peeled and quartered. Remove before serving.

Lemon dressing: Instead of vinegar, use one-fourth cup lemon juice.

"French-style" French dressing: Do not mix dressing in advance. Rub the salad bowl with a cut clove of garlic before arranging greens. At serving time, sprinkle the greens with olive oil, vinegar, salt, dry mustard and freshly ground pepper. (Use proportions above, but reduce amounts to suit the size of your salad.) Toss greens and serve at once.

This recipe is similar to Thousand Island Dressing. A bit rich, but particularly good on Chef's Salad, since it blends a variety of tastes.

CORAL DRESSING FOR TOSSED SALAD

½ cup mayonnaise or salad dressing
½ cup commercial sour cream
¼ cup vinegar
Dash of salt and pepper

1 teaspoon sugar
¼ cup chili sauce
¼ teaspoon salt

Fold the mayonnaise and sour cream together, then add the remaining ingredients, blending well. Keep refrigerated. *Makes about one and one-fourth cups.*

A simple cucumber salad is often the perfect touch for a menu—crisp, refreshing and mild-flavored.

SWEDISH–STYLE CUCUMBERS

2 cucumbers, washed and peeled
2 tablespoons chopped parsley
1 teaspoon salt

⅛ teaspoon pepper
⅛ teaspoon sugar
⅓ cup vinegar

Slice the cucumbers paper-thin. (A potato peeler will do a good job, as will the slicing blade found on a metal grater.) Place a thin layer in the bottom of a mixing bowl. Sprinkle with a little of the parsley, salt, pepper and sugar. Add another layer of cucumbers, then seasonings and repeat until cucumbers are used. Add the vinegar, using just enough for it to peep up around the edges. Press down firmly with a plate which fits snugly, and let stand at room temperature one hour. Then pour off all the vinegar, pressing slices down again to squeeze it out. Chill two hours, then turn into serving dish. *Makes four servings.*

CUCUMBERS IN SOUR CREAM

Follow recipe above, but add two tablespoons of minced sweet onion or scallions along with the parsley. After the cucumbers have marinated at room temperature, pour off the liquid and add one-third cup of sour cream.

Here's the Greek version of green salad, slightly exotic and just the right note with roast lamb, shish-kabob, or for an international buffet.

SALATA

1 head lettuce, cored, washed and
   shredded
3 tomatoes, peeled and chopped
4 scallions (green onions), peeled
   and minced
1 cucumber, peeled and minced

2 green peppers, seeded and minced
1 bunch water cress, chopped
3 tablespoons vinegar
1 teaspoon salt
12 ripe olives, pitted and halved
⅓ cup olive oil

About twenty minutes before salad is to be served, combine all the ingredients except the olive oil in a serving bowl. Toss well. Sprinkle the olive oil over the top of the salad. Let stand at room temperature fifteen minutes. *Makes six generous servings.*

Simple coleslaw becomes a party spectacular when you serve it in a gorgeous red cabbage.

RED AND WHITE SLAW

1 medium to large head red cabbage
1 small head white cabbage
1 cup commercial sour cream

1 cup salad dressing or mayonnaise
¼ cup cider vinegar
1 tablespoon onion salt

Remove any wilted leaves from red cabbage. Peel back one row of outer leaves; with a sharp paring knife or grapefruit knife cut a circle in top of head, leaving a half-inch rim. Hollow out head to use as salad "bowl." Chop the removed cabbage to make four cups. Shred or chop fine the white cabbage to make four cups. Toss red and white cabbage together in a large bowl. Mix remaining ingredients and pour over cabbage. Toss again. Pack into hollowed red cabbage head, saving any extra slaw for refilling when level gets low. Cover head with plastic wrap and refrigerate until serving time. *Enough coleslaw for eight to ten guests.*

Have you tried combining other vegetables (and fruits—consider apples, pineapple) with cabbage to make a salad? Tastes even better.

CARROT AND CABBAGE SLAW

⅔ cup (small can) evaporated milk
⅓ cup vinegar
1 tablespoon sugar
1 envelope Italian-style salad-dressing
  mix

1 large head (2½ lbs.) cabbage,
  cored, quartered and washed
4 carrots, washed and peeled

If possible, make this salad the day before it is to be served. The flavor improves as it chills in the refrigerator. Start by making the dressing: shake milk, vinegar, sugar and salad-dressing mix together in a tightly capped jar. Next grate the cabbage and carrots together. Combine them with just enough dressing to moisten. Cover and chill. At serving time, drain before turning into dish. *Makes eight servings.*

Here's a dilly of a salad—a slaw with a different flavor, in tomato baskets. Good with chicken, pork, ham.

SLAW–STUFFED TOMATOES

4 medium-size tomatoes
½ teaspoon dried dill weed or dill
  seed
¼ teaspoon salt
Few grains of pepper

¼ teaspoon dry mustard
2 tablespoons vinegar
¼ cup salad oil
¼ cup evaporated milk
3 cups finely shredded cabbage

Dip each of the tomatoes into a pan of rapidly boiling water to loosen skins, then rinse in cold water, peel and chill. Measure dill weed, salt, pepper, mustard, vinegar, oil and milk into a jar. Cover tightly and shake until creamy. Add to cabbage, toss and chill. At serving time, core tomatoes and turn cut side down. Then cut each *almost* to the bottom, into six sections. Put one tomato on a bed of lettuce on each of four plates. Spread tomato sections apart and fill with coleslaw. *Makes four salads.*

Here's a salad which uses vegetables easily found in the colder months. It's especially good with baked ham.

WINTER SALAD SURPRISE

½ cup light corn syrup
½ cup wine vinegar
¼ cup cooking oil
1 teaspoon dry mustard
¼ teaspoon pepper

1½ teaspoons garlic salt
6 cups finely shredded cabbage
3 cups grated carrots
2 tablespoons grated onion
1 cup diced cooked beets

To make the dressing, combine corn syrup, vinegar, oil, mustard, pepper and garlic salt. Whir in a blender or beat with rotary beater until creamy and well mixed. Combine with remaining ingredients. Chill, covered, at least two hours. *Makes eight servings.*

This sort of salad tastes just right at a harvest supper. Looks pretty, too!

GARDEN PATCH SALAD

1 package frozen lima beans
2 cups shredded lettuce
2 cups shredded red cabbage
1 cup chopped green onions
½ cup sliced radishes
2 large tomatoes, cut into wedges
1 cup green pepper strips

1 envelope classic salad-dressing mix
¼ cup vinegar
⅔ cup cooking oil
2 tablespoons water
½ cup commercial sour cream
½ cup crumbled blue cheese
Spanish onion rings for garnish

Cook beans as package directs. Drain and chill. Mound lettuce in center of salad bowl; arrange all vegetables in pie-shaped wedges around bowl. Combine remaining ingredients (except onion) to make dressing; put in a sauceboat, serve separately. Garnish salad with the Spanish onion rings. *Makes eight servings.*

Particularly attractive for buffet service, this salad is all in tones of green. Please note: no dressing, except the chutney!

EMERALD SALAD

3 green peppers, diced
4 cucumbers, peeled and diced
4 stalks celery, diced

2 packages cooked frozen peas,
   drained
½ cup chutney
Iceberg lettuce

Combine green pepper, cucumbers, celery and cooked peas in a large bowl. Chop chutney into small pieces and add to vegetables. Stir and refrigerate a half-hour or longer. Near serving time line individual salad bowls with lettuce leaves. Drain vegetable mix and mound over lettuce. *Makes eight servings.*

You'll find Artichoke Hearts Vinaigrette on page 124.

We really believe that packaged potatoes make some of the best potato salads. The two recipes which follow use dehydrated potato products. But you can make the first one with fresh potatoes—just cook them until not quite tender, then slice and proceed to add sugar, vinegar, etc.

REALLY WONDERFUL POTATO SALAD

2 cups packaged sliced potatoes
2 teaspoons sugar
3 tablespoons vinegar
3 tablespoons cooking oil
½ cup chopped celery

¼ cup chopped sweet onion
¼ cup chopped green pepper
Dash of pepper
½ cup Party Dressing (below)

Cook the sliced potatoes as package directs. When done, drain. Blend sugar, vinegar and cooking oil and pour over hot potatoes. Cool. Add remaining ingredients, toss lightly to blend. Chill. *Serve on lettuce to six.*

Party Dressing

⅔ cup sugar
2 teaspoons dry mustard
3 tablespoons cornstarch
1 teaspoon salt

2 eggs
½ cup vinegar
½ cup water
2 cups (1 pint) mayonnaise

In a saucepan stir together sugar, mustard, cornstarch and salt. Blend in eggs. Gradually add mixture of vinegar and water, stirring constantly. Cook, stirring every minute, over moderate heat until mixture thickens and is shiny. Cool slightly and fold in the mayonnaise. Keep refrigerated.

If you like your potato salad to contain all sorts of interesting tastes besides potatoes, you'll like this recipe.

QUICK POTATO SALAD

The basic potato mixture:

2 packages (6 oz. each) scalloped
 potatoes
6 cups hot water

½ cup wine vinegar
¼ cup butter or margarine
1⅓ cups cold water

Open the boxes of scalloped potatoes, remove seasoning packets, place potatoes in a saucepan of hot water. Bring to a boil, reduce heat and simmer until tender, about fifteen minutes. Turn into a colander, rinse with cold water, drain. Turn into a bowl; sprinkle with vinegar, cover and chill. Now melt the butter. Add the packets of seasoning and the cold water. Cook over medium heat, stirring constantly, until mixture boils. Then cover and chill.

The vegetables and dressing:

½ cup mayonnaise
2 tablespoons prepared mustard
½ cup chopped peeled cucumber
½ cup diced celery

½ cup finely chopped or grated
  carrot
¼ cup minced parsley
4 hard-cooked eggs, sliced

When both mixtures are cold, blend the mayonnaise and mustard into the seasoning sauce. Then combine potatoes, sauce, vegetables and eggs and fold together. Place in a serving bowl (lined with lettuce if you like) and garnish with additional vegetables. Cover; chill until serving time. *Makes twelve servings.*

Here's a salad to serve hot or cold—either way, it's delicious. Good with chicken, and absolutely superb with franks or other cooked sausages.

GERMAN POTATO SALAD

4 lbs. potatoes of uniform size
¾ cup boiling water
¾ teaspoon instant bouillon or 1
  bouillon cube
1 medium-size onion, peeled, washed
  and finely chopped
1 egg yolk

½ cup vinegar (wine vinegar
  preferred)
½ cup cooking oil
1½ teaspoons salt
2 teaspoons sugar
½ teaspoon freshly ground pepper

Wash the potatoes and remove any eyes or spots. Without peeling, cook in boiling salted water, covered, ten to fifteen minutes or until sharp fork will penetrate no more than one-half inch. Meantime, stir boiling water and bouillon together. When potatoes are barely tender, drain and dry by shaking over low heat. Cool only enough so you can peel and slice them very thin. Toss gently with bouillon and onion. Beat remaining ingredients together with a fork and pour over potatoes. Serve at once or cool and chill. Mixture may also be reheated. *Makes eight servings.*

Most boys like macaroni salad almost as much as potato salad and (shh!, don't tell) it's somewhat easier and quicker to make.

MACARONI VEGETABLE SALAD

3 quarts water
1 tablespoon salt
1 package (8 oz.) elbow macaroni
½ cup chopped celery
½ cup chopped green pepper
¼ cup chopped scallions (green onions)

1 tomato, diced
¼ cup minced parsley
½ cup mayonnaise
1 teaspoon salt
¼ teaspoon pepper
1 tablespoon prepared mustard

Bring the water to a rapid boil, add the tablespoon of salt and then the macaroni gradually so water continues to boil. Stir occasionally and cook twelve to fifteen minutes or until tender. Drain macaroni in a colander, then rinse in running cold water to cool it. Drain well. Combine macaroni with celery, green pepper, scallions, tomato and parsley. Combine remaining ingredients and blend into salad. Chill and serve in a bowl lined with crisp greens. *Makes eight servings.*

This salad is so attractive it should be the starred item on the menu. With open-face grilled cheese sandwiches, it makes a complete light meal.

BEAN BASKET SALAD

4 large tomatoes
1½ cups cooked frozen baby lima beans
1 tablespoon chopped parsley
Salt and pepper to taste

4 strips crisp bacon, chopped fine
1 small onion, peeled and grated
2 tablespoons minced celery
Chiffonade Dressing (below)

Wash tomatoes and cut a slice from top of each. Use a teaspoon to scoop out pulp (save it for other uses if you wish). Then slice a ring from top of hollowed tomato for use as a decorative handle. To lima beans, add parsley, salt and pepper to taste, bacon, onion, celery and enough Chiffonade Dressing to coat thoroughly (about one-third cup). Pile back into tomato baskets; arrange handle as if on a basket, tucking ends into salad. Chill. Serve with remaining Chiffonade Dressing. *Serves four.*

Chiffonade Dressing: Measure into a jar one-fourth cup olive oil, one-fourth cup vinegar, one-half teaspoon salt, one-eighth teaspoon paprika, one teaspoon sugar, one mashed, hard-cooked egg and one teaspoon Worcestershire sauce. Cover tightly and shake for about one minute.

How about a three-course lunch for four, all in one salad bowl? Guests can help themselves; you'll need three sets of salad servers, three plates for each guest and three salad dressings (see below).

SOUP–TO–NUTS SALAD

Make the first course early:

1 can consommé madrilene
½ lb. jumbo shrimp

1 cup drained pimiento-stuffed olives

Chill the madrilene overnight. Cook shrimp the morning of your lunch; refrigerate. Slide madrilene out of can and cut into cubes at party time. For this course prepare Coral Dressing (see page 144).

Make the second course—easy:

1 cucumber, peeled
2 tomatoes, cut into wedges
1 carrot, halved lengthwise
4 oz. salami, cut into wedges

4 oz. Swiss cheese, cut into strips
4 oz. ham, cut into strips
1 bunch radishes, sliced
1 cup ready-seasoned croutons

Flute the cucumber by running a fork down the sides; slice. Make carrot shavings with potato peeler; curl, fasten with toothpicks and "set" in bowl of ice water. Cover meats and cheese. Chill everything. You'll need Classic French Dressing (page 144) for this salad.

Make the third course sweet:

1 can (No. 1 flat) pineapple rings
1 pint strawberries, washed
2 firm bananas, sliced

1 can (11 oz.) mandarin oranges
1 cup miniature marshmallows
⅓ cup walnut halves

Drain pineapple rings; cut in half. Remove strawberry caps. Sprinkle banana slices with lemon juice to prevent browning. Drain oranges. Refrigerate everything. For dessert salad, use the Cherry Pink dressing below.

Half an hour before lunch arrange all three courses in a long lettuce-lined salad bowl or platter. Separate the three courses with neat rows of parsley or water cress; cover the salad bowl with plastic film and chill till serving time. *Makes four servings.*

Cherry Pink Dressing

½ cup commercial sour cream
⅓ cup mayonnaise

2 tablespoons lemon juice
3 tablespoons grenadine syrup

Combine ingredients in a bowl, stirring well to blend thoroughly. Chill before serving with the dessert salad. *Makes about one cup.*

Here's a way to make conversation—a select-it-yourself salad. Serve the elements separately in an attractive arrangement and let guests choose their own combinations.

TUNA 'ROUND THE BOWL

1 can (about 7 oz.) solid pack tuna	2 carrots, cut into shavings with
Crisp salad greens	vegetable peeler
2 cucumbers, peeled, cored and sliced	Bottled Italian salad dressing
8 small scallions, trimmed well and	1 cup mayonnaise
washed	3 tablespoons shredded Parmesan
2 small tomatoes, sliced thin	cheese
1 green pepper, cut into strips	

Open tuna and turn out onto a plate to drain. Select a large shallow salad bowl or a tray with deep sides to hold the salad. Line it with greens. In the center arrange cucumber slices. Next, with a slotted turner pick up whole round of tuna and place it prominently on the lettuce. Arrange the remaining foods in attractive patterns around the tuna. Keep covered and cold until ready to serve. Present it to your guests with a choice of Italian dressing or mayonnaise mixed with cheese. *Makes four to six servings.*

AVOCADOS

Here's how to peel and slice avocados: Cutting around stone, halve the fruit lengthwise with a knife. Twist to pull halves apart. To peel, run blade lightly down center back of skin only; pull off skin. Slice; then dip the pieces in citrus juice to prevent darkening.

At a splendid feast, the salad below might be a first course. Serve two to each person as a main luncheon dish. Pretty, too.

TUNA–STUFFED AVOCADO

½ cup tuna fish, drained and flaked	2 avocados, peeled, cut in half length-
⅓ cup diced boiled potato	wise, pitted and brushed with lemon
¼ cup diced celery	juice
2 tablespoons minced green onion	1 package (3 oz.) cream cheese
1 teaspoon salt	3 tablespoons milk
¼ cup mayonnaise	Water cress, lemon for garnish
¼ cup cooked peas	French dressing
Lettuce, washed and patted dry	

In a mixing bowl, combine tuna fish, potato, celery, onion, salt and mayonnaise. Mix well. Add peas and toss lightly to avoid crushing. Line four salad plates with lettuce. Place one-fourth of the tuna mixture in the center of each plate. Over each tuna-vegetable mound, place an avocado half, cut side down. Blend cream cheese and milk. Place softened cream cheese in a pastry bag and flute a one-inch band of cream cheese down the center of each avocado. Garnish with water cress and a lemon wedge. Sprinkle French dressing over lettuce leaves. *Makes four servings.*

This cold tuna-and-rice salad has some surprising ingredients—makes a piquant summer lunch conversation piece.

BLUE CHEESE–TUNA SALAD

1 cup uncooked rice	½ cup chopped cucumber
1½ cups mayonnaise	2 cans (about 7 oz. each) tuna fish
½ teaspoon pepper	drained and flaked
½ cup diced celery	¾ cup blue cheese, crumbled
½ cup chopped onion	Lettuce and cucumber for garnish

Cook rice according to package directions, draining if necessary. While still hot, add mayonnaise and combine. Cool twenty minutes. Add pepper, celery, onion and cucumber and toss to combine. Fold in tuna and blue cheese. Chill. Serve on a platter of lettuce leaves, garnished with sliced unpeeled cucumber. *Makes ten servings.*

Fruit salads—particularly the tart-sweet variety—fit especially well on the menu when the main dish is a casserole with some vegetables in it. This one has a marvelous dressing which you can use with many fruit salads.

RING–A–LING SALAD

1 small head lettuce	½ sweet (Bermuda) onion, sliced
1 bunch water cress	2 oranges, peeled, seeded and cut
2 cups torn spinach leaves	crosswise into slices

Wash the greens thoroughly and pat them crisp and dry in toweling. Place in a serving bowl. Pull onion slices apart into rings and add to greens. Cover with damp paper towel and refrigerate. Store oranges separately. Make Ring-a-Ling Dressing (page 154). At serving time, add oranges and just enough dressing to moisten greens. *Serve remaining dressing with the salad to six.*

Ring-a-Ling Dressing

1 cup cooking oil	⅓ cup chili sauce
½ cup vinegar	½ teaspoon salt
½ cup honey	Dash of pepper

Place all ingredients in a jar, cover and shake to blend. Store in the refrigerator.

The salad below is twice blessed—since it doubles as dessert.

TROPICAL FRUIT SALAD

2 cans (1 lb. each) grapefruit sections	¼ cup brown sugar
1 can (1 lb. 14 oz.) pineapple chunks	2 tablespoons lemon juice
1 jar (8 oz.) maraschino cherries	2 bananas, sliced
¼ cup commercial sour cream	Romaine lettuce leaves
¼ cup mayonnaise	

At least eight hours before your party—or the night before—drain syrup from grapefruit, pineapple and cherries. Combine sour cream, mayonnaise, brown sugar and lemon juice. Combine bananas with drained fruit. Add the dressing and toss gently. (Use only enough dressing to coat the fruit.) Place in a large strainer in a bowl and chill. Near party time, arrange fruit in a bowl lined with washed, dried leaves of crisp Romaine. Serve with the reserved dressing in a sauceboat. *This recipe serves eight, may be doubled for a large party.*

Apple and celery salad is easy to make, sure to be welcome and takes to a variety of changes.

WALDORF SALAD

3 red eating apples	½ cup mayonnaise or salad dressing
¼ cup lemon juice	(use just enough to moisten)
½ cup chopped celery	Lettuce leaves
½ cup chopped walnuts	

Wash the apples. Without peeling, quarter and core, then chop into bite-size pieces. Mix with lemon juice. Add celery, walnuts and mayonnaise. Taste and add salt if desired. *Serve on lettuce leaves to six.*

NOTE: Walnuts may be omitted if desired. Or you may add one or all of the following: one-half cup chopped dates; one-half cup seedless raisins; one-half cup miniature (or cut-up regular size) marshmallows.

DO–AHEAD SALADS

The salads which follow win honors as the easiest kind for cooks with last-minute nerves. You can make them a full day in advance, and in those frantic hours just before the party, they'll be absolutely no bother to you. If you're timid about making a molded salad, brush up on these rules.

Tips on Making Molded Salads and Desserts

Choosing molds: If your kitchen includes a wide choice of molds of various sizes and shapes, rejoice! But if not, don't despair. You can mold gelatine mixtures in mixing bowls, loaf pans, glasses, foil containers, even paper cups. For best results, the mold should be light metal (your salad will set faster, unmold more easily). Very tall molds or those with many deeply cut designs may be risky—sometimes part of the mixture will stick.

Simplest fruit mold: Pour dissolved gelatine mixture into mold and add self-layering fruits: orange slices, grapes and most canned fruit will sink to the bottom; slices of fresh apple, banana, peaches, pears and strawberries will float. (Note: Never use fresh or frozen pineapple in a gelatine mold. It contains a substance which causes the mold to collapse! Canned pineapple, though, works fine.) After adding fruits, just chill until firm.

Fancy fruited mold: For a beautiful top design, first pour an eighth of an inch of dissolved gelatine mixture into the bottom of the mold and chill until almost firm. Next place prepared fruit in pretty patterns, remembering that mold will be inverted. Add several spoonfuls of slightly thickened gelatine to anchor the fruit. Chill until almost set. When remaining gelatine is the consistency of unbeaten egg whites, fold in more fruit. (This step distributes the fruit evenly.) Turn into mold and chill until set.

Two-textured mold: Pour half the prepared gelatine mixture into a mold and chill until firm. Refrigerate remaining mixture until it's slightly thicker than unbeaten egg whites. Then beat until light and foamy. Pour over clear gelatine in mold. Chill until firm.

Rainbow mold: For two or more contrasting layers, pour prepared gelatine mixture in mold and chill until not quite set. Pour a second mixture of different color over the first. Chill until firm; repeat as desired.

How to unmold: Fill a pan or bowl large enough to accommodate mold with warm—not very hot—water. Loosen the mold gently around the edge with the tip of a paring knife. Dip the mold into warm water almost to the rim. Then place a serving dish face down over the mold. (It's a wise idea to moisten the plate with water, so if gelatine does not fall in the center, it will slide easily into position.) Now grasp the mold tightly with fingers, pressing down onto serving dish with thumbs. Still holding tight, turn mold and dish over together and shake until you hear and see the mold slip out. Rx for stubborn molds: Place a hot, wet dish towel over the inverted container. Or dip again in warm water. Or carefully insert a knife between mold and salad, following a line in the mold, all the way to the bottom to break suction. Then reinvert with serving dish. Molded salads and desserts should be refrigerated until the moment they are served.

This recipe is a surprising one—it sets much faster than most molds, tastes deliciously rich, has its dressing right in the salad. Note: It includes lots of meat and cheese, too, which means you can serve it as a main dish.

SOUFFLÉ PARTY SALAD

First, a "dressing" mixture for the refrigerator freezing section:

2 packages lemon-flavored gelatine	1 cup mayonnaise
2 cups hot water	1 teaspoon salt
1 cup commercial sour cream	

Dissolve the lemon gelatine in hot water. With a rotary beater, blend in sour cream, mayonnaise and salt. Pour into two ice cube trays and chill in freezing unit for fifteen minutes or until firm about one inch from edge but still soft in center. Meantime, get ready:

1½ cups chopped ham	⅔ cup drained chopped cucumber
½ cup diced Cheddar cheese	½ cup chopped celery
2 cups finely chopped lettuce	¼ cup chopped green pepper
8 radishes, sliced	

Pick out a pretty two-quart mold and choose some of the above ingredients to decorate it. (Just put the radish slices, strips of green pepper or pieces of ham in place to help accentuate the design of the mold. When you're filling the mold, be careful not to disturb them.) When the mayonnaise mixture is properly chilled, turn it into a bowl and whip with a rotary beater until fluffy. Fold in the remaining ingredients. Turn this mixture into the mold. Chill in refrigerator until firm—about one hour (longer if you like). Unmold by loosening around edge with pointed knife, then dipping lightly and quickly into hot water. Place serving platter on top, invert both together. Garnish with salad greens and tomato wedges. *Makes eight servings.*

Everybody loves this salad. It's made in two layers, the flavors are perfectly balanced and—well, you know how men feel about corned beef and cabbage.

CORNED BEEF AND CABBAGE MOLD

For corned beef layer:

1 envelope unflavored gelatine
½ cup cold water
¼ teaspoon salt
2 tablespoons lemon juice
¾ cup mayonnaise

¼ cup minced onion
½ cup chopped sweet pickle
½ cup diced celery
1 can (12 oz.) corned beef, finely
  diced

Soften gelatine in cold water; place over boiling water and stir until dissolved. Add salt and lemon juice. Cool. Mix in mayonnaise and remaining ingredients. Turn into an eight-inch square pan or a mold which holds the same amount and chill until almost firm.

For cabbage layer:

1 envelope unflavored gelatine
½ cup cold water
¾ cup hot water
½ teaspoon salt
2 tablespoons sugar

2 tablespoons lemon juice
¼ cup vinegar
2 tablespoons chopped pimiento
2 cups finely shredded cabbage

Soften gelatine in cold water. Add hot water and stir until gelatine is dissolved. Add salt, sugar, lemon juice and vinegar. Chill until mixture is consistency of unbeaten egg white. Fold in pimiento and cabbage. Turn out on top of almost firm first layer. Chill until firm. Unmold onto serving platter (or cut into nine squares and place on each diner's plate). If desired, garnish with slices of olive and lettuce cups filled with tomato and onion slices. *Makes nine servings.*

A real luncheon sparkler—orange juice jellied and served in its own cup!

JELLIED ORANGES

4 medium oranges
1 envelope unflavored gelatine
½ cup sugar

⅛ teaspoon salt
½ cup water
¼ cup lemon juice

At about one-third of the distance below the top, cut each orange in two. Press out the juice, being careful not to break skins, and measure one and one-fourth cups. (Remove seeds but do not strain.) In a small pan, mix gelatine with sugar, salt, water and lemon juice. Cook over medium heat, stirring constantly, until gelatine dissolves. Add orange juice and blend in well. Pour into orange shells and chill until firm. Serve each shell on a bed of lettuce with a mound of cottage cheese. *Serves four.*

A carbonated beverage adds sweetness and spiciness to this molded salad.

TOMATO VEGETABLE ASPIC

1 can (No. 2) tomato juice	2 bottles (7 oz. each) lemon-lime
1/3 cup chopped celery leaves	carbonated beverage
1/3 cup chopped onion	2 envelopes unflavored gelatine
2 tablespoons sugar	1 tablespoon lemon juice
1 1/4 teaspoons salt	1 cup finely diced celery
1/2 teaspoon monosodium glutamate	1 cup finely diced green pepper
1 bay leaf	

To tomato juice, add celery leaves, onion, sugar, salt, monosodium glutamate, bay leaf, and simmer ten minutes. Pour one bottle lemon-lime into bowl. Sprinkle gelatine over surface. Let stand five minutes. Remove tomato juice from heat and strain into a large bowl. Add gelatine and lemon juice and stir until gelatine is dissolved. Add second bottle of lemon-lime. Chill until as thick as unbeaten egg whites. Mix celery and green pepper and fold into tomato mixture. Turn into a two-quart mold. When ready to serve, unmold on a platter and garnish with fresh greens. *Makes eight servings.*

Coleslaw is delicious and, of course, popular. But it's spectacular, too, when it's molded into pretty shapes. Try it at a card party with tiny sandwiches—or at a supper, with baked ham.

MOLDED COLESLAW

2 envelopes unflavored gelatine	1/4 teaspoon cayenne pepper
1 1/2 cups water	1 1/2 cups mayonnaise
2 teaspoons salt	1 tablespoon grated onion
1/4 cup lemon juice	1/2 cup chopped pimiento
1/2 teaspoon Worcestershire sauce	6 cups finely shredded cabbage

Sprinkle gelatine over water in a saucepan. Place saucepan over low heat and stir until gelatine is dissolved. Remove from heat and add salt, lemon juice, Worcestershire sauce and pepper. Cool. Gradually stir into mayonnaise in a bowl. Fold in remaining ingredients. Turn mixture into eight individual molds or a one-and-one-half-quart mold. Refrigerate until firm. Unmold by dipping mold in warm water, then loosening around edge with tip of a knife. Place plate on top of mold and turn upside down. Garnish with lettuce leaves. *Makes eight servings.*

Here's a good recipe for gatherings of the clan. You can mold it, as detailed here, or chill it in flat pans to be cut in squares and served with a spatula.

MINTED FRUIT MOLD

not so much pepper mint

3 envelopes unflavored gelatine
¼ cup sugar
½ cup water
3 bottles (7 oz. each) lemon-lime
  carbonated beverage
6 drops green food coloring

1 teaspoon peppermint extract
1 tablespoon lemon juice
1 can (No. 2) pineapple tidbits
1 jar (8 oz.) stemless maraschino
  cherries
2 bananas, sliced

Place gelatine in a saucepan. Add sugar and water. Bring to a boil over medium heat, stirring constantly, until gelatine and sugar are dissolved. Remove from heat. Stir in lemon-lime beverage. Then add food coloring, peppermint extract and lemon juice. Chill mixture until it is the consistency of unbeaten egg whites. Fold in remaining ingredients; pour into a six-cup mold (decorate outer edge of mold with some of the fruit before filling if desired). Chill until completely set. Dip mold for a moment into a pan of hot water; place a serving plate on top and invert together. *Makes twelve servings.*

Many people like frozen fruit salad for a light lunch or supper, served with simple small sandwiches of ham or chicken and a hot beverage. The old-fashioned method was to freeze the salad in the fruit can, but now we can use freezer jars and be assured of long-term storage.

FROZEN FRUIT ROLL

4 cups peeled, cut-up fresh fruit
2 teaspoons ascorbic acid mixture for
  freezing fruit

⅓ cup sugar
2 packages (8 oz. each) cream
  cheese, softened

Prepare the fruit by cutting it into small pieces. (Apples, strawberries, melon, peaches, pears and grapes make a good combination.) Place in a bowl with the ascorbic acid and sugar. Toss well. Fold in softened cream cheese. Pack in thoroughly washed and cooled tapered half-pint freezer jars, leaving one-half inch head space at top. Cap with sterilized lids. At once, place upright in freezer until salad is frozen hard. Label and date the jars, and stack in freezer. When ready to use, run cool water over cap for two minutes and slide out entire contents of jar. Slice roll and arrange on lettuce leaves. Sour cream or mayonnaise may be used as a topping. *Makes five half-pints, four servings in each.*

Added Touches

$\mathcal{T}$HE DISHES in this chapter are to your menu as gloves and shoes are to a new dress—accessories. Just as the perfect handbag highlights a suit, so an ideal first course can illuminate a meal.

When you're going to have guests, you'll undoubtedly be looking for a delicious soup to start the menu with—or perhaps a homemade bread to provide an accent better than anything you can buy. But why wait? Try these treasures in your everyday cooking, too.

FIRST–COURSE DRINKS

TOMATO JUICE COCKTAILS

1 can (46 oz.) tomato juice
⅛ teaspoon Tabasco sauce

1 tablespoon lemon juice
1 teaspoon Worcestershire sauce

Combine all ingredients in a pitcher, then pour into glasses. Garnish each with a slice of lemon. *Makes eight servings.*

Sophisticated, but also delicious. Serve these for your first course on the front porch on a sultry summer evening.

LIME MINT JULEP

1 bunch fresh mint, washed and
   patted dry
½ cup lime juice (about 3 limes)

8 teaspoons sugar
2 small bottles quinine water
4 lime slices

Frost four tall glasses. Into each break three sprigs of mint, then add one tablespoon lime juice and two teaspoons sugar. Stir, crushing leaves against sides of glass with the back of a spoon to bring out the mint flavor. Pack glasses with crushed ice. Portion remaining lime juice into the glasses, then fill with quinine water. Trim each glass with a slice of lime and another sprig of mint. *Makes four servings.*

You *do* need a blender for this recipe—nothing else can blend the fresh vegetable taste quite so smoothly.

TOMATO–PLUS COCKTAIL

4 medium-size tomatoes, diced or
  2½ cups tomato juice
1 large cucumber, diced
¼ medium-size onion, sliced
2 tablespoons celery leaves

2 tablespoons parsley sprigs
1 tablespoon lemon juice
1½ teaspoons salt
⅛ teaspoon Tabasco sauce

Place all ingredients in blender jar. Cover and blend until smooth—about two minutes. Strain and pour over ice cubes in a large pitcher. *Makes four servings.* (To double this recipe, make it twice—to avoid overloading the blender.)

GOLD FIZZ

For each serving: Pour two tablespoons of defrosted grapefruit juice concentrate over ice cubes in a tall glass. Fill glass with lemon-lime carbonated beverage; stir once. For eight, you'll need three cans of grapefruit juice, seven seven-ounce bottles of lemon-lime beverage.

RELISHES

This relish is equally good cold or reheated. Let the weather and the rest of the menu govern your decision. A good dish for a picnic barbecue!

RELISH TOMATOES

3 pounds tomatoes, cored and diced
3 green peppers, seeded and diced
3 medium-size onions, peeled and
  chopped
¼ cup cooking oil

1 teaspoon salt
¼ teaspoon pepper
1 teaspoon sugar
¼ cup vinegar
½ teaspoon dry mustard

Combine the tomatoes, peppers and onions. Heat the cooking oil in a large skillet, add the tomato mixture and sprinkle with salt, pepper and sugar. Cook gently, turning and stirring occasionally, three minutes or until vegetables are slightly softened. Add vinegar and mustard and stir to mix. Remove from heat and spoon into storage jars. Refrigerate. Serve cold or reheated. *Makes six servings.*

At holiday dinners add a special touch to a family favorite.

CRANBERRY ORANGE SAUCE

2 cans (1 lb. each) whole cranberry sauce	2 teaspoons grated orange peel
	4 teaspoons orange juice

Three hours before you plan to serve it, open the cranberry sauce, turn it into a bowl with the other ingredients and chill to blend flavors. *Makes eight to ten servings.*

We like this fruit relish *best* when served with baked ham—but it also blends well when roast pork or turkey is on the menu.

SPICED PINEAPPLE

1 can (No. 2) pineapple chunks or slices	3 whole cloves
¼ cup vinegar	3 allspice berries
¼ cup brown sugar	1 three-inch stick of cinnamon

Drain the syrup from pineapple into a saucepan. Add remaining ingredients (reserving fruit) and bring to a boil. Reduce heat and simmer twenty minutes to make a sweet-sour spicy syrup. Add pineapple and simmer one minute, then remove from heat. Cool briefly, then chill. Remove spices. Pineapple may be served in its syrup, but provide a fork or slotted server. *Enough for eight side-dish servings.*

This is the original New Orleans Pepper Relish, which is an absolute necessity for Po' Boy franks-in-buns. Delicious, too, as a side dish.

PEPPER RELISH

4 sweet red peppers	⅔ cup vinegar
4 green peppers	⅔ cup sugar
4 sweet onions	1 tablespoon salt

Wash the peppers and discard core and seeds. Peel and wash onions. Cut all in half lengthwise, and then into very thin slices. Cover with boiling water and let stand five minutes. Drain, then add vinegar, sugar and salt. Bring to a boil in a saucepan, then reduce heat and simmer, covered, five minutes. Store in the liquid. Serve hot or cold, using a perforated spoon. *Makes about six cups, or about eighteen side-dish servings.*

SOUPS

Soup—hot or cold—is often the perfect answer for a light snack, or a welcoming, pace-setting first course.

CHILI CHEESE SOUP

4 cans condensed chili soup   1 cup (about) grated Cheddar cheese
4 soup cans of water

Reconstitute soup as label directs. Heat until piping hot. Pour into soup tureen and sprinkle top with grated cheese. Pass extra cheese with soup. *Serves up to twelve.*

TOMATO MINESTRONE SOUP

This is a snap! For six, mix five cups of water with two cans condensed minestrone soup and two cans of tomato soup.

PIMIENTO CHEESE SOUP

2 jars (4 oz. each) pimientos   2 cups chicken broth
2 cans condensed cheese soup

Press pimientos through a coarse sieve (or buzz in blender with cheese soup). Combine all ingredients together; refrigerate now if desired. At serving time, slowly bring to a simmer. *Pour into eight mugs.*

TOMATO BACON SOUP

8 to 12 slices bacon   2 soup cans of water
2 cans condensed tomato soup   12 sprigs parsley

Fry bacon over low heat until it's crisp. Combine soup and water in a saucepan. Heat to boiling point. Pour one-fourth cup soup into a blender container. Add the bacon and parsley and blend about twenty seconds or until finely minced. Add to soup in pan. Stir. Serve with cracker snacks. *Fills six soup plates.*

NOTE: If you haven't a blender, mince the parsley and bacon and stir into the soup.

SOUP ON THE ROCKS

Pour two cans of undiluted beef broth over ice cubes in a pitcher. *Serve in mugs or glasses to six.*

GAZPACHO

(*Cold Vegetable Soup*)

1 can condensed tomato soup	¼ cup olive oil
1 soup can water	2 tablespoons wine vinegar
1 cup thinly sliced cucumber	1 small clove garlic, minced
½ cup finely chopped green pepper	Dash of Tabasco sauce
¼ cup minced onion	Salt and black pepper to taste

Combine all ingredients in a large bowl. Cover bowl and refrigerate for at least four hours or overnight. Stir gently and pour into bowls set in containers of crushed ice. Garnish with thin lemon slices. *Makes four servings.*

CELESTIAL MANDARIN SOUP

1 quart chicken broth	1 cup diced cooked pork
1 can (12 oz.) frozen won ton soup	1 tablespoon barbecue or steak sauce
2 cups chopped cabbage	½ cup sliced scallions
1 cup green peas, fresh or frozen	

Bring the chicken broth to a boil and add all remaining ingredients. Bring back to a boil, then boil ten minutes or until cabbage is tender-crisp. *Makes eight servings.*

SOUP–DEE–DO

4 cans condensed minestrone	Grated Parmesan cheese
1 lb. brown-and-serve pork sausages	

Prepare minestrone, adding water as directed on label. Cut sausages into small pieces and brown. Add to soup and simmer five more minutes. Serve in chowder bowls with cheese available for each guest to sprinkle on soup. Delicious with hot, buttered onion rolls. *Makes eight servings.*

FESTIVAL CREAM SOUP

2 tablespoons minced scallions (green onions)
2 tablespoons butter or margarine
2 tablespoons flour
1 teaspoon salt
½ teaspoon freshly ground pepper
3 cups milk

½ teaspoon celery salt
1 can (about 7 oz.) tuna fish, drained and flaked fine
2 tablespoons minced pimiento
2 tablespoons minced green pepper
¼ cup thinly sliced canned water chestnuts

Cook scallions in butter over low heat until soft, not brown. Stir in flour, salt and pepper and allow to bubble over low heat about one minute. Remove from heat. Very slowly stir in milk. Add celery salt, flaked tuna, pimiento, green pepper and water chestnuts. Return to low heat. Cook until thickened, stirring constantly. (Do not let boil.) Serve hot, topped with grated Cheddar cheese. *Makes enough for six soup cups or four rimmed soup plates.*

EASY BORSHT

2 cans (1 lb. each) sliced beets
2 beet cans of water

2 cans condensed beef broth
3 frankfurters, sliced

Combine sliced beets and water in a large saucepan. Cover and simmer one hour. Beets will be pale in color and should be discarded. Add broth and frankfurters and simmer ten minutes to blend flavors. Season with salt and pepper to taste. Serve hot. *Makes eight servings.*

LUSCIOUS SHRIMP CHOWDER

2 tablespoons cooking oil
2 onions, chopped
2 cloves garlic
1 can condensed tomato soup
5 cups boiling water
½ cup green peas
½ cup whole kernel corn

5 potatoes, peeled and cubed
2 teaspoons salt
¼ teaspoon chili powder
¼ teaspoon marjoram
1 package (3 oz.) cream cheese
2 cups milk
¾ lb. cleaned uncooked shrimp
4 eggs

Heat oil in a deep saucepan. Add onions and garlic and cook until brown. Remove garlic. Add tomato soup, water, peas, corn, potatoes and seasonings and cook twenty minutes. Meantime, soften cream cheese in a bowl and gradually blend in milk. Next stir in soup. Return to pan. (From this point on, soup must *not* boil.) Add shrimp; cook slowly ten minutes more. Beat eggs in a bowl. Gradually stir in some of the soup, then return to pan over low heat and heat through. *Makes ten servings.*

SUNDAY MORNING CHOWDER

2 cans condensed cream of chicken soup	1 can (6 oz.) small shrimp, drained
1 teaspoon curry powder	2 tablespoons butter
2⅔ cups milk or light cream	Paprika
	Chopped parsley

Stir a little of the soup into the curry powder in a large saucepan. Then blend in remaining soup and slowly stir in milk or cream. Heat gently until very hot but do not boil. Five minutes before serving add shrimp. Pour into serving bowls and top each serving with a dot of butter and a sprinkle of paprika and chopped parsley. *Makes six servings.*

BREADS

More than one hostess has built a reputation on always serving an interesting bread at her dinner parties. If you live in a metropolitan area, you can scour the town for the good breads of other nations—Swedish *limpa*, crisp-crusted loaves of French or Italian bread, pumpernickel, caraway rye, *panettone*. You can try cheese bread, cinnamon bread, oatmeal bread and see what suits your taste. But even the smallest town has a wonderful array of breads to enrich your meals—in brown and serve, heat and serve, in complete mixes, canned refrigerator style. And of course, you can make bread yourself—and that's the very nicest way of all.

Yeast Doughs—Tips for Success

Treat yeast like a baby—keep it snug and warm and free from drafts—and it will grow up into a big loaf of bread or lots of hot rolls or dozens of delicious doughnuts.

Dissolve the yeast by stirring it into warm (not hot) water; yeast needs warmth to work, but it can be killed by high temperatures. Stir only until yeast granules are dissolved. Your recipe will indicate how much water to use. Some old recipes tell you to dissolve yeast in milk. Don't! Instead, stir yeast into one-fourth cup of warm water; when dissolved, mix the yeast with milk—using one-fourth cup less milk than amount recipe calls for.

Scald the milk. If your recipe calls for milk, scald it to give dough better texture. (Exception: canned or dry milk needs no scalding.) To scald, bring milk just to boiling point, then cool. Stirring in other ingredients, (shortening, eggs, salt, sugar) will hasten cooling. When a drop of milk mixture on your wrist feels lukewarm, combine with yeast.

Work in the flour. To make yeast products light, flour must be thoroughly worked in with "wet" ingredients by beating or kneading. This develops a substance called gluten which traps the yeast-formed air.

Knead the dough. If recipe calls for kneading, here's how: turn dough onto floured board; flour hands and lift far edge of dough toward you (1), then (almost in the same movement) press down on the edge with

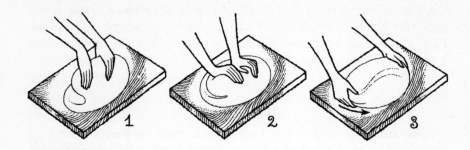

heels of hands as though pushing the dough away (2). Turn dough one-quarter way around on board (3); fold, push and turn again in quick rhythm. Repeat several minutes till dough is smooth, satiny, tightly stretched and springy.

Let dough rise in a warm place, free from drafts. A good rising method: nest bowl of dough in a larger bowl which has been warmed by rinsing in hot water; pour enough warm water into larger bowl so that all but the top two inches of the bowl holding the dough are surrounded by water; cover with a towel. Another good method: put bowl of dough in an unheated oven; put large pan of hot water on shelf below bowl; close oven door to maintain temperature. In winter, you can also set the bowl near (not on top of) a radiator. Dough has risen enough when it's double in size and when two fingers inserted leave a deep impression after withdrawal.

HOT BUTTERED FRENCH BREAD

For perfection—hot buttery bread with a crisp crust—follow this method. Slice down through a small loaf of French, Vienna or Italian bread, almost to the bottom of the loaf. Make the cuts about one inch apart. Spread the slices apart and spread with softened butter. (If you like, add a little garlic powder or a mixture of your favorite herbs to this butter before spreading.) Place the loaf on a piece of aluminum foil. Bring foil up around loaf, folding ends to seal but leaving a small opening in top. Bake at 350°F. (moderate) about fifteen minutes.

Of all the flavored breads, we think this one is the most delectable. Tastes marvelous at dinner and takes well to a variety of sandwich fillings. And—extra blessing—no kneading!

HERB BREAD

1 package active dry yeast	1½ teaspoons *"fines herbes"* blend
1¼ cups warm (not hot) water	½ teaspoon nutmeg
2 tablespoons shortening	½ teaspoon ground sage
2 tablespoons sugar	3 cups sifted flour
2 teaspoons salt	

Sprinkle yeast over water; stir to dissolve. Add shortening, sugar, salt, herbs, nutmeg, sage and half the flour. Beat at medium speed in electric mixer one minute. Stop, scrape bowl well, then beat another minute. Add remaining flour and blend with a spoon until smooth. Now cover with a clean cloth and let rise in a warm place until double in bulk, about half an hour. Beat down with twenty-five strokes of spoon. Put in greased nine-by-five-inch loaf pan. Let rise again till double, about forty minutes. Bake at 375°F. (moderate) forty-five to fifty minutes. Tap loaf lightly— if it sounds hollow, it's done. Butter top crust. Turn out, cool, slice.

Most extravagantly delicious, this California special may be served with a meal—but it's really a snack in itself. If you like, make the cheese spread ahead and refrigerate it until baking time.

ZOMBIE BREAD

1 lb. sharp Cheddar cheese	¼ teaspoon pepper
½ cup minced parsley	¼ teaspoon garlic powder
Juice of one lemon	½ lb. butter, melted
1½ teaspoons salt	2 loaves French bread

First grate the cheese. Use a grater that makes those little slivers; don't grate it too fine. Then mix the cheese, parsley, lemon juice, salt, pepper and garlic powder. Beat in melted butter to make a paste. Refrigerate at this point if you like, but warm at room temperature before using. At spreading time, split the loaves of bread in half, lengthwise. Make vertical cuts in each half loaf at two-inch intervals. Be careful not to cut all the way through to the bottom crust. Spread cut surfaces with the cheese paste and let stand for about two hours. Twenty minutes before serving time put the four halves on a large cookie sheet and bake at 350°F. (moderate) until cheese is slightly melted and browned. *Makes six servings.*

STEP–BY–STEP MAKING OF MUFFINS

Before you begin, preheat the oven to 425°F. (hot). Then get out the muffin pans (our recipe fills twelve medium cups). Grease these—generously on the bottoms, lightly on the sides—using a dab of oil or shortening on a smitch of waxed paper for smooth coating.

Here are the ingredients for making our marvelous muffins:

2 cups sifted flour	1 egg, beaten
3 teaspoons baking powder	1 cup milk
1½ teaspoons salt	3 tablespoons cooking oil or melted
3 tablespoons sugar	butter

To measure flour: First, place about two cups of flour in a sifter. Sift onto a square of waxed paper. Gently lift flour into measuring cup and level off. (Cut across with a straight knife without packing down.) Empty the cupful of flour into sifter placed in mixing bowl, then fill cup once more, pour into sifter. Add baking powder, sugar and salt to the flour, mix them lightly and sift mixture into bowl.

Beat egg in a separate smaller bowl until foamy. Add one cup milk, warmed to room temperature if there's time. Now add the oil or butter. Beat together briefly.

To mix batter: Pour the liquids into the dry ingredients; using just a few efficient strokes, stir mixture together *only* until flour is dampened throughout. Don't overmix. The batter *should* be lumpy.

To bake: Spoon batter into the muffin tins, filling them just two-thirds full. Pour a little water into any unfilled cups to prevent scorching pan. Bake twenty minutes or until firm and browned. Rush the muffins to the table while they are still hot. Or if you're not quite ready to serve them, turn the muffins on their sides in the muffin cups to prevent sogginess.

Success is assured if you have a good oven and a fine recipe—or is it? When the muffins are undersized, peaky, full of tunnels, they have been overbeaten. Stir *only* till flour is dampened. Remember: cakes need lots of beating, muffins very little.

Some easy variations: For a hearty one, add one cup of grated Cheddar cheese to the sifted dry ingredients. Some sweet versions: increase sugar to one-third cup, add a half-teaspoon of cinnamon plus two-thirds of a cup of diced dried apricots (presoaked in water for one hour) *or* chopped walnuts *or* seedless raisins.

Very good at dinner and just heaven freshly baked at breakfast time.

OATMEAL BUTTERMILK MUFFINS

¾ cup buttermilk pancake mix	1 egg
¼ cup sugar	¾ cup milk
1 teaspoon baking powder	3 tablespoons butter or margarine,
¼ teaspoon salt	melted
¾ cup quick rolled oats	

Mix together pancake mix, sugar, baking powder, salt and quick rolled oats. Combine egg, milk and melted butter and stir until thoroughly mixed. Add to dry ingredients and stir just long enough to moisten. Fill greased muffin cups two-thirds full. Bake at 400°F. (hot) for twenty-five minutes. *Makes six medium-size muffins.*

Raisin-Oatmeal Muffins: Fold in one-half cup raisins before pouring batter into greased muffin cups.

BASIC BISCUIT BAKERY

The same ingredients (below) make two different biscuits—plus a shortcake. Amounts and baking times vary. *Each recipe serves four.*

Ingredients	Drop Biscuits	Rolled Biscuits	Shortcake
Sifted flour	2 cups	2 cups	2 cups
Baking powder	2 teaspoons	2½ teaspoons	3 teaspoons
Salt	1 teaspoon	1 teaspoon	1 teaspoon
Sugar	—	—	2 tablespoons
Shortening	¼ cup	¼ cup	⅓ cup
Milk	1 cup	¾ cup	¾ cup
Bake at	450°F. (very hot)	450°F. (very hot)	450°F. (very hot)
Time	10 to 12 min.	10 to 12 min.	15 to 17 min.

Measure dry ingredients and shortening into bowl; cut in shortening with a pastry blender. (Cutting in makes biscuits light, flaky.) Push blender repeatedly—at different angles—to bottom of bowl, cleaning blades often. Continue until mixture is like coarse corn meal, then rapidly stir in almost all the milk with a fork. If flour is not completely absorbed, add the remaining milk; stir in—don't beat. Drop dough by tablespoonfuls on a greased cookie sheet for drop biscuits.

To shape rolled biscuits or shortcake: Turn dough out on a floured surface; fold it over and press out flat again. Repeat about ten times, then roll out to desired thickness, keeping in mind that biscuits rise to double height in baking. Use a metal cutter to make rounds or cut the dough into squares with a knife. If you like biscuits with soft, white sides, let sides touch on baking sheet. If you want crusty sides, set biscuits one inch apart. Bake until top is dark golden brown and crisp.

Country Shortcake: Prepare two cups sugared, sliced strawberries. Mix shortcake dough as directed above. Shape into a six-inch round. Bake on u..greased pan. Split in half. Butter cut sides. Whip one cup heavy cream. Fill shortcake with most of the strawberries, half of the cream. Cover top with remaining cream and garnish with fruit.

Lots of people love whole-wheat flavor, but whole-wheat flour is hard to get. What to do? Why, use whole-wheat cereal, of course.

WHEATEN BREAD

1¾ cups sifted flour	2 eggs
1 tablespoon baking powder	¼ cup cooking oil
1 teaspoon salt	¼ cup milk
5 tablespoons sugar, divided	1 teaspoon cinnamon
⅔ cup instant whole-wheat cereal	

Sift together into a bowl flour, baking powder, salt and three table-spoonfuls of the sugar. Stir in whole-wheat cereal. Beat eggs; set aside one tablespoonful for brushing top. Add remaining eggs, oil and milk to dry ingredients. Stir with a fork until mixture forms a ball. Knead lightly about ten times and press into an ungreased eight-inch round cake pan. Brush top with reserved beaten egg. Combine remaining two tablespoons sugar with cinnamon and sprinkle over top. Bake at 425°F. (hot oven) ten to twelve minutes or until done. Serve hot, *cut into eight spicy wedges.*

Here's a mix-made quickie, especially good with chili.

CHEESE CORN BREAD

1 package (10 oz.) yellow corn bread easy mix	¾ cup grated Cheddar cheese

Prepare batter (in the plastic mixing bag) according to directions on box, adding egg and milk called for. Add one-half cup of the grated cheese to bag, mix, and pour into special pan enclosed in the package. Sprinkle with remaining one-fourth cup grated cheese. Bake at 425°F. (hot) twenty minutes. *Makes six servings.*

Try this one sliced and spread with cream cheese and jelly for delightful tea sandwiches. So good you can eat it almost like cake!

BANANA WALNUT BREAD

2 cups sifted flour
1 teaspoon salt
1 teaspoon baking soda
½ cup butter or margarine
1 cup sugar
2 eggs

1 cup mashed ripe bananas
  (2 to 3 bananas)
1 tablespoon vinegar plus milk to
  make one-half cup
¾ cup chopped walnuts

Sift flour, salt and baking soda together. Beat butter with a wooden spoon until light. Gradually blend in sugar. Add eggs one at a time, beating until fluffy after each addition. Add sifted flour mixture alternately with mixture of mashed banana and soured milk, beating well after each addition. Fold in chopped walnuts. Pour into a greased loaf pan (nine by five by three inches) and bake at 350°F. (moderate) sixty-five to seventy-five minutes or until done. Turn out of pan onto a rack; cool several hours before serving. *Makes one loaf.*

Canned refrigerator rolls are delicious as they are, of course. But to add your own signature, you might like to try one of the variations below.

SCALLION ROLLS

1 stick soft butter or margarine
1½ tablespoons finely chopped
  scallions (green onions)

1 package (8 oz.) refrigerator
  butterflake rolls

Combine soft butter and chopped scallions. Open package of rolls and separate into twelve sections. Gently pull apart (or cut) the top of each roll and fan it out a bit; spread the opening with butter mixture. Place in twelve small muffin cups, cut side up. Bake as package directs. *Makes twelve.*

HERB CRESCENTS

2 packages (8 oz. each) crescent
  refrigerator rolls
½ cup (1 stick) softened butter

2 teaspoons parsley flakes
1 teaspoon ground rosemary

Separate crescents and place on two greased cookie sheets. Combine rest of ingredients and spread evenly over crescents. Roll up and bake as package directs. *Makes sixteen.*

Fruit Desserts

*E*ACH TIME fruit appears as a dessert at your lunch or dinner, give yourself a gold star. Every fruit offers a beauty bonus. The more frequently you eat fruit, the closer you'll be to the true beauty that comes from within.

Freezing and canning have made it quite easy to have your favorite fruits the year around. But when fruit is in its season and coming to you from nearby areas, it is at its very best. Besides nibbling it between meals, make it into something special that everyone can enjoy.

When you work with the fresh-fruit recipes in this chapter, remember that fruits vary in acidity. Taste during the making and add more sugar if needed. When recipes call for mashed fruit, use a fork. Puréeing may be done with a blender or a food mill. Strain berry purées before you use them to remove seeds.

APPLES

There are many kinds of apples. Some are ideal for eating in the hand or for salads but when baked tend to lose their shape. Others give excellent results when baked but are too tart for salad use. And some varieties can perform in any role.

Especially for salads and snacks

    Red Delicious   Winesap
    Golden Delicious   All-purpose varieties

For pies and sauces

    Greening   Rome Beauty
    Lodi (yellow transparent) All-purpose varieties

For all purposes

Baldwin	McIntosh
Cortland	Newtown Pippin
Grimes Golden	Northern Spy
Jonathan	

Buying guide: Choose apples which have a fresh aroma and are free from blemishes. Two to three medium-size apples equal a pound, will make two cups, diced. Store apples in a plastic bag in a cool place.

Baked apples: Wash and core apples (use the corer at both ends of each apple). Remove top third of peel and set apples in a baking pan. Now bring to a boil a half-cup each of corn syrup and water, one-fourth teaspoon cinnamon, one teaspoon grated lemon peel, one tablespoon butter and two tablespoons sugar (enough for four apples). Pour over apples; bake at 350°F. (moderate) an hour, basting often. Serve with ice cream or cream.

Pies and sauces: For quickest preparation, cut apples into quarters first, then peel them and cut away the core before you slice them. You'll need six to seven cups of sliced apples, or about two and a half pounds, to fill a nine-inch pie shell.

Salads and snacks: For nibbling, make quick, pretty apple flowers with a corer-sectioner; just press it down and the apple falls away from core in snack-size pieces. To make a tangy salad tower, alternate thick orange slices, sweet onion rings and thin apple slices. For looks (and nutrition), leave skin on apples. To prevent browning, which happens if uncooked apples aren't eaten as soon as they're cut: dip the slices in orange, pineapple or grapefruit juice or in lemon juice diluted with a little water.

We think a cobbler tastes best served with "pour cream"—heavy cream almost too thick to pour. Or you might want to try the recipe below with ice cream (vanilla or butter pecan) instead.

APPLE COBBLER

4 cups sliced, pared cooking apples	2 tablespoons butter or margarine
1½ cups plus 1 tablespoon sugar, divided	½ teaspoon salt
1 teaspoon cinnamon	4 teaspoons baking powder
1 teaspoon nutmeg	⅓ cup shortening
2¼ cups flour, divided	1 egg, well beaten
2 tablespoons lemon juice	½ cup milk

Arrange the apples in the bottom of a greased nine-inch-square baking dish. Combine one and one-half cups of sugar, the cinnamon, nutmeg and one-fourth cup of the flour and sprinkle the mixture over the apples. Then sprinkle with lemon juice and dot with butter. Mix and sift together into a bowl two cups of flour, the salt, baking powder and one tablespoon of sugar. With a pastry blender or two knives, cut in the shortening until the mixture looks like coarse crumbs. Add egg and milk and stir just until moistened. Turn out on a lightly floured board. Pat or roll out and cut into two-inch rounds with sharp cutter. Arrange over apples. Bake at 425°F. (hot) twenty-five to thirty minutes, until browned. *Serves eight.*

Here, a delicious version of baked apples.

JAM APPLES

6 baking apples   ¾ cup (or more) peach jam
2 cups leftover cake crumbs

Core the apples and fill each cavity with one-third cup cake crumbs. Top each with two tablespoons jam. Place in a shallow pan. Bake at 350°F. (moderate) thirty to forty minutes or until soft. Baste occasionally with a little additional jam. *Serve hot or cold to six lucky people.*

At an on-the-go sort of party, caramel apples make a nice dessert to eat in the hand. Easy to fix, too.

CARAMEL APPLES

2 lbs. caramels   10 medium-size McIntosh apples,
¼ cup strong brewed coffee   washed and dried
10 wooden skewers   1 cup chopped walnuts (about)

Place caramels and coffee in the top of a double boiler and heat over boiling water, stirring often until caramels are melted and the sauce is smooth. Insert a wooden skewer into the stem end of each apple. Dip into the hot caramel sauce, turning until surface is completely coated. Press bottom of each apple into chopped nuts, then place (nut side down) on waxed paper or aluminum foil and chill in the refrigerator until firm. *Makes ten.*

Here's an appealing dessert to whip up from pantry-shelf ingredients.

QUICK PINK–APPLE PARFAIT

⅓ cup brown sugar   2 cans (1 lb. each) appleberry sauce
⅓ cup graham cracker crumbs   Whipped cream
⅓ cup chopped walnuts

Combine brown sugar, graham crumbs and walnuts. Select six parfait glasses and half fill them with appleberry sauce. Cover with a layer of crumb mixture. Fill to the top with more appleberry sauce and chill. Top with whipped cream and *serve to six*.

To end a meal in a blaze of glory, try these!

APPLES AFLAME

4 Winesap apples
2 tablespoons chopped walnuts
2 tablespoons brown sugar
2 tablespoons raisins

1 small bottle lemon-lime soda
4 sugar cubes
Lemon extract

Core the apples, hollowing out cavity. Remove part of skin in a long strip, to make barber pole stripes. Combine walnuts, brown sugar and raisins and divide into each apple. Place in a baking pan and bake at 350°F. (moderate) fifty minutes, basting twice during baking period with lemon-lime soda. Before serving, soak sugar cubes in lemon extract, place one on each apple and light! *Serves four, spectacularly!*

Sliced apples in syrup, nestling under a tender shortcake crust with a special top treatment:

CINNAMON APPLE PUFFS

¾ to 1 cup sugar
1 cup water
3 drops red food coloring
1½ lbs. (4 to 5) cooking apples, such
   as greenings

1½ cups sifted flour
½ teaspoon salt
2 teaspoons baking powder
¼ cup shortening
¾ cup milk

Place sugar (amount depends on tartness of apples), water and food coloring in a saucepan. Bring to a boil and boil about five minutes until syrup forms. Remove from heat. Peel, core and slice apples. Place in a six-by-nine-by-two-inch greased baking dish. Pour syrup over apples. Now mix the biscuit topping. Sift the flour, salt and baking powder together into a mixing bowl. With a pastry blender, cut shortening into flour until mixture looks like coarse corn meal. Stir in milk to make a soft dough. Over apples drop six to eight rounded spoonfuls of dough (number of puffs depends on servings desired). With top of spoon, make a small rounded dent in the top of each spoonful of dough and fill with Cinnamon Topping (below). Bake at 450°F. (very hot), or 425°F. if oven-glass dish is used, for about twenty-five minutes or until biscuit is browned. Serve warm, topped with cream (plain or whipped). *Serves six to eight.*

Cinnamon Topping: Combine two tablespoons melted butter, two table-spoons sugar and three-fourths teaspoon ground cinnamon.

BERRIES

Blackberries, blueberries, raspberries and strawberries all have similar rules for storing and washing. Give them a gentle cold-water shower in a strainer. For strawberries, use a strawberry huller or the point of a paring knife to trim off the green cap and the white core below the cap. To keep berries firm, refrigerate in a single layer in a shallow pan; never wash them until ready to use.

Here's an amusing dessert to make in a hurry.

SHORT-CUT STRAWBERRY SHORTCAKE

6 slices white bread	1 pint sliced, sugared, fresh straw-
Butter	berries or 1 package (10 oz.) frozen
¼ cup sugar	strawberries, thawed
½ teaspoon cinnamon	Pressure-packed whipped cream

Trim crusts from bread and butter both sides lightly. Combine sugar and cinnamon, dip bread into that mixture and press into large muffin cups. Bake at 400°F. (hot) ten minutes. Use hot or cold: fill with straw-berries and top with whipped cream. *Serves six.*

As you read this recipe, you'll see that the basic idea is quite simple— so simple you may make it often. But for a party, add the do-ahead whipped cream hearts; they add the glamour!

JELLIED STRAWBERRIES
WITH WHIPPED CREAM HEARTS

1 package strawberry gelatine	1 package (10 oz.) frozen sliced
1½ cups boiling water	strawberries
	½ cup heavy cream

Empty gelatine into a mixing bowl; pour boiling water over it, stirring with a wooden spoon till dissolved. Add frozen block of strawberries and let stand two minutes, then break block into smaller pieces. Stir occasionally until fruit is entirely defrosted—about twenty minutes. Refrigerate till serving time. (It will set to a soft jell.) Whip the cream till soft peaks form. Spoon evenly into ice cube tray; freeze several hours or overnight. Cut in hearts with a tiny cookie cutter. *Serves four.*

This is a shortcake in a new shape.

BLUEBERRY ROLY–POLY

1 pint (about 2 cups) blueberries	⅓ cup sugar (about)
A few drops of lemon juice	2 eggs
2 cups biscuit mix	⅓ cup light cream

Wash and drain the blueberries. Sprinkle with lemon juice and two tablespoons sugar (depending on sweetness of berries). Toss and set aside. Combine biscuit mix and one-fourth cup sugar in a large bowl. Beat one egg lightly, add with cream to the mix. Stir with a fork until combined. Turn out on a board dusted with additional biscuit mix. Knead eight to ten times. Roll out into a ten-by-twelve-inch rectangle. Beat second egg. Brush half on surface of dough. Sprinkle berries evenly on top. Press berries lightly into dough. Starting on one long side, roll up dough. Place roll, seam side down, on a greased shallow pan (like a jelly roll pan). Brush with remaining egg. Bake at 375°F. (moderate) for forty-five minutes. Roly-Poly is good made with peaches or strawberries, too. *Serves eight.*

Although it's true that the guests must wait for the soufflé, never the impatient soufflé for the guests, the reward makes it all worthwhile. Actually, it bakes in just about the time it takes to eat the main course.

RASPBERRY SOUFFLÉ

¾ cup strained, puréed raspberries	1 tablespoon cornstarch
¼ cup sugar (about)	1 tablespoon water
2 tablespoons lemon juice	4 egg whites

Strain purée to remove the seeds; place in a saucepan. Add lemon juice, then sugar to taste. Bring to a boil over medium heat, cook for three minutes. Combine cornstarch and water; stir into boiling fruit. Cook, stirring constantly until thickened. Set aside. Rub the inside of a one-and-one-half-quart casserole dish with butter; dust with sugar. Beat egg whites until soft peaks form. Gently but quickly fold warm fruit mixture into egg whites. Pour into prepared casserole. Bake at 375°F. (moderate) for twenty-five minutes. Remove from oven and serve immediately. Good with blueberries, peaches, nectarines or plums, also. *Serves four.*

Although this recipe takes three steps, the results are party-big, party-rich and party-pretty.

CHERRY PIZZA

First make the crust:

1½ cups sifted flour	2 tablespoons butter or margarine
¾ teaspoon salt	3 to 5 tablespoons milk
⅓ cup shortening	

Sift flour and salt into a bowl. Cut in shortening with a fork or pastry blender until dough looks like coarse corn meal. Cut in the butter until it looks like large peas. Now toss dough lightly with a fork and gradually sprinkle milk over it. Continue tossing until dough clings to fork. On a large baking sheet roll out two-thirds of dough into a ten-by-fourteen-inch rectangle. Turn up the edges to make a one-inch standing rim; flute the rim with your fingers. Roll out remaining dough and cut into half-inch strips for latticed top crust.

Add a coconut "crumble":

½ cup butter or margarine	1 cup sifted flour
1 cup brown sugar, firmly packed	1 cup flaked coconut

Combine all the ingredients in a bowl and mix them together with a pastry blender or fork. Sprinkle two-thirds of this mixture evenly over the rolled-out pastry on your baking sheet. Save the remainder to sprinkle around edge of filling later.

For the filling you'll need:

¾ cup sugar	1 teaspoon lemon juice
3 tablespoons cornstarch	½ teaspoon salt
1 can (1 lb.) red sour pitted cherries with liquid	¼ teaspoon red food coloring
	¼ teaspoon almond extract
1 tablespoon butter or margarine	¾ cup coarsely chopped walnuts

Mix sugar and cornstarch in a saucepan. Slowly add the liquid from the cherries. Stir over medium heat till thickened. Remove from heat. Stir in

remaining ingredients plus drained cherries. Spread on crumble-topped pastry carefully. Sprinkle remaining crumble mix around edge. Arrange pastry strips diagonally over top, sealing to fluted edge when possible. Bake at 400°F. (hot) twenty to twenty-five minutes or until golden brown. Serve hot (with ice cream if you like) or cool.

CITRUS FRUITS

Besides being good for you, citrus fruits add color and appeal to many a party menu. Here are some cutting-up tricks.

Citrus Cups, to hold salad dressings: Cut off top quarter of a lemon or lime. Scoop out pulp and cut a thin slice from bottom of fruit so cup will stand without tipping. Notch edge if desired.

Orange Fancies, for salads and the like: The first step is to peel the oranges. With a sharp knife, using a slight sawing motion, cut peel in one long continuous spiral (1). Another method: cut off stem end and score peel

as shown (2), but don't cut into "meat." Now, starting at stem, pull away each section of peel. Except for parties, don't remove the white membrane which clings to the meat—it is believed to have health values.

Orange sections (for salads, jellied molds, cake trim and meat garnish): Peel. Cut halfway between segment walls so membrane is in center of section (3). Or peel and cut just inside segment walls for natural sections minus membranes.

Chunks for dunks: Halve an unpeeled orange lengthwise. Halve lengthwise again, then cut crosswise. For smaller chunks, make two more lengthwise cuts, then cut crosswise.

Punch tricks and cake trimmings all start with thin slices of unpeeled fruit. For wheels: Stud peel with whole cloves. Or notch edge of peel

◀ *At a coffeehouse party, the beverages (pages 300–302) are the party.*

with kitchen shears. For bow ties: Cut two wedges from opposite sides of slices and add a cherry-on-a-toothpick in the center. For an Aladdin's lamp (4): Cut across center of an orange slice but not through the opposite peel. Cut away "meat" from half the slice. Curl the remaining strip of peel to form lamp handle; secure with a toothpick. Add a bit of cherry for flame. For butterflies (5): Slice just to center of orange or lemon slice, twist into "wings" for cake garnish.

Pretty gift to make: a pomander ball. An old-fashioned pomander ball adds a fresh, spicy scent to drawers or closets. For each, you'll need: a firm orange; two small boxes of whole cloves; two tablespoons each of ground orris root (buy at drugstore) and cinnamon. Stud orange closely all over with cloves. Dry in a warm place two weeks. Put ground spices in a bag, add orange, shake and let stand two hours. Remove; roll on flat surface to shake off excess spices. Crisscross a pair of yard-long ribbons; place orange at cross. Tie each ribbon at top of orange, then tie all tightly together at the crossing.

Grapefruit "on the half-shell" is most often called for; here's how to prepare it: Choose a grapefruit heavy for its size, cut it in half (if you like, core with kitchen scissors) then cut around each section, to

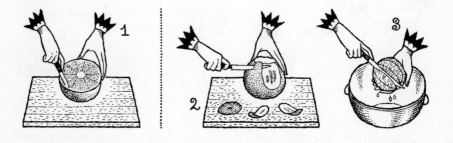

loosen it from membrane (1). A curved knife helps. Extras: Fill center with cherries, grapes, crushed candy, berries, syrup or honey. Or dot the halves with butter, brown sugar and cinnamon, and broil them slowly!

Sectioning grapefruit is easy, especially if the fruit is well chilled. For salads and cocktails, cut peel off in strips from top to bottom, cutting deep enough to expose pulp (2). You may have to do more trimming to remove all the white membrane. Working over a bowl, cut along sides of each dividing membrane to center with a sharp knife and slip the sections out (3). Save the fresh juice you've caught in the bowl—delicious for drinking or stirred into mayonnaise dressing!

This particular recipe for ambrosia bears the Florida stamp. Particularly nice after a dinner featuring ham or pork.

GRAPEFRUIT AMBROSIA

3 grapefruit
2 oranges
1 tangerine

1 cup quartered pitted dates
½ cup chopped pecans
½ cup flaked coconut

Peel and section the grapefruit and oranges. Remove the peel and white membrane from tangerine. Pull apart into sections and cut into thirds with scissors, removing seeds. Drain these fruits and toss with dates, pecans and coconut. Chill in serving bowl at least one hour. *Serves six.*

MELON

Make a habit of using melon—cantaloupe, honeydew, Persian, casaba—whenever it's in season. It's high in vitamins, high in refreshing flavor, good at any meal. And we hardly need to mention watermelon!

HOW TO MAKE MELON BALLS

Halve cantaloupe or similar melon and remove seeds. (Cut watermelon into thick slices instead of halves.) With a tiny melon scoop or rounded measuring spoon, cut out balls, using a circular motion.

FOUR SUMMER FRUITS

The following fruits come into season about the same time. Here's how to prepare them.

Peaches, nectarines: Remove skins with vegetable peeler. (If skin clings, skewer fruit on tines of fork and dunk in boiling water one minute, then in cold water.) To slice, make long cuts down fruit, using the pit as a backstop; separate slices. Sprinkle sliced fruit with lemon juice to prevent browning.

Pears: If underripe, store in a paper bag and ripen at room temperature. Quarter, peel and core fruit. Use lemon juice to prevent browning.

Plums: Peel with a vegetable peeler; slice like peaches.

PEACH MOUSSE

1 cup mashed peaches	1 tablespoon lemon juice
½ cup sugar (about)	¾ cup heavy cream, whipped

Combine fruit with lemon juice; sweeten to taste. Fold mixture into whipped cream. Pour into a refrigerator tray. For frozen mousse, freeze until firm (about three hours). For a half-frozen, spoonable whip, leave in food section of refrigerator till a half-hour before serving—then put in freezer. Other flavors: replace peaches with strawberries, blackberries, blueberries, bananas or nectarines. *Serves four.*

PINEAPPLE

Fresh pineapple has a clear, sharp, refreshing sweetness and is especially welcome after a heavy meal. Some preparation tips below.

PINEAPPLE RINGS

Cut off top of pineapple. Stand fruit upright on a cutting board and—working downward from the top—cut away thick slices of skin with a sharp knife (1). When fruit is completely pared, remove the "eyes." To do this

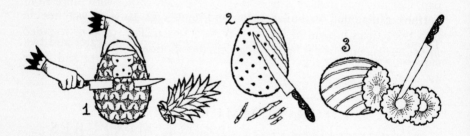

cut shallow, full-length wedges directly over each diagonal row of eyes (2). Lift out wedges and discard. Now turn pineapple on its side and slice it into rings. With tip of paring knife cut out the hard center core (3). If desired, cut each pineapple ring into small wedges.

DRIED FRUITS

Maybe you've found out what a satisfying nibble food dried fruits make. Ready for a change now?

PLEASINGLY PLUMP PRUNES

1 package (1 lb.) dried prunes
1 cup seedless raisins
1 lemon, thinly sliced
6 whole cloves

1 small cinnamon stick
3 bottles (7 oz. each) lemon-lime
carbonated beverage

Place all ingredients in a bowl or similar container with a cover. Add cover and refrigerate for two days. The prunes will plump magically, without cooking. Delicious as is for breakfast. For dessert, add heavy cream or whipped cream.

DATE DELITE

1 tablespoon butter or margarine
1½ cups brown sugar, firmly packed
¾ cup hot water
1¼ cups sifted flour

2 teaspoons baking powder
2 cups chopped pitted dates
2 cups chopped walnuts
Topping (below)

Beat butter and brown sugar together with wooden spoon; gradually add hot water. Sift flour and baking powder into sugar mixture and stir in. Add dates and walnuts. Stir until well mixed. Pour into greased eight-by-eight-by-two-inch pan. Immediately make topping. Pour this over the batter. Bake forty to forty-five minutes at 375°F. (moderate). Cool in pan. Cut into two-inch squares and serve in dessert dishes with sauce from bottom of pan. Top with whipped cream if desired. *Serves eight.*

Topping: Combine one tablespoon butter, three cups hot water and two cups brown sugar in saucepan. Stir over low heat until butter and sugar are dissolved.

SOME IDEAS FOR FRUIT MIXTURES

If there's anything better than one fruit, it's several. Here are some novel ways to combine them.

Have you a champagne taste on a soda pop budget? No matter. Here's a way to satisfy the first with the last. The idea is borrowed from the French, who steep their fruit macedoine in champagne.

LIVELY FRUIT COMPOTE

Over diced fresh fruit or drained canned fruit (any kind or several kinds) pour a bottle of lemon–lime carbonated beverage, using just enough to cover the fruit. Chill thoroughly, two or three hours. Lively, tangy, delicious.

Try the fruit lover's version of frozen ice cream pops.

FREEZER FRUIT POPS

Turn a can of fruit cocktail into frozen-pop molds. Freeze until firm. One No. 303 can makes four pops.

Here's another pretty way to serve summer's bounty of fresh fruit— try it for an outdoor supper.

RAINBOW FRUIT DESSERT

Fill a tray with crushed ice. On it arrange a rainbow—three wide bands —of differently colored fruits. Start on the outside with a band of bite-sized watermelon chunks. Next, place a row of cantaloupe balls, then a row of honeydew balls. Supply toothpicks so guests may dip fruit in a choice of flavored sweet syrups cupped in scooped-out limes (see page 181). To make the syrups, mix well one cup of sugar, one-third cup of lime juice, one-third cup of water. Divide into three bowls. Flavor one with peppermint extract, one with powdered ginger, leave one plain. Scoop out limes and fill with syrup.

This dessert is particularly appropriate for a *luau* meal—or indeed any party meal when the main course has been rich and guests want a feast for the eyes as well as a bit of something sweet. But note: it takes about twenty minutes to put this extravaganza onstage, so plan your party to allow for your absence in the kitchen.

FLAMING SNOW MOUNTAIN

2 oranges, peeled, seeded and
  sectioned
2 apples, cut in eighths, cored and
  dipped in lemon juice
16 maraschino cherries
16 pineapple chunks
2 quarts crushed ice
¼ cup lemon extract

Prepare the fruit and keep it chilled until serving time. The crushed ice can perhaps be bought at your local icehouse. If not, run four trays of ice cubes through an electric or mechanical ice crusher, or crush in a canvas bag with a wooden mallet. Firmly pack a cone-shaped vase or a mold with the crushed ice. Invert on a serving plate. (Or shape crushed ice with hands into one large or two smaller mountains.) Scoop out a hole in the top to hold a bowl for the "flaming crater." Attach fruit to mountain with toothpicks. (If you have a freezer, you can shape the mountain and crater and stud with toothpicks, then freeze. At dessert time, add fruit, etc.) In the crater hole, place a small metal bowl covered with one or two layers of heavy-duty foil inside and out. Fill with lemon extract. Bring to table and ignite extract. Guests eat the chilled fruit from the mountain, and may dip it in flaming extract. *Serves eight.*

This dessert-centerpiece is as rewarding to the eye as to the taste.

FROSTED FRUIT CENTERPIECE

Frozen fruits—frosted over with snowy crystals—make a strikingly beautiful summer centerpiece. Use different varieties and colors: red strawberries, plums and purple grapes accented with golden pears. Arrange them in a silver dish or crystal bowl. Or use fresh leaves or ferns and pyramid the fruits on top. Set your creation on the dinner table immediately before sitting down. By dessert time (about an hour later), fruits will be nicely defrosted, and your centerpiece ready to eat.

To make the centerpiece, just arrange fruit in a serving dish or on foil, place in freezer or ice cube part of refrigerator for twenty-four hours.

Whole fruits: Wash plums, pears, apricots, nectarines, berries and peaches and freeze them whole, uncut, unsliced.

Melons: Before freezing, slice watermelon, cantaloupe and honeydew into wedges. Or make melon balls and heap them back into their shells. For fancier shapes, slice melon thinly and make stars and half-moons with cookie cutters.

Citrus fruits: Peel and section oranges and grapefruit before freezing.

Special handling: Strawberries, pineapple slices and grapes are better with a light brushing of lemon juice and a whisper of granulated sugar. Short-cut: brush with thawed lemonade concentrate.

Pies

*I*N MANY FAMILIES, pies may appear once or twice a week—and two kinds of pie for company is standard practice. Most of us now, though, are so figure-conscious that we put pie into the special-treat category and usually serve it after a meal which has been lighter than average.

Certainly fruit pies, made with peak-of-the-season ripe fruit are a clearly marked road to a man's heart. And just as certainly, some of the refrigerator pies—cloudy chiffons and rich cream pies—make a big hit with the ladies. Therefore, pie lovers, unite! All is not lost!

HOW TO ROLL AND BAKE A PIECRUST

Make a pastry dough using the following recipe or one of the packaged mixes. Follow the mixing directions. When dough clings together in a smooth nonsticky ball, it's ready to roll out. Flour a pastry cloth or board; rub a rolling pin (the ball-bearing type is best) with flour. Cut the ball in half; flatten one half into a smooth round with palm of hand.

Roll from the center outward. Use light strokes; lift pin up just before you get to the edge of the dough (1). Keep edge round. If a crack forms, roll toward it from both sides (2). To test size, invert your pan onto the round. Dough should extend at least one inch beyond pan so you can make a border. It should extend two inches for a fluted edge.

Fold dough in half, then quarters. (Lightly dust with flour any sticky places on top surface.) Loosen from board with long edge of spatula if necessary. Move dough to pan gently to avoid tearing. Lay folded dough in pan with point exactly in center (3). Unfold, without pulling or stretching. If there is a bubble under the surface, lift pastry and refit.

For a one-crust pie, trim edge even and fold extra pastry underneath to make a high rim (4). Lock firmly to pan edge by crisscrossing with fork.

Or flute, pinching and twisting as shown (5). If crust is not to be filled before baking, prick every inch of surface to prevent bubbles.

To make a top crust: Roll a second round of pastry. Slit to let steam escape and place over filling. Fold both edges under; press to the pan with a fork (or flute). Use water to "glue" any tears in pastry.

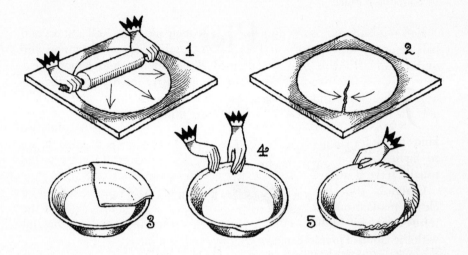

Problem: Crust is too small. If you have trouble rolling out pastry big enough to fit pan, use a bit more dough—for a one-crust pie, up to three-fourths of the mix package. Crust will be thicker but still tender.

Problem: Dough sticks to board. Try this: Roll dough between two pieces of floured waxed paper. As you roll, flip packet over a few times to see if paper wrinkles; lift paper and smooth it if necessary. After rolling, lift off top paper, invert dough into pan, peel off bottom paper.

HOMEMADE PASTRY

2¼ cups sifted flour	¾ cup shortening
¾ teaspoon salt	5 tablespoons ice-cold water

Sift flour and salt into a mixing bowl. With a pastry blender or two knives, cut in shortening. Sprinkle ice water over mixture gradually, using a fork and a stirring-tossing motion to blend it in lightly. When dough clings together in a ball, it's ready to roll out; follow preceding directions. Enough for a two-crust pie, or two one-crust pies.

For a trial run, start with this American classic.

EASY APPLE PIE DANDY

Homemade Pastry (page 189)
½ cup sugar
1 teaspoon cinnamon
¼ teaspoon nutmeg

2 cans (No. 2) sliced apples
1 tablespoon lemon juice
1 egg

Roll out half the pastry and line a nine-inch pie pan. Roll out second half of pastry for top crust and set aside. Combine sugar, cinnamon and nutmeg and stir this into the drained sliced apples. Add lemon juice. Turn mixture into lined pie pan. Cut slits in pastry for top crust, then fit over apples. Trim and seal edges. Beat the egg until foamy and brush it over the top crust. Bake at 425°F. (hot) forty minutes.

This shortbread pie crust is patted out, not rolled. The result tastes even better than regular blueberry pie!

BLUEBERRY SHORTBREAD PIE

First make the filling:

3½ tablespoons quick-cooking tapioca
¾ cup sugar
¼ teaspoon salt
¼ teaspoon cinnamon

1½ cups water
3 cups blueberries, divided
1½ tablespoons lemon juice

Combine tapioca, sugar, salt, cinnamon, water and one and one-half cups of washed fresh blueberries in a saucepan. Cook over medium heat, stirring and mashing berries with a fork or potato masher. Remove from heat when mixture comes to a boil and let stand fifteen minutes. Then stir in lemon juice and remaining blueberries. Let cool.

Make the shortbread crust:

½ cup softened butter or margarine
¼ cup sugar

1¼ cups sifted flour

Mix butter and sugar, then add flour and blend until crumbs are formed. Mix well with hands until mixture reaches a soft dough stage. Press evenly into sides and bottom of an eight-inch round cake pan. Prick bottom crust all over with a fork. Bake at 325°F. (slow) thirty-five to forty minutes. Cool in pan. Remove carefully. If shell sticks to pan, warm a few seconds over low heat, then invert. Fill with blueberry mixture and *serve to six.*

This version of apple pie (it blushes bright red) is just right at holiday party time.

CRANBERRY APPLE PIE

1 package (2 sticks) piecrust mix	¼ teaspoon salt
1 teaspoon cinnamon	¼ cup water
½ teaspoon nutmeg	1½ cups fresh cranberries
4 tablespoons boiling water	½ teaspoon grated lemon peel
1½ cups sugar	2 tablespoons butter
3 tablespoons cornstarch	1½ cups sliced cooking apples

Crumble piecrust mix into a bowl. Combine cinnamon, nutmeg and water; stir into mix. Shape dough into a ball. Cut off a little less than half and reserve for lattice top. Roll out remaining dough into a circle one inch larger than an inverted nine-inch pie pan and fit smoothly into the pan. Combine sugar, cornstarch and salt in a saucepan, stir in water and cook over low heat, stirring constantly, until syrup thickens and begins to boil. Stir in washed, drained berries; cook till they pop, then stir in lemon peel and butter. Put apples in pie pan, pour berries on top. Now roll dough for top into six-by-ten-inch rectangle. Cut into ten strips, half-inch wide. Moisten rim of bottom crust with water, lay strips across top of pie, fold bottom crust over ends of strips. Press to seal edges, then crimp with tines of fork. Bake at 425°F. (hot) thirty minutes or till crust is browned. Cool; *serve to eight.*

Cherry pie may in time outrank apple as America's favorite dessert. Here's a good one.

LATTICE CHERRY PIE

1 box (10 oz.) piecrust mix	½ teaspoon cinnamon
1 cup sugar	2 cans (No. 2) pitted tart red cherries
1 tablespoon flour	4 drops red food coloring
1 tablespoon cornstarch	1 tablespoon butter

Prepare piecrust dough (using both sticks) according to package directions. After fitting bottom crust into a nine-inch pie pan, roll out second half of dough and cut into long strips with a pastry wheel or knife. Next, combine in a saucepan the sugar, flour, cornstarch and cinnamon. Drain cherries, reserving one-half cup of liquid. Add liquid gradually to sugar mixture and stir to combine. Cook over medium heat, stirring constantly, until mixture thickens and begins to boil. Stir in food coloring. Pour over drained cherries and mix lightly. Pour into pastry-lined pie pan.

Dot with butter. Now make the lattice top. Place a strip of dough across top of pie near one edge. Place another strip over the first—going in the crosswise direction. Continue placing strips until entire pie has been covered with lattice work. Press strips to edge of bottom crust, using water to "glue" them in place. Fold outer edge of pastry over ends of strips, pressing firmly. Flute edge if desired, or make crisscross marks with fork. Cut paper drinking straws in thirds and insert in each opening to let juices bubble up. Or place a cookie sheet under the pie to catch any drips. Bake at 425°F. (hot) for thirty-five to forty-five minutes until golden. Cool; *serve to eight.*

This is a wizard's recipe: follow the directions accurately and you'll see the filling set without cooking—before-your-eyes magic! Tangy lime, in an easy meringue pie.

MAGIC LIME MERINGUE PIE

1 nine-inch crumb crust, baked and cooled	2 eggs, separated
	Few drops of green food coloring
1 can (14 oz.) sweetened condensed milk	⅛ teaspoon salt
	¼ cup sugar
½ cup lime juice	

Prepare Nutty Graham Crust (page 193) or your own favorite. Then in a mixing bowl, blend condensed milk, lime juice, egg yolks and enough food coloring to tint pale green. Turn into baked crust. In a clean bowl use a rotary beater to beat egg whites and salt until stiff but not dry. Add sugar one tablespoon at a time and continue to beat until mixture holds stiff points when beater is withdrawn. Pile on top of filling, spreading with spoon so it touches inner edge of crust. Bake at 325°F. (slow) for eighteen minutes. Chill well.

Even though you won't be able to "stick in your thumb and pull out a plum" (they're all sliced) you'll think this summer pie tastes as good as Christmas!

PLUM MERINGUE PIE

2 cups sliced, pitted fresh red plums	3 egg yolks
⅔ cup water, divided	1 nine-inch pie shell, baked and cooled
3 tablespoons quick-cooking tapioca	
¾ cup sugar	Meringue (page 193)
¼ teaspoon salt	

Place plums and one-third cup of the water in a saucepan and bring to a boil. Combine tapioca, sugar and salt in a small mixing bowl. Then add to plums along with remaining one-third cup of water. Cook and stir until mixture boils. Remove from heat and cool slightly. Beat egg yolks until thick and lemon colored. Add plum mixture gradually to beaten yolks, mixing well. Cool thoroughly. Pour into pie shell. Top with meringue, spreading it carefully to edges, and bake at 425°F. (hot) five to ten minutes or until meringue is lightly browned. *Serves seven.*

Meringue: Beat three egg whites until soft peaks form, then add six tablespoons of sugar, two tablespoonfuls at a time, beating after each addition. Continue beating until mixture stands in stiff peaks.

NUTTY GRAHAM CRUST

1¼ cups graham-cracker crumbs, finely rolled
½ cup finely chopped walnuts

2 tablespoons sugar
½ cup butter or margarine, melted

Combine crumbs, nuts and sugar. Add butter and mix until blended. Turn into nine-inch pie pan. Press firmly to bottom and sides of pan. Bake at 350°F. (moderate) about eight minutes. Cool.

If you've never eaten a pie made from dried fruits—like the one below— you have a real treat in store.

TRIPLE–TREAT FRUIT PIE

1 cup dark raisins
1 cup water
1¼ cups cooked or "plumped" dried prunes
1¼ cups cooked dried apricots
½ cup reserved apricot or prune liquid
½ cup sugar

4 teaspoons cornstarch
Dash of salt
¼ teaspoon cinnamon
3 tablespoons lemon juice
1 tablespoon butter
1 package (10 oz.) pastry mix (two sticks)

Combine raisins and water and slowly bring to a boil. Drain and combine with cooked prunes and apricots. In a saucepan combine re-served apricot or prune liquid with sugar, cornstarch, salt and cinnamon and bring to a boil. Cook until thickened. Remove from heat and stir in lemon juice and butter. Make up pastry dough according to package directions. Divide dough in half and use one half to form bottom crust for pie. Roll out second half and cut into half-inch strips. Fill pastry-lined pan with the mixed fruit; pour thickened sauce over fruit. Arrange pastry strips across top of pie in lattice effect. Bake at 375°F. (moderate) forty-five minutes or until browned. *Serves seven.*

NOTE: To "plump" one pound of dried prunes, place in a large refrigerator jar, add one quart of cold water, cover. Refrigerate at least twenty-four hours before using.

Plain peach pie can qualify as food for the gods, and this coconutty version is even more delectable.

PEACH COCONUT PIE

4 cups sliced fresh peaches
1 teaspoon lemon juice
⅔ cup sugar
1½ tablespoons quick-cooking tapioca
1 nine-inch pie shell, unbaked

⅓ cup firmly packed brown sugar
¼ cup flour
3 tablespoons softened butter or
 margarine
¾ cup flaked coconut

Combine peaches, lemon juice, sugar and tapioca in a large bowl and let stand. Prepare pastry shell. Combine brown sugar, flour and butter and mix with a pastry blender or fork until crumbs form. Stir in coconut. Sprinkle one-third of this mixture over bottom of pie shell. Fill with the peach mixture. Top with remaining crumbs. Bake at 425°F. (hot) thirty-five to forty-five minutes or until juice boils with heavy bubbles. *Serve warm to six.*

This recipe will earn you credit with your friends as being a fabulous cook. And no wonder—it's a fabulous pie!

MOCHA MARVEL PIE

2 envelopes unflavored gelatine
½ cup cold water
1 cup hot water
3 teaspoons instant coffee powder
2 cups (12 oz. jumbo package)
 semisweet chocolate pieces
4 eggs, separated

½ teaspoon salt
2 teaspoons vanilla
¾ cup sugar, divided
1½ cups heavy cream, divided
1 nine-inch pastry shell, baked and
 cooled

Sprinkle gelatine over cold water; let stand. Bring hot water to boil. Add instant coffee and stir. Stir in chocolate (save a quarter-cup to garnish top) and heat, stirring constantly, until melted. Set aside a half-cup of this mixture. Add gelatine to remainder, stir to dissolve, and remove from heat. In a medium-size mixing bowl beat egg yolks well with rotary beater. Beat in salt, vanilla and a half-cup of the sugar. Slowly stir in chocolate-gelatine mixture. Chill until slightly thickened. Meanwhile, beat egg whites until foamy, then beat in gradually the remaining one-fourth cup sugar. With clean, dry beater beat one-half cup of heavy cream until soft peaks form. Fold egg whites into chocolate mixture gently but thoroughly, then fold in whipped cream. Chill about ten minutes or till mixture mounds when dropped from a spoon. Turn into a baked pastry shell, mounding high in the middle. Pour reserved chocolate mixture in parallel ribbons across pie's surface. Swirl a knife across chocolate from one side of pie to other to give marbled effect. Chill pie until firm (about three hours). Whip remaining heavy cream, mound around edge of pie, dot with chocolate pieces. *Nine rich servings.*

The cool, refreshing flavor of this chiffon pie makes it a pleasure to meet —and eat—after a dinner of baked ham, for instance.

LIME CHIFFON PIE

2 cups chocolate cookie crumbs
⅓ cup melted butter
1 cup sugar (about)
1 envelope unflavored gelatine
¼ teaspoon salt
4 eggs, separated

½ cup lime juice
¼ cup water
1 teaspoon grated lemon peel
Green food coloring
½ cup heavy cream
½ teaspoon cream of tartar

To make crumbs, place cookies between sheets of waxed paper and crush with a rolling pin. (Or crush in electric blender.) Combine with melted butter and one-fourth cup of sugar; press into bottom and sides of a nine-inch pie pan. Bake at 350°F. (moderate) for eight minutes. Cool. For filling: Mix gelatine, salt and one-third cup of sugar in top of double boiler. Beat egg yolks, lime juice and water together; stir into gelatine. Cook over boiling water, stirring constantly until gelatine is dissolved, about five minutes. Remove from heat, stir in lemon peel. Add food coloring to make mixture a medium pastel green. Refrigerate gelatine mixture, stirring occasionally, till it mounds slightly when dropped from spoon. Meanwhile, whip heavy cream; chill. Next, beat egg whites with cream of tartar till stiff but not dry, then slowly beat in one-third cup sugar. The mixture should hold stiff peaks when the beater is removed. Fold gelatine into egg mixture, then fold in whipped cream. (Skip liquid at bottom of bowl.) Pour filling into pie shell; chill until firm. At serving time decorate with more whipped cream if desired. *Serves eight.*

Evaporated milk here cuts the cost—in pennies and in calories—of having a light, rich, flavorful pie.

PINEAPPLE CHIFFON PIE

1 can (No. 2) crushed pineapple with syrup	1 teaspoon grated lemon peel
1 envelope unflavored gelatine	¼ teaspoon salt
3 eggs, separated	⅔ cup (small can) evaporated milk, chilled
½ cup sugar	1 nine-inch pie shell, baked and cooled
2 tablespoons lemon juice	

Drain crushed pineapple thoroughly but save one-fourth cup of the syrup. Over this, sprinkle gelatine and let stand five minutes. Combine in a double boiler egg yolks, one-fourth cup of the sugar, lemon juice, lemon peel and salt. Stir in crushed pineapple and cook, stirring, over hot water ten minutes. Remove from heat, stir in softened gelatine until dissolved. Cool, then chill until as syrupy as unbeaten egg white. Next, in a large bowl beat egg whites until stiff; gradually add remaining one-fourth cup sugar, beating until egg whites are smooth and shiny and hold peaks when beater is removed. Whip chilled evaporated milk until it holds soft peaks. Beat pineapple-gelatine mixture with a rotary beater and fold into meringue. Fold in whipped evaporated milk. Pour into baked pie shell; chill several hours or overnight in refrigerator until firm. *Serves seven.*

NOTE: To chill evaporated milk, empty it into an ice cube tray, place in freezing section fifteen minutes or until tiny ice crystals form around the edge but center remains soft.

Feeling daring? Here's a recipe to match your mood; good, too.

PEANUT–BUTTER CREAM PIE

1½ cups sugar	3½ cups scalded milk
6 tablespoons cornstarch	½ cup peanut butter
½ teaspoon salt	2 teaspoons vanilla
½ cup cold milk	1 ten-inch pie shell, baked and cooled
4 egg yolks	

In mixing bowl, combine sugar, cornstarch and salt. Add cold milk and egg yolks and beat until smooth. Stir half of the scalded milk gradually into the egg mixture. Then pour this mixture into remaining scalded milk and cook over hot water, stirring occasionally, until thickened. Stir in peanut butter, continuing to cook until mixture is well blended and has a sheen.

Remove from heat and stir in vanilla. Pour into baked pie shell. Cool. Make meringue. Spread over top of pie. Bake at 300°F. (slow) until golden brown. Cool. *Serves eight to ten.*

Meringue: With a rotary beater or electric mixer, beat four egg whites until soft peaks form. Add four tablespoons sugar gradually, continuing to beat until stiff and shiny.

NOTE: To scald milk, place it over moderate heat until it begins to bubble around the edges and the surface shines, then remove from heat at once.

Here's a special kind of homemade piecrust—made from homemade cookie crunch. This filling is delicious, but you can experiment with other flavors, too.

BUTTER CRUNCH–LEMON CHIFFON PIE

First make Butter Crunch for the crust:

½ cup butter, softened
¼ cup brown sugar, firmly packed
1 cup sifted flour

¼ cup chopped pecans or walnuts
¼ cup flaked coconut

Mix all ingredients with hands. Spread in a thirteen-by-nine-inch pan. Bake at 400°F. (hot) for fifteen minutes. Remove from oven and stir with spoon. Cool slightly. *Makes two and one-half cups.* Press one and three-fourth cups hot Butter Crunch against bottom and sides of a nine-inch pie pan. Chill.

Now prepare the filling:

1 cup sugar, divided
1 envelope unflavored gelatine
⅔ cup water
⅓ cup lemon juice

4 eggs, separated
1 teaspoon grated lemon peel
½ teaspoon cream of tartar

Combine one-half cup of the sugar, gelatine, water, lemon juice and lightly beaten egg yolks in a saucepan. Cook over medium heat, stirring constantly, just until mixture comes to a boil. Stir in the lemon peel. Remove pan from heat and place in cold water. Cool until mixture mounds slightly when dropped from a spoon. Meanwhile, combine egg whites and cream of tartar. With rotary beater or electric mixer, beat until foamy. Gradually add remaining half-cup of sugar, continuing to beat until stiff peaks form when beater is raised. Fold lemon mixture into stiffly beaten egg whites. Turn into prepared crust. Sprinkle remaining Butter Crunch evenly over filling. Chill for one hour. *Serves eight.*

For a very special boy, a very special valentine. And it's so simple to make, angel pie. Just spin together our pink push-button pastry in an electric mixer and add the filling: a cloud of cherry ice cream parfait (translated, in any boy's language, as perfect) frosted with a puff of whipped cream. Pink, of course. Add a fanfare of tiny hearts around the rim. And that's it. Make one and see—he'll love you for it.

PINK ANGEL PIE

For Pink Push-button Pastry:

⅔ cup white vegetable shortening	⅓ cup boiling water
8 drops red food coloring	2 cups sifted flour
½ teaspoon almond extract	1 teaspoon salt

Place shortening, food color and almond extract in a small mixing bowl. Add boiling water all at once and immediately combine ingredients with electric mixer. Set mixer at slow speed until ingredients are blended, then beat at high speed. (If you use a rotary beater or a wire whisk, stir slowly first, then beat vigorously.) After the mixture thickens enough to form soft billows when beater is raised, fold in the flour and salt with a rubber scraper. Set mixer on slow speed again and beat until a moist, crumbly dough is formed. Set aside three-fourths cup of dough for other uses. Shape remaining dough into a ball and roll out between sheets of waxed paper into an eleven-inch circle. Peel off top piece of paper and invert dough into a nine-inch pie pan, then peel off the other piece of paper. Trim off a one-inch strip of pastry from the outer edge (use for making hearts as described below). Turn under the new outer edge and press to pan rim with fingers. Prick all over with a fork. Now cut out thirty valentine hearts. Use a one-inch heart cutter. Or use a bottle cap to cut rounds, then shape hearts this way: cut a small V from top of circle; trim lower part of circle into a point directly opposite. Moisten hearts, "paste" to pie rim. Bake at 375°F. (moderate) fifteen minutes or until golden. Cool.

For Pink Parfait Filling:

1 can (1 lb. 14 oz.) pitted Bing cherries	1 tablespoon lemon juice
	1 teaspoon grated lemon peel
1 package cherry-flavored gelatine	1 pint cherry-vanilla ice cream

Drain cherries, saving the syrup. Measure one and one-fourth cups syrup into a saucepan and heat to boiling point. Add gelatine; stir to dissolve. Now remove from heat, add lemon juice and peel, and blend in ice cream by spoonfuls. Refrigerate until it looks like whipped cream, about twenty minutes. Meanwhile, halve cherries. Fold these into chilled mixture and pour into pie shell. Refrigerate until filling is set, about two hours. Before serving, add:

Pink Puff Topping. Whip one cup heavy cream with four drops of red food coloring and two tablespoons confectioners' sugar. Top pie. *Serves eight.*

In a cherry-flavored crumb crust, a pretty pink lemonade pie. What does the thickening? The marshmallows.

PINK LEMONADE PIE

1½ cups finely rolled vanilla wafer crumbs
6 tablespoons melted butter or margarine
1 tablespoon maraschino cherry syrup

1 can (6 oz.) frozen pink lemonade
1 lemonade can of water
8 oz. marshmallows
1½ cups heavy cream
1 teaspoon sugar

Combine crumbs, butter and cherry syrup well. Reserve one-fourth cup for topping and pat remaining crumbs into a nine-inch pie pan, pressing firmly against sides and bottom. Chill three hours. Combine lemonade and water in a saucepan. Heat, but do not boil. Add marshmallows and stir over low heat until melted. Chill mixture until cool and thickened. Whip one cup of cream until soft peaks form. Fold into mixture, blending well. Pile into chilled crumb crust. Whip the additional cream with sugar and use to garnish top of pie, sprinkling reserved crumbs around edges. Freeze solid and wrap in heavy foil. Remove from freezer about thirty minutes before serving. *Serves six to eight.*

This parfait pie has its calories somewhat reduced by using *soft ice cream,* the type you buy at a "frozen custard" stand. You may use regular ice cream if figures don't count!

ORANGEADE PARFAIT PIE

1 nine-inch crumb shell or rice cereal shell (page 200)
1 can (6 oz.) frozen orange juice concentrate, thawed

½ cup water
1 package orange-flavored gelatine
1 teaspoon grated orange peel
1 pint vanilla-flavored soft ice cream

When crust is prepared, heat orange juice concentrate with water in a saucepan until it begins to boil. Add gelatine, remove from heat and stir until dissolved. Add orange peel, then the ice cream, one heaping tablespoon at a time, stirring until melted. Refrigerate until thickened but not set (about thirty minutes), then turn into the pie shell. Chill until firm and garnish with thin orange slices and swirls of sweetened whipped cream if desired. *Serves seven.*

Honey Rice Pie Shell

1 cup brown sugar, firmly packed	2½ tablespoons butter or margarine
1½ tablespoons light corn syrup	4 cups honey-flavored rice cereal
⅓ cup milk	

Combine sugar, syrup, milk and butter in a saucepan and cook over medium heat, stirring constantly, until sugar dissolves. Continue to cook until mixture reaches soft ball stage (238°F. on candy thermometer). Turn cereal into a large bowl, pour cooked syrup over it and mix to coat. Turn into a greased nine-inch pie pan and press to bottom and sides of pan to form a thick shell.

This tastes rather like a chocolate cream. The dessert is modest in size but big on flavor.

CHOCOLATE CROWN CHEESE PIE

For the graham-cracker crust:

1¼ cups fine graham-cracker crumbs	⅓ cup melted butter
(20 square grahams)	⅓ cup sugar

Combine ingredients. Press on bottom and sides of a nine-inch pie plate. Chill until ready to use.

For the filling and crown:

1 package (8 oz.) cream cheese	¼ cup lemon juice
2 tablespoons butter or margarine	2 tablespoons grated lemon peel
½ cup sugar	1 package (6 oz.) semisweet chocolate
1 egg	pieces
2 tablespoons flour	3 tablespoons light cream
⅔ cup milk	

Soften cheese and butter at room temperature, then cream until fluffy. Beat in sugar and whole egg. Next stir in flour. Gradually stir in milk, then lemon juice and peel. Pour into unbaked graham crust. Bake at 350°F. (moderate) thirty-five minutes. Turn heat off, but let pie remain in oven with door ajar until cool. When cool, melt semisweet pieces over hot (not boiling) water. Remove from heat and blend in cream. Spread over cheese filling. Chill until serving time. *Serves eight.*

This pie is different from start to finish. Tastes like ice cream and cookies, but better than either.

SUPREME CREAM PIE

First make oatmeal-nut crust and cookies:

1 cup shortening	1½ cups sifted flour
¾ cup light brown sugar, firmly packed	1 teaspoon salt
	1 teaspoon baking soda
¾ cup granulated sugar	3 cups old-fashioned or quick-cooking
2 eggs, well beaten	oatmeal
1 teaspoon vanilla	½ cup chopped nuts

Beat shortening until fluffy; gradually beat in both sugars, then eggs and vanilla. Sift together flour, salt and soda. Stir in. Fold in oatmeal and nuts. Use about one and one-third cups of this mixture, patted out thin, to line a nine-inch pie pan. Press firmly into plate; flute the edges. Pat out another one-half cup of mixture in a pie pan to look like a large cookie. Bake both at 350°F. (moderate) twenty to twenty-five minutes or until light brown. Cool. Remove large "cookie" from pan, crumble, and use to top filling. (Remaining cookie dough may be shaped into a roll, wrapped in waxed paper and chilled overnight. Next day, cut into slices one-fourth inch thick, bake on an ungreased cookie sheet at 350°F. about ten minutes.)

Now make Supreme Cream Filling:

¼ cup cornstarch	3 egg yolks, slightly beaten
⅔ cup sugar	2 tablespoons butter
¼ teaspoon salt	½ teaspoon vanilla
1½ cups milk	½ cup vanilla ice cream
½ cup light cream	

Blend cornstarch, sugar and salt in top of double boiler. Gradually add milk, stirring constantly, then cream. Cook over boiling water until thickened, stirring constantly. Then cover and cook ten minutes more, stirring occasionally. (Very low direct heat may also be used; time will be briefer.) Slowly add a little hot mixture to the beaten egg yolks, then stir them into hot mixture. Cook five minutes more, stirring constantly over boiling water. Remove from heat. Add butter, vanilla and ice cream. Mix well. Cool. Pour into cooled baked oatmeal shell. Sprinkle with crumbled topping. Chill about three hours. *Serves eight.*

In the baking, this pie filling separates into two layers like a cake-top pudding. Try it hot with vanilla ice cream.

CHOCOLATE CAKE PIE

3 tablespoons shortening	6 tablespoons cocoa
⅔ cup sugar	1 cup milk
2 eggs, separated	1 nine-inch pastry shell, unbaked
2 tablespoons flour	

Beat shortening until fluffy and gradually beat in sugar. Then beat in egg yolks. Mix flour and cocoa and stir into egg mixture. Stir in milk. Beat egg whites until stiff but not dry. Fold in. Pour into unbaked shell. Bake at 375°F. (moderate) forty minutes. *Serves six.*

This is rather like pecan pie, but the almonds give a more subtle flavor. Good warm or cold, with or without whipped or ice cream.

GOLDEN DREAMY PIE

Homemade Pastry (½ recipe, page 189)	½ cup light corn syrup
	½ cup dark corn syrup
1 cup chopped blanched almonds	⅓ cup butter, melted
3 eggs	¼ teaspoon salt
⅔ cup sugar	

Roll out pastry one inch larger than eight-inch pan. Sprinkle with three tablespoons of the chopped almonds and roll these lightly into the pastry. Fit dough loosely into pan and flute edges. Chill while making filling. Using an electric or rotary beater, beat together eggs, sugar, both syrups, butter and salt. Pour into pastry shell. Sprinkle remaining almonds over top. Bake at 375°F. (moderate) forty-five minutes or until firm. *Serves six.*

If you like things "the most," you'll like this. Pecan pie is good, but chocolate makes it better!

CHOCOLATE PECAN PIE

1 cup pecan halves	4 egg yolks
Homemade Pastry (½ recipe, page 189)	½ cup sugar
	¼ teaspoon salt
¼ cup butter or margarine	1¼ cups light corn syrup
2 squares (1 oz. each) unsweetened chocolate	1 teaspoon vanilla

Chop enough pecan halves fine to make one-fourth cup. Now make up pastry or piecrust mix for a one-crust pie, but add chopped pecans before adding liquid. Roll out on a floured pastry cloth or board to a ten-and-one-half-inch circle. Fit loosely into a nine-inch pie pan. Make a standing rim and flute edge. For filling, melt butter or margarine and add chocolate over hot, not boiling water. Set aside to cool. In a bowl, beat egg yolks slightly. Gradually beat in sugar and salt. Blend in corn syrup, vanilla and the chocolate-butter mixture. Fold in remaining pecan halves. Pour into pastry shell. Bake at 450°F. (hot) ten minutes. Turn down oven to 325°F. (slow) and bake forty minutes or until firm. *Serves eight to ten.*

For gourmet refrigerator raiders, or for anybody hungry for something really special, this is it! Triple chocolate, in crust, filling and cream topping.

MIDNIGHT'S MOST DIVINE PIE

1 envelope unflavored gelatine
½ cup sugar, divided
¼ teaspoon salt
¼ teaspoon cinnamon
1 cup milk
3 eggs, separated
3 squares unsweetened chocolate

½ teaspoon vanilla
¼ teaspoon cream of tartar
2 cups heavy cream
1 baked nine-inch chocolate pie shell
 (see below)
Grated semisweet chocolate

Mix gelatine, one-fourth cup of the sugar, salt and cinnamon in heavy saucepan. Blend in milk and beaten egg yolks. Add unsweetened chocolate. Heat slowly, stirring constantly until chocolate melts and mixture is slightly thickened (don't boil!). Add vanilla. Pour into bowl. Cool until mixture mounds when dropped from spoon. In a large bowl, beat egg whites with cream of tartar until foamy. Add remaining one-fourth cup sugar gradually and continue beating until meringue stands in stiff peaks. Beat the cooled chocolate mixture until smooth. Gradually fold into the meringue, then whip one cup of heavy cream until soft peaks form. Fold in. Pour into baked chocolate shell. Chill. Before serving, top with the additional heavy cream, whipped, and garnish with grated semisweet chocolate. *Serves eight to ten.*

CHOCOLATE PIE SHELL

1 cup sifted flour
¼ teaspoon salt
⅓ cup shortening

2 tablespoons grated semisweet
 chocolate
2 tablespoons water

Sift flour and salt into a bowl. Cut in shortening until the size of small peas. Sprinkle chocolate over mixture, then water. Toss-stir with fork until dough clings together in a ball. Roll out and line a nine-inch pan. Bake at 400°F. (hot) about twelve minutes. *Makes one nine-inch shell.*

Cakes

*O*NE REASON cake is such an effective party dessert is that it can be as spectacular and artistic as your skill and imagination can make it. You can bake a cake in pans of different shapes, cut it up to look like various objects and decorate it as formally or as whimsically as you please. Cakes are made for show-off cooks.

First in this chapter comes a Calendar of Cakes—one for every month of the year, just to get your imagination rolling. Then you'll find ideas for using packaged mixes. Next are some really-worth-making cakes from scratch, including cheesecake. Following these are some helpful tips on frosting and decorating. And finally, there's the famous Seventeen Birthday Cake that involves a little of everything.

P.S. If you've never made a cake before, turn to page 20 for valuable tips on mixing and baking.

A CALENDAR OF CAKES

JANUARY—and snow-time almost everywhere. Celebrate with mugs of hot spiced tea or cocoa and one big snowball, or lots of little ones.

BIG SNOWBALL

You'll need two packages of angel cake mix. Follow package directions. Make one cake at a time. Bake each in an ungreased three-quart mixing bowl (metal or ovenproof glass) until dark golden brown, ten minutes longer than package directs. Cool upside down in bowl three hours. (Balance bowl on two cans: be sure only rim of bowl rests on cans.) Remove from bowl, set right side up. Trim top crusts from both cakes; cut a three-inch hole through center of each; lift out "holes" (use for a few small snowballs). Using a mix, make a fluffy white frosting. Frost cut surface of each cake; fill hole with Fortune Favors (below). Put the two together to form ball. Frost all over and sprinkle with flaked coconut.

SMALL SNOWBALLS

Bake a box of angel cake mix in a tube pan. Cool; remove from pan. Trim off top crust. Cut cake into three layers. Cut into rounds (about eighteen) with a two-inch cookie cutter, using just a little pressure and a rotary motion. Coat rounds with white frosting made from a box of mix; roll in flaked coconut (two packages), "packing" gently with hands into spheres. When frosting is hard, tuck a wrapped Fortune Favor (below) into a fold of ribbon; insert into ball with the point of a knife.

Fortune Favors

Buy tiny toy charms and write prophecies on small strips of paper to go with each. ("Life will be a song" for a trumpet; "You're going to meet a cut-up" for scissors, etc.) Tie fortune and charm to ribbon; let each guest draw one and be surprised! Use candy for favors if you prefer.

FEBRUARY—It's time for Valentine's Day. Make the most of it by making hearts by the dozens to give your beaux (and friends and family). These easy angel food hearts can be party decorations-and-dessert.

PLACE CARD CAKES

1 package (1 lb.) angel cake mix   6 bottles ruby red sugar crystals
2 packages fluffy white frosting mix

Make up angel cake as package directs. Divide batter in half and turn into two pans approximately eleven by seven by one and one-half inches. Bake as directed or until cakes test done. Cool upside down in pans, placing pans over supports of equal height so that air will circulate under cakes. When cakes are thoroughly cooled, remove from pans and cut into heart shapes. Use paper pattern measuring about four inches high, three and one-half inches at its widest point. Cut six hearts from each layer. Now make up frosting mix following package directions. Use to ice top and sides of each heart. Smooth frosting with a knife blade dipped in hot water. Then cover sides of each cake with ruby red sugar crystals. To write names on cakes, you can use red decorating frosting in tubes or cans, or tint remaining frosting red. Fit cake decorator with fine writing tip and fill container with tinted frosting. Write desired names on cake tops with frosting gently squeezed through tip. Decorate cakes with candy hearts, or make hearts with tinted frosting. *Makes twelve cakes.*

MARCH—Have a ball, Mardi Gras style, and serve this authentic New Orleans cake, richly fruited and spiced.

KING'S CAKE

1 box (1 lb. 4 oz.) spice cake mix
⅓ cup orange juice
2 teaspoons brandy extract
1 cup chopped glacéed fruit
½ cup currants
½ cup raisins

½ cup chopped pecans
¼ cup flour
Packaged white frosting mix
Red food coloring
Gumdrops for decoration

Preheat the oven to 350°F. (moderate). Place cake mix in a large mixing bowl and prepare according to package directions, but substitute the orange juice and brandy extract for one-third cup of water called for. In a separate bowl combine fruit and nuts with flour, then fold into cake batter. Pour the mixture into a greased and floured crown-shaped ring mold (two-quart size) and drop in the royal symbols (king's penny, queen's ring), one to each side of the cake. The pair finding these become monarchs of the ball. Mark on the mold which side to serve to the boys, which to the girls. (For a really big party, double the recipe; have one cake for girls, one for boys.) Bake cake at 350°F. (moderate) two to two and one-quarter hours, or until a toothpick inserted in the center comes out clean. Remove cake from oven, cool five minutes on rack, then invert. When cool, make up frosting mix and tint it pink. Decorate with gumdrops cut into jewel-like shapes and sizes. *Serves twelve.*

APRIL—Spring is on its way. Flowers will be everywhere, so put one made of cake on your table, with each slice cut and frosted in advance. And you can choose any color or flavor!

DAISY CAKE

1 package yellow cake mix
1 package (3 oz.) gelatine dessert, any flavor
¾ cup water
⅓ cup cooking oil
4 eggs

1 teaspoon grated lemon peel
½ teaspoon almond extract
1 can (3½ oz.) flaked coconut
1 package fluffy white frosting mix
Yellow food coloring

Empty cake mix into the large bowl of an electric mixer. Add the next six ingredients. Beat three minutes at medium speed until smooth and creamy. Fold in one cup of coconut; pour batter into a nine-inch square pan which has been lined with waxed paper. Bake at 350°F. (moderate) for sixty-five to seventy minutes or until cake top springs upward when touched lightly. Cool for ten minutes, then turn out of pan onto a wire rack. When thoroughly cooled, cut a two-and-one-half-inch circle from exact center. From each of the four quarters, cut three wedges, then round the wide ends of each to make petals (see diagram). Frost the daisy petals and round flower center in white. Tint a little coconut with yellow food coloring and sprinkle over frosted center. Arrange into daisy on large plate.

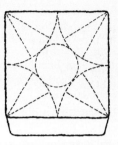

NOTE: Cake may also be baked in a nine-by-thirteen-inch pan if desired.

MAY—and time for showers. Make it a shower of flowers with the recipe below.

ROSY CUPCAKES

1 package (1 lb. 2 oz.) yellow cake mix	2 teaspoons rose water (buy it at the drugstore)

Prepare cake mix according to package directions. Add rose water to batter and stir to combine. Place two-inch paper baking cups in small cupcake pans. Pour about one tablespoon of batter into each paper cup to fill it halfway. (If there are unused sections, fill with a little water.) Bake at 375°F. (moderate) for twenty-five minutes. Now make beautiful frosting roses to top these cakes following directions on page 230.

To make a crepe-paper leaf holder for your cupcakes, cut a four-inch square of crepe paper. Fold in half, then in half again to make a smaller square. Hold square so uncut corner is at lower left. Make a mark one inch away from this corner on each adjoining side—at left edge and lower edge. Draw a curving line from each point to the upper right corner to make a leaf shape. Cut out; open to form four-leaf cupcake holder. Set cupcake in center. Pull four leaves up and glue to the paper baking cup surrounding cupcake. Top with a frosting rose.

JUNE—the month of farewell parties. Make yours a sumptuous gesture —like this cake, which can be made well in advance. It's a star in its own right, served with soft drinks and coffee, or a perfect ending for supper with the crowd.

COCO–MOCO REFRIGERATOR CAKE

1 package chiffon cake mix
1 lb. marshmallows
½ teaspoon salt
⅔ cup water
2 tablespoons instant coffee

1 package (12 oz.) semisweet
chocolate pieces
1 pint heavy cream
¼ teaspoon vanilla extract

Make up chiffon cake mix according to package directions. Bake in a ten-inch tube pan. Cool thoroughly, then slice cake horizontally into seven equal layers. Combine marshmallows, salt, water and instant coffee in a saucepan and stir, over moderate heat, until melted. Remove from heat and add semisweet chocolate pieces. Stir until chocolate is melted. Allow to cool to room temperature. Whip cream until stiff, and fold in vanilla. Fold flavored whipped cream into cooled chocolate mixture. Use to fill each layer, then to frost top and sides of restacked cake. Refrigerate several hours or overnight. *Makes plenty for twenty.*

Coco-Moco Loaf: For a ten-serving version of the cake, make up chiffon mix and pour into two nine-by-five-by-three-inch loaf pans. Bake at 350°F. (moderate) about forty-five minutes. Save one loaf for snacks; slice the other into seven equal layers. To fill and frost: divide recipe amounts above (for marshmallows, salt, etc.) in half.

JULY—How about a patriotic picnic? If you have it at home, you can completely assemble and decorate the cake before guests arrive. If you're traveling far, carry the cake in its pan, add decorations at dessert time.

FLAG CAKE

1 block (5 oz.) old-fashioned peanut
candy or 5 oz. of peanut brittle
1 cup seedless raisins

1 cup red, white and blue gumdrops
plus additional large ones for decoration
1 package (1 lb. 4 oz.) yellow cake mix

Roll the peanut candy into coarse crumbs (you should have about one cup). Measure raisins and gumdrops and set aside. Make up the cake mix following package directions. Pour half the batter into a greased and floured ten-inch round cake pan (a spring-form pan may be used). With a spatula, lightly mark the surface of the batter into nine even pie-shaped wedges. Then working clockwise, sprinkle surface of first wedge with one-third of the raisins, next wedge with one-third of the gumdrops, the next one with a third of the peanut candy crumbs. Repeat until all ingredients are used. Spoon remaining batter gently over entire surface of cake. Bake at 350°F. (moderate) about forty-five minutes, then invert. Decorations will have sunk and will now be on the surface. Place on a serving plate. Surround with large gumdrops (assorted colors) each bearing a tiny American flag. *Serves nine.*

AUGUST—It's carnival weather. Wouldn't it be fun to have the crowd in before or after you all go to the fair? Here's the cake—you plan the rest of the menu!

CARNIVAL CAKE

1 package (18 oz.) orange chiffon cake mix	1 tablespoon lemon juice 1 teaspoon grated orange peel, if
1 package regular vanilla pudding mix	desired
1 cup orange juice	½ cup heavy cream

Prepare orange chiffon cake using ingredients called for on package. Bake in a ten-inch tube pan until golden; cool thoroughly. Meantime, empty pudding mix into a saucepan and stir in orange juice, lemon juice and, if desired, orange peel. Cook slowly, stirring constantly, until mixture thickens and begins to boil. Remove from heat, cover and cool one hour. Now whip the cream until soft peaks form. Beat pudding with a wire whisk until fluffy. Fold in whipped cream. Cut cooled cake carefully into three even layers. Spread filling between the layers. Now you are ready for frosting.

Confetti Frosting

1 package (14 oz.) creamy white frosting mix	¼ cup hot orange juice 3 tablespoons lemon juice
2 tablespoons soft butter	½ lb. colored mint wafers

Empty frosting mix into small bowl of electric mixer. Add butter, orange juice and lemon juice. Beat at medium speed until well blended and smooth. Cover entire outside surface of cake with frosting. Cut mints into confetti-like pieces; scatter over top of cake. *Serves twelve.*

SEPTEMBER—Are you looking forward to the first big game? Celebrate or console your favorite football team and their dates with this one.

FIFTY-YARD SPICE CAKE

1 package spice cake mix	Yellow frosting (from a tube or
1 package (13 oz.) caramel fudge frosting mix	pressure can)

Prepare the cake mix following package directions and bake in two round pans, one ten-inch and one eight-inch. Cool. Cut layers in half to make four half-moons. Now make up the frosting mix. Turn layers bottom (flat side) up and frost. Stand the two larger half moons on a serving plate with cut surfaces down, rounded edge up, and press frosted sides together. Press one small half to each side. With a sharp knife, smooth off corners to trim cake to football shape (nice nibbling for the cook!). Brush off crumbs. Coat thinly with caramel frosting and let set about thirty minutes. Frost again. Make the football's laces with yellow frosting, then trim with paper pennants, yellow chrysanthemums.

OCTOBER—Time to invite all the ghosts, goblins and monsters you know to a Halloween party. The cake is a jack-o'-lantern with scary black eyes!

JACK-O'-LANTERN CAKE

1 package devil's food cake mix   Food coloring
1 package fluffy lemon frosting mix

Grease and flour two ovenproof mixing bowls (two quarts each) for pans. Prepare cake batter as package directs; divide equally into two bowls. Bake fifty to sixty minutes or until toothpick inserted in center comes out clean and dry. Cool cakes in bowls five minutes; turn out on wire racks, cool thoroughly. Trim off tops of cakes absolutely flat; put together to form ball. Save scraps trimmed from tops, and press together to form a neat pumpkin stem. Now make up packaged frosting. Tint one-half cup green and frost pumpkin stem. Tint rest of frosting to a pumpkin orange (use yellow and red food color) and frost cake. If desired, make indentations to simulate pumpkin shell, then place stem on top of cake. To make pumpkin face, cut holes in frosting so dark cake shows through. Use a sharp, pointed knife. Wipe knife clean after each cut and dip it in hot water to get a clean edge on the frosting. To serve, use a long knife and cut from top to bottom into crescents. *Serves ten.*

NOVEMBER—when spice tastes so good! Whether it's a party for Election Day or one around Thanksgiving time, fruitcake is in order. This one is so quick and easy that you'll want to bake it again in December to give to your friends.

TWELVE-MINUTE FRUITCAKE

1 can (9 oz.) crushed pineapple   ½ teaspoon baking soda
1 package (14 oz.) date-bar mix   2 eggs
1 cup raisins   1 cup (8 oz. jar) candied fruits and
2 tablespoons light molasses   peels
2 teaspoons apple pie spice   1 cup (4 oz. can) chopped walnuts

First preheat oven to 350°F. (moderate). Bring pineapple to a boil. When it's boiling, pour into a large bowl and add inner envelope of date filling from package of date-bar mix. Add raisins, molasses, spice and soda; stir. Now blend in the crumbly mixture from the date-bar package. Add eggs and beat vigorously about forty strokes, then beat in the candied fruit and nuts. Pour the batter into a greased and floured pan or fancy mold (choose one which holds six cups of liquid) and bake an hour and a quarter. Or use muffin tins (lined with paper baking cups) and reduce baking time to thirty minutes. If you use shallow cake pans, baking time will be about an hour. To check timing, insert a toothpick in center of cake—when it comes out clean, cake is done. Cool on a rack, then loosen from pan and turn out. Refrigerate to "ripen" at least twenty-four hours before serving. Store it in the refrigerator.

DECEMBER—and that special season! Because so much of Christmas entertaining is impromptu, a cake that has freeze-ability is especially helpful. And that's what appears below.

QUICK–MIX YULE LOGS

You can make our yule logs several days before a party or—if you have a freezer—three or four weeks ahead. To freeze, follow the directions below, then place the frosted and decorated logs on a cookie sheet and freeze solid (three to five hours). Remove from the freezer, wrap each log individually in plastic wrap or foil, seal the edges and return to the freezer. Thirty minutes before serving, unwrap logs and defrost. For half-frozen logs (mmm!), defrost only fifteen minutes before serving.

First make the yule log cakes:

1 package white cake mix	1 teaspoon rum extract
1 teaspoon nutmeg	Water called for on package
2 egg whites	

Preheat oven to 350°F. (moderate). Then prepare eleven well-scrubbed, six-ounce frozen-juice cans (save them ahead). Grease and flour insides, and set cans on a cookie sheet. Blend cake mix and nutmeg in large bowl of electric mixer. Add egg whites, rum extract, water; blend and beat as package directs. Fill each prepared can with scant half-cup of batter. Bake about twenty-two minutes, or until toothpick inserted in center comes out clean. To cool: leave cakes in cans five minutes after you take them from the oven, then slip a table knife inside cans to loosen the cakes and slide them onto a cake rack. When thoroughly cooled, use an apple corer to remove centers. Insert corer as far as it will go into cake, pull it out and insert again—repeating until cake center is neatly extracted (1). Now repeat at opposite end of the log to form a hollow tunnel.

Next, prepare Chocolate Bark Frosting:

1 package creamy white frosting mix	6 tablespoons softened butter
1 package creamy chocolate frosting mix	2 tablespoons instant coffee
	½ cup boiling water

Empty both packages of frosting mix into a large mixer bowl. Add butter, instant coffee and water and blend, then beat with mixer until frosting is smooth and creamy. Spoon some of the frosting into a cake

decorator. (Use only metal coupling at the end; do not use a decorating tip.) Squeeze frosting into the hollow center of each log—working first from one end, then from the other (2). Smooth off any excess frosting so ends are flat. Using a knife or spatula, coat outsides of logs with frosting. As you finish each, run a table fork through frosting to create bark effect. Let frosting set half an hour; then, using frosting-in-tubes, trim with Christmas symbols: candles, bells, etc. *Makes eleven logs, each a portion.*

NOTE: For extra glow, set your yule logs ablaze. Use sugar lumps saturated with lemon extract. Make three "boats" to hold the sugar: use about an eight-inch square of heavy-duty foil for each; fold square twice (to make four thicknesses) and shape it into a boat, pinching ends together to make it leakproof. Place the boats on a tray behind logs, put three or four soaked sugar lumps in each and set a match to the sugar. Add more sugar lumps as flames die down.

MORE CAKES FROM MIXES

Here's how to make a good thing better—add bananas and spice to pineapple upside-down cake, then top it with a spicy, creamy sauce.

For a holiday crowd: Quick-Mix Yule Logs (page 211) ▶

TWO-FRUIT UPSIDE-DOWN CAKE

¼ cup butter or margarine
½ cup brown sugar, firmly packed
1 can (No. 2) sliced pineapple

1 package (1 lb. 4 oz.) spice cake mix
2 ripe bananas
Whipped Spice Topping (below)

Choose a pan nine or ten inches square or thirteen by nine by two inches. Grease it well with butter or margarine. Dot the bottom with the one-fourth cup of butter. Sprinkle brown sugar over this. Drain pineapple, reserving the syrup, and arrange a layer of as many slices as the pan will hold. (If you like, fill centers with maraschino cherries.) Turn cake mix into bowl. Mash bananas until creamy. Place in a one-cup measure and fill to the one-cup mark with pineapple syrup. Use this for one cup of the liquid called for on package and mix according to directions. Gently pour over pineapple slices. Bake at 375°F. (moderate) or 350°F. (if you are using a glass pan) fifty-five to sixty minutes or until cake is well browned and pulling away from pan at edges. Let stand in pan ten minutes, loosen around edges with sharp knife, then invert over serving dish. Serve warm with Whipped Spice Topping, below. *Serves nine to twelve.*

Whipped Spice Topping

1 cup undiluted evaporated milk
2 tablespoons lemon juice

½ teaspoon cinnamon
2 tablespoons sugar

About an hour before cake is to be served, pour evaporated milk into an ice cube tray and place in freezing unit until soft ice crystals form around edge. At dessert time, turn this into a bowl and whip one to two minutes or until soft peaks form. Add lemon juice; whip until very stiff. Fold in cinnamon and sugar. Serve at once.

The added oatmeal transforms yellow cake mix into a more homespun dessert. And the topping adds just the right country-kitchen touch.

HONEY FLAKE CAKE

1 package yellow cake mix
1½ cups quick-cooking oatmeal, uncooked

1 cup honey
⅓ cup grated orange peel
6 tablespoons melted butter

Prepare cake mix according to package directions, adding oatmeal to dry ingredients. Pour batter into two greased eight-inch square or nine-inch round pans. Bake at 350°F. (moderate) for twenty-five to thirty minutes. Turn cakes out of baking pans and cool on separate plates, right

◀ *Party pretty, of course: Petite Doughnuts (page 255).*

side up. At serving time, combine melted butter, honey and orange peel in a saucepan. Heat till bubbly, pour over cakes and serve. *Serves twelve.*

At a record party, serve a cake which looks like a stack of records. Cream cheese makes it extra-rich.

PLATTER CAKE

1 package devil's food cake mix	¼ teaspoon salt
2 packages (3 oz. each) cream cheese	1 package (1 lb.) sifted confectioners'
3 tablespoons milk	sugar
1 teaspoon vanilla	For decoration: confectioners' sugar
1 cup quick chocolate drink mix	and semisweet chocolate pieces

For one cake: Prepare cake mix as package directs and bake in three eight-inch round layer pans. Baking time will be a little less so watch frequently for doneness. Cool on wire racks. Meantime, soften cream cheese at room temperature, then blend with milk and vanilla. (If available, an electric mixer is a big help.) Stir in chocolate mix and salt. Gradually add sugar, beating until consistency is smooth-spreading. Spread between cake layers, then on top and sides. To make record grooves you can use a fork, but if you want them to be perfectly even, buy a new coarse-tooth comb and wash well. Hold end of comb in center of cake and make a sweeping circle to form grooves. Groove side of cake to look like stacked records. Now trace and cut out a round of cardboard the same size as the cake pans. In the center, cut out a three-inch circle. Hold opening over center of cake and sprinkle confectioners' sugar through it to simulate label. Center with a "hole"—a semisweet chocolate piece.

When you feel like having an all-out dessert, there's no better way than cake topped with ice cream and sauce!

CHOCOLATE SUNDAE CAKE

2 tablespoons melted butter	1 teaspoon vanilla
1 can (5 oz.) slivered almonds	¼ teaspoon almond extract
2 tablespoons sugar	1 quart vanilla ice cream
1 package devil's food cake mix	1 cup prepared chocolate sauce

Melt butter in a nine-by-thirteen-by-two-inch baking pan. Sprinkle with almonds and sugar. Make up cake mix—adding vanilla and almond extract to liquid called for in package directions. Pour mix over almonds in pan.

Bake. Cool five minutes; invert onto a plate. Save half the cake for another meal. Cut remainder into six pieces. Before serving, top with ice cream, sauce. *Makes six Sundae Cakes.*

Some call this a cookie, some a cake. By any name, it tastes as sweet!

PILGRIM CAKE BARS

1 package (14 oz.) gingerbread mix
4 eggs, separated
1 cup apricot jam
⅔ cup water (approximately)

¼ teaspoon cream of tartar
½ cup sugar
½ cup chopped walnuts

Preheat oven to 325°F. (slow). Grease two eight-inch square pans and line with white paper. Empty mix into a large mixing bowl. Place egg yolks in a glass measuring cup and add enough water to make one-half cup. Add this to mixing bowl; stir to blend. Beat one-half minute in electric mixer on low speed or seventy-five strokes by hand. Add one-half cup water and beat one-half minute at low speed. Pour half of batter into each prepared pan and bake twenty minutes. While cakes are still warm, spread each with one-half cup of the jam. Beat egg whites until foamy; add cream of tartar and beat until soft peaks are formed when beaters are withdrawn. Gradually add sugar (two tablespoons at a time) and beat until meringue is shiny and firm peaks are formed. Spread half of meringue on each cake and sprinkle each with one-fourth cup chopped walnuts. Bake at 450°F. (very hot) until meringue is golden and walnuts are lightly toasted, about five minutes. Cut cakes into bars. *Makes twenty.*

Rich and moist, tart and sweet, and most appetizing to behold. Try it!

HEART OF GOLD SPONGECAKE

1 package angel cake mix
1 cup lukewarm water
2 tablespoons sugar

3 egg yolks, unbeaten
2 tablespoons grated orange peel
⅓ cup orange juice

Open package of angel cake mix. Pour water into a large mixing bowl and sprinkle egg-white mixture over it. Stir to moisten and beat to very stiff peaks. Then beat in sugar. Place flour mixture in a small bowl. Add egg yolks, orange peel and juice. Beat to blend, about one-half minute. Pour batter, one-fourth at a time, over egg whites and fold in. Bake in ungreased ten-inch tube pan at 375°F. (moderate) thirty-five to forty minutes. Cool upside down in pan. Then make up frosting (page 216) and top cake. Keep chilled. *Serves twelve.*

Orange-Cheese Frosting: Soften one package (3 oz.) cream cheese. Blend in one-fourth cup orange juice. Sift, then measure two and one-half cups confectioners' sugar, then resift gradually into cream cheese, mixing well. Blend in one teaspoon vanilla. Spoon frosting over top and sides of cake, making "driplets."

Refrigerator cakes may be made a day ahead; they really improve by waiting. Try different kinds—this one is deliciously fruit-filled.

RING–A–BERRY ANGEL CAKE

1 package angel cake mix	2 cups heavy cream
1 package (10 oz.) frozen raspberries, thawed	¾ cup confectioners' sugar
	2 teaspoons vanilla
1 package (12 oz.) frozen sliced peaches, thawed	1 teaspoon almond extract
	½ teaspoon salt
1 can (5 oz.) toasted slivered almonds	

Bake the angel cake in a ten-inch tube pan, cool and brush off crumbs. Then with a sharp knife and gentle sawing motion, cut a deep channel 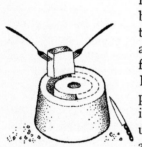 in top of cake: make the cuts one inch in from both edges and straight down *almost* to the bottom (see illustration). Pull the cut section out and crumble it. Combine with thawed, drained fruit (set aside a few attractive pieces of fruit for last-minute decoration) and the almonds. Now place the remaining ingredients in a large mixing bowl and beat with rotary or electric beater until the heavy cream stands in soft peaks. Set aside about two-thirds cup of whipped cream. Fold remainder into fruitcake mixture and spoon back into scooped-out cake. Top with the plain whipped cream and chill. Just before serving, dot the saved fruit around the top. *Serves ten.*

This do-ahead version of strawberry shortcake tastes cool and rich.

STRAWBERRY TALL CAKE

1 package angel food cake mix	1 envelope unflavored gelatine
2 packages (12 oz. each) frozen whole strawberries, thawed	2 cups heavy cream, divided
	Fresh strawberries for garnish, if desired

Prepare and bake cake mix as package directs, using tube pan. Tunnel out cake as follows. Insert paring knife (a serrated edge is best) straight down into top surface of cake about one-half inch from outer edge. Cut all around cake, keeping half-inch margin. Next cut around center hole, staying half-inch from edge. (Don't cut through bottom of cake.) Gently tear out center section, leaving just the outer shell of the cake. Tear removed cake into small pieces and set aside. Drain thawed strawberries, reserving syrup in saucepan. Sprinkle gelatine over syrup to soften. Bring to a boil over medium heat, stirring constantly. Remove from heat, cool, and then refrigerate until mixture mounds. Beat until light and fluffy, then beat one cup of the cream until soft peaks form. Fold gelatine mixture into cream, then fold in cake pieces and drained strawberries. Turn mixture into tunnel of cake. Whip remaining cream to frost cake top and sides. Garnish with strawberry slices. Refrigerate six hours or overnight. *Serves ten to twelve.*

Part of the luxury of this luxurious cake is that you can prepare it all in advance.

CHOCOLATE TORTE

1 package angel cake mix
3 cups heavy cream
6 tablespoons quick chocolate-drink
   powder

3 tablespoons confectioners' sugar
1½ cups walnut meats
1 cup orange marmalade
½ cup finely snipped raisins

Follow package directions to prepare angel cake mix and bake in a ten-inch tube pan at 375°F. (moderate) for thirty-five to forty-five minutes. Cool upside down at least two hours. Cut into four equal layers, using a sharp knife and sawing motion. To make the fillings and frosting: Combine in a large bowl the cream, drink powder and sugar. Beat with electric mixer or rotary beater until stiff and peaky. Chop enough walnuts fine to make one-half cup. Chop remainder coarsely and reserve for decoration. In a smaller bowl, combine one cup of this cream with finely chopped walnuts. In a third bowl, combine marmalade and raisins. Now place bottom layer of cake on a serving dish; frost cut surfaces with half the chocolate cream-nut mixture. Top with second cake layer. Spread all of the marmalade-raisin mixture on cut surface of this, then cover with the third layer. Frost this with the remaining chocolate cream-nut mixture; top with fourth cake layer. Now frost the entire cake with chocolate cream. Decorate sides with the coarsely chopped walnuts. Refrigerate until ready to use. *Serves twelve.*

THE CAKES YOU BUY

Even if you start with a fully baked cake, you can add the special touch of flavor and ingenuity that makes a dish *your* recipe. Examples follow.

Ready-baked poundcake may be used in some pretty, delicious ways.

PRETTY PETITS FOURS

Slice half a twelve-ounce pound cake into one-inch-thick slices. To form diamonds and triangles, cut slices in half lengthwise, then cut diagonally. Set pieces on a rack over waxed paper. Now make frosting: Combine in a saucepan two tablespoons shortening, one-fourth cup light corn syrup and three tablespoons water. Bring just to a boil over moderate heat, stirring constantly. Remove from heat; add one six-ounce package of semisweet chocolate pieces. Stir until smooth. Cool several minutes, then pour over cake tops. Return excess frosting from paper to double boiler; resoften over hot water and frost sides with a spatula. While frosting is still moist, decorate cake tops with silver shot, pink- or green-tinted coconut, snips of marshmallows. *Makes about two dozen little cakes.*

COCONUT TAFFY SLICES

Use six one-inch-thick slices of poundcake. Set slices on a cookie sheet. Mix three tablespoons butter or margarine with one-fourth cup brown sugar, two tablespoons light cream, a dash of salt and one-half teaspoon vanilla. Stir in one-half cup flaked coconut. Spread over cake slices. Bake at 375°F. (moderate) ten minutes or until lightly browned. Top with whipped cream if desired. *Serves six.*

Here's a homey and delectable combination.

ORANGE DATE LAYER CAKE

1 package regular vanilla pudding mix	1 package (7½ oz.) chopped dates
1½ cups orange juice	2 cake layers, 8 inches in diameter
4 teaspoons grated orange peel, divided	1 loaf-size package creamy white frosting mix

Place the pudding mix in a medium saucepan. Gradually stir in orange juice. Place over moderate heat. Stirring constantly, bring the mixture to a boil and cook until thickened. (Keep stirring all the while!) Remove from heat. Stir in three teaspoons of the orange peel and the chopped dates. Cool thoroughly. Then place one of the cake layers, rounded side down, on a serving platter. Cut some waxed paper into five-inch squares. Tuck these under the cake to protect the platter from any drips of frosting. Spread the cooled filling to within one-half inch of the edge of the top of the layer. Add second layer, rounded side up. Now make up frosting mix, following package directions, but mix in the remaining teaspoonful of grated orange peel. Use a rubber spatula to place dollops of frosting (about one-third cup at a time) on sides of cake. Spread smoothly all over sides with a second, flexible metal spatula. (Two spatulas help avoid getting crumbs from the cake back into the bowl of frosting.) When sides are frosted, use same procedure to frost the top smoothly. You can swirl it attractively, or try for perfect smoothness. Let frosted cake stand at least one hour before cutting. *Serves ten to twelve.*

ORANGE CREAM CAKE

Arrange four one-fourth-inch-thick slices of poundcake on the bottom of an ice cube tray. Peel and cut oranges to make one cup of sections (saving the juice) and add one-half cup sugar; mix well. Moisten cake with the reserved juice. Over cake arrange one banana, sliced. Beat one-half cup heavy cream until peaks form. Fold into orange mixture. Pour over bananas. Place in freezer at least three hours. Cut into rectangles. *Serves six.*

CAKES FROM SCRATCH

For most of the people, most of the time, cake mixes fill the bill, admirably. But for some of the people, some of the time, there's nothing like a homemade cake—moist and rich, and your own creation. Here are some suggestions, each with its own special quality.

The cake is white, the chips are chocolate, the pecans add distinction.

CHOCOLATE CHIP CAKE

2½ cups sifted cake flour
4¼ teaspoons baking powder
1 teaspoon salt
1½ cups sugar
⅔ cup shortening

1¼ cups milk
1 teaspoon vanilla
5 egg whites (⅔ cup), unbeaten
1 cup chopped pecans
⅓ cup semisweet chocolate pieces

Sift together flour, baking powder, salt and sugar into a mixing bowl. Add shortening, milk and vanilla. Beat for one and one-half minutes in electric mixer, scraping sides of bowl frequently, or 225 strokes by hand, until batter is well blended. Add egg whites and beat one minute more (150 strokes). Grease and flour a pan thirteen by nine by two inches, or ten inches square. Sprinkle chopped pecans evenly over bottom. Pour half the batter into pan, sprinkle on three tablespoons chocolate pieces and top with the last of the batter and remaining chocolate pieces. Bake at 350°F. (moderate) for thirty-five minutes. Frost with Glossy Chocolate Frosting (page 226). *Cut into sixteen squares.*

This is a poundcake rich, long-keeping and large enough for a crowd.

BOSTON PARTY CAKE

3 cups sifted all-purpose flour	2 cups sugar
3 teaspoons baking powder	4 eggs, separated
¼ teaspoon salt	1 cup milk
1 cup butter	1 teaspoon vanilla

Sift flour, baking powder and salt together. In a large mixing bowl, beat butter with a wooden spoon or electric mixer until fluffy and soft. Gradually add sugar and continue to beat until light and fluffy. Beat egg yolks lightly. Add to butter-sugar mixture and beat until well combined. Add dry ingredients alternately with milk, beating after each addition. Stir in vanilla. Beat egg whites until stiff but not dry. Gently fold into batter. Pour into greased nine-inch spring-form pan or tube pan. Bake at 350°F. (moderate) one hour and ten minutes for the spring-form, about fifty minutes for the tube pan. When done, top should spring back when lightly touched, and a cake tester inserted deeply should come out clean. Cool cake ten minutes in pan. Then loosen with spatula, remove pan and cool upside down. Frost with Boston Butter Cream (below). Reserve one-half cup to tint lightly with food coloring, if desired, and decorate cake. When frosting has set, wrap cake in transparent plastic film or foil. *Serves twenty generously.*

Boston Butter Cream

1 lb. confectioners' sugar	1½ teaspoons vanilla
½ cup butter (1 stick)	1 egg white

Sift confectioners' sugar. With electric mixer or with a wooden spoon, beat butter until fluffy. Slowly beat in about half the sugar. Add vanilla, then egg white, beaten until foamy. Add remainder of sugar gradually, beating until fluffy. Use to frost Boston Party Cake above.

A "priceless treasure" kind of chocolate cake, with applesauce to make it moist, spices and black walnuts to make it unique.

CHOCOLATE APPLESAUCE SURPRISE CAKE

2 cups less 2 tablespoons sifted cake flour	1½ cups sugar
¼ teaspoon salt	3 eggs, separated
½ teaspoon baking soda	1 teaspoon vanilla
1 teaspoon baking powder	½ cup cocoa
½ teaspoon cinnamon	⅓ cup boiling water
¼ teaspoon cloves	1 cup applesauce
¼ teaspoon allspice	½ cup buttermilk
6 tablespoons butter or margarine	⅔ cup raisins
	½ cup chopped black walnuts

Sift together the flour, salt, baking soda, baking powder and spices. Set aside. Cream butter. Gradually add sugar, beating until light and fluffy. Stir in lightly beaten egg yolks and vanilla. Combine the cocoa and boiling water and blend into egg-sugar mixture along with the applesauce. Add flour mixture alternately with buttermilk, beating well after each addition. Combine raisins and nuts, and coat lightly with flour. Fold into batter. Fold in stiffly beaten egg whites. Pour into a greased nine-by-nine-by-two-inch-pan. Bake at 350°F. (moderate) for forty-five minutes. Cool at least thirty minutes. Cut into squares. Serve warm or cold, with whipped cream.

Here's a cake with baked-on bottoming. Flip side: topping!

CARAMEL COCONUT UPSIDE–DOWN CAKE

Prepare the caramel sauce first:

1½ cups brown sugar, firmly packed	2 tablespoons water
½ cup butter or margarine	

Combine ingredients in a saucepan. Cook over low heat, stirring constantly until dissolved.

And now the cake:

1¼ cups sifted flour	¼ cup cooking oil
½ cup brown sugar, firmly packed	1 teaspoon vanilla
2 teaspoons baking powder	2 eggs
½ teaspoon salt	1 cup flaked coconut
⅓ cup milk	

Sift flour, brown sugar, baking powder and salt together through a strainer into a mixing bowl. Add milk, oil and vanilla. Beat thoroughly.

Add eggs one at a time. Beat well after each one is added. Grease a nine-inch ovenproof glass cake or pie plate. Sprinkle with coconut. Top this with the caramel sauce. Carefully distribute cake batter over all. Bake at 350°F. (moderate) forty minutes or until cake springs back when lightly touched in center. Cool ten minutes. Invert onto a serving plate. Best served warm with whipped cream or ice cream on top. *Serves eight.*

Chiffon cakes seem made for parties since they are firm enough for eating in the hand, yet tender and sweet.

LEMON CHIFFON CAKE WITH LEMON FILLING

2 cups sifted flour
1½ cups sugar
3 teaspoons baking powder
1 teaspoon salt
½ cup cooking oil
¾ cup water
1 tablespoon grated lemon peel

7 eggs, separated
½ teaspoon cream of tartar
1 package lemon pudding and
  pie filling mix
2 cups heavy cream
¼ cup confectioners' sugar

Sift flour, sugar, baking powder and salt together into a mixing bowl. Measure and combine the oil, water, lemon peel and egg yolks. Shape a little well in the flour mixture. Pour in oil-yolk mixture. Beat with a wooden spoon until smooth. To the egg whites in a large bowl, add cream of tartar. With an electric mixer at high speed or a rotary beater, beat until the whites form very stiff peaks when the beater is raised. (Turn the bowl, push whites toward beaters with a rubber scraper occasionally to ensure even whipping.) Gradually pour the egg yolk mixture over beaten whites, folding with a rubber scraper until just blended. When yolk mixture is thoroughly folded in, turn into an ungreased ten-inch tube pan. Bake at 325°F. (slow) for fifty-five minutes. Raise heat to 350°F. (moderate) and bake ten to fifteen minutes more. (The top of the cake should spring back when lightly touched.) Invert pan so top crust is air-cooled. Some pans have rests. If yours does not, balance the rim of pan on three objects of equal height. When cool, loosen around edges with a long knife or spatula. If necessary, bang bottom of pan on table. Brush off crumbs, place cake on a serving plate and you're ready to frost. Make up the lemon pudding mix as package directs and cool thirty minutes. Use as much as needed to frost top and sides of cake with a thin glaze. Let set about thirty minutes. Then pour heavy cream into a medium-size mixing bowl. Whip with an electric mixer or rotary beater until slightly thickened. Add confectioners' sugar, one tablespoon at a time, and continue to whip until soft peaks form. Refrost entire cake with the cream. Garnish with paper-thin lemon slices or a border of grated lemon peel. Chill until serving time. *Serves twelve.*

This lime chiffon cake tastes refreshing—just as you would expect!

LIME SPECIAL CAKE

2¼ cups sifted cake flour
1½ cups sugar
3 teaspoons baking powder
1 teaspoon salt
½ cup cooking oil
6 eggs, separated

¾ cup cold water
2 teaspoons lime juice
1 teaspoon grated lime peel
½ teaspoon cream of tartar
Lime Fluff Frosting (below)

Sift flour, sugar, baking powder and salt together into a mixing bowl. Make a well in the center; pour in oil, egg yolks, water, lime juice and peel. Beat with a wooden spoon until smooth. Add cream of tartar to the egg whites in a large bowl. Beat with rotary beater or electric mixer until very stiff. Pour egg yolk mixture gradually over egg whites, folding carefully until just blended. Pour right away into an ungreased ten-inch tube pan. Bake at 325°F. (slow) one hour and ten minutes or until top springs back when lightly touched. Turn pan upside down over a small funnel to cool thoroughly. Then loosen around edge, remove cake from pan and frost.

Lime Fluff Frosting

½ cup butter or margarine
¼ teaspoon salt
4 cups sifted confectioners' sugar,
   divided

3 tablespoons lime juice
2 teaspoons grated lime peel
Few drops of green food coloring

Cream butter with salt. Add one cup of the sifted confectioners' sugar and beat until creamy. Add alternately, creaming constantly, remaining sugar and the lime juice. When light and fluffy, beat in grated lime peel and food coloring. Makes a ten-inch cake; *serves fourteen.*

This is the sort of recipe which you can make your personal specialty. Not everyone thinks of making a cake roll, and really, it's so easy!

CHOCOLATE MINT ROLL

To make the roll:

½ cup sifted cake flour
1 teaspoon baking powder
¼ teaspoon salt
¼ cup cocoa

4 eggs
⅔ cup sugar
1 teaspoon vanilla
2 tablespoons water

Grease a fifteen-by-ten-inch jelly roll pan and line the bottom with waxed paper. Grease again. Preheat oven to 375°F. (moderate). Mix and sift onto a sheet of waxed paper the sifted cake flour, baking powder, salt and cocoa. Separate eggs—placing whites in a medium-size bowl, yolks in a larger bowl. Beat yolks with electric mixer or rotary beater until lemon yellow. Gradually beat in vanilla and half (one-third cup) of the sugar. Continue to beat until very thick; gradually beat in water. Wash and dry beater; beat whites until stiff but not dry. Gradually beat in remaining sugar, then gently fold whites into yolks with a rubber spatula or flat spoon. Sift dry ingredients—a quarter cup at a time—over egg mixture; fold in gently after each addition. Turn batter into pan, spreading evenly into corners. Bake fifteen minutes or until cake springs back when touched. First loosen cake from sides of pan with a sharp knife, then invert it onto a clean kitchen towel well dusted with confectioners' sugar. Gently pull off

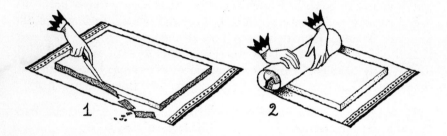

waxed paper from bottom of cake and trim off hard edges all around (1). Start at a narrow end and gently but firmly roll up cake and towel together (2). This step prevents cooled cake from cracking. Place roll, with loose end on bottom, on cake rack to cool thoroughly. When cool, unroll cake, then spread evenly with the Cream-Mint Filling (below). Roll up cake (without towel), starting at same end as before (3). Roll should be not so tight that filling squishes out nor so loose that there are gaps in roll. Place roll on a serving plate with small squares of waxed paper under edges to keep frosting off the platter. Spread with Chocolate Frosting, using spatula to make swirls. Remove paper squares; refrigerate till serving time.

Cream-Mint Filling

1 cup heavy cream	¼ cup crushed peppermint-flavored
2 tablespoons confectioners' sugar	hard candies or after-dinner mints

Whip cream and sugar until soft peaks form. Fold in crushed candy.

Chocolate Frosting

3 squares unsweetened chocolate	4 tablespoons hot coffee
3 tablespoons butter	2 cups sifted confectioners' sugar

Melt chocolate and butter over hot water. Add half the coffee to the sugar; stir until blended. Stir in chocolate-butter mixture. Add enough remaining coffee to make frosting easy to spread, stiff enough to swirl.

Variations

Here are five alternate fillings for your chocolate roll:

Ice-cream filling: Spread cake with one and one-half pints of soft ice cream. Roll up, frost; freeze until firm.

Almond-cream filling: Add one teaspoon almond extract and one-fourth cup toasted, finely chopped almonds to one cup heavy cream, whipped. Fold in lightly.

Coffee-cream filling: Add two teaspoons each of instant coffee and sugar to one cup of heavy cream, whipped.

Pistachio filling: Add one-half cup blanched, chopped pistachio nuts to one cup of heavy cream, whipped.

Brandy-cream filling: Whip one cup of heavy cream and fold in one teaspoonful artificial brandy flavoring.

Many boys feel that the ability to make a good cheesecake is the mark of a truly good cook. Start practicing!

CHEESECAKE

1 box (6 oz.) zwieback	3 eggs, beaten
½ cup (1 stick) butter, softened	2 teaspoons vanilla, divided
1 teaspoon cinnamon, divided	¼ teaspoon salt
4 packages (8 oz. each) softened cream cheese	1½ teaspoons grated lemon peel
1½ cups sugar, divided	1 pint commercial sour cream

Crush zwieback between sheets of waxed paper with a rolling pin to make crumbs. Combine with butter and a half-teaspoon of the cinnamon. Press into bottom and halfway up sides of a nine-inch spring-form pan. Beat cream cheese until fluffy. Gradually beat in one cup of the sugar. Add eggs, one teaspoon of the vanilla, salt, lemon peel. Beat until well combined; turn gently into pan. Bake at 350°F. (moderate) one hour and fifteen minutes or until a knife inserted into center of cake comes out clean. Meantime, combine sour cream with the remaining half-cup of sugar, one teaspoon vanilla and one-half teaspoon cinnamon. When cake is done, spread sour-cream mixture over top and bake another five minutes. Cool on a rack, remove sides of pan and place on serving dish. Refrigerate till party time. *Serves up to twelve.*

FUN WITH CAKE FROSTING

There are endless ways to frost every cake—different recipes, different designs. As you may have noted, many of our cake recipes suggest a specific frosting. (You'll find these grouped together in the index.) But to help you experiment, here is a whole collection of chocolate frostings, each delicious in its own different way. (You'll find instructions for fancy decorating beginning on page 228.)

GLOSSY CHOCOLATE FROSTING

¼ cup water
2 squares (1 oz. each) unsweetened chocolate
½ cup sugar

4 egg yolks
1 cup butter or margarine
1 teaspoon vanilla
2 cups sifted confectioners' sugar

Place water, chocolate and sugar in a saucepan and cook over low heat, stirring constantly until mixture is smooth. Remove from heat, stir a little into egg yolks, then add egg yolks to chocolate and beat thoroughly. Cool this mixture. Beat butter in a mixing bowl until fluffy; gradually beat in vanilla and confectioners' sugar. Blend well. If you wish, save some of this white frosting for decorating. Add the cool chocolate mixture and beat until thick in consistency. Spread evenly over top of thoroughly cooled cake. *Frosts a thirteen-by-nine-by-two-inch cake.*

COCOA–COFFEE FROSTING

1 lb. (3½ cups) sifted confectioners' sugar
⅓ cup cocoa
Dash of salt

1 teaspoon vanilla
3 tablespoons strong hot coffee
2 tablespoons melted butter
Chopped assorted nuts, if desired

Combine sugar, cocoa, salt and vanilla. Gradually add hot coffee, using enough to bring to spreading consistency. Blend in butter. Spread on top and sides of cake and sprinkle with chopped nuts. *Enough to frost outside of two nine-inch layers.*

CHOCOLATE VELVET

4 squares unsweetened chocolate
1 cup sifted confectioners' sugar
2 tablespoons hot water

2 eggs
6 tablespoons butter

Melt unsweetened chocolate in the top of a double boiler over hot water. Remove from heat, add sugar and hot water and stir until well blended. Add eggs, one at a time, beating until combined. *Enough to frost two eight- or nine-inch layers.*

QUICKIE CHOCOLATE FROSTING

Bake your cake in a large rectangular pan. While it's hot from the oven, sprinkle with two cups (12 oz. package) semisweet chocolate pieces. Bake at 350°F. (moderate) five minutes. Remove from oven; spread semisweet pieces with a spatula. Cool; then cut cake into squares and serve.

MOCHA FUDGE FROSTING

1 package (6 oz.) semisweet chocolate pieces	2 teaspoons instant coffee powder
1½ cups sifted confectioners' sugar	2 tablespoons soft shortening
	¼ cup hot milk

Melt the chocolate pieces over hot, not boiling, water. Stir in sugar, coffee, shortening and milk. Remove from heat and beat with a wooden spoon until smooth. *Use to frost twelve medium-size cupcakes.*

This frosting dries dull, smooth and white and is ideal if you intend to decorate further.

WHITE WHITE FROSTING

1 egg white	⅛ teaspoon salt
1 cup sifted confectioners' sugar	¾ teaspoon vanilla

Beat the egg white until stiff but not dry. Add the sugar, a little at a time, beating after each addition. Add salt and vanilla and continue to beat until mixture forms peaks when beater is lifted. *Enough to frost top of thirteen-by-nine-inch cake.*

You'll like this to serve with fruitcake, or perhaps with a rich coffeecake.

HARD SAUCE FROSTING

4 tablespoons butter or margarine	Dash of salt
1¼ cups sifted confectioners' sugar	1 teaspoon vanilla

Beat butter until soft, then gradually beat in remaining ingredients. *Tops one nine-inch cake.*

CAKE DECORATING

The pastry tubes you will need to make the decorations which follow are sold in sets—with a cloth pastry bag or metal decorator. Most good housewares departments carry such sets and a selection of tube sizes and

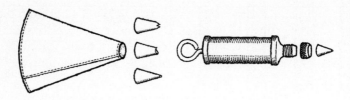

styles. If you are unable to find what you want locally, you may order from A. Thomsen & Co., 37-28 56th St., Woodside, New York 11377.

If you plan to use more than one color of frosting (recipe on page 230) to decorate a cake, it saves time to make disposable paper cones. To make: Fold a twelve-inch square of waxed paper in half to form a triangle. Holding long side of triangle horizontally in left hand, bring the lower left corner up to top point of triangle to form a half-cone (1). Hold points together with right thumb and index finger. Now take lower

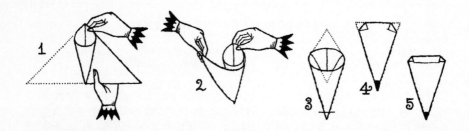

right corner in left hand and wrap it around half-cone so that the three points meet (2). Fold points down into cone (3) and scissor off end of cone, making opening large enough to hold tube. Insert tube and fill about two-thirds full of frosting. Pinch top of cone together; fold corners in toward middle (4); fold down to seal cone (5).

Lily of the Valley: Make on waxed paper, chill, then transfer to cake. (If you're a pro, make right on cake.) First, with a leaf tube (No. 65, 66 or 67) and green frosting squeeze out long ribbons for leaves (1). To add flowers, use petal tube (No. 59 or 79) and white frosting. Hold pastry bag so that tube opening is straight up and down (wider part at bottom). Force out frosting—without moving tube—till a little curl forms (2). When flowers are made (3), use plain tube (No. 1, 2 or 3) and yellow frosting to make center dots (4).

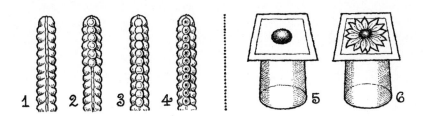

Daisy Flowers: For ease, make a little revolving pastry stand to shape daisies on. Invert a glass or jar. "Glue" a cardboard square on it with a bit of frosting. Then "glue" on a waxed paper square. Next, stiffen some white and yellow frosting by adding extra confectioners' sugar. Flatten a ball of yellow frosting with hands to form daisy center; put on waxed paper (5). Make petals with petal tube (No. 59 or 79), white frosting. Press tube on edge of ball to anchor petal, then pull up and toward you so petal arcs, reducing pressure on bag to form pointed end (6). Turn glass, make next petal. Repeat, making three rows, one on top of the other. Chill till firm on waxed paper, then remove from paper and transfer to cake.

Easy Roses: With wide part of rose tube (a No. 127 is best) resting on a jar with "pastry stand" (see Daisy Flowers above) press out icing—slowly

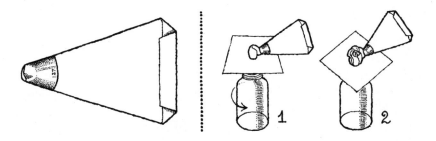

turning jar counterclockwise to form tight center petal (1). Repeat, pressing out second petal (about one-half inch long) against center petal. Continue, making petals slightly overlapping, until rose is desired size (2). Chill; place roses on cake.

Writing: With a toothpick, sketch greeting on the iced cake. Insert small-holed writing tube in paper cone; add frosting. Turn down flap and squeeze icing through tube, following outline. Or cut a very small hole in tip of paper cone and gently press out the frosting.

Leaves: Use leaf tube (No. 65, 66, or 67). Point tube down on sheet of waxed paper and as you force out icing (varying pressure to notch the leaf edge), pull cone back slowly. Pull cone up for point. Chill to harden; put on cake; add stem with writing tube.

MIX–EASY FLOWER FROSTING

¼ cup butter or margarine
½ cup vegetable shortening

1 package (12 oz.) creamy white
   frosting mix
Food colorings

Put butter in small bowl of electric mixer. Add shortening; blend at low speed. Slowly add frosting mix. Beat until combined. Tint as desired. Makes enough flowers to trim a two-layer cake (or one tier of the Seventeen Birthday Cake on page 231).

When you want really spectacular roses, as you might for the top of cupcakes at a bridal shower, this is the way to make them:

GIANT FROSTING ROSES

To tint frosting use red food coloring. Leave half of frosting (see page 231) in mixing bowl and tint it medium pink. Divide the rest into two parts; tint one pale pink, one a dark pink. You can make two types of roses. Give some dark centers, medium pink petals. For the others use medium pink centers, pale pink petals.

For decorating ease, make roses on waxed paper over a jar; turn jar as you press out petals. "Glue" paper to jar cap with frosting. Use rose tube No. 127 in pastry bag.

To make rose. First squeeze a round mound of frosting from your pastry bag for a base. Wrap frosting tightly around this, starting about halfway up, to form bud center (1). As you squeeze, hold tube straight (wide part of opening at the bottom); hold bag still, rotate jar. Finish bud with one row of four overlapping petals, each about one inch wide (2). Slant tube slightly outward for this, so petals will begin to "open." If you intend to shade your roses, you will need another color frosting now for outer petals. To save switching colors and pastry bags, make all rose centers first. As you finish each one, put it in the refrigerator to firm it.

To finish rose. Make as many rows of lighter, outer petals (with about four petals to a row) as you wish. Hold base of tube against rose, slant top decidedly outward now (3). Chill or freeze roses; attach to mix-made cupcakes with a little frosting an hour or so before the party (4).

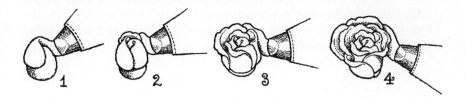

ROSE CREAM FROSTING

Combine three cups vegetable shortening and one pound butter at low speed on electric mixer (or use wooden spoon). Slowly add four pounds confectioners' sugar and four teaspoons almond extract. Beat until light and fluffy. Tint. *Yield: forty-eight roses.*

THE SEVENTEEN BIRTHDAY CAKE

For a real wingding of a birthday: Make all three tiers of the fabulous pink iced cake which follows, set roses frozen in ice cubes bobbing in the punch bowl, stack the hi-fi with slow, dreamy dance records—and have a ball. If you're planning a surprise party for someone in your crowd, you can divide up the cake-making among three or four friends and share the fun with fifty or more! The cake can serve up to seventy.

For smaller parties, make just the top two tiers (or the bottom tier only) and invite ten to twelve couples.

Start with a mix. We like white, but the varieties to choose are endless.

To make the cake:

6 packages white cake mix   12 egg whites
Water called for on package

To bake the cake, buy or borrow:

1 or 2 nine-by-thirteen-inch pans   2 eight-inch-square pans
2 seven-by-eleven-inch pans   10 wooden skewers

Prepare pans each time you use them: Grease bottom and sides, line bottom with waxed paper, grease again. We suggest you begin baking two days before party; wrap layers in foil or plastic film till you assemble the whole cake.

To make bottom tier: Prepare three packages of white cake mix, one at a time. Use egg whites only (no yolks). Bake each in a prepared nine-by-thirteen-inch pan. Cool five minutes, turn onto wire rack, peel off the paper and cool thoroughly.

To make top two tiers: Prepare one package of cake mix and divide batter equally into two prepared seven-by-eleven-inch pans. Bake and cool as above. Make up another package and divide equally into two prepared eight-by-eight-inch pans. Bake and cool. Make up last package of mix and divide between one seven-by-eleven-inch pan and one eight-by-eight-inch pan. Bake and cool.

Fill and frost the cake: First prepare your fillings (see page 233) and split your layers. We suggest you do this the day before your party. To split the layers, place toothpicks around the sides of each layer (halfway between top and bottom) to guide your cutting. Then halve each layer into two thin layers. Use a long meat knife or bread slicer—preferably with a serrated edge—and work slowly.

For the bottom tier: Split the three nine-by-thirteen-inch layers as described above. Now cut a piece of cardboard eight by twelve inches and set one split layer, cut side down, on this cardboard liner. Spread layer with a scant cup of filling. Cover with another layer, cut side down, and spread with a different filling. Continue (building up the corners with filling if layers tend to droop there) until sixth layer is in place, cut side down. Now trim browned edges, making sides absolutely perpendicular. Frost (see page 233) top and sides of tier; set aside.

For the middle tier: Stack the three seven-by-eleven-inch layers; cut one inch off the shorter side to make them seven by ten inches. Unstack and split layers as above. Set one split layer on a cardboard liner cut to six and one-half-by-nine inches. Fill and stack each layer just as you did for bottom tier, but use only one-half cup of filling per layer. Trim edges and frost.

For the top tier: Stack the three eight-inch layers and trim into oblongs of four and one-half by five and one-half inches. (Use the scraps to line a bowl of vanilla pudding for the family.) Unstack and split the layers as above. Use only five of these to make seventeen layers in all (that is, unless you're eighteen!). Set one layer on a four-by-five-inch cardboard liner, spread with one-third cup of filling. Continue stacking and filling just as you did for bottom and middle tiers. Trim the edges and frost top and sides.

To assemble cake: Whether you are making the top two tiers only or all three tiers, here is how to build up your cake. Slide your bottom tier to table's edge, carefully put hands under cardboard and lift tier to a pretty tray or a large piece of cardboard covered with foil. With a toothpick lightly trace on top of frosting the area in which your second tier will rest. (The area should be equally distant from sides, but only one inch from back edge of bottom tier.) To support the second tier, so that it will not rest too heavily on the cake below it, you will need long wooden skewers—often called hibachi skewers. To make the skewers exactly the right length, just insert one into the bottom tier inside the marked area, then remove it and break it off at frosting level. Break the rest the same size. Place five skewers and join to bottom tier with a little frosting. To add third tier: mark off area with toothpick, put remaining skewers inside marking, lift tier into place.

To decorate your cake: Use the picture facing page 244 as a guide. To make the lilies of the valley (which are a snap) see page 228. (For frosting daisies and roses, see page 229.) You may also use fresh stemless flowers to decorate your cake instead of frosting flowers. Or combine the two, using real posies with the lilies of the valley that you make. When your cake is decorated, add the candles—tall flower tapers cut to size and squiggled with frosting from a pastry tube till they seem vined with wee rosebuds and green leaves.

The fillings: You will need five packages (twelve ounces each) of creamy white frosting mix to fill the seventeen-layer cake. Prepare according to package directions, but make these changes.

When you make fruit fillings (you can use almost any flavor preserve), use only three tablespoons of water per package of frosting mix. Then, to each three-fourths cup of frosting, add one-fourth cup of jam. Cherry, damson plum, black or red raspberry jams make luscious fillings. Or use preserves like strawberry, peach, pineapple or thick blueberry. If color is pale, add food coloring. If filling is thin, add more frosting to stiffen it.

Tint small portions of frosting with food coloring to fill some layers; add a few drops of orange, lemon or mint flavoring extract; stir in chopped nuts or coconut.

Make mocha filling for one or two layers. For this, blend three tablespoons quick chocolate-drink powder, one-half teaspoon instant coffee and one cup frosting.

Swirl melted semisweet chocolate into some plain white frosting to create an easy marble filling for a layer or two.

The frosting on the cake is pale and pink. Start with three packages of creamy white frosting mix; prepare according to package directions, tint with red food coloring.

More Desserts and

Sweet Saucery

This chapter is full of really *special* desserts—from chocolate candy baskets to triple-flavored ice cream *bombes*. To select an appropriate one for your special meal, ask yourself these three guideline questions:

Does it suit my menu, and the time of year? Generally, if the main course has been heavy and rich, the dessert should be light and fruity. Although cold desserts may be served in summer or winter, hot desserts are most welcome in the chillier seasons.

Does it suit the tastes of my guests? Although you rarely know each person's individual food dislikes, you usually know what foods are not "in" with your crowd. And remember that boys tend to like heartier (let's face it, more high-caloried!) desserts than girls. Girls put more emphasis on prettiness and love interesting combinations.

Can I make the recipe fit my time plan? This depends on the rest of your menu and how the party will proceed. Some hostesses plan for a break between main course and dessert when guests can dance or chat—this leaves the cook time to arrange for something spectacular in the way of a sweet. But if you're having a dinner before a prom, for instance, and know that everyone will be rushed, it's best to choose a dessert that can be snatched from the refrigerator or freezer and served immediately.

PERFECT CUSTARD

Custard is an eat-for-beauty dessert, and what's more, delectable. Here are the basic instructions, plus some special flourishes for company.

Scald the milk or cream. Exception: evaporated milk, which can be used just as it comes from the can. To scald, heat gently over medium heat until a film begins to form on top and tiny bubbles appear around the edge. Remove from heat. Meanwhile, preheat oven to 325°F. (slow).

Beat the eggs with a wire whisk or fork till lemon colored and slightly frothy. For richness, replace one of the whole eggs called for with two yolks—see Company Custard below. Next beat in sugar, salt, flavoring.

Add milk to eggs gradually, beating with a whisk as you pour. It's important not to add the scalded milk all at once or the heat from the milk will cook the eggs too quickly.

Strain the custard into your baking dish—to remove tiny lumps of egg and ensure smoothness. Use a buttered ovenproof baking dish or small individual custard cups. For a party touch, line bottom of the baking dish with coconut, brown sugar or cut-up marshmallows. Sprinkle nutmeg on top if desired.

Set baking dish in a pan on the oven rack, then pour hot water into the pan—to within one inch of top of baking dish if possible. Custard made with nonhomogenized milk bakes in about one hour. Custard made with homogenized milk may take longer. Cup custard bakes quicker. Custard is done when a knife inserted deep into center comes out clean.

Cool the custard, then chill it. To unmold: run spatula all around dish, then invert onto serving plate. Serve with sauce or fruit.

Plain Custard

4 eggs
1 quart milk (or 2 tall cans evaporated milk)

½ cup sugar
½ teaspoon salt
1 teaspoon vanilla

Make as directed above. Sprinkle the top of the custard with nutmeg and bake one hour. Serve warm or chilled. *Makes six servings.*

Company Custard

4 eggs, (or for added richness, 3 eggs plus 2 yolks)
½ cup sugar
½ teaspoon salt
1 teaspoon vanilla

4 cups half-and-half (a milk-cream combination sold in pints)
1 cup flaked coconut
2 cups sliced strawberries, lightly sugared

Make as directed above. Line a one-and-one-half-quart casserole with coconut and gently pour in custard. Bake about one hour and fifteen minutes, then cool and chill. Unmold and top with strawberries. *Serves six.*

Maybe you'll feel wicked when you eat this, but it tastes so good you won't stop. Ideal for dinner parties.

CHOCOLATE MOUSSE PARFAIT

2 packages (6 oz. each) semisweet chocolate pieces
4 eggs, separated
⅔ cup water

½ cup light brown sugar, firmly packed
2 teaspoons vanilla
20 vanilla wafers, rolled into fine crumbs

Place chocolate in the top of a double boiler and melt over hot (not boiling) water. Remove from water. Combine egg yolks and water and beat slightly, then add melted chocolate slowly, beating rapidly. In a separate bowl and with a clean beater, beat the egg whites until stiff but not dry. Beat in brown sugar gradually until stiff, glossy and peaked. Gently fold in chocolate mixture and vanilla. Chill until slightly set. In eight parfait glasses, put alternate layers of chocolate mixture and cookie crumbs, ending with chocolate. Refrigerate until serving time, then top each with puffs of whipped cream and chocolate shavings. *Serves eight.*

This dessert always seems to us like a little miracle. See if you agree.

LEMON CAKE–TOP PUDDING

3 tablespoons butter or margarine
⅔ cup sugar
2 eggs, separated
2 tablespoons lemon juice

1 teaspoon grated lemon peel
2 tablespoons flour
1 cup milk

Beat the butter until fluffy, then gradually beat in sugar. Beat the yolks of the eggs into this mixture along with lemon juice and peel. Fold in flour. Gradually stir in milk. Beat the egg whites until stiff but not dry and fold thoroughly into the yolk mixture. Pour into a two-quart casserole. Set in a pan of hot water. Bake at 375°F. (moderate) thirty to forty minutes until puffed, golden and quite firm on top. Good hot or cold. *Serves four to six.*

Here's a quick and easy dessert with an exciting taste.

PECAN–O

1 box vanilla instant pudding
1 cup dark corn syrup
¾ cup evaporated milk

1 egg, beaten
1 cup chopped pecans

Combine vanilla pudding with syrup, then stir in evaporated milk and egg. Add pecans and turn into five custard cups. Bake at 375°F. (moderate) forty minutes. *Serve, warm or cold, to five.*

Lovely, smooth, and almond-flavored. Rich, of course, but—who cares!

ALMOND CREAM

1 cup sugar	2 tablespoons butter
2 tablespoons cornstarch	½ cup blanched shredded almonds
2 cups milk	1 cup heavy cream
2 whole eggs or 7 egg yolks, well beaten	½ teaspoon almond extract

In a saucepan, mix sugar with cornstarch, then slowly stir in one-half cup milk. Stir in remaining milk and bring to a boil, stirring constantly. Place eggs, butter and almonds in a bowl and slowly stir in about half the hot mixture. Return to saucepan and stir over low heat until thickened. Refrigerate until cold. Whip cream until it forms soft peaks, then fold in with almond extract. Keep cold until ready to serve. Enough to top generously one ten-inch chocolate angel food cake or two nine-inch layers, or makes *eight servings as a pudding.*

MOLDED DESSERTS

Molded desserts are a great gift to the cook who would serve a thing of beauty—made well in advance. If you're not sure how to go about it, consult the general directions on page 155.

Not high in calories, but picture-pretty. Make this one often.

PINEAPPLE PERFECT

1 can (No. 2) crushed pineapple or pineapple tidbits	5 tablespoons sugar, divided
2 tablespoons lemon juice	½ cup ice cold water
½ teaspoon grated lemon peel	1 teaspoon vanilla
1 envelope unflavored gelatine	½ cup nonfat dry milk powder

Drain the pineapple, saving syrup. Place the syrup in a two-cup measure and add enough water to make one and one-half cups. Pour into a saucepan, add lemon juice and peel and bring to a boil. Meanwhile, combine gelatine with two tablespoons of the sugar. Pour boiling liquid over gelatine and stir until dissolved. Refrigerate until as thick as unbeaten egg whites. Meanwhile, place ice water and vanilla in a small bowl (preferably of an electric mixer). Sprinkle dry milk over surface and beat until peaks form, about ten minutes. Gradually add remaining three tablespoons of the sugar, beating constantly. Continue beating until mixture is thick enough to hold soft peaks (about five minutes). Beat gelatine mixture until foamy, then pour into whipped dry-milk mixture and fold in, along with pineapple. Pour into a five-cup mold and chill until set, about three hours. Unmold and garnish with flower petals made of slivered maraschino cherries or gumdrops in gay colors. *Serves eight.*

Jellied fruit desserts can be works of art if you exercise "TLC" (tender, loving care). Here's the way:

JELLIED FRUIT SPECTACULAR

4 cups pineapple-grapefruit drink
2 tablespoons grenadine syrup
2 teaspoons rum extract
2 envelopes unflavored gelatine
1 can (14 oz.) pineapple chunks, drained

11 extra-large strawberries, washed and hulled
2 large navel oranges, peeled and sliced
1 cup drained canned sliced peaches

Place pineapple-grapefruit drink, grenadine and rum flavoring in a saucepan and sprinkle gelatine over it to soften. Stir and cook over low heat until gelatine is dissolved. Choose a fancy two-quart mold. Into it pour one-eighth inch gelatine mixture. Chill until set but not firm; meantime prepare the fruit. Select a few pieces of each kind of fruit to arrange in a pretty pattern which will enhance the top design of your mold. Add another thin layer of gelatine mixture to anchor fruit, and chill again. (This time, it won't take so long to "almost set.") Repeat until all fruit and gelatine are used. Chill overnight. *Serves ten.*

Cool and fruity, pink and delectable!

MANDARIN CHERRY MOLD

1 tall can (1⅔ cups) evaporated milk
1 can (No. 2½) fruit cocktail
1 jar (8 oz.) maraschino cherries
1 cup marshmallows
2 envelopes unflavored gelatine
Red food coloring

¼ teaspoon almond extract
2 tablespoons lemon juice
½ teaspoon salt
⅓ cup chopped almonds, toasted
Cherries and whipped cream for garnish

Chill evaporated milk thoroughly in the refrigerator. Drain fruit cocktail and cherries separately, saving syrups. Chop the cherries fine. Into the top of a double boiler, measure one cup of fruit cocktail syrup and one-half cup maraschino syrup. Add marshmallows and gelatine. Cook over boiling water, stirring occasionally until marshmallows melt. Then cool until mixture begins to jell. To the chilled evaporated milk in a cold bowl, add a few drops of red food coloring, the almond extract, lemon juice and salt. Beat until stiff. With same beater, beat the jellying mixture until fluffy. Fold both mixtures together along with drained fruit cocktail, chopped cherries and toasted almonds. Turn into a casserole or loaf pan holding seven cups. Chill until firm (at least three hours). Unmold and garnish with slivers of cherries and whipped cream. *Serves twelve.*

A richer pineapple mold for un-calorie-conscious days. The snowball shape can be best made by using—not a mold—but a mixing bowl!

PINEAPPLE SNOWBALL

1 envelope unflavored gelatine
⅛ teaspoon salt
½ cup sugar, divided
2 eggs, separated
1¼ cups milk

1 can (9 oz.) crushed pineapple, drained
¼ cup chopped maraschino cherries
1 cup heavy cream, whipped

Mix gelatine, salt and one-fourth cup of the sugar in a large saucepan. Beat together egg yolks and milk; stir into gelatine mixture. Place over low heat and stir constantly until the gelatine is dissolved and the mixture has thickened slightly. Remove from heat; stir in crushed pineapple and maraschino cherries. Chill until mixture is slightly thicker than unbeaten egg white. Lightly beat with whisk or rotary beater. Beat egg whites until stiff, but not dry. Gradually add remaining one-fourth cup sugar and beat until very stiff. Fold into gelatine mixture; whip cream until soft peaks form. Fold half of it into gelatine. Refrigerate remainder. Turn pineapple mixture into a five-cup mold; chill until firm. One hour before serving, unmold on a platter. Place remaining whipped cream in pastry tube fitted with rosette point. Cover entire surface of snowball with tiny rosettes. Garnish with bits of chopped cherries for color. Return to refrigerator until dessert time. *Serves twelve.*

A kiss for every strawberry heart! That's what you get when you serve our Heart of Cream. It's the lightest, prettiest, easiest party dessert—a streamlined version of the French cheesecake called *cœur à la crème.* Make it today and freeze it until party time if you like, or make it the morning of your party and chill till serving time.

HEART OF CREAM

2 envelopes unflavored gelatine
½ cup cold water
1 pint cottage cheese, pressed through a fine sieve
2 cartons (4 oz. each) whipped cream cheese
½ teaspoon salt
1 cup sugar
¼ cup lemon juice

1 teaspoon grated lemon peel
1 teaspoon vanilla
1 cup heavy cream
Honey Crumb Crust (below)
1 pint fresh strawberries or 1 package (1 lb.) frozen whole strawberries, drained
Silver dragées

In the top of a double boiler (off the heat) sprinkle gelatine over water and let stand five minutes. Then place over boiling water and stir until dissolved. Combine sieved cottage cheese, cream cheese, salt, sugar, lemon juice, peel and vanilla in a large bowl. Stir in dissolved gelatine. Whip cream until soft peaks form. Gently fold in. Carefully pour mixture into a nine-inch heart-shaped layer pan. (Or use a round pan; later fake a heart shape with your strawberry garnish.) Sprinkle Honey Crumb Crust evenly over mixture in pan. Refrigerate four hours or until set. If you make cake ahead, store in freezer; put in refrigerator the morning of party. At serving time dip mold briefly in hot water. With a sharp knife, loosen the very top edge of mold, then in one spot run knife right to the bottom to break the vacuum. Put serving plate over mold and invert both together. To garnish: Wash, core and cut strawberries in half, and trim to heart shape. Use to decorate cake as shown; add dragées. Keep cold. *Serves ten.*

Honey Crumb Crust

½ cup honey graham cracker crumbs
2 tablespoons melted butter or margarine

1 tablespoon sugar
¼ teaspoon cinnamon
¼ teaspoon nutmeg

Place cracker crumbs in a small bowl. Add remaining ingredients; stir until well blended. Spread evenly over top of cheese mixture.

NOTE: To vary Heart of Cream, top your cake with a bright, shiny fruit glaze for a change the second or third time you make this dessert.

Strawberry Glaze

1 package (16 oz.) frozen whole strawberries

2 tablespoons cornstarch
2 or 3 drops red food coloring

Thaw frozen strawberries at room temperature. Then drain thoroughly, reserving syrup. Add water if necessary to make one cup of liquid. Measure cornstarch into a saucepan and gradually stir reserved liquid into cornstarch. Stir in the food coloring. Bring mixture to a boil, stirring constantly. Continue to cook, stirring until mixture is thick and clear. Arrange strawberries in bottom of pan, pour cornstarch mixture over berries; cool. Gently pour cheese mixture into pan. Sprinkle with crumb mixture; chill till firm. Unmold.

Cherry Glaze

1 can (16 oz.) dessert cherries
2 tablespoons cornstarch

2 or 3 drops red food coloring

Drain dessert cherries and reserve liquid. Add enough water to make one cup. Measure cornstarch into saucepan. (If you use unsweetened water-pack cherries, stir into the cornstarch one-fourth cup sugar.) Add liquid to cornstarch and stir. Bring to a boil, stirring constantly. Continue to cook, stirring, until mixture is thick and clear. Arrange cherries in bottom of pan. Pour cornstarch mixture over them; cool. Add filling, then crumbs. Chill.

Pineapple Glaze

Prepare pineapple glaze the same way as you would the glazes above, using one can (20 oz.) crushed pineapple in place of strawberries, yellow food coloring in place of red.

Sometime try this in a melon mold, garnished with whipped cream and whole berries.

STRAWBERRY GELATINE TORTE

1 cup boiling water
1 package strawberry-flavored gelatine
4 eggs, separated
½ cup sugar
1 cup heavy cream

1 pint strawberries, washed, picked over and mashed, or 1 package (10 oz.) frozen strawberries, thawed
6 oz. vanilla wafers, rolled into fine crumbs

Stir boiling water into gelatine until completely dissolved. Set in the refrigerator to cool until it's like unbeaten egg white. Beat egg yolks until light and lemon colored. Mix these in the top of a double boiler with sugar. Cook over hot (not boiling) water until light in color and thick, stirring constantly. Cool. Place egg whites in a large mixing bowl and beat until shiny with stiff peaks. Then in a separate bowl, beat cream until soft peaks form. Fold gelatine, yolk mixture and cream into egg whites. Fold in strawberries. Line a nine-by-twelve-inch glass baking dish with half the wafer crumbs. Pour mixture over crumbs, top with remaining crumbs. Chill at least two hours. Cut in squares. *Serves ten.*

This recipe is not so high in calories as baked cheesecake, but it's very high on rich flavor.

PINEAPPLE CHIFFON CHEESE TORTE

1½ cups finely rolled zwieback crumbs	¼ cup sugar
	½ cup softened butter

Mix crumbs, sugar and butter with hands until well combined. Set aside one-third cup of crumbs. Press remainder in thin layer against bottom and sides of nine-inch spring-form pan. A spring-form pan has a ringlike side which clamps on and off—and keeps the cake pretty and intact. If you haven't a spring-form pan, use a two-quart casserole or pudding pan and serve from it.

For the filling, step one:

2 envelopes unflavored gelatine	2 cups creamed cottage cheese, sieved
½ cup orange juice	
2 egg yolks	1 cup (9 oz. can) crushed pineapple with syrup
¼ cup sugar	
1 teaspoon salt	3 tablespoons lemon juice
½ cup milk	1 tablespoon grated lemon peel

Sprinkle gelatine over orange juice to soften. In a saucepan, beat egg yolks, sugar, salt and milk together. Cook over moderate heat, stirring every minute (a wire whisk is ideal) until custard thickens. Remove from heat. Add softened gelatine and stir until dissolved. Cool the mixture. Add cottage cheese, crushed pineapple with syrup, lemon juice and peel.

For the filling, step two:

2 egg whites	1 cup heavy cream
¼ cup sugar	

Beat egg whites until foamy, add sugar gradually, continuing to beat until mixture holds points when beater is withdrawn. Fold into cottage-cheese mixture. Beat cream until soft peaks form and fold into mixture. Pour into crust. Sprinkle reserved one-third cup of buttered crumbs over top. Chill until set. When ready to serve, unclamp, remove sides of spring-form pan. Place cake (on bottom of pan) on a serving platter and *cut into ten to twelve rich servings.*

This is like biting into pink clouds, all soft and cold and airy, with a thick whipped-cream richness you can stand your spoon up in. Make it with fresh or frozen fruit—make it today!

THE FROU-FROU

First pick your favorite fruit:

Strawberries: You will need two pints. Remove caps and rinse berries thoroughly under running water.

Raspberries: Pick over two pints of berries; remove any bruised fruit. Place in strainer and wash.

Peaches: Peel and slice two pounds. Sprinkle with lemon juice to prevent the fruit from browning.

If you use fresh fruit: Place in a bowl, add one-half cup of sugar and mash with a fork. Let stand at room temperature for two hours before using.

If you use frozen fruit: Thaw two packages (ten ounces each) at room temperature for three hours. Mash the fruit before using, but do not add sugar.

To make the Frou-Frou you will need:

Sugared, mashed fruit (amounts above)	**⅛ teaspoon salt**
1 envelope unflavored gelatine	**¼ teaspoon almond extract**
4 eggs, separated	**½ cup sugar**
1 tablespoon lemon juice	**1 cup heavy cream**

Place fruit in a strainer over a bowl; let syrup drain off. Pour three-fourths cup syrup into top of a double boiler. Sprinkle gelatine over syrup. Beat egg yolks lightly; stir into gelatine mixture; place over simmering water. Cook, stirring constantly until gelatine is dissolved, about five minutes. Remove from heat, stir in lemon juice, salt, almond extract. Cool; refrigerate till thick as unbeaten egg white. Press fruit through a fine sieve, combining it with any remaining juice. Beat egg whites until they stand in peaks. Add sugar gradually, beating until mixture is stiff and shiny. Beat gelatine mixture with a rotary beater until smooth; add the sieved fruit and beat until blended. Fold gelatine mixture carefully into egg-white mixture. With a clean beater, whip the cream until soft peaks form. Gently fold into fruit mixture. Turn into a one-and-one-half-quart serving dish or six medium-size glasses or eight small glasses. If you like, garnish the glasses with sliced fruit before filling. Chill in refrigerator until mixture is set. Garnish with a topping of additional fruit if desired.

Frou-Frou Soufflé: You will need a soufflé dish with straight sides. Add a paper collar to the sides: use a piece of waxed paper (be sure it's long enough to go around dish and overlap a bit where ends meet). Fold paper in half to make a long strip and tie it around outside of dish, leaving an inch-and-a-half collar extending up beyond rim of dish. Fill with Frou-Frou mixture to top of collar. Chill. Peel off collar at serving time. Frou-Frou puffs above dish.

Frozen Frou-Frou: When you freeze it, Frou-Frou becomes like ice cream, only better. Use freezerproof containers only. To store, after mixture is frozen firm, wrap in plastic film, and tape to seal.

FROZEN DESSERTS

This is so good you'll feel guilty! But all those dairy products mean it's one more way (a heavenly one) to get your milk!

HEAVEN ON ICE

¼ cup butter
1 cup slivered blanched almonds
1 cup graham cracker crumbs
3 eggs, separated
1 cup heavy cream
½ cup sugar

1 package (3 oz.) cream cheese, softened
½ cup commercial sour cream
2 teaspoons grated lemon peel
¼ cup lemon juice

To make the crust: Melt the butter in a small saucepan. Add the almonds and graham-cracker crumbs; mix well and let cool. To make the sherbet: Beat egg whites until stiff; set aside. Whip cream until soft peaks form; set aside. Beat egg yolks until thick and lemon colored. Gradually beat in sugar. Add the cream cheese and sour cream, stir until blended, then stir in the lemon peel and juice. Now fold in whipped cream and egg whites.

To assemble: Spread half the crumb mixture in the bottom of a nine-by-nine-by-two-inch pan (or a double ice cube tray). Ease sherbet over this, then sprinkle rest of crumb mixture over all. Place in freezing section. Freeze overnight at regular setting of refrigerator or four hours at coldest setting. If covered with foil, sherbet will keep many days without forming ice crystals. If they appear, mellow at room temperature ten minutes. *Serves eight.*

On your day, the Seventeen *Birthday Cake (page 231)* ▶

Next time you have a pizza party, you might top it off with a dessert inspired by Italian-American restaurants.

SPUMONI AMERICANO

3 pints regular or "soft" vanilla ice cream
3 tablespoons chopped walnuts
¼ cup finely chopped glacéed fruit

½ square (½ oz.) unsweetened chocolate, grated
Few drops of green food coloring
¼ cup flaked coconut
Few drops of red food coloring

To begin, have ice cream slightly softened and all other ingredients ready. Place one pint of ice cream in a bowl and fold in walnuts. Turn into a one-and-one-half-quart decorated mold. With back of spoon, spread mixture so it is evenly distributed over bottom and up sides of mold. Return to freezer. Into the second pint, fold the glacéed fruit, the grated chocolate and enough food coloring to make a delicate green. Smooth this over bottom and sides of first layer, leaving center hollow. Return to freezer. Into the third pint fold coconut and enough food coloring to make it medium pink. Fill the hollow with this mixture. Cover mold and set in freezer till very hard. At serving time, unmold and slice. *Serves eight.*

For the discriminating guest—and for fun, too—serve ice cream in a crinkly candy cup.

CHOCO–MINT ICE CREAM BASKETS

1 package (6 oz.) semisweet chocolate pieces
2 teaspoons shortening
1 or 2 drops peppermint flavoring

1 pint vanilla ice cream
Chocolate shavings or chopped walnuts for garnish

Place chocolate and shortening in the top of a double boiler over hot (not boiling) water and cook until melted. Remove from heat, add peppermint flavoring and stir well to combine. Have ready six holders, each made from two paper baking cups (double-thick to keep sides from collapsing). Pour equal amounts of the melted chocolate into the six cups and swirl each until sides and bottom are coated with a thick layer. Store in freezer on a sheet of aluminum foil until chocolate has hardened. Working with one at a time and with a light hand, peel the paper away from the chocolate shells and return to freezer. Just before serving, fill each cup with a small scoop of vanilla ice cream and top with chocolate shavings or chopped nuts. *Serve at once to six.*

◀ *On Valentine's Day, serve Heart of Cream (page 240) and enjoy the compliments.*

This made-a-day-ahead dessert is a delight to your guests and a pleasure to their hostess.

SHERBET COCONUT BALLS

1 pint lemon sherbet	1 pint raspberry sherbet
1 pint lime sherbet	1 can flaked coconut
1 pint orange sherbet	

Let sherbets warm to a consistency easy for scooping. Spread coconut in a pie plate. Make small neat scoops of sherbet and roll each in coconut, then hurry it into the freezer. Work fast to prevent melting. Count on four small scoops for each guest. When they have refrozen firm, arrange them attractively in a freezerproof serving dish (silver is ideal) and store in freezer until party time. Guests can help themselves to desired flavors. *Serves eight.*

This tastes so marvelous you'll think you're eating in Paris. Your all-American home freezer makes it possible.

FROSTY CHOCOLATE RUSSE

8 ladyfingers	⅔ cup light brown sugar
6 tablespoons water	½ teaspoon vanilla
3 tablespoons rum extract	Dash of salt
1 package (6 oz.) semisweet chocolate pieces	1 egg yolk
	¾ cup heavy cream, whipped
1 package (3 oz.) cream cheese, softened	

One hour before starting, set freezer or ice cube compartment at coldest setting. Split ladyfingers and cut in half crosswise. Line a one-quart freezerproof serving dish with ladyfinger sections, cut side up. Combine water and rum extract and brush it over ladyfingers. Melt the chocolate pieces over hot, not boiling, water. Remove from water; cool. Blend cream cheese, sugar, vanilla and salt thoroughly with a wooden spoon. Beat in egg yolk; stir in cooled chocolate; fold in whipped cream. Spoon into serving dish. Freeze. Thaw ten to fifteen minutes before serving. *Serves six.*

Parties are often made memorable by the unexpected. Ice cream sandwiches are old hat—but not the giant size!

GIANT ICE CREAM SANDWICH

Make up a box of brownie mix; bake in a jelly roll pan twenty minutes at 350°F. (moderate). Cool; halve crosswise. Stand a half-gallon brick of ice cream on end, halve to make two thin slices; put slices between brownie layers. Wrap in plastic film, freeze. Thaw ten minutes. Slice and *serve to eight.*

This delicious ice cream is particularly good after an oriental main dish.

GINGER ICE CREAM

1 quart vanilla ice cream	8 gingersnaps, rolled into fine crumbs
2 teaspoons powdered ginger	

Soften ice cream slightly in a bowl and stir in ginger with a wooden spoon until blended. Return to container and store in freezer until hard. Place a large scoop of ice cream in each serving dish and dust tops with gingersnap crumbs. *Serves eight amply.*

When chocolate is frozen, wondrous things happen. Keep these pop sticks in your freezer, ready for the boy who drops in casually. Or choose this recipe for a dessert when you're barbecuing outdoors.

CHOCOLATE POP STICKS

⅔ cup water	2 cups heavy cream
1 envelope unflavored gelatine	2 teaspoons vanilla
1 lb. marshmallows	16 frozen pop sticks (available at
½ teaspoon salt	dime store)
2 packages (6 oz. each) semisweet chocolate pieces	

One hour before starting, turn your freezer or ice cube compartment to the coldest setting. Mix water and gelatine in a large saucepan. Add marshmallows and salt; melt over medium heat, stirring constantly. When combined, remove from heat; add chocolate pieces and stir briskly until chocolate is completely melted. Let cool fifteen minutes. Beat cream until it stands in soft peaks; add vanilla, fold into chocolate mixture. Tear off two strips of foil, each nine inches wide. Fit each into a nine-inch square pan, letting ends extend. Pour half of the mixture into each pan. Place pans on a freezing surface in freezer and freeze until firm (four hours or overnight). When ready to form pops, bring a saucepan of water to a full boil. Remove one pan from freezer. Turn out frozen mixture on a piece of foil. Peel off foil liner (1). Cut chocolate block in half. Mark one half (do not cut through) into eight pops. Now dip eight pop sticks in the boiling water and press one down the center of each pop (2). Dip a pastry brush in boiling water and brush the top surfaces of both halves of the chocolate block, then flop the brushed sides together (3). Now cut through to make eight pops. Separate pops a bit; return to freezer. Repeat pop-

making procedure with second pan of chocolate. Freeze pops five hours or overnight before coating (see below). Eat at once or store in freezer. *Makes sixteen pop sticks.*

Rich Chocolate Coating

2 packages (6 oz. each) semisweet   ¼ cup vegetable shortening
  chocolate pieces

Melt chocolate and shortening together in the top of a double boiler over hot (not boiling) water. Stir to blend mixture, then spoon a little onto one surface of a pop stick and quickly spread with a knife. Repeat to coat all surfaces. Enough to cover sixteen pop sticks.

If you have a freezer, you know it can open new paths to old pleasures— like these now-you-can-do-it-yourself pops. Buy the sticks at the dime store or the tongue depressors (even better) at your drugstore.

NEAPOLITAN ICE CREAM POPS

1 can (3½ oz.) flaked coconut   Wooden pop sticks, spoons or tongue
2 packages (1 pint each) strawberry-   depressors
  vanilla-chocolate brick ice cream

Cover an area of the freezer with a piece of aluminum foil. Sprinkle the coconut on a sheet of waxed paper. Cut ice cream into thirds. Dip wooden pop sticks into water and insert the wet part into short ends of ice cream bars. Quickly roll each pop in the coconut, covering the ice cream. Freeze for one hour or until firm, then wrap pops in transparent plastic film or foil and store until needed. *Makes six.*

Toasted Coconut Pops: Before beginning, spread coconut in a shallow pan and toast at 350°F. (moderate) until a pale golden color. Use in place of plain coconut in preceding recipe.

Almond Pops: Instead of coconut, use a six-ounce can of blanched almonds. Chop fine, then toast in a shallow pan at 350°F. (moderate) fifteen minutes or until golden, stirring occasionally.

Parfait means perfect—as anyone who tastes this can testify.

CAFÉ AU LAIT PARFAIT

1 pint vanilla ice cream	Mocha Sauce (below)
1 pint chocolate ice cream	Coffee Whipped Cream (below)

This dessert may be made in advance and frozen, but it's at its best if you put it together at party time. Use nine six-ounce parfait glasses. Into each spoon alternate layers of vanilla ice cream, Mocha Sauce and coffee ice cream, letting sauce marble through the ice cream as much as possible. Top with Coffee Whipped Cream. *Serves nine.*

Mocha Sauce

1 package (6 oz.) semisweet chocolate pieces	1¼ cups sifted confectioners' sugar
2 tablespoons butter or margarine	½ cup hot black coffee

Place chocolate and butter in the top of a double boiler and cook over hot, not boiling, water until melted. Add sugar and coffee and stir until smooth. Remove from heat and chill.

Coffee Whipped Cream

1 cup heavy cream	1 tablespoon instant coffee
1 tablespoon sugar	

Combine ingredients in a small mixing bowl and chill one hour. Then whip with electric mixer or rotary beater until soft peaks form.

For an informal party, there's nothing more convivial than letting your guests help themselves to their wildest sundae fantasies.

BUFFET OF SUNDAES

Buy an assortment of ice cream flavors in advance of the party. The day before, scoop the assorted flavors into a freezerproof serving dish; cover bowl with a piece of foil and put it in the freezer until serving time. The toppings are easy! You can buy sundae toppings in ten-ounce jars all ready to serve. Try chocolate caramel and vanilla caramel, pineapple, peach, black raspberry, strawberry, butterscotch and walnut. Serve some from-your-own-kitchen versions too: the syrupy portion of cherry preserves is perfect—or try any other fruit preserve on your shelf. For garnishing, whip two cups (for ten people) of heavy cream before party and refrigerate. Place in serving dish at dessert time, and set everything on the buffet.

LUNCH–COUNTER SUNDAE SAUCES

Try this different way of presenting a buffet of sundaes. Set up a quick lunch counter in the breakfast room, complete with catchup bottle, mustard jar, pickle dish, etc. But here's the fun: there's raspberry sauce in the catchup bottle, butterscotch in the mustard jar and the pickle relish is chopped red and green maraschino cherries, all ready to top the guests' choices of ice cream. Other ideas: salt and pepper shakers filled with silver shot and chocolate sprinkles; coconut-flake coleslaw. The recipes follow.

In the Tabasco bottle:

Cinnamon Red Hot Sauce

¼ cup tiny red cinnamon candies   ¼ cup water
¼ cup light corn syrup

Place all ingredients in a saucepan. Bring to a boil over moderate heat, stirring constantly. Boil without stirring two minutes. Remove from heat; cool. *Makes three-fourths cup.*

In the steak sauce bottle:

Satiny Chocolate Syrup

½ cup light corn syrup   1 cup (6 oz. package) semisweet
¼ cup water   chocolate pieces
¼ cup milk

Place corn syrup and water in a saucepan. Heat, stirring constantly, until mixture just comes to a full boil. Remove from heat; stir in milk and chocolate pieces and continue stirring until no lumps remain and the sauce is shiny and smooth. Serve warm or cool. *Makes one and one-third cups of syrup.*

In the mustard jar:

Instant Butterscotch Topping

1 package butterscotch instant-   ⅔ cup dark corn syrup
    pudding mix   ⅔ cup evaporated milk

Combine pudding and syrup in bowl. Mix well. Gradually add milk, stirring constantly. Stir until well blended and smooth, then let mixture stand ten minutes to thicken. *Makes one and one-third cups.*

In the catchup bottle:

Raspberry Jazz

1 teaspoon cornstarch
1 tablespoon water
½ cup bright red currant jelly

½ cup light corn syrup
1 package (10 oz.) frozen raspberries, thawed

Combine cornstarch and water in a saucepan. Add other ingredients. Bring to a boil over medium heat, stirring constantly. Boil one to two minutes, until mixture begins to thicken slightly and becomes clear. Remove from heat and strain. *Makes one and one-third cups.*

DESSERT SAUCES

There is an astonishing array of ready-to-use sundae sauces available at most supermarkets. But sometimes you want to add your own unique touch to ice cream, puddings or cakes. Plan on at least three tablespoons of sauce for each serving of dessert—or one cup for five servings.

PINE–APPLE MINT SAUCE

½ cup crushed pineapple
4 drops peppermint flavoring

½ cup applesauce

Combine ingredients and chill. *Makes one cup.*

MAPLE NUT SAUCE

½ cup walnuts
½ cup pecans
½ cup blanched almonds

1½ cups maple syrup
½ cup light cream

Put walnuts, pecans and almonds through coarse blade of food chopper. Mix with maple syrup and cream. Heat and serve. *About three cups.*

EASY RASPBERRY MELBA

1 package (10 oz.) frozen raspberries, thawed

1 jar (12 oz.) bright red currant jelly

Empty raspberries with syrup into blender container. Add jelly. Cover container and blend at low speed forty-five seconds or until well blended. Strain. *Makes two cups.*

CHOCOLATE MINT SAUCE

1 package chocolate instant pudding ½ teaspoon peppermint extract
⅔ cup light or dark corn syrup ¾ cup evaporated milk

Place pudding, corn syrup and peppermint into bowl. Stirring constantly, gradually add evaporated milk. Continue stirring until well blended. Let stand ten minutes to thicken. *Makes one and one-fourth cups.*

HONEYCOMB SUNDAE SAUCE

1 cup raisins 1 cup light cream
1 cup walnuts ½ cup honey
½ cup dates

Put raisins, walnuts and dates through fine blade of food chopper. Mix with cream and honey in saucepan. Cook until hot. Serve over vanilla, butter pecan or rum raisin ice cream. *About three cups.*

HOT FUDGE SUNDAE SAUCE

¼ cup butter 1 teaspoon vanilla
⅓ cup undiluted evaporated milk 1 cup sifted confectioners' sugar
1 package (6 oz.) semisweet
chocolate pieces

Place butter and milk in a saucepan. Bring to a boil over medium heat, stirring constantly. When butter has melted, remove from heat and immediately stir in semisweet chocolate pieces and vanilla. Stir until chocolate has completely melted; then stir in confectioners' sugar. Ladle over scoops of ice cream—vanilla or chocolate. Or refrigerate until serving time, then reheat. *Makes one and one-fourth cups.*

Specials for the
Deep-Fat Fryer

ALTHOUGH deep-fat frying has its special rules, the results you get from following them are rather special, too. Deep-fat fried foods can add elegance to many menus—and you know how boys go for doughnuts!

Read the simple general directions before you tackle the recipes which follow. You'll be rewarded with crisp, delicately crusted goodies—everything from appetizers to fruit drops.

DEEP-FAT FRYING

Use a good deep-fat fryer. An electric one has an automatic heat control, which keeps the temperature of the cooking oil at the desired degree and comes with its own self-draining fry basket (1). If you haven't an electric

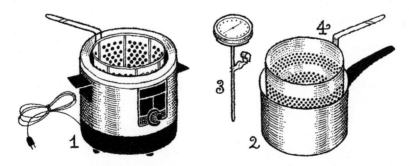

deep-fat fryer, use a straight-sided pan—at least three-quart size (2). Unless you can set your range unit as you set your oven (to 350°F. etc.), you will need a deep-fat thermometer (3) to test the temperature of the fat. A metal frying basket (4) makes it easier to handle "small frys" like shrimp, potatoes.

For best results, fry foods in cooking oil, lard or vegetable shortening (not butter or olive oil). Fat should cover foods but be three inches below top of fryer for spatter-protection. (Moisture on foods sometimes causes spattering; dry them with a paper towel if necessary.) When fat is heated to correct temperature, lower food gently into fryer with a slotted pancake turner, spoon or basket. Fry in small amounts to keep fat temperature even. Most foods need one turning.

Drain fried foods thoroughly. Let them "drip dry" a minute over the fryer when you take them out; then put them on several layers of paper toweling. To keep first batch of food hot while you finish frying, put it in a 300°F. (slow) oven, in a baking pan lined with paper towels.

To reuse frying fat, cool it, pour through a strainer lined with cheesecloth, cover and refrigerate. To help remove onion, fish or other strong odors from fat: cool first, add a few slices of raw potato, then reheat, stirring occasionally. Cool again and strain as above.

Our *best* doughnut recipe, sweet and spicy, with that special richness that sour cream adds.

SUGARPLUM DOUGHNUTS

4 cups sifted flour	1 whole egg plus 3 yolks
3 tablespoons baking powder	1 cup sugar
½ teaspoon baking soda	1 cup commercial sour cream
2 teaspoons salt	½ teaspoon grated orange peel
½ teaspoon nutmeg	½ teaspoon grated lemon peel
½ teaspoon cinnamon	Fat for deep frying

Sift together flour, baking powder, baking soda, salt, nutmeg and cinnamon. With electric mixer or rotary beater, beat eggs until thick and yellow. Gradually beat in the sugar. Next beat in the sour cream and fruit peels. Remove from mixer; stir in flour mixture. Turn out on floured board. Flour a rolling pin and roll out dough to half-inch thickness. Cut into desired shapes. If possible, let stand thirty minutes before frying, so doughnuts will hold shape better. Heat fat to 375°F. Lower doughnuts into fat with slotted spatula. Fry golden brown, about two minutes on each side. Drain on paper toweling. Sprinkle with confectioners' sugar, or shake two or three doughnuts in a bag with cinnamon-sugar (one teaspoon cinnamon to one-half cup granulated sugar.) Or frost and decorate as desired. *Makes about three dozen.*

Petite Doughnuts

Make up the recipe for Sugarplum Doughnuts, but cut the doughnuts in petite size. Use a tiny round or heart-shaped cutter (one and one-half to two inches). Make the holes in the center with the small end of a large funnel. When you've cut all the doughnuts you can, reroll scraps and cut. Fry as usual, and drain. *Recipe yields six dozen tiny doughnuts.*

Frost some with chocolate. Use this shiny chocolate glaze: Combine in a saucepan two tablespoons each of butter and water with one-fourth cup light corn syrup. Bring to a boil over moderate heat. Add one package (six ounces) semisweet chocolate pieces; stir until smooth. Cool; then stir in one-half cup confectioners' sugar. *Makes one and one-half cups.*

Dip some in a tinted glaze. First make a white glaze: lightly beat one egg white with a fork or wire whisk. Gradually beat in one cup sifted confectioners' sugar. Makes one-half cup. Divide glaze and tint to pretty pastels with food coloring. Spear doughnuts with a fork, dip into bowl and coat one or both sides; set on wire rack to dry before handling.

Add the finishing touch. *While glaze is still wet*, sprinkle on sugar crystals, candy beads, coconut flakes or dragées. *When glaze is dry*, make tiny flowers or designs with jelly frosting-in-a-tube.

If you start with a hot-roll mix, you get yeasty "raised" doughnuts with very little work. Yummy!

SPEEDY DOUGHNUTS

1 package hot-roll mix	½ teaspoon grated lemon peel
½ cup warm water	½ teaspoon nutmeg
2 egg yolks	3 tablespoons sugar
½ cup commercial sour cream	Fat for deep frying

Remove the yeast packet from a package of hot-roll mix and dissolve the yeast in warm water. Blend in egg yolks, sour cream, lemon peel, nutmeg and sugar. Add the dry roll mix and beat together until well combined. Let rise in warm place, free from drafts, from thirty to sixty minutes until double in size. Turn out onto a floured board. Roll out dough to one-fourth-inch thickness and cut into doughnuts, removing centers as you cut. Reroll scraps and cut. Let rise half an hour until doubled. Fry and add sugar or glaze. *Makes eighteen regular or three dozen tiny doughnuts.*

REFRIGERATOR DOUGHNUTS

Take one can of refrigerator doughnuts, some cooking oil or fat, an electric frying pan or deep-fat fryer and you have the ingredients for an instant party. Doughnuts (even the holes) are fun to watch while cooking, and their fragrance calls, "Come and eat!" The canned variety takes happily to sugar coating or chocolate glazing.

Chopped cranberries are a piquant surprise in these homey doughnuts.

CRANBERRY DOUGHNUTS

½ cup sugar	¼ teaspoon salt
1 egg	½ cup milk
1 tablespoon butter or margarine	½ cup chopped, washed, fresh
1½ cups sifted flour	cranberries
2 teaspoons baking powder	Fat for deep frying
½ teaspoon cinnamon	Cinnamon-sugar
½ teaspoon nutmeg	

Beat sugar, egg and butter together until creamy. Mix and sift flour, baking powder, cinnamon, nutmeg and salt. Add a little at a time to sugar mixture, alternating with the milk. Fold in cranberries. Make the cinnamon-sugar by mixing one-half cup sugar with one teaspoon cinnamon. Heat the fat (which should be at least two inches deep in fryer) to 360°F. Drop dough by measuring out tablespoonfuls into hot fat, being careful not to overcrowd. Fry about four minutes or until medium brown on all sides. Drain on absorbent paper; then roll, while still hot, in cinnamon-sugar. *Makes about twenty-four "hen's-egg size" doughnuts.*

Chocolate-frosted heart-shaped doughnuts—now there's the way to a boy's heart!

SWEET HEARTS

½ cup warm, not hot water	2 egg yolks
1 package active dry yeast	Fat for deep frying
2½ cups biscuit mix	Chocolate Glaze (page 258)
3 tablespoons sugar	

Measure warm water into a bowl and sprinkle in yeast. Stir until dissolved. Add biscuit mix, sugar and egg yolks. Beat vigorously about 130 strokes until well blended. Then turn out on a surface well dusted with biscuit mix. Knead twenty times until smooth. Roll out one-fourth inch thick. Cut into rounds with a doughnut cutter. Indent at tops and pull bottoms into a point to form heart shapes. Cover and let stand in a warm place, free from drafts, forty-five minutes. Fry, a few at a time, in deep fat heated to 360°F. until golden on one side. Turn and brown second side. Remove from fat; drain on absorbent paper. Cool and frost with Chocolate Glaze. *Makes eighteen.*

Chocolate Glaze

2 tablespoons shortening	1 cup (6-oz. package) semisweet
2 tablespoons light corn syrup	chocolate pieces
1 tablespoon water	

Combine shortening, light corn syrup and water in a saucepan. Bring just to a boil over moderate heat, stirring constantly. Remove from heat. With a wooden spoon, stir in chocolate pieces until smooth (two to three minutes). Dip doughnuts in this mixture, then let stand on a wire cake rack over waxed paper until frosting sets. If desired, decorate tops with fluffy white frosting put through a cake decorator in a lacy pattern. *Enough frosting for eighteen doughnuts.*

Call it an appetizer, call it a snack—either way, it's a change of pace.

TASTE TEASERS

1 cup mashed liverwurst	½ teaspoon salt
1 cup ground uncooked beef	Pepper to taste
2 tablespoons minced onion	Fat for deep frying

Combine all ingredients. Shape into balls one inch in diameter. Fry in deep hot fat (375°F.) one minute or until browned. Drain on absorbent paper. Serve on toothpicks. *Makes twenty-four Taste Teasers.*

The Japanese deep-fry their favorite vegetables, thus adding a crunchy, crisp texture. It's a method especially designed for those of you who are trying to gain weight! Look for Crisp-Fried Mixed Vegetables on page 128.

A treat for breakfast, these frittered bananas also gracefully accompany a main dish.

FRENCH–FRIED BANANAS

1 cup pancake mix	1 tablespoon cooking oil
1 cup milk	3 medium-ripe bananas
1 egg	Fat for deep frying

Place pancake mix, milk, egg and oil in a bowl and beat until just blended. Then peel and slice the bananas crosswise into one-inch pieces. Dip pieces one at a time into batter to coat, then lower into fat heated to 375°F. Fry about three minutes or until golden brown and tender. Drain on paper towel; *serve at once to six.*

Delicious at a brunch, and a fine complement for a ham or pork dinner.

APPLE CORN FRITTERS

2 eggs
⅔ cup milk
1½ cups sifted flour
½ teaspoon salt
1 tablespoon sugar

1½ teaspoons baking powder
¾ cup drained whole-kernel corn
1 cup diced canned apple slices
1 tablespoon cooking oil
Fat for deep frying

Beat the eggs and beat in milk. Sift together the flour, salt, sugar and baking powder. Add to egg mixture and stir only until free of lumps. Add corn and apple slices, folding in gently. Add oil. Heat fat to 375°F. Drop batter by tablespoonfuls into fat, then fry about three minutes, turning once, until dark golden brown. Drain on absorbent paper. Serve plain or with syrup. *Makes twenty-four.*

If you took all your favorite fruitcake ingredients and deep-fried them puffy light, what would you have? Try the recipe below and find out what "delicious" means.

DEEP–FRIED FRUIT DROPS

2 cups sifted flour
¼ teaspoon salt
3 egg yolks
⅔ cup sugar
⅔ cup buttermilk
½ teaspoon baking soda
2 tablespoons melted butter

¾ cup finely chopped nuts
¼ cup chopped mixed candied fruit
¼ cup chopped raisins
1 tablespoon grated orange peel
3 tablespoons orange juice
Fat for deep frying

Sift flour and salt together and set aside. Beat egg yolks until lemon colored and gradually stir in sugar. Combine buttermilk and baking soda and stir into yolk mixture. Then add flour, blending well. Stir in melted butter. Combine nuts, fruits and orange juice and fold into batter. Drop by teaspoonfuls into fat heated to 325°F. Turn once to brown evenly. Fry until golden and cooked through. *Makes twenty-four.*

Doughnuts gone to heaven? Maybe! These little sweet puffs taste deliciously rich hot, but they're good cool, too.

GOLDEN NUGGETS

1 package (14½ oz.) hot-roll mix	½ teaspoon cinnamon
⅓ cup warm (not hot) water	¼ teaspoon nutmeg
2 egg yolks, lightly beaten	1 cup chopped walnuts
2 tablespoons dark brown sugar	1 cup seedless raisins
1 small can (⅔ cup) evaporated milk	Cooking oil
¼ teaspoon salt	

Remove yeast packet from hot-roll mix; sprinkle over warm water, in a large bowl. Stir to dissolve. Add egg yolks, sugar, milk, seasonings and dry mix from hot-roll mix package. Stir until well combined. Then beat fifty strokes with a wooden spoon. Stir in nuts and raisins. Cover and let rise in a warm place for about one hour. Pour oil at least three inches deep into a high-sided saucepan or deep-fat fryer. Heat to 365°F. Drop dough by soupspoonfuls into fat and fry for about two minutes or until golden brown on both sides. (Add just a few dough nuggets at a time so temperature of fat will not drop too far.) Drain nuggets on absorbent paper, then drizzle them with an orange glaze. To make glaze: mix one cup sifted confectioners' sugar with three tablespoons frozen orange juice concentrate. For variety: glaze half the nuggets, then sugar-coat the rest by shaking them—while they're still hot—in a paper bag containing one-fourth cup sugar and one-fourth teaspoon cinnamon. *Makes about two dozen.*

These little twists are made in many European countries with names which, translated, mean everything from lover's knots to little lies—or less romantically, rags. In Romania (in case you're having a United Nations party), they're called *Minciunele*.

FRIED CAKE TWISTS

2 egg yolks	1 egg white
¼ cup evaporated milk	1¾ cups biscuit mix
2 teaspoons grated lemon peel	Fat for deep frying

Beat egg yolks, milk and lemon peel together. Beat the egg white until stiff but not dry and fold into the yolk mixture. Add biscuit mix and beat and work with back of spoon until well blended and easy to handle. (Add a little more biscuit mix if needed.) Then flour a board lightly with biscuit mix. Roll out half the dough to one-sixteenth inch thickness (paper thin). Cut with a pastry wheel or knife into five-by-two-inch rectangles. Make a lengthwise slit one inch long in center of rectangle. Pass one end of rectangle through slit to make a twist knot. Then fry, three or four at a time, in fat heated to 360°F. Turn once and remove when golden brown. Drain on absorbent paper. Sprinkle with confectioners' sugar. *Makes twenty-four to thirty twists.*

Here's a quick route to jelly doughnuts—or a reasonable facsimile. And they're always done in the middle, too!

SANDWICH DOUGHNUTS

1 loaf thin-sliced white bread (18 slices)
1 cup strawberry jam (about)
1 cup milk
1 tablespoon melted shortening
1 egg
1 cup pancake mix
Fat for deep frying
1 cup granulated or confectioners' sugar

Trim crusts from bread and arrange in sandwich pairs. Spread half the slices with jam; close sandwiches. Cut each into four tiny sandwiches (rectangles or triangles). Make pancake batter with milk, shortening, egg and pancake mix, following package directions. Heat the fat to 375°F. Dip each sandwich into batter, making sure it is completely covered. Use one or two forks to drain slightly, then drop into deep hot fat at once. Fry until brown on both sides. Remove and drain on paper towel. Put sugar in paper bag, then shake doughnuts, two or three at a time to cover with sugar. *Makes three dozen.*

THE
PARTY
COOKBOOK

The Party Notebook

So YOU'RE GIVING A PARTY! If it's your first boy-girl party, maybe you're suffering from butterflies. Will everyone come? Will they like the food? Will they have a good time? What will they think of you? Will they ask you to their next party?

To make sure all the answers come out in your favor, take the time to plan every step of your party in advance. Everything will probably turn out just a little different from your expectations, but plans help keep you calm and that's part of the secret of being a perfect hostess.

Most good hostesses share one secret word—*love*. A successful hostess loves her guests, and she loves having them with her. So she's ready and eager to plan for their needs in advance—eager, too, to make the party one they'll remember with joy. She thinks through everything her guests will need, and she organizes herself to provide it all—right down to a fresh-from-the-wrapper cake of soap and more than enough clean guest towels.

When her guests arrive, she greets them with genuine pleasure and quickly makes them feel at home by disposing of wraps, introducing them to any strangers, providing a start for conversation.

She isn't pushy and she doesn't give orders to make sure the party meets a schedule. Instead she suggests, sets the scene, starts things going. The guests themselves provide the action, but the hostess may cleverly start it with the help of one or two good friends. She knows that the best party fun is spontaneous, resulting from the atmosphere and the right combination of guests. She knows that if she has chosen the right ingredients, fun is bound to come of its own accord.

Everybody invites her to their parties—after all, they want to be asked back to *her* house!

MASTERMINDING A PARTY

First, choose a date. Check it against conflicts—club meetings, big games, other parties. Choose it far enough in advance to avoid the latter.

Decide how many you'll invite. This depends on the type of party and where it will take place—inside or out, at home or elsewhere.

Make a list of guests' names. Will you invite them by couples or singly? Will you add some strangers to the group to make conversations more interesting? Is one of your guests apt to clash with another? If so, is the party big enough to avoid this?

Plan the focus of the party. Will it be at a regular mealtime? Will it include a late supper? If it's a record party, do you want guests to bring their own favorite disks? Will you spotlight some special activity like dancing or Ping-pong? Do you want your guests to dress in a special way, as they might for a *luau* or a Halloween party?

Think out your decorations. A strong theme and an effective setting to carry it out often make a party more fun—especially if you and your guests are not experienced party-goers as yet. Consider where the party will be held, and how that room or rooms will look with the decorations you have in mind. Consider the cost of decorations, too—if you're not careful, they can cost more than the food!

Invite your guests. Depending on the kind of party, you can use handmade invitations to fit your theme, or printed ones, or simply invite guests at school or by telephone. Get a definite idea of how many are coming.

Plan your menu. It's even more fun if it fits your party theme. You can use a very simple menu, but try to spark it with one all-out dish. If your party hour is late morning for brunch, or late afternoon for snacks, make sure you keep the food light so your guests will be able to have their dinners too. Evening snacks are different—since breakfast is a long way away, they can be as substantial or rich as you please. Consider your time schedule, too. If your menu includes some dishes which can be made well ahead and refrigerated or frozen, precious party-day time will be saved. If you're having a large crowd, it's especially wise to stay with well-liked and familiar foods, but add the little touches that make this menu distinctively yours.

Compose a shopping list. Once you know how many guests (about) are coming, you can plan on definite quantities to buy. Always figure on "too much" rather than "just enough." New hostesses often tend to underestimate the number of bottles of sodas or amounts of punch their guests will consume; plan on plenty! As you make your list, better check on the staple foods, too. You *could* make a cake without salt, but it wouldn't taste as good.

Set aside time for advance preparation. Perhaps your party is in a game room and you can put up your decorations a day ahead. Certainly there is some part of the menu you can prepare in advance.

Make a time plan for the party day. Once this is made—and posted in the kitchen—you'll find you can let the list do most of the worrying. Include on it: the hour to start early preparation of the food; time to tidy the party room and perhaps the house; time to set the table; one hour (at least) to dress and relax; thirty minutes for unforeseen emergencies; a check list of operations involved in serving the food.

It's your party now—relax and enjoy it!

WHAT EVERY GIRL SHOULD KNOW

Since you presumably are a girl, we should face something together. Only a boy can explain why it is that boys eat *what* they do the *way* they do. We've invited a guest editor, a regular contributor to *Seventeen*, to tell you—

What To Feed a Boy

by Jimmy Wescott

There are, of course, certain ground rules for giving a party that are good to know about. When you're hostessing the fellows, remember: Mother's best china is not for this taffy pull. Boys who can thread their way through a football line or shoot a basket with one finger are curiously unable to keep from dropping plates for any length of time. I remember at one party there was quite a battle between a slice of cold beef and my fork, and the meat won. The fork broke away just where the tines meet the handle, and I was forced to hide the two pieces in a water cress salad nobody was patronizing.

There are wheels within wheels at parties, too. Like—should you order crunchy or creamy peanut butter? Now, there's much to be said for both sides. If you're eating creamy peanut butter and a pretty girl asks you a question, you can jam it on the roof of your mouth before you answer her. If it's crunchy peanut butter, you can answer right away, but you have to keep your teeth closed to keep the tidbits in as you talk.

Butter can be tricky. If it's cool and you drop it on the rug, you can pick it up and put it back on the serving dish. But if it's warm and you drop it on the rug, your only chance is to drop a brownie over it and move away quick.

Paper plates—except for the plastic-y kind—are no answer either. If you're eating anything with sauce or gravy, the plate usually absorbs more of it than you do. For years I thought one girl's mother made a terrible apple pie until I discovered I'd eaten the plate along with it.

The main thing you girls should remember is that boys are capable of eating more food than you or your parents or the grocery man are capable of imagining. A fellow is *always* hungry, even after dinner. So be sure that the forage is on the sturdy side. There are no hours in the day or night when it is possible to suppose that a group of teen-age fellows will eat any less than a platoon of Kodiak bears which has been on a two-week hunger strike for sweeter honey. Boys regard eating as a serious occupation, requiring full attention and entered into with a high sense of adventure, primarily centered around the idea of eating something of everything in sight and then going back for a rerun of the choicest tidbits on the table. Remember the boy's point of view and your party will be fun.

And now, let's mix Mr. Wescott's opinions with fact—the foods which have proved, survey after survey, to be most popular with boys.

TO EAT SITTING DOWN

Boys like a good solid home plate to slide into and stay with semipermanently in a restful posture. Another thing boys like— small servings. This is so that they can go back for six or seven helpings without seeming greedy.—J.W.

Guaranteed sit-and-eat
successes:

Spaghetti and meat balls
Fried chicken
French fried potatoes
Sloppy Joes
Salads—potato and macaroni, coleslaw, jellied fruit salad
Chocolate cake
Apple or cherry pie
Anything à la mode

TO NIBBLE WHILE STANDING

Boys are at ease with finger food. It's the kind of hand-to-mouth living that appeals to them for several good reasons: they can eat the food quicker, thus getting into position for grabbing another portion; they can take bigger mouthfuls, providing a healthful stretching of the jaws; and it leaves their hands free to talk in sign language while they are eating, a kind of conversation in which the male animal excels. Hamburgers, pizza, potato chips and the like are what may be called a good running start for any party, to be eaten on the move while rushing about to insult old friends and meet new ones.—J.W.

Favorite pick-up foods:

Crackers and potato chips, with sour-cream onion dip

Pizza—plain or with mozzarella, sausage, or mushrooms

Hamburgers—with lettuce, tomato, pickles, mustard and catchup

Ham and cheese—the most popular sandwich

Watermelon and other fruits

Chocolate fudge, with nuts or without, peanut brittle

Brownies and Toll House cookies, also peanut butter and oatmeal-raisin

TO DRINK

Every boy's stomach is like a bottomless well. Into it, he pours an endless stream of liquids to create an inner balance of satisfaction. When ordering these life-giving supplies, think of the maximum amount—then just double it. Have ice—tons of it, bergs of it—and your party will be rated cool.—J.W.

Top life-giving supplies:

Colas

Lemon-lime soda

Tropical fruit punch

Milk drinks, especially those made with ice cream

IN GENERAL

In spite of their occasional resemblance to hurricanes or noc-
turnal predators, boys are conservatives, which means they like
to go easy on the garlic, if and when it's used. They are also
temperature-conscious and believe that anything hot should be
very hot, anything cold *really* cold and never the bane (in between) shall meet. And while no one, least of all themselves,
expects boys to be civilized, most of them will get into their best
threads for a party, and they are unhappy when required to
balance plates of hot stew or tossed salad on a well-pressed
knee.—J.W.

FIFTY-FOUR EXCUSES FOR A PARTY

By the calendar:

1. New Year's Day egg nog party
2. Midyear exams are over
3. Groundhog Day
4. Lincoln's Birthday
5. Valentine's Day
6. Mardi Gras (the day before Lent begins)
7. Washington's Birthday
8. The first day of spring
9. Easter brunch or tea
10. First baseball game of the season
11. Memorial Day
12. Last baseball game of the season
13. School's out
14. Graduation
15. Independence Day
16. Labor Day
17. School's in
18. First football game of the season
19. Columbus Day
20. United Nations Day
21. Halloween
22. Election Day
23. Last football game of the season
24. First basketball game of the season
25. Thanksgiving week end

26. Beginning of Christmas vacation
27. Christmas Eve
28. Christmas Day
29. New Year's Eve

By your mood:

30. To introduce a new friend
31. To say good-by to an old friend
32. It's your birthday
33. It's a friend's birthday
34. Everyone's going to college
35. Split-up before summer vacation
36. Shower for someone getting married
37. To get acquainted with a new class
38. Last club meeting of the year
39. Pre-prom dinner or dessert
40. Post-prom supper
41. Pre-game luncheon
42. Victory or defeat dinner
43. Paint-the-garage party
44. After skiing or sledding party
45. Ice-skating barbecue
46. Clean-up-our-town party
47. Hay ride
48. Box social for charity
49. After-church brunch
50. Someone's going to Europe
51. Swimming party
52. Bring a present for the needy party
53. Family and best beau get-acquainted dinner
54. Kite-flying picnic

TWENTY-TWO CAPSULE PARTIES

Following is a series of bright party ideas, offering just enough information to get you started thinking. The recipes are listed in the index.

TEA DANCE—BOSTON STYLE

Not every party seems just right for a holiday or a Sunday afternoon, but a tea dance is! It helps you expand a crowded social calendar, makes a new and pleasant time to be dancing to records. Invite a crowd—nobody wants to sit down at a tea dance—and keep the refreshments light and easy to eat:

Hot Tea   Iced-Tea Punch
Cream Cheese and Date Nut Bars
Ham Asparagus Rolls   Open Hearts
Chinese Chicken Sandwiches
Boston Party Cake

MEXICAN DINNER

Plan your party decorations around a color theme of red, green and yellow, with shiny Mexican silver and simple earthenware. Play Mexican records and tell that boy to bring his guitar! The menu is the sort that gets all the tricky kitchen work out of the way early, leaves time for you to slip into your fullest, gayest skirt and be at ease. The food:

Paella Pronto
Ring-a-Ling Salad   Zombie Bread
Hot Mocha Milk   Iced Tea
Sherbet Coconut Balls
Nutty Crunch Cookies

BUFFET BEFORE A SHOW

For a well-timed dinner before a theater or movie date, follow this plan: Serve an appetizer in the living room to greet arriving guests and help them get acquainted if necessary. Choose main-course foods which can be kept deliciously hot or deliciously cold with ease. Have a dessert of the "it's all ready" variety, so when the time comes, you've nothing to do but pass it, eat and leave! One menu suggestion:

Tomato Juice   Chips and Dips
Baked Glazed Ham
Macaroni Salad   Sliced Tomatoes
Cold Vegetable Relishes   Assorted Breads
Layer Cake
Coffee   Milk

RECORD PARTY

The trick is to be as fancy-free the night of your party as your guests. The menu below is a complete one, yet it takes a minimum of party time. Bake the brownies in advance, have the hot snacks ready for baking.

Then oven time—not your time—is all that's needed. Just the Hot Spiced Milk need be warmed at evening's end. For a novel way to serve the colas and fruit, make a cooler from a dish pan. Wrap chicken wire around the outside and into this weave fresh leaves and flowers from the garden. Fill it with ice cubes and bottled sodas. Leave the center open and at party time, arrange pears (cut into wedges for easy eating) around a bunch of fresh grapes. The menu:

Pigs in Blankets
Portable Pizzas
Fresh Fruits   Bottled Colas
and later on:
Brownies   Hot Spiced Milk

Birthday Dessert Party

What better time to serve birthday cake than at dessert time? And what better kind of birthday refreshments than something different enough to be newsy? Plan for dessert in the dining room followed by games in the living room—whatever your crowd knows and enjoys playing. The food:

Nutcracker Sweet
Junior Ice Cream Sodas
Mints   Nuts

Party on the Porch

One of the pleasantest summer parties is an outdoor-indoor porch party. Invite a few close friends—as many as your porch will comfortably hold. The night air is sure to be filled with some fairly close harmonizing, so try to include a guitar or ukulele player in the group. A few big floor pillows provide extra seating space; a string of paper lanterns adds a festive touch. Set up a small refreshment table in an out-of-the-way place—then sit back and just relax. Your menu:

Tiny Finger Sandwiches
Chilled Peeled Watermelon Wedges
Punch

Sukiyaki Party

Say skee-yah'-kee—it means one of the gayest parties you've ever given—and one of the easiest. From the moment your guests arrive, everybody becomes Bob-*san* or Alice-*san* and it's "shoes off!"—old Japanese custom. Everybody sits around a low table (bricks and a piece of plywood, or a low, long coffee table) watching you, cook-*san*, prepare the meal. Use an electric skillet to prepare the sukiyaki in the Japanese tradition before your guests. Meantime, guests can practice their chopstick work (instructions below). Forks may be faster, but chopsticks pick up more party fun. Decorate with paper lanterns, tiny paper parasols and magic water flowers. For party favors: oriental puzzles. For laughs: yo-yos. For food:

Sukiyaki
Oriental Rice
Ginger Ice Cream   Fortune Cookies
Tea

Chopstick Primer: Mount the following instructions on colored paper and place them on the party table.

Place a stick in crotch of thumb. Hold stick in place with tip of third finger.
Place second stick between tip of thumb and side of index finger, with index finger resting a bit on top of stick.
Move second stick by moving index finger up and down. *Don't* move first stick. Adjust sticks until you can make tips meet easily.
You're on your own! Pick up tiny morsels of sukiyaki between tips of sticks and convey to honorable mouth. No fair bending over dish!

SLUMBER PARTY

Your crowd may have its own favorite ways of staving off sleep, but if not here are some ideas to get you started: listen to records; dance; try new hair styles; paint your toenails; play Ghost; play cards; tell fortunes. Serve a midnight snack—that should *really* wake everybody up. And have something marvelous for breakfast the next day.

Midnight Snack

Apple Dreams   Strawberry Milk Shakes

Next Morning

Pineapple-Orange Juice
Eggs à la Duke   Buttered English Muffins
Milk   Coffee   Café au Lait

Have a Snow Ball

Roughly translated, this means a supper party after skiing, skating, tobogganing, etc. Since you'll want to be out in the snow enjoying the fun, pick a menu that is mostly do-ahead, with a minimum of last-minute fussing. Warming up will be Activity Number One (accompanied by hot soup) and after a good dinner inspires a mellow mood, it will be time for accordion, guitar, close harmonies and far-into-the-night discussions. Serve:

Mugs of Tomato Minestrone Soup
Salty Snack Sticks
Dunk-a-Bobs and Dips
Carrot and Cabbage Slaw   Potato Puff
Ring-a-Berry Angel Cake
Milk   Hot Tea

Valentine Supper

Quickest way to a boy's heart: a meat-and-potatoes meal that's special yet unsuspectedly easy. The supper is timed for busy midweek cooking. Make your dessert the night before; fix the salad when you come home from school—then relax and dress while the roast cooks itself.

Tiny Roast Beef
Pan Roasted Potatoes
Sliced Tomato Salad
Jellied Strawberries with Whipped Cream Hearts
Milk   Coffee

Washington's Birthday Brunch

No school today, and don't waste a minute of it! Get the day off to a bright and early (well, not too early) holiday mood with a brunch—then take off afterward for ice skating or a hike or a movie matinee. It's the easiest party going! If you want to invite a real crowd, skip the eggs in the menu and serve buffet style.

Orange Juice
Swiss Eggs with Bacon Rings
Cherry Whirls
Milk   Coffee

DUDE RANCH PARTY

You *could* invite everyone for March 2—Texas Independence Day! Why? Just for fun. Texas teens have the day off from school, but our menu is geared to the other forty-nine states: everything on it can be made the night before and stored in the refrigerator. Just reheat the chili while you decorate the table and you're set!

Rio Grande Chili Bowls
Finger Salad
Buffet of Sundaes
Cocoa

MARDI GRAS BUFFET

Festoon the party room with balloons—it's Carnival night in New Orleans. Pick a savory pork Creole, a cake sprinkled with candy confetti— and take your feast (it's mostly made ahead) to the table in twenty minutes! For added gayety, issue invitations on balloons: write on blown up balloons with a marker pen, deflate and mail.

Spicy Pork Creole
Rice   Red and White Slaw
Assorted Soft Drinks
Carnival Cake

SPRING SEMESTER LUNCHEON

Launch the new term with a Saturday lunch—just for girls and girl talk, uninterrupted. The menu, like all good menus, is planned to fit the party mood: light and cheery. The chicken is flavored with just a hint of lemony freshness, the rolls are dainty—everything is pretty and feminine.

Spring Chicken
Asparagus Tips   Green Salad
Sesame Rolls
Pears à la Mode
Milk   Tea

BRUNCH ON THE PATIO

For this party—which can begin any time between ten and twelve noon, choose foods which are easy to keep warm as you wait for your guests.

Hearty breakfast food is in order, but always with the glamour touch. Plans for later: basking in the sun; playing darts; records; team contests on the Sunday crossword.

Grapefruit Juleps
Corn Nugget Waffles
Hot Orange Honey   Maple Syrup
Whipped Butter
"Branded" Canadian Bacon
Coffee   Milk

Mexican Fiesta

Tell the girls to wear colorful summer skirts, white blouses, hoop earrings. Have the boys drape bright beach towels over one shoulder for serapes. Decorate with bright red or orange tablecloths (paper or burlap); cut "silver" Mexican motifs—like fighting cocks—of aluminum foil, hang dried red peppers and sombreros. What to play? Your guitar, of course, and maybe pin the tail on the burro. Dance to the Mexican Hat Rock—*Olé!*

Hot Sweet Italian Sausages   Hamburgers
Chili Bean Rice
Crisp Lettuce Salad
Cinnamon Cookies
Coffee   Milk   Cold Drinks

Polynesian Luau

Everyone wears sandals or thongs and bright-colored *leis*. Girls can dress in *muumuus* with flowers in their hair. Boys might wear gay shirts, straw beach hats. Decorate with blossoms galore (maybe floating in a kiddy pool), totem poles with cardboard masks, a large blanket for serving on the grass, *luau* style. Play Hawaiian records. Make a grass skirt and have a hula contest. Let the boys judge, then give them a chance. *Aloha!*

Ham and Beef Teriyaki
Pineapple Raisin Rice
Carrot and Celery Sticks
Pineapple Juice   Coffee   Milk
Coconut Cake

Japanese Moon-Watching Party

Girls might wear elaborate hairdos, long earrings; boys might wear coolie hats. Everybody wears kimonos, thong sandals and very bright smiles.

Decorate with Japanese lanterns, low tables, tatami mats, chrysanthemums. Paint bright dragons and flowers on window screens with water color (washes off with a hose). You might play Pick Up Sticks with chopsticks while you listen to Japanese records. Watch the moon rise. *Sayonara!*

Chicken and Shrimp Shoyu
Pickled Watermelon Rind   Cucumber Spears
Almond Mushroom Rice
Tea   Milk   Cold Drinks
Ice Cream sprinkled with Candied Ginger

STACK-TABLE BUFFET

This dinner party adapts to dining room service, living room eating. Use the tables already in your living room, add a set of stack tables and the dining room chairs and count on one or two (you know who) guests sitting on the floor at a coffee table. Set the places in advance with mats, silver and napkins, so guests will know where to go. The menu:

Gold Fizz   Dagwood Jrs.
Frankfurter-Corn Bread Casserole
Green Beans with French Fried Onion Rings
Dill Spears
Cheesecake
Milk   Coffee

SIT-DOWN PICNIC

Even for your own dining room, picnic-style planning pays off. Prepare your hot foods to keep very hot for fifteen or twenty minutes; then you can add last-minute touches to the table in a leisurely way, not feel panicked if guests call for one more dance. With this menu you can serve the first course in the living room, everything else in the dining room:

Cheese Dip with Assorted Dunkers
Harvest Stew
Garden Patch Salad   French Bread
Cranberry Apple Pie
Coffee   Milk

TRAY PARTY

Assemble enough trays (borrow extras from a friend) to have one for each guest. When you set the buffet table, leave a margin at the edge

At a record hop, a Platter Cake (page 214), of course! ▶

nearest the guests for trays to slide along, cafeteria style. Provide paper mats, silver rolled in a napkin at the start of your cafeteria line. Wherever possible, have food already portioned into small dishes.

Pimiento Cheese Soup
Chicken Bombay with Walnut Rice
Hot Buttered Biscuits   Emerald Salad
Lime Chiffon Pie
Milk   Coffee

PARTY ON WHEELS

This type of service could be used on porch, patio or rumpus room. Everything goes anywhere! Seat your guests at card tables. One rolling cart will serve three tables. Place the first course on the card tables, main dish and dessert on the tea cart. Everybody can relax—only the four-wheeled butler need work from table to table.

Tomato Juice Cocktail
Ham and Cheese Pie
Sliced Tomatoes   Celery Curls
Herb Crescents
Pink Punch Torte
Milk   Coffee

◀ *Exciting dessert party: Cookies and Dips (pages 367–368).*

{ 17 }

Pancakes, Waffles and Other Breakfast Party Breads

*P*ANCAKE-MAKING is such a lark, it can make any occasion a party—even if your family are your only guests. Here you'll find our favorite pancake and waffle recipes, along with others for luscious coffeecakes and dressed-up yeast breads. Use them to make a breakfast worth getting up for. Turn to them, too, when you're hungry for a sweet afternoon snack or when you want to "bake a present" for the new girl next door.

Consult this chapter also when you're planning a company breakfast or brunch. Though your main dish will probably be one with eggs, meat or cheese, a fragrant homemade bread will put your own signature to the menu in the most distinctive—and tasteful!—way.

And speaking of company, remember that a pancake party provides its own entertainment! Let the guests flip their own cakes, then have the fun of mixing and matching a variety of fillings and toppings. Suggestions for an array of them follow, after some tips on the right equipment and basic methods of procedure.

PERFECT PANCAKES

Heat the griddle slowly if you are making pancakes on the stove. For controlled, all-over, even heat use a griddle or skillet made of cast iron, aluminum or other heavy-gauge material. (The two-burner size is handy for speeding up a party-size batch of pancakes.) If you use an electric frying pan or griddle, set the automatic control to the temperature recommended by the manufacturer, usually at about 400°F.

Test the griddle to see if it is hot enough for cooking: drop a little water on it from the tip of a spoon. The water should dance and skitter around the griddle. If it turns to steam without dancing, the griddle is not hot enough. To grease the griddle: use a tiny natural-bristled brush to coat pan lightly with oil or unsalted shortening before cooking the first pancake. Further greasing may not be necessary. If pancakes begin to stick, it's time to add a bit more oil.

Mix batter only until blended; don't worry about little lumps. To mix: shake batter in a jar, whirl it briefly in a blender, or beat it with a spoon or rotary beater. If you want thin pancakes (to roll around a filling), add extra milk to the batter. If you plan to stir nuts, berries or other fruit into the batter, thicken it first with extra pancake mix. (Thicker pancakes need slower cooking.)

Pour the batter from a pitcher or tip of a large spoon onto a hot griddle. (If it's a party, you can use a silver ladle!) Allow room for turning pancakes. When top is puffy with air bubbles that have not yet broken, pancakes are ready for turning. To keep "seconds" hot place between the folds of a towel in a warm oven. At clean-up time, brush crumbs from griddle. Follow manufacturer's directions for cleaning.

BASIC PANCAKE BATTER

1 cup milk	1 tablespoon oil or melted butter or
1 egg	margarine
	1 cup pancake mix

Mix ingredients until just blended. Cook, following directions above. *Makes eight.*

For Orange Pancakes: Before mixing the basic matter, add two tablespoons of undiluted frozen orange-juice concentrate.

CHOCOLATE PANCAKES

1 egg	1½ cups pancake mix
1½ cups milk	½ cup quick chocolate-flavored
	drink mix

Combine as above and cook as directed. *Makes ten pancakes.*

To write on pancakes: Use extra-heavy chocolate batter. Measure one-half cup prepared basic batter. Add to it, one tablespoon of pancake mix and two tablespoons quick chocolate-flavored drink mix. Drizzle this from spoon tip (or use a pastry tube with a large tip) onto the uncooked side of pancake *just* before it's ready to turn.

Corn meal pancakes have a country flavor that appeals to boys. Delicious with brown-and-serve sausages, butter and warmed maple syrup.

CORNCAKES

1 egg	1 package (10 oz.) yellow corn bread
¾ cup milk	mix in plastic mixing bag

Add egg and milk to corn bread mix and blend in the mixing bag as directed. Pour out to form pancakes on hot greased griddle. Turn when brown. *Makes eight pancakes; serves three to four.*

These wonderful pancakes are amazingly light and tender. So delicious you can just top them with pats of butter—they don't really need syrup!

GRANDMA'S HOTCAKES

2 cups buttermilk	1 cup plus 2 tablespoons unsifted
2 teaspoons baking soda	flour
¾ teaspoon salt	⅔ cup sugar
½ cup commercial sour cream	¾ teaspoon baking powder
2 eggs	¼ cup corn meal
½ cup regular oatmeal, uncooked	

Pour buttermilk into a mixing bowl. Add soda and salt. Stir in sour cream until mixture foams. Add eggs and beat with a spoon. Add oatmeal. Sift flour, sugar, baking powder and corn meal into mixture and beat until smooth. Heat griddle and grease. Pour batter onto griddle to make small cakes. When bubbles on pancakes begin to break, turn and brown the other side. Add syrup, honey, or preserves if desired. *Serves four to six.*

Pancake Toppings

Pancakes take on new dimensions when offered with varied toppings.

ORANGE HONEY

1 cup honey	½ cup frozen orange-juice
6 whole cloves	concentrate

Combine the ingredients in a small saucepan. Place over medium heat and simmer five minutes. Remove cloves. Good either hot or cold.

BERRY–GOOD SAUCE

¾ cup syrup drained from any frozen berry   2 teaspoons cornstarch

Combine two tablespoons fruit syrup with cornstarch. Heat the remaining syrup to boiling point. Stir in cornstarch mixture and simmer, stirring constantly until syrup thickens. Serve hot.

BUTTER FLUFF

½ cup butter   ¾ cup honey

Beat butter until fluffy with a wooden spoon (or electric mixer). Gradually add honey; beat until well combined. Use on hot pancakes.

SOME ADDITIONAL TOPPERS

Mix warmed applesauce with a little apple-pie spice, spoon over pancakes; add a sprinkling of brown sugar.

Heat a thawed package of frozen berries; serve with a ladle or pour from pitcher.

Combine chopped nuts, toasted coconut and shaved maple sugar and sprinkle over pancakes.

PANCAKE FILLINGS

Spoon one of the following fillings onto the uncooked side of a pancake. Cover with more batter. Turn and complete browning.

Sliced bananas sprinkled with brown sugar.

Thawed and drained frozen raspberries or strawberries.

Canned crushed pineapple, well drained.

Appleberry sauce or applesauce mixed with a little sugar.

Jam or jelly—whipped until it can be drizzled from the tip of a spoon.

Crisp, crumbled Canadian bacon or fried brown-and-serve sausage bits or diced cooked ham.

Packaged chopped dates or raisins mixed with chopped nuts and sugar.

Canned sour red cherries—halved, spooned over the pancake, then sprinkled with sugar.

Serve these as a brunch spectacular or to conclude an elegant dinner.

ORANGE DESSERT PANCAKES

4 eggs
⅔ cup milk
1 cup pancake mix
1 cup (2 sticks) butter or margarine
½ cup sugar

2 tablespoons grated orange peel
2 teaspoons grated lemon peel
⅔ cup orange juice
1 teaspoon Angostura bitters

Beat eggs with rotary beater until light. Beat in milk, then pancake mix. For Orange Sauce: Melt butter or margarine (in a chafing dish if you have one). Stir in sugar, grated peels and orange juice. Cook over low heat five minutes or until slightly thickened. Add bitters, mixing well. Keep warm. Now make the pancakes. With butter or margarine, lightly grease a six-inch cast-iron skillet. Heat thoroughly over moderate heat. Hold skillet with one hand and pour two tablespoons batter with the other, using ladle or two-tablespoon-size serving spoon. Immediately swirl skillet with a circular motion to spread batter over the bottom of the pan. Cook until bubbles form all over surface. With narrow spatula, loosen edges. Turn. Cook one minute more. Repeat to make sixteen. Pour a little sauce on each pancake. Roll up. Heat gently in remaining sauce one minute, beating frequently. Serve with sauce. *Enough for six.*

For glamorous midnight suppers: Make pancake batter and fruit filling in advance; refrigerate. Cook and fill at party time.

FRENCH OOH–LA–LA PANCAKES

2 eggs
1⅓ cups milk

⅔ cup pancake mix
Butter or margarine

Beat eggs and milk together. Stir in pancake mix. Place one teaspoon of butter in an eight-inch crêpe pan or a heavy cast-iron skillet and heat. Pour two to three tablespoons batter in pan. Shake pan rapidly from side to side and around so that batter coats bottom. Cook until slightly golden (lift edge to peek); turn, cook the other side. *Makes ten.*

Pineapple Apricot Filling

2 jars (4¾ oz. each) strained apricots
2 flat cans (No. 1) crushed pineapple, drained

½ teaspoon allspice
¼ teaspoon nutmeg
Confectioners' sugar

Combine strained apricots with pineapple. Add spices. Spoon a little of this filling onto each pancake. Roll; dust with confectioners' sugar. *Filling is ample for ten pancakes.*

This marvelous combination is rich enough to make a dessert party all by itself.

BROWNIE PANCAKES A LA MODE

Chocolate Pancake Batter (page 279)
½ cup finely chopped walnuts
1 pint vanilla ice cream
1 cup heavy cream, whipped
Prepared chocolate sauce

Make up the chocolate pancake batter. Pour one-fourth cup batter onto heated griddle. Sprinkle with nuts. When bubbles appear, turn and cook second side. Place a large spoonful of ice cream on each pancake. Fold pancake in half over ice cream and place a dab of whipped cream on top. Drizzle chocolate sauce over all. Repeat, serving immediately as each pancake is complete. *Makes ten.*

Pancakes don't have to be sweet. In fact, they're a wonderful feature of French and Italian lunch and dinner cooking. Much more exciting than a piece of toast! Try these:

HAM AND SWISS CAKES

4 slices boiled ham
Butter
1 can condensed cream of asparagus soup
¼ teaspoon mace
Basic Pancake Batter (page 279)
¼ lb. Swiss cheese, grated

Cut ham slices in half and sauté in a small amount of butter. Combine asparagus soup with mace. Heat in a saucepan. Use the Basic Batter to make eight pancakes. Place four pancakes on individual serving plates. Stack two pieces of sautéed ham on each pancake. Sprinkle each with two tablespoons grated cheese; top with another pancake. Pour asparagus sauce over top; sprinkle with additional cheese. *Serves four.*

PANCAKES CHICKEN ROMA

2 cans condensed cream of chicken soup
2 tablespoons lemon juice
1 cup light cream
1 package (10 oz.) frozen peas
2 cans (5 oz. each) boned chicken
French Ooh-la-la Pancakes (page 282)
½ cup mayonnaise

Place soup in a saucepan. Stir in lemon juice and light cream. Bring slowly to boiling point. Reduce heat. Simmer for five minutes. Meanwhile, cook peas according to package directions. Drain. Add peas to sauce along with chicken. Stir in mayonnaise just before serving. Double the recipe for French Ooh-la-la Pancakes and use to make twenty pancakes. Spoon a little filling onto each cake and roll up. Serve with extra sauce as a topping. *Makes twenty small cakes or enough for six people as a luncheon dish.*

A gourmet's delight, this—and just the recipe to try when you're tired of the same old thing. Everything's different!

FRENCH–FRIED FOLDOVER PANCAKES

Basic Pancake Batter (page 279)　　Fat for deep frying
½ pint creamed cottage cheese　　½ cup light corn syrup
½ teaspoon cinnamon　　2 tablespoons lemon juice
¾ teaspoon grated lemon peel　　Commercial sour cream
2 teaspoons sugar

Make eight pancakes; follow basic batter recipe, but omit egg. Cook pancakes on one side only, on an electric griddle preheated to 400°F. Remove from griddle and cool on a towel. Meanwhile, combine cottage cheese, cinnamon, lemon peel and sugar. Spoon onto the uncooked side of each cooled pancake. Fold pancakes over, pinching edges together. Drop into cooking oil heated to 375°F. Fry for two minutes on each side. Remove. Drain on absorbent paper. Combine corn syrup and lemon juice and drizzle over each pancake or top each with a mound of sour cream. *Makes eight.*

Now here's a complete brunch in one pancake!

COMPLETE BREAKFAST PANCAKES

Buckwheat pancake mix　　6 eggs
3 strips bacon, fried crisp and drained　　¼ cup milk
¼ cup melted butter or margarine　　Salt and pepper to taste
½ cup grape jelly or orange
　marmalade

Prepare buckwheat batter (use buckwheat mix and directions for Basic Pancake Batter, page 279), crumble bacon and add. Cook pancakes on lightly greased griddle until browned on both sides. Spread with melted butter and jelly and keep warm. Beat eggs well, add milk, salt and pepper and scramble in greased skillet. Transfer buckwheat cakes to baking sheet. Place eggs on half of face of each cake. Fold the other half over to form a half-moon. Dot with butter and jelly. Heat in oven at 375°F. (moderate) until jelly is slightly melted. *Serve hot to six girls—or to two boys and two girls.*

These pancakes are not fried but baked. They make a delectable dessert.

CREAM CHEESE FRITTERS

1 package (8 oz.) cream cheese	¼ teaspoon salt
1 large egg	2 tablespoons flour

Soften cream cheese at room temperature, then cream until very soft. Beat in egg until fluffy. Stir in salt and flour. Drop by tablespoonfuls onto greased cookie sheets to make eight pancake shapes. Near serving time, bake at 375°F. (moderate) twenty minutes or until browned and crusty. Serve with warm maple syrup and a sprinkling of cinnamon as a dessert. *Serves four.*

WAFFLES

Naturally, any topping that tastes good with pancakes will taste equally good with fluffy waffles, so check over the toppings on page 280. And waffles always make people feel you've done something special for them.

OLD-FASHIONED AIRY WAFFLES

3 cups sifted flour	⅓ cup vinegar
1½ teaspoons baking soda	2 cups undiluted evaporated milk
1 tablespoon sugar	1 cup water
¾ teaspoon salt	½ cup butter or margarine, melted
3 egg yolks	2 egg whites

Sift flour, soda, sugar and salt together onto waxed paper. Measure egg yolks, vinegar, evaporated milk and water into a large pitcher or a bowl with a pouring spout. Beat until combined. Add butter and sifted dry ingredients to the milk mixture and stir well. Beat egg whites until stiff but not dry. Fold into batter. Pour on preheated waffle iron, using about one cup of batter for each double waffle. Bake until the waffle stops steaming. *Makes twelve.*

For Nut Waffles: Before you fold in egg whites, stir in three-fourths cup of chopped salted mixed nuts.

Here are two toppings that will transform plain waffles into a hearty main dish for brunch or supper.

PINEAPPLE–HAM WAFFLE TOPPING

1 can (14 oz.) pineapple tidbits
2 tablespoons butter or margarine
¾ cup chopped green pepper
3 tablespoons flour
1½ cups undiluted evaporated milk

3 cups diced cooked ham or luncheon
  meat
¼ teaspoon Tabasco sauce
⅛ teaspoon paprika

Drain the pineapple, reserving syrup. To this syrup, add enough water to make one and one-half cups. Set aside. Melt butter slowly in a skillet (an electric one makes it easy to keep topping hot for company while waffles bake). Add green pepper and cook slowly until soft. Sprinkle with flour. Slowly stir in water-syrup mixture and cook until mixture thickens and comes to a boil, stirring constantly. Then add evaporated milk, ham, Tabasco and paprika. Heat through and ladle over waffles. *Tops eight waffles.*

TUNA VELOUTÉ WAFFLE TOPPING

2 cans (7 oz. each) tuna
1 bottle (7 oz.) pimiento-stuffed
  olives
¼ cup butter or margarine

⅓ cup flour
3 cups clear chicken broth
¼ cup cream (light or heavy)

Drain the tuna, reserving its oil, and flake. Drain olives, halve and set aside. In a skillet (electric if desired) over low heat, melt the butter. Add the oil drained from tuna, then stir in flour. Add chicken broth gradually, stirring constantly. Cook, stirring, until thickened. Now add the drained flaked tuna and olive halves, along with cream. If desired, season with paprika. Keep warm in skillet. *Tops six waffles.*

Try this recipe when there's a boy or two on the breakfast-date calendar —we've never known one who could resist the spell of its hidden gold!

CORN NUGGET WAFFLES

3 cups buttermilk pancake mix
3 cups milk
3 eggs

⅓ cup melted butter or margarine
1½ cups drained canned whole-kernel
  corn

Measure pancake mix into large bowl. Next, beat the milk and eggs together. Stir into pancake mix, along with cooled melted butter and corn.

Beat vigorously until batter is fairly smooth. Ladle into preheated waffle iron. Serve waffles as they are made, or keep hot in very slow oven (250°F.) wrapped in a kitchen towel; use towel or napkin to separate layers. The number of waffles varies with iron. *Serves eight.*

Just imagine these waffles for dessert, spread with orange marmalade and topped with a scoop of vanilla ice cream. Or imagine them for breakfast, with butter melting in the crevices and Orange Honey (page 280) to top them. Stop imagining! Start mixing!

WONDERFUL ORANGE WAFFLES

2 eggs, separated
1 tablespoon orange juice
1⅔ cups milk (about)
¼ cup melted shortening or cooking oil

2 cups sifted flour
1 tablespoon sugar
½ teaspoon salt
3 teaspoons baking powder
2 teaspoons grated orange peel

Place egg whites in mixing bowl and beat until stiff but not dry. Set aside. Place orange juice in two-cup glass measure, then add milk to make one and two-thirds cups. Combine with egg yolks and liquid shortening. Sift together flour, sugar, salt and baking powder and add to yolk mixture. Beat until blended. Stir in orange peel, then fold in egg whites. Use a scant cup to fill a preheated waffle iron, close and bake until waffle stops steaming. *Makes four large waffles.*

Fun for breakfast? Of course. Fun for after a date, too, sometime when you're thinking "but there's nothing in the house."

FRENCH–TOASTED HAM SANDWICHES

3 eggs
¼ cup maple-blended syrup
¼ teaspoon salt

6 thin slices ham
12 slices bread
¼ cup butter or margarine

Beat eggs; add maple syrup and salt. Beat until well combined. Place one folded slice of ham between two slices of bread. Heat two tablespoons of the butter in a skillet until bubbling. Using a kitchen fork, dip both sides of sandwich into egg mixture. Brown on both sides in hot butter. Cut in half and serve immediately. *Serves six.*

For one: Beat one egg with one tablespoon maple syrup and a pinch of salt. Make a sandwich with one slice of ham, two slices of bread. Dip in egg. Fry on one side; pour remaining egg mixture over top before turning to brown other side.

BREADS FROM THE OVEN

You can have homemade pecan buns in a hurry when you start with refrigerator biscuits.

PECAN BUNS

⅔ cup brown sugar
⅔ cup butter or margarine
⅔ cup chopped pecans

½ teaspoon cinnamon
2 packages refrigerator biscuits

Combine brown sugar, butter, pecans and cinnamon in a baking pan thirteen by nine by two inches. Melt over low heat. Cut the biscuits in half, down the length of the can. Roll each of the halves in the mixture to coat, then place in pan. Bake at 425°F. (hot) fifteen minutes. Remove from oven and turn to coat tops again. *Serve warm to six.*

This breakfast cake is rich enough to be a dinnertime dessert.

APPLE CAKE

5 medium-size apples
⅓ cup brown sugar
½ teaspoon cinnamon
2 whole eggs plus 2 egg yolks
½ cup sugar

1 teaspoon grated lemon peel
2 cups biscuit mix
2 tablespoons butter or margarine,
   melted

Peel, core and slice the apples, then sprinkle them with a mixture of brown sugar and cinnamon. Mix eggs, egg yolks and granulated sugar in a bowl. Add lemon peel, biscuit mix and melted butter and mix until well blended. Pour half the batter into an eight-by-eight-by-two-inch square pan. Cover with about half the apple slices. Spread remaining batter over them. Decorate top in an attractive pattern with remaining apple slices. Bake at 375°F. (moderate) forty-five to fifty minutes. If desired, top with hard sauce or whipped cream. *Serve hot or cold to twelve.*

Homemade coffeecake, hot from the oven—is there anything better?

CRUMBLY NUT COFFEECAKE

To make the cake:

2 tablespoons sugar
1 egg
¾ cup milk

2 cups biscuit mix
½ cup raisins, lightly floured

In a bowl, combine sugar with egg, milk and biscuit mix. Beat vigorously for half a minute. Fold in raisins. Turn into a greased nine-inch square pan.

To make the topping:

½ cup sugar
¼ cup flour
½ teaspoon cinnamon

½ cup chopped pecans
2 tablespoons soft butter

Blend sugar, flour, cinnamon, pecans and butter until crumbly. Sprinkle over batter. Bake at 400°F. (hot) twenty-five minutes. *Cut into nine squares.*

SWEET YEAST BREADS

If you've never worked with yeast doughs, find out the little tricks on pages 167 and 168. Then proceed to the recipes following.

These pinwheels aren't nearly so hard to make as authentic Danish pastry, but they're equally delicious. Try them for a Coffee House Party.

PINWHEEL PASTRIES

1 box (13½ oz.) hot-roll mix
1 cup (2 sticks) butter or margarine
¼ cup warm (not hot) water

½ cup scalded milk
¼ cup sugar
3 egg yolks, divided

Empty flour from box of hot-roll mix into a large bowl. Using pastry blender, cut in butter. Sprinkle yeast from the mix packet over warm water. Stir until dissolved. Cool the milk until lukewarm, then stir sugar into milk. Add dissolved yeast, milk and two lightly beaten egg yolks to flour-butter mixture. Stir with a wooden spoon until flour is absorbed. Refrigerate, covered, several hours or overnight. Divide into fourths; roll out one-fourth of chilled dough on a well-floured board into an eight-by-twelve-inch rectangle. (Note: Be sure board is generously dusted with flour, and check the dough during rolling to 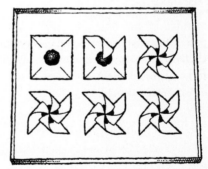 be sure it's not sticking; reflour board as needed.) Cut rolled dough into six four-inch squares. Transfer squares to cookie sheet, leaving one inch between squares. Put a tablespoonful of one of the fillings (page 290) in the center of each square. Now, to shape them into pinwheels, make a cut from each corner halfway to the center of each square; bring alternate points to the center—overlapping them as you would to make a paper pinwheel (see illustration). Let rise in a warm draftless place for about a half-hour. Bake at 350°F. (moderate) for five minutes. Brush surface with remaining egg yolk beaten with a little water. Bake five minutes longer or until golden brown. Repeat procedure with remaining three-fourths of the dough. *Makes two dozen.*

Prune Filling

1 box (1 lb.) dried prunes
½ cup sugar

½ teaspoon cinnamon

Cook prunes until tender. Remove pits, chop prunes until fine and combine with sugar and cinnamon.

Apricot Filling

Easiest of all: open a jar of good apricot preserves and spoon onto dough.

Almond Filling

1 can (4½ oz.) blanched almonds
¼ cup soft butter or margarine
¼ cup sugar

1 egg
1 teaspoon almond extract

Blend almonds in electric blender at high speed until very fine. (Or use rotary grater.) Cream butter and sugar. Add egg and extract; beat until fluffy. Stir in the almonds.

Cheese Filling

1 package (8 oz.) cream cheese
1 egg yolk
2 teaspoons lemon juice

½ teaspoon grated lemon peel
¼ cup sugar

Let cheese stand at room temperature until soft. Place cheese in mixing bowl or small bowl of electric mixer. Add egg yolk; beat until fluffy and well combined. Beat in lemon juice, grated peel and sugar. Chill an hour or two before using.

Because of their pretty red filling, these little sweeties *look* their best on holidays like Christmas, Valentine's Day, Washington's Birthday. But they *taste* their best every time!

CHERRY WHIRLS

1 box (14½ oz.) hot-roll mix
1 teaspoon cinnamon

1 cup (2 sticks) soft butter
2 jars (1 lb. each) cherry preserves

Prepare hot-roll mix as package directs, using egg and water called for but adding cinnamon to flour mixture. Let dough rise half an hour or until double in bulk. Roll dough thin on well-floured board to make a fifteen-by-twenty-inch rectangle. Spread butter on half the rectangle and fold in half, pinching edges together. Spread entire top surface with butter and fold in half again. Now cut dough in half. Roll one half into a twelve-by-sixteen-inch rectangle. Spread with butter, fold in half, joining long edges. Spread again with butter. Drain preserves (save syrup for sundaes) and spoon half the cherries over buttered surface. Roll up to form a long roll and cut into sixteen pinwheels. Put each pinwheel into a buttered two-inch muffin cup. Now roll, fill and cut second half of dough. Let all rise half an hour, then bake at 375°F. (moderate) twenty minutes or until golden. *Makes thirty-two.*

This yeast coffeecake roll has even better keeping qualities than old-fashioned Stollen, and it's sweet, moist and tender.

FROSTED PECAN–FRUIT ROLL

To make the dough:

1 package active dry yeast	1 teaspoon salt
½ cup warm (not hot) water	1 cup shortening
4½ cups sifted cake flour	3 egg yolks, beaten
3 tablespoons sugar	1 cup milk, scalded and cooled

Sprinkle yeast over warm water and stir until dissolved. Sift flour, sugar and salt into large bowl. Cut in shortening, using pastry blender or two knives. Combine egg yolks, cooled milk and yeast; blend into flour, beating well and adding a little more cake flour if needed to make a very soft sticky dough. Cover bowl and refrigerate overnight. Turn out on a lightly floured board. Knead lightly until dough is smooth enough to roll. Divide into four parts. Roll out each part into a very thin rectangle about eleven by eighteen inches.

To make the filling:

2 cups coarsely chopped pecans, divided	1 cup sifted brown sugar, firmly packed
1 cup golden seedless raisins	1 teaspoon cinnamon
1 cup coarsely chopped pitted dates	1 cup cherry preserves
	3 egg whites

Combine one cup of the chopped pecans with all the other ingredients except the egg whites. Beat egg whites until stiff but not dry. Spread each rectangle with one-fourth of egg white, then sprinkle with one-fourth the fruit mixture. Roll up lengthwise as for jelly roll and pinch seam together. Place rolls seam side down on a greased cookie sheet. Let rise forty-five minutes in a warm place, free from drafts. Bake at 400°F. (hot) thirty to thirty-five minutes or until tops are firm when tapped. Cool a little. Frost with Butter Cream Frosting (below), then sprinkle each roll with one-fourth cup chopped pecans. Serve warm or cold. *Makes thirty-two slices.*

Butter Cream Frosting

¼ cup butter or margarine	1 teaspoon vanilla
2 cups sifted confectioners' sugar	⅓ cup milk, cream or evaporated milk

Cream butter until fluffy, then gradually blend in sugar, vanilla and as much milk as needed to bring to thin spreading consistency.

Cherry desserts have a standing invitation to appear for February holidays, but this rich cherry ring wins friends the year 'round.

HOLIDAY CHERRY RING

3½ cups sifted flour	½ cup undiluted evaporated milk
½ cup sugar	½ teaspoon grated lemon peel
½ teaspoon salt	2 eggs, beaten
¼ cup butter or margarine	1 jar (8 oz.) maraschino cherries
2 packages active dry yeast	1 can (1 lb. 13 oz.) fruit cocktail
½ cup warm (not hot) water	Spicy Sauce (page 293)

Sift together flour, sugar and salt. Cut in butter. Stir yeast into warm water. Add to flour. Stir in milk, lemon peel and eggs. Beat until glossy (about three minutes). Cover; let rise in a warm place forty-five minutes or until doubled in bulk. Meantime drain cherries, saving the syrup. Set aside ten cherries and chop the rest fine. Stir into the risen dough. Spoon dough into a greased nine-inch ring mold. Let rise twenty minutes until doubled. Bake at 400°F. (hot) twenty-five minutes. Drain fruit cocktail, saving syrup. Make the sauce (page 293) as cake bakes, then turn cake out onto a slightly concave platter (to hold the good sauce). Pour sauce slowly over cake, basting often, until syrup is absorbed. Before serving, pile fruit cocktail in the center of cake and top with the reserved cherries. *Serves sixteen.*

Spicy Sauce

Reserved syrups from fruit cocktail
and cherries
1 teaspoon whole allspice
1 teaspoon whole cloves
2 sticks cinnamon

1 strip lemon peel
½ cup sugar
1 bottle (7 oz.) lemon-lime
carbonated beverage
2 teaspoons rum extract

Place the fruit syrups in a saucepan. Add the remaining ingredients except the rum extract. Simmer ten minutes. Stir in rum extract, then strain and use over Holiday Cherry Ring (page 292).

Beverages

*A*S PREVIOUSLY NOTED, good parties require an ample supply of refreshing things to drink. Examples follow.

MILK AND MILK DRINKS

Milk, just as it comes from the carton, is too often omitted at parties, according to many boys we talk to. Take their advice. Arrange to have a few extra quarts on hand the next time you're entertaining.

Or, even better, make a marvelous milk combination drink. Some of those which follow call for whole milk, some for nonfat dry milk, which shaves a few calories if you're weight-watching.

WEIGHT–LOSER'S BANANA FLIP

1 cup ice water	1 small banana, sliced
3 tablespoons instant nonfat dry milk powder	1 teaspoon lemon juice

Place ice water in a bowl or shaker. Sprinkle dry milk over water, stir until blended. In a small bowl, beat together until blended banana slices and lemon juice, using a rotary beater. Add liquefied milk and beat until blended. Pour into glass. Garnish with a dusting of powdered ginger. *Makes one glass. Calories: 169.*

NOTE: In a blender, just pour in the water, add all remaining ingredients, then blend thirty seconds at high speed until frothy.

WEIGHT–GAINER'S STRAWBERRY NOG

1 cup ice water
⅓ cup instant nonfat dry milk
   powder

2 tablespoons strawberry preserves
1 egg

Place ice water in a mixing bowl. Sprinkle dry milk over water, stir until blended. Add strawberry jam and egg to the liquefied milk. Then, with rotary beater or electric mixer, beat until light and foamy. *Makes one Strawberry Nog. Calories: 322.*

NOTE: In a blender, place water, jam and egg. Sprinkle dry milk over surface. Blend until foamy, about twenty-five seconds on high speed.

CHOCOLATE FIZZ

1 cup chilled club soda
1½ cups vanilla or chocolate ice
   cream

2 tablespoons chocolate syrup
2 tablespoons nonfat dry milk powder

Combine ingredients in shaker or jar of electric blender. Cover and shake or run blender until foamy. *Pour into two glasses and serve.*

BLENDER STRAWBERRY SHAKES

3 medium scoops strawberry ice cream
1½ cups milk

1 tablespoon quick strawberry-flavored
   drink mix

Combine in a blender, blend twenty seconds until foamy. *Makes three glasses*—repeat to serve more.

CARAMEL NOG

½ cup sugar, divided
1 cup boiling water
3 eggs, separated
3 cups cold milk

½ cup light cream
¼ teaspoon salt
½ teaspoon nutmeg

First make a caramel syrup. Place six tablespoons of the sugar in a heavy skillet. Stir constantly over low heat until the sugar dissolves and becomes a golden brown. Slowly stir in boiling water and continue to cook and stir until smooth syrup forms. Chill. When cooled, beat the egg whites until foamy, add the remaining two tablespoons of sugar and beat until stiff peaks form. Beat the egg yolks until thick and pale yellow. Fold into whites. Combine remaining ingredients with caramel syrup and fold into eggs. Serve with a sprinkling of additional nutmeg. *Fills six large glasses, even more punch cups.*

PINK PARTY MILK SHAKES

1 cup pineapple juice, chilled
2 tablespoons grenadine syrup
1 teaspoon lemon juice
2 tablespoons sugar

2 cups milk, chilled
⅓ cup crushed ice
1 pint vanilla ice cream

Combine the first four ingredients and stir until well blended. Add milk and ice. With an electric or rotary beater, beat until frothy. Strain out ice. Pour into tall glasses. Top with a scoop of ice cream. *Serves four.*

HOLIDAY EGGNOG

2 quarts commercial eggnog
1 cup heavy cream, whipped
2 egg whites

2 tablespoons sugar
Freshly ground nutmeg

Pour eggnog into punch bowl. Fold in heavy cream, whipped. Beat egg whites until foamy. Add sugar and continue beating until mixture forms stiff peaks. Fold into eggnog. Sprinkle surface lightly with nutmeg. Or ladle into punch cups and sprinkle each with nutmeg. *Makes twenty four-ounce servings or enough for eight people.*

To keep eggnog cold: Get an extra quart of eggnog and pour into ice cube trays with dividers in place. Add nog-cubes to bowl before serving.

HOT MOCHA MILK

¼ cup instant coffee powder
⅓ cup quick chocolate-flavored drink mix

¼ cup sugar
5 cups very hot milk

In a heatproof pitcher, blend coffee powder, chocolate drink mix and sugar. Add milk and stir until well combined. (A delicious drink for an automobile trip—put it in a vacuum jug previously rinsed with hot water.) *Serves five generously.*

HOT SPICED MILK

4 quarts milk
2 cups evaporated milk, undiluted
2 teaspoons nutmeg
2 teaspoons ground cloves

3 tablespoons sugar
½ teaspoon salt
Cinnamon sticks

Heat all the ingredients except the cinnamon sticks together in a large kettle. Stir from time to time and do not allow to boil. When hot, pour into mugs, garnish each with an extra-long cinnamon-stick stirrer. *Makes twenty-four six-ounce cupfuls.*

ICE CREAM SODAS—AT HOME

3 tablespoons syrup or sweetened
  mashed fruit
¼ cup milk or 2 heaping tablespoons
  whipped cream

6 oz. (about) bottled soda, any flavor
1 to 2 scoops ice cream, any flavor

Spoon syrup or fruit into a ten-ounce glass. Add milk or cream, then half-fill the glass with soda. Drop in the ice cream and fill the glass almost to overflowing with a final, foaming cloud of soda, poured against the side of the glass, not on top of ice cream. *Makes one.*

Hot Strawberry Soda: To make the sauce, thaw a ten-ounce box of frozen sliced strawberries. Add one-half cup light corn syrup; heat five minutes. Use hot with vanilla ice cream, milk and chilled strawberry soda.

Black Knight: Blend half a scoop of chocolate ice cream with one tablespoon chocolate syrup. Add a dash of cinnamon and nutmeg. Stir to mix. Add more ice cream and enough cola to fill glass.

Peacherino: To make sauce, thaw a ten-ounce box of frozen sweetened sliced peaches; rub through a sieve; add one-half teaspoon almond flavoring. Use with butter pecan or peach ice cream and ginger ale.

Root Beer Rave: Vanilla ice cream, milk, one-eighth teaspoon ginger, root beer—and stir.

The Last Straw: Use the largest glass you can find (oh, bigger than that!) and pile—in order: vanilla ice cream, sweet pitted Bing cherries, orange sherbet, peach sauce (above), strawberry ice cream, hot strawberry sauce (above). Fill to the brim with lemon-lime soda, then smother in whipped cream and top with a maraschino cherry.

JUNIOR ICE CREAM SODAS

12 bottles (7 oz. each) lemon-lime
  soda, chilled

1 quart strawberry ice cream or lemon
  ice

Have ready eight squat six-ounce glasses. Cut party straws to just the right length for these glasses with a razor blade or a very sharp knife. At party time, place a scoop of ice cream or sherbet in each glass, top with lemon-lime soda. *Serve with straws and teaspoons to eight.*

BOTTLED SODAS

Certainly the simplest way to provide refreshment at parties is to have on hand a virtually inexhaustible supply of bottled sodas. The cardinal rule: have enough. A minimum supply for a record hop would be three bottles per person. Every crowd has different flavor preferences—try to suit them. Generally, you'll need lots of colas, lots of lemon-lime, a smaller selection of other fruit flavors, ginger ale and root beer.

At an informal party, you may serve sodas from the bottle, glamorized as suggested below, or perhaps provided with a paper or fabric jacket. Have straws, of course. For slightly more dressed-up parties, use paper cups or glasses.

Refrigerating soda for a crowd of twenty or more can be a problem. Some suggestions: Use ice cubes and paper cups. Or borrow a large insulated container and buy ice in a twenty-five-pound block. Set the ice block in the container, then fill with sodas. The block melts more slowly than cubes and chills the sodas rapidly. For an outdoor party use a washtub, and fill it with ice cubes and bottled sodas in layers.

Be sure to have at least three bottle openers (the larger the better) and provide a spot for guests to discard empty bottles and caps.

Glamour Touches for Bottled Soft Drinks

Mock Champagne: Wrap a square of aluminum foil smoothly over the top of a bottled soda, conforming it to the bottle's shape. Around the neck, wrap a piece of bright red sticky tape, cross it at one side. If you want to do this for a big crowd, consult directions in the Prom Planner's Guide (page 406).

On the Colorful Rocks: Tint the water you use to make ice cubes with food coloring to match your color scheme. Fill a foil-covered tub with the cubes and rest bottles on them.

Soda Cartwheel: On a lazy Susan or other round tray with a rim, heap cracked ice. Arrange bottles of chilled cola like the spokes of a wheel, bottoms at outside edge. At center, place a cluster of flowers or fruit.

Soda Surprises: Serve a tray of assorted sodas with an assortment of soda fountain extras—lemon wedges, grenadine syrup, maraschino cherries and their syrup. Let guests mix-match their own treats.

COLA EGGNOG

2 eggs, separated	2 tablespoons confectioners' sugar
2 bottles cold cola beverage	¼ teaspoon vanilla

Slightly beat the egg yolks and combine with cola in a bowl. Beat egg whites until stiff but not dry, then beat in the sugar and vanilla. Fold half of the beaten whites into the cola. Pour into serving glasses and top each with the remaining whites. Sprinkle with cinnamon, if desired. *Fills two tall glasses or four punch cups.*

COLA SNOWSTORM

Beat together a pint of vanilla ice cream and three-fourths cup of cola beverage. For a party touch: top with whipped cream (tint it pink) and a shaving of unsweetened chocolate.

COLA–TONIC COOLER

4 bottles (10 oz. each) quinine water
2 bottles (12 oz. each) cola beverage

2 packages (10 oz. each) frozen
  sliced strawberries

Chill quinine and cola thoroughly. Let strawberries thaw about one hour at room temperature. Combine in a punch bowl. *Makes three quarts, a hospitable amount for eight or ten people.*

COLA FRUIT FIZZ

2 cans (6 oz. each) frozen lemonade
  concentrate
1 jar (8 oz.) maraschino cherries

2 oranges, sliced
8 bottles (6 oz. each) or 2 large
  bottles (26 oz. each) cola beverage

In advance, combine lemonade, cherries and oranges and keep chilled, along with cola. At serving time, place all in a punch bowl and stir to combine. *Makes about twenty punch-cup servings.*

GOOD COFFEE

Begin right—with the right grind of coffee. Each type of coffeepot requires a special kind. If the grind is too fine for the pot, the coffee will be muddy; if it's too coarse, the brew will be weak.

The vacuum pot (1) needs the finest grind—"vacuum" or "silex." Water bubbles up from lower container, mixes with coffee, and the brewed coffee returns to serving pot.

The percolator (2) needs coarse "regular" grind. Coffee is measured into the basket. When the water below it, in the pot, comes to the percolating point (just below boiling) it will travel up the hollow stem, bubble over top and drip down through coffee.

The drip coffee maker (3) needs medium "drip" grind. Coffee is measured into basket; rapidly boiling water is poured in top and moves downward, extracting flavor. Before serving coffee, remove top half of pot.

For each cup of perfect coffee, use one coffee measure (two level table-spoons) of coffee plus three-fourths cup water. Never use the pot to make less than three-fourths of its capacity—that is, don't make less than six cups in an eight-cup pot. For instant coffee (which seems to taste better by the potful) use one teaspoon (more or less to taste) per cup.

For a crowd, brew coffee like this: Tie a pound of regular grind coffee in a large piece of cheesecloth (leave room for coffee to expand). Bring eight quarts of water to a rapid boil, reduce heat till water stays below boiling point, then add coffee sack and tie it to pot handle. Brew about ten minutes. (4) Push sack up and down occasionally. *Don't* boil. Remove sack, press out brew. *Serves forty.*

Clean your coffee maker after each use. Wash it thoroughly with suds, rinse well and dry. Use steel wool pads to scour aluminum pots; use a baking soda solution plus plastic scouring pads to loosen stains in glass, enamel, ceramic and stainless steel coffeepots. If you have an electric pot, follow the directions of the manufacturer for cleaning.

Never boil coffee. All good coffee makers are styled to bring water and coffee together just a few degrees below the boiling point. It's better to keep coffee warm (very low heat) than to reheat it.

CAFÉ AU LAIT

Make four cups of coffee. Heat a quart of milk and pour it into a pitcher. Now—with the pitcher in one hand and the coffeepot in the other—pour the milk and coffee simultaneously into each cup. *Serve while frothy to five or six—with seconds.*

WITCHES' BREW

1 quart milk
3 cinnamon sticks
¼ cup sugar

4 cups hot coffee
½ cup quick chocolate-flavored drink
mix

Bring milk, cinnamon and sugar to simmering point in large saucepan. Reduce heat and cook ten minutes till cinnamon flavor is released. Add chocolate mix to the milk; combine with fresh hot coffee. *Serves eight.*

VIENNESE VELVET

1 quart vanilla ice cream
6 cups hot double-strength coffee

1 cup heavy cream, whipped

In each of six tall goblets, place a scoop of ice cream and a metal spoon. Pour hot coffee carefully against side of glass until glass is two-thirds full. Add a second scoop of ice cream, fill to brim with coffee. Garnish with whipped cream. Use iced-tea spoons for the first half, drink the rest with a straw. *Delicious for six.*

NOTE: To make double-strength coffee, use regular amount of ground coffee but half the water.

Five recipes guaranteed to make a sensation at your Coffee House Party!

THE SUNDAE SPECIAL

A layer of meringue
¼ cup strong cold coffee
1 scoop pistachio ice cream

Whipped cream for garnish
Pistachio nuts

Make the meringue an hour before the party and refrigerate. To make it: Beat two egg whites till stiff but not dry. Slowly add one-fourth cup sugar; beat till meringue holds stiff peaks. Enough for eight drinks. For each: Pour coffee into a slender glass. Spoon meringue over coffee to make a two-inch layer. (Seal against sides of glass so coffee won't rise.) Carefully spoon ice cream over meringue, add a mound of whipped cream and a sprinkling of pistachios. Serve with a spoon for stirring. *Makes one.*

CINNAMON SPOON

To each cup of hot coffee add a few whole cloves and whole allspice. Keep warm over low heat three minutes; then strain into cups. Stir with a cinnamon stick, add a mound of whipped cream, garnish with ground nutmeg. (A half-pint of cream, whipped, tops twelve drinks.)

POUF CAFÉ

1½ cups strong coffee, cooled
Cracked ice

Liquid artificial sweetener or sugar
(optional)

Fill electric blender container half full of cracked ice. Add coffee. Blend until thick and foamy. Add sweetening if desired. *Serve in four tall glasses.*

ESPRESSO INFERNO

1 level teaspoon instant espresso
  coffee
½ cup boiling water
1 tablespoon brown sugar

¼ teaspoon orange extract
1 orange slice
1 sugar cube

Place instant coffee in a small glass (not fine crystal). Pour boiling water into glass down the side of a spoon. Stir in brown sugar and orange extract. Slit orange slice, place on glass. Add sugar cube saturated in orange extract. (Make a pinhole in cube; secure to orange with toothpick.) Ignite cube and *serve to one.*

COFFEE HOUSE TWIST

For four Twists you need: two cups of cocoa, two cups of strong coffee and one ice cube tray each of pink and chocolate milk cubes. (Recipes are below; use four pink and four chocolate cubes in each glass.) Have everything ready in the refrigerator when guests arrive. To serve: alternate cubes in glass, fill halfway with cocoa, add coffee, stir once.

For pink milk cubes:

2 cups nonfat dry-milk powder
2 cups water

Few drops of red food coloring
1 teaspoon rum extract

Combine milk powder, water and food coloring; stir in extract. Pour into an ice tray and put in the freezer.

For chocolate milk cubes:

1 cup instant sweet cocoa
1 cup hot water

1 cup cold water
2 cups nonfat dry milk powder

Mix cocoa with hot water. Add cold water and milk; stir to combine and pour into ice tray. Freeze.

GOOD TEA

Keep tea fresh: Store it for not more than six months in a tight canister or jar, away from spices or aromatic foods.

Bring cold water to a full boil. Pour over tea leaves while water is still boiling.

Use crystal-clean pot or cup made of glass, china or earthenware. Preheat it with hot or boiling water for the best brew.

To make tea for one: Pour boiling water over tea bag in a cup. Let stand three to five minutes, bobbing tea bag occasionally. Press tea bag with spoon and remove. Or use instant tea, following label directions.

For more: Use one tea bag for each cup of tea, plus one for the pot. Hold tight to the bags as you pour in boiling water, then secure them by replacing cover. Time the brewing as above, remove bags and stir. Always make tea like this for full flavor—add very hot water to dilute, if it is too strong for your taste.

For iced tea: Try instant tea, using label directions. Or for two, brew extra strong hot tea (three tea bags, two cups boiling water). Pour over ice. Place a metal spoon in glass to prevent breakage from sudden temperature changes.

DIXIE ICED TEA

½ cup loose tea or 15 tea bags
  (remove tags)
4 lemons, sliced thin

¾ cup superfine sugar
2 quarts fresh cold water

When tea is measured, place lemons and sugar in a two-and-one-half-quart pitcher. Bring the water to a full boil and remove from heat. Add the tea all at once. Let stand five minutes. Stir once, then pour into the pitcher. (Strain carefully if you have used loose tea.) Serve at once in ice-filled glasses with additional sugar and lemon if desired. Or keep at room temperature (to prevent clouding) removing lemon slices after two hours. *Fills ten glasses.*

TEA FOR A CROWD

Hot: In the morning, make a tea concentrate. Bring one and one-half quarts of water to a boil. (A glass saucepan is good.) Add one-fourth pound of loose tea. Stir, then steep five minutes. Strain and store at room temperature. At party time fill a two-quart teapot with one cup concentrate and five cups very hot water. Stir and serve. Refill pot as needed. *Makes enough tea for fifty-two.*

Iced: Mix the full recipe of concentrate (one and one-half quarts) with five quarts of cold water. Pour over ice cubes in glasses.

Tea Trimmers

Whenever you serve hot tea, offer your guests milk (never cream, which spoils the flavor), wedges of lemon and sugar—in tiny cubes or granulated. For fun, try cinnamon-stick stirrers. Whenever you serve iced tea, provide wedges of lemon or bottled lemon juice, superfine sugar. Pleasant changes: add orange juice, fresh or frozen concentrate, to sweeten and flavor; or lemon-lime soda (no sugar necessary).

FRUIT DRINKS AND PUNCHES

Some of the refreshing fruit drinks which follow are suggested for private parties—maybe just you and a friend on the patio, watching the sun go down. Others are for larger groups—six to twelve.

But when the party gets really big, or when you're looking for a different recipe for the next school dance, turn to page 395, where the giant-size punches begin.

FLORIDA FREEZE

6 thin slices of orange
6 maraschino cherries
1 pint orange sherbet

1 quart fresh or frozen reconstituted
   orange juice
½ teaspoon Angostura bitters

Garnish rims of six eight-ounce glasses with halved orange slices and maraschino cherries. Place sherbet in large bowl of electric mixer. Turn to medium speed and begin adding orange juice, a little at a time. Add bitters. Beat until well combined and frothy. *Serves six.*

PARTY PUNCH

1 package tangerine instant soft-drink
   mix
½ cup sugar

2 quarts cold water
1 to 2 cans (6 oz. each) frozen
   lemonade concentrate

Put soft-drink mix into a tall pitcher. Add sugar, cold water and one can of lemonade concentrate. Stir to combine. Taste; add as much more lemonade as desired. Chill, add ice and *serve to six.*

SWIMMER'S PUNCH (HOT OR COLD)

1 can (46 oz.) pineapple-grapefruit
  juice drink
1 bottle cranberry juice cocktail
2 bottles (7 oz. each) lemon-lime
  soda

1 lemon, cut in thin slices
16 whole cloves
4 tablespoons honey

Combine all ingredients in a large kettle and heat. Hold just below simmering point for fifteen minutes. Strain if desired. Cool, then chill. At party time, heat or serve cold, depending on the mood of the group. *For six.*

ROSE WATER PUNCH

¼ cup rose water
1 quart cold water
1 can (6 oz.) frozen lemonade
  concentrate

1 can (No. 2) crushed pineapple,
  drained
2 cups cracked ice
Fresh rose petals

Combine all ingredients except rose petals in a large bowl or pitcher. Ladle into punch cups; garnish each with a fresh rose petal. *Serves six.*

NOTE: Get rose water at your drugstore.

BLENDER LIME PUNCH

1 can (6 oz.) frozen limeade
  concentrate, thawed
1 package (12 oz.) frozen mixed
  melon balls, thawed, or 1 ripe
  papaya, cut up

1 pear, peeled and cut up
3 cups water
2 cups cracked ice
Few drops of green food coloring

Since the total amount of this recipe would overfill the blender, place half of each ingredient called for in blender jar. Cover and blend until smooth, about one minute. Repeat with remaining ingredients. Mix and *serve in six tall glasses or twelve punch cups.*

BRAZILIAN FRUIT FRAPPÉ

1 cup grapefruit juice
1 cup pineapple juice
1 ripe banana, cut up
1 teaspoon rum extract
1 teaspoon almond extract

1 teaspoon grenadine syrup
1 tablespoon lemon juice
1 tablespoon honey
1 tablespoon flaked coconut
1 cup finely cracked ice

Place all ingredients in electric blender jar. Blend one minute. *Serve in tall glasses to three.*

PINK POLYNESIAN FOAM

2 cans (No. 2) pineapple-grapefruit
  juice drink
6 cups orange juice

1 cup lemon juice
1 cup grenadine syrup
Cracked ice

Measure the fruit juices and flavorings into a pitcher and stir to blend. To make the punch foamy, fill the electric blender or a shaker jar one-third full of cracked ice. Add about one-fourth of the fruit juice mixture and agitate until foamy. Repeat to make enough to serve guests, preparing more as needed. *Makes fourteen large servings, enough for eight people.*

CRANBERRY PINEAPPLE PUNCH

1 can (46 oz.) pineapple-grapefruit
  juice drink
1 cup canned whole cranberry sauce

½ cup crushed pineapple
1 quart ginger ale
Ice cubes

Have all ingredients cold. At serving time, mix together in punch bowl, adding enough ice cubes to keep punch cold. *Makes three quarts or sixteen punch cup servings.*

ISLANDER'S PUNCH

1 can (46 oz.) pineapple juice
1 can (46 oz.) tropical fruit punch
½ cup grenadine syrup
3 bottles (7 oz. each) lemon-lime
  carbonated beverage

¼ cup lemon juice
1 can (No. 2) pineapple chunks
Maraschino cherries

Chill all ingredients at least three hours. Combine liquids in punch bowl. Stir, add ice cubes and garnish with pineapple chunks and a few maraschino cherries. *Fills thirty four-ounce punch cups, enough for ten people.*

SIX–FLAVOR PUNCH

2 tablespoons tea packaged with
  orange and sweet spice
2 quarts boiling water

1 can (46 oz.) pineapple-grapefruit
  juice drink
½ cup honey

Put tea in boiling water and steep for ten minutes. Strain and add the pineapple-grapefruit juice and honey. Pour into pitcher. Chill; add ice at serving time. *Makes twenty six-ounce servings, plenty for ten.*

SPICY PINEAPPLE GRAPEFRUIT PUNCH

1 can (46 oz.) pineapple-grapefruit
   juice drink
2½ cups water
1 stick cinnamon
1 teaspoon whole cloves

½ teaspoon whole allspice
Peel of one orange, cut up
3 tea bags
½ cup sugar
¼ cup lemon juice

Chill pineapple-grapefruit drink. Place water, spices and orange peel in a saucepan. Bring to a boil over moderate heat. Simmer fifteen minutes, then strain. Add tea bags and allow to steep five minutes. Remove tea bags and add sugar and lemon juice. Stir until sugar is dissolved; then cool and refrigerate. When ready to serve, combine with chilled pineapple-grapefruit juice drink. Serve from a two-and-one-half-quart pitcher or ladle from a punch bowl. *Makes twenty-four half-cup servings or punch for eight to twelve people.*

Dips and Nibbles

$\mathcal{T}$o SERVE DIPS WITH FLAIR, the secret word is variety—several dips, plus an assortment of dunkables—crisp rye wafers, saltines, potato chips and sesame wafers. You'll find some crackers already packed in assortments: browse around the cracker counter and see what's new. Visit the vegetable department, too, for more crisp dunkers: celery, radishes, carrots to cut into sticks, cauliflower, white turnips to cut into strips. You can arrange your trays of vegetables and crackers well in advance. Cover both with transparent plastic wrap; refrigerate the vegetable tray. Make the dips in advance and refrigerate them too. For a big crowd, divide each dip into several small bowls so you can keep some cold while the party progresses. An avid dipper can easily consume one-third cup of dip (given enough chips or crackers!); plan amounts accordingly.

COMPANY DIP

Soften one package (three ounces) cream cheese and gently blend in one-half pint commercial sour cream. Stir in one package or can of dehydrated onion soup. To ripen flavor refrigerate at least one hour in a pretty bowl. Garnish top with chopped chives or parsley. Serve surrounded by crisp rye crackers and celery sticks.

NOTE: Onion dip may also be made with onion-flavored salad dressing mix or the special mix made just for dips.

CREAM CHEESE–PICKLE DIP

1 package (8 oz.) cream cheese
1 dill pickle
3 tablespoons dill pickle juice

½ teaspoon onion salt
½ teaspoon paprika

Different and *delicious*: Vanilla Game Cookies (*pages 357–358*) ▶

Warm cheese to room temperature, then place in a bowl. Beat with a wooden spoon until soft. Chop dill pickle fine. Stir pickle juice into cream cheese to get desired dip consistency. Add chopped pickle, onion salt and paprika. Keep in refrigerator until ready to serve. *Makes about one cup.*

CUCUMBER DIP

½ cucumber (about)
1 package (8 oz.) cream cheese

¼ teaspoon Worcestershire sauce
Dash of garlic salt

Scrub cucumber well. Do not peel. Shred it fine and drain thoroughly to make one-fourth cup. Combine with remaining ingredients. Serve with potato chips. *Makes about one cup.*

CHEDDAR CHEESE DIP

2 cups (½ lb.) grated Cheddar
  cheese
½ cup salad dressing or mayonnaise
1 can condensed cheese soup

¼ teaspoon onion powder
1 teaspoon parsley flakes
1 teaspoon lemon juice

Combine ingredients and refrigerate in serving bowls till party time. Serve with crackers for dipping. *Makes about three cups.*

CHILI DIP

1 bottle (12 oz.) chili sauce
1 tablespoon lemon juice

1 can (7 oz.) tuna, drained and
  flaked
½ teaspoon chili powder

Combine all ingredients and spoon into a serving dish. Refrigerate. *Makes about two cups.*

AVOCADO DIP

2 very ripe avocados
2 tablespoons lemon juice
4 drops Tabasco sauce
1 teaspoon salt

1 small bunch green onions, peeled,
  washed and finely chopped
1 large tomato, diced

Peel avocados, cut in half and discard stone. In a bowl combine avocados, lemon juice, Tabasco and salt. Mash with a fork or place in a blender container and blend until smooth. Stir in onions and diced tomato. Place in small bowls or dishes; chill until serving time. *Makes about one and one-half cups.*

◀ *Easy to enjoy: Fruitcake Bonbons (pages 353–354).*

BLUE CHEESE DIP

½ pint commercial sour cream
1 teaspoon instant minced green
onion

1 wedge (3 oz.) packaged blue cheese

Place sour cream and instant minced green onion in a bowl. Crumble blue cheese into sour cream; mix well. Or blend in an electric blender for two seconds. Chill. *Makes one and one-fourth cups.*

TASTY TUNA DIP

1 can (7 oz.) chunk-style tuna,
drained and flaked
1 package (3 oz.) cream cheese,
softened
3 to 6 tablespoons mayonnaise
1 tablespoon capers, chopped

½ teaspoon soy sauce
1 teaspoon prepared horse-radish
¼ teaspoon garlic salt
¼ teaspoon celery salt
¼ teaspoon onion salt
¼ teaspoon monosodium glutamate

Make early in the day if desired. In a medium-size bowl, combine all ingredients. (If you prefer a thinner dip, use the larger amount of mayonnaise.) Refrigerate till serving time. To serve, arrange spread in a bowl on a tray; surround with corn chips. Guests spread or dunk their own. *Makes about one and one-half cups.*

SHRIMP DIP

1 package (8 oz.) soft process
American cheese
1 package (8 oz.) cream cheese
1 tablespoon catchup
1 tablespoon Worcestershire sauce

1 tablespoon mayonnaise (optional)
1 cup finely chopped onion
Garlic salt to taste
1 package (8-10 oz.) frozen shrimp,
cleaned, cooked and chopped

Blend cheeses. Add catchup, Worcestershire sauce, mayonnaise, onion and garlic salt to taste. Continue to beat until very creamy. Add shrimp. Keep cold until serving time. Makes about a quart or *enough for eight to twelve guests.*

SHRIMP AVOCADO DUNK

2 ripe avocados
1 cup commercial sour cream
2 tablespoons chili sauce

1 teaspoon salt
1 cup cooked shrimp, chopped small

Remove the skin and pits from avocados and mash in a bowl with fork. Blend in sour cream, chili sauce and salt, then fold in shrimp. Serve in a bowl in center of tray surrounded with potato chips, corn chips, pretzels, crisp crackers. *Makes two and one-half cups.*

SAMPAN GRUB

1 can (7 oz.) salmon
1 avocado, peeled, pitted and cubed
1 onion, peeled and diced
¼ cup mayonnaise

Salt, pepper, vinegar to taste
1 tomato, diced
1 can (4½ oz.) pitted ripe olives,
    drained and chopped

Combine all ingredients except tomato and olives in electric blender. Mix until smooth. Pour into serving bowl; stir in tomatoes and olives. Serve with potato chips and crackers. *Makes about two and one-half cups.*

SPICED CRANBERRY NUT DIP

2 cups fresh cranberries
1 orange, quartered and seeded
¼ cup water
1 cup sugar

⅛ teaspoon cinnamon
⅛ teaspoon nutmeg
⅛ teaspoon allspice
½ cup chopped salted peanuts

Put cranberries and orange through food chopper. Combine in a saucepan with water, sugar and spices. Cook over medium heat until thickened, about fifteen minutes. Stir in peanuts. For a smoother consistency, you may place all the ingredients in a blender and run about two minutes, stopping blender and shifting contents one or two times. Delicious as a spread for crackers or toast at holiday time. *Makes about two cups.*

LITTLE SNACKS

Here is a collection of recipes for finger foods. Some are the type you place in party bowls in several areas of the room to keep your guests happy until it's time to eat! Some can provide all the "refreshments" needed at an informal gathering. Put the hot bites on a warmer of some kind, the cold ones on a tray lined with salad greens.

SPICY POPCORN

Use each of the tasty variations below with two quarts of freshly popped, unsalted corn. (See how to pop corn on page 366.) Dot it with one-fourth cup of butter, sprinkle with the seasoning called for, then place it in an ovenproof bowl in a slow oven (300°F.) for ten minutes. Toss well to combine; serve at once.

Pizza Popcorn: Sprinkle over popcorn one cup grated Parmesan or Romano cheese, one teaspoon salt, one-half teaspoon orégano and heat. For parties, serve with a dip of heated undiluted condensed tomato soup.

Chili Corn: Combine two tablespoons chili seasoning mix and one-half teaspoon salt. Add to popcorn and heat.

Barbecue Corn: Combine two teaspoons barbecue seasoning and one teaspoon salt. Sprinkle on popcorn; heat.

Onion Zings: Sprinkle two teaspoons onion salt over popcorn; heat.

Curry Corn: Mix one teaspoon curry powder and two teaspoons salt. Sprinkle over the popcorn; heat.

Garlic-ity Splits: Season popcorn with two teaspoons garlic salt; heat.

Poppycorn: Mix two teaspoons poppy seeds, one teaspoon salt, one cup grated American cheese. Sprinkle over the popcorn and heat.

Salad Mix-Up: Combine one-fourth teaspoon salt and one tablespoon *dry* salad dressing mix. (Choose your own favorite flavor. We like a blue cheese mix.) Sprinkle this over the popcorn; heat.

PARTY MIX

¾ cup butter or margarine, melted
¾ teaspoon each garlic salt, onion salt, monosodium glutamate
½ teaspoon celery salt
1½ tablespoons Worcestershire sauce

⅛ teaspoon Tabasco sauce
7 cups bite-size shredded wheat, rice or corn biscuits
1 cup broken pretzel sticks
2 cups salted mixed nuts

Combine butter and seasonings in a measuring cup. Spread cereal, pretzels and nuts in large roasting pan, distributing evenly. Pour the seasoned butter over cereal and toss lightly to coat. Bake at 275°F. (very slow) one hour, stirring every ten minutes. *Makes about two quarts, or enough to serve a party of eight.*

NOTE: Other crisp nonsweetened cereals may be used according to taste.

CHEESE PUFFS

1 cup sifted flour
⅓ cup butter or margarine
¼ lb. natural Cheddar cheese, grated

¼ teaspoon salt
2 tablespoons cold water
1 teaspoon Angostura bitters

Place flour in a bowl, add butter and, with a pastry blender or two knives, cut in until like coarse corn meal. Stir in cheese and remaining ingredients, toss-stirring dough until it clings together. Form into small balls, about one inch in diameter. Place on a greased baking sheet and bake about twenty minutes at 375°F. (moderate) until slightly browned. *Makes about three dozen.*

CHEESE PILLOWS

1 stick piecrust mix
1 cup grated Cheddar cheese

2 teaspoons Worcestershire sauce

Crumble piecrust mix into a bowl. Add cheese and Worcestershire sauce. Mix well. Roll out one-half inch thick. Cut into tiny squares. Bake at 325°F. (slow) twenty minutes or till browned and firm. *Snacks for four.*

BRAZIL NUT CHIPS

1 lb. Brazil nuts
1 teaspoon salt

¼ cup butter or margarine, melted

To shell the Brazil nuts: Place in a saucepan and cover with cold water. Bring to a boil and boil three minutes. Drain. Cover with cold water, let stand one minute, then drain. Crack gently and pull out meat. You should have one and one-half cups of shelled nuts.

Now toast the chips: Cover nut meats with cold water. Bring slowly to a boil and simmer five minutes. Drain and cool. Cut lengthwise into paper-thin slices. Spread one layer deep in a shallow pan. Sprinkle salt and butter over surface. Bake at 350°F. (moderate) twelve to fifteen minutes, stirring once or twice during baking. Delicious eaten as salted nuts or sprinkled over chocolate ice cream. *Makes two cups.*

SESAME SWISS SQUARES

For every four squares you make, you will need: two oblong crisp rye crackers; one slice of process Swiss cheese; one-fourth teaspoon sesame seeds; one teaspoon prepared mustard. Break each crisp rye cracker in half and spread with mustard. Cut cheese slices in quarters. Place one on each cracker and spread again with mustard. Sprinkle with sesame seeds. Place on a broiler pan set five inches from heat source. Broil until cheese is bubbly and lightly browned (about three minutes). *Serve hot, two to each guest.*

CURRIED RYE CRACKERS

2 tablespoons butter or margarine
¼ teaspoon curry powder

13 crisp rye crackers

Blend butter with curry powder and spread evenly on crackers. Place on rack in a shallow pan and bake at 350°F. (moderate) five minutes. Serve hot or cold. *Makes thirteen curried crackers.*

CHEESE TOASTIES

3 cans condensed cheese soup
⅓ cup light cream
¼ teaspoon Tabasco sauce
1 tablespoon minced parsley

2 tablespoons lemon juice
1 loaf French bread, cut into
    one-inch cubes

In advance: Combine soup, cream, Tabasco, parsley and lemon juice in a saucepan. Bring mixture to a simmer over moderate heat. Toss bread cubes in cheese mixture until well soaked, then spread cubes on a rack over a foil-covered baking sheet. Cover and chill cubes and sauce.

At serving time: Bake cubes at 425°F. (hot) for ten minutes; reheat sauce. When cubes are baked, brown for about a minute in the broiler. Serve with toothpicks for guests who want to dip the Toasties in the hot sauce. *Hearty snacking for four.*

SUNSHINE PILLOWS

1 package (3 oz.) cream cheese,
    softened
1 egg yolk
⅛ teaspoon baking powder

⅛ teaspoon onion powder
4 slices white bread
1 can (2¼ oz.) deviled ham
Butter

Mix cream cheese, egg yolk, baking powder and onion powder and blend well. Remove crusts from bread. Cut each slice into four squares. Spread generously with deviled ham. Spread egg mixture over deviled ham. Grease cookie sheet generously with butter. Bake at 350°F. (moderate) seven minutes. *Makes sixteen.*

MIDGET BURGERS

10 slices bread
Softened butter or margarine
1 lb. ground beef
2 tablespoons grated onion

1 tablespoon Worcestershire sauce
1 teaspoon salt
¼ cup chili sauce

Toast bread on one side in broiler. Cut four one-and-one-half-inch rounds from each slice. Lightly butter rounds on untoasted side. Combine ground beef, onion, Worcestershire and salt. Shape mixture into forty marble-size balls (one heaping teaspoon each) and place one on buttered side of each bread round, leaving a border of bread showing. Make a thimble-size indentation in center of balls. Broil four inches from heat for five to six minutes or till meat is done and edges of bread are toasted. Fill indentations with chili sauce. Serve hot. *Makes forty.*

HURRY CURRY CURLS

First make the crust:

1 cup sifted flour
½ teaspoon salt
½ teaspoon ginger

½ teaspoon monosodium glutamate
⅓ cup butter or margarine
3 to 4 tablespoons cold water

Sift together flour, salt, ginger and monosodium glutamate in a mixing bowl. Cut in the margarine or butter until particles are the size of small peas. Sprinkle with cold water while tossing and stirring lightly with a fork. Add just enough water to hold together. Form into a ball. Roll out to one-eighth-inch thickness on a lightly floured board or pastry cloth; cut into strips one-half inch wide.

Now make the dip:

½ teaspoon curry powder
3 tablespoons melted butter or
  margarine

½ cup crushed potato chips

Stir curry into melted butter or margarine; dip pastry strips, one at a time, in curry butter. Roll in crushed potato chips. Hold ends and twist, then place on an ungreased cookie sheet. Bake at 450°F. (hot) for eight to ten minutes or until golden. Serve at once or, if you wish to make them ahead of time, recrisp in moderate oven just before serving. *Makes about four dozen Curls.*

20

Cold Sandwiches and Other Cold Snacks

WHETHER you're making sandwiches for a crowd, the school lunch box or a midnight snack, bread is in the picture. What kind? Any kind, as long as it's fresh! These tips will help you enjoy bread at its best.

Store bread either in the refrigerator or in a room-temperature breadbox. Refrigerated bread dries out more quickly but is less apt to mold. (You can prevent this drying out to some extent by putting the wrapped bread in a plastic bag. A plastic bag should also be added to the original wrapper if you freeze bread.)

Unsliced bread and rolls can be freshened even after several days. Wrap in aluminum foil and heat at 350°F. (moderate). Or place in a clean but unwaxed paper bag and sprinkle the outside of the bag lightly with water, then heat in oven.

Turn really dry bread into croutons to garnish your next green salad—just cube the bread and fry it in garlic-flavored oil or butter.

Even leftover party sandwiches have a future if they've been kept cold to prevent spoilage. Sandwiches made with a meat, fish or cheese filling can be dipped in very thin pancake batter and fried in shortening until golden brown. Top with a sprinkling of chopped parsley and serve warm.

HAM AND EGG SALAD SANDWICHES

5 eggs	8 slices bread
1/3 cup mayonnaise or salad dressing	4 slices boiled ham
1½ teaspoons salt	Water cress, paprika, olives and
Pepper to taste	pickles for garnish

Hard-cook the eggs, cool and chop fine. Combine with mayonnaise, salt and pepper. At serving time, toast and butter bread. On four slices, arrange ham. Top with a few sprigs of water cress. Cover with remaining toast, butter side *up*. Spread with egg salad mixture, using one-third cup on each. Sprinkle with paprika. Cut diagonally into quarters. Serve with a nest of water cress filled with an olive and a sweet pickle. *Serves four.*

SEAFARE SPECIAL

1 can (7 oz.) tuna
¼ cup chopped celery
2 strips bacon, fried crisp, drained and crumbled
1 tablespoon vinegar
2 teaspoons minced onion

¼ cup mayonnaise or salad dressing
Salt and pepper to taste
8 slices pumpernickel bread
4 lettuce leaves
8 thin apple slices, cored

Drain tuna and flake. Combine with celery, bacon, vinegar, onion, mayonnaise, salt and pepper. Butter pumpernickel. Spread four slices with tuna filling, top each with two slices of apple and a lettuce leaf. Cover with remaining bread, cut in half and *serve to four.*

WESTERN SALAD FILLING

½ green pepper, washed, seeded and chopped fine
¼ cup chopped onion
1 teaspoon salt
1 teaspoon sugar

Dash of pepper
4 hard-cooked eggs, chopped
2 cans (2¼ oz. each) deviled ham
½ cup mayonnaise or salad dressing

Mix ingredients together in the order listed and blend well. Taste and add more salt and pepper if desired. Makes about two cups to use as a spread for crackers or a *filling for six sandwiches.*

TEA SANDWICHES

You don't *have* to serve tea with them, but these small and dainty sandwiches are just right when you want a variety of tiny bite-size treats.

OPEN HEARTS

Select a two-inch heart-shaped or round biscuit cutter. With it, cut two hearts or rounds from each of sixteen slices of white bread, avoiding crusts. Soften half an eight-ounce package of cream cheese with two teaspoons milk. Use to spread half the hearts. With a smaller cutter of same shape, cut the center from remaining half of hearts. Place the outlines over hearts spread with cream cheese, matching edges. In center hole place a washed, hulled strawberry or a fresh cherry. *Makes sixteen.*

DAGWOOD JRS.

24 slices salty party rye bread
2 cans (4½ oz. each) deviled ham
24 thin slices liverwurst

2 cans (5 oz. each) chicken spread
Mayonnaise
Parsley flakes

Spread each slice of bread thinly with deviled ham. Add a slice of liverwurst; spread chicken over this. Pipe borders with mayonnaise (put it through a pastry tube). Garnish with parsley. Cover with aluminum foil, shaped to form a hood which doesn't touch sandwiches. Chill until party time. *Makes two dozen.*

CHINESE CHICKEN SANDWICHES

½ cup chopped canned water
   chestnuts
1 jar (6½ oz.) boned chicken,
   drained and chopped
1 teaspoon instant minced green
   onion

½ teaspoon salt
Dash of pepper
¼ cup mayonnaise
12 slices white bread
¼ cup minced parsley (about)

Combine all ingredients except bread and parsley in mixing bowl. Chill. From each slice of bread, cut four tiny rounds. Spread with chilled mixture. Garnish with parsley. Cover with transparent plastic wrap and refrigerate until ready to serve. *Makes forty-eight.*

HAM ASPARAGUS ROLLS

18 thin slices white bread
⅓ cup mayonnaise

1 can (No. 2) white asparagus
18 thin slices boiled ham

Trim crusts from bread and arrange on board. With rolling pin, flatten bread thoroughly. Spread thinly with mayonnaise. Drain asparagus. Cover each piece of bread with boiled ham slice. Place asparagus at one edge and roll from this edge to the other. Arrange on platter seam side down. Cover with foil or transparent plastic wrap. Chill until ready to use. *Makes eighteen.*

CREAM CHEESE AND DATE NUT BARS

Cream cheese (half an 8 oz. package)
2 tablespoons milk

1 package (1 lb.) date nut bread

Soften cream cheese at room temperature, then blend with milk, beating until easy to spread. Open bread package and place half the slices on cutting board. Spread with cream cheese. Top with remaining slices, matching crusts. Cut each sandwich into four bars. *Makes thirty-two.*

DATE NUT RIBBONS

Make a four-decker sandwich using sliced date nut bread and softened cream cheese. Press stack firmly together. Trim sides square. Cut, crosswise, into quarter-inch slices. *Each makes twelve ribbons.*

"BACON" SLICES

1 small loaf white bread, unsliced
Softened butter

1 can (4½ oz.) deviled ham

Trim crusts from loaf of bread. Then cut four thin lengthwise slices from bottom (use remaining bread for stuffing or other fancy sandwiches). Use a rolling pin to roll each slice thin. Spread all inside surfaces of bread with butter and fill with deviled ham as you stack in layers. Wrap firmly and tightly in foil. Chill well. Then cut down into thin slices crosswise. *Makes about twenty slices.*

SPECIAL SANDWICH BUTTERS

You can make the most everyday sandwich taste unusual if you spread it with a specially seasoned butter. Such butters are especially appropriate in tea sandwiches since butter is often the only filling. Imagination and experimentation should help you create your own originals. (Suggestions: Tabasco sauce, toasted sesame seeds, poppy seeds, mustard or curry powder combined with butter.) Here are two recipes to get you started.

Scallion Butter

2 scallions (green onions)
1 tablespoon lemon juice

½ cup (1 stick) butter or margarine

With a paring knife, trim off root and peel the scallions. Discard the green except for its lower two inches. With a French knife, chop scallions very fine. Cream butter until fluffy. Beat in lemon juice and scallions. Use to spread bread for sandwiches of chicken, roast beef, hard-cooked egg, tuna and cheese, or as a filling for ribbon or pinwheel sandwiches. *Makes one-half cup.*

Olive Nut Butter

½ cup chopped ripe olives   ¼ cup softened butter
½ cup chopped walnuts

Combine olives, walnuts and softened butter in a bowl. Spread on slices of white, whole wheat or pumpernickel bread. Top with second slices and cut into shapes desired. *Makes four regular sandwiches or twelve small tea sandwiches.*

PASTEL RIBBONS

Spread one slice of white bread with cream cheese tinted pink. Top with a second slice. Spread with cream cheese tinted green and top with third slice. Press firmly together; trim crusts. Wrap in foil and chill. Cut stack into four equal slices. Then cut each slice into thirds, crosswise. *Makes twelve ribbons.*

GEOMETRIC SANDWICHES

Butter one slice of dark bread. Spread with desired filling—deviled ham, liver pâté, egg or tuna salad. Top with buttered white bread. Press firmly together. Trim crusts. For finger sandwiches, cut into slices about one-half inch thick. *Makes six.* For triangles, cut sandwich in half diagonally. Cut these two triangles in half again and repeat process until you have *eight small triangles.*

MOSAICS

Using a large, round cookie cutter, cut out two white and two whole-wheat bread rounds. With a small round cutter, remove centers from one each of white and dark rounds. Insert small dark round into hole in white ring; small white round into hole in dark ring. Spread the two large rounds with favorite filling. Cover the white round with the dark ring; dark round with the white ring. *This makes two mosaics; repeat to make more sandwiches.*

SANDWICH SPECTACULARS

These sandwiches may be the perfect answer when you need something that looks fabulous and tastes unique at a really important party. Like old-fashioned sandwich loaves, they take a little preliminary fussing, but each is grand enough to make the party table sparkle, and each will be talked about for days.

THE SEVENTEEN–LAYER BANQUET SANDWICH

(*From Appetizer Through Dessert*)

This sandwich spectacular is—truly—a meal in itself. Nine servings of eight courses of delectability. Each serving is a tall wedge-shaped sandwich. Assemble them into a cake shape and trim with candles for a birthday party. Or trim with olives, pickles and carrot curls for *any* party. Serve it (with a cake server) sideways on each plate, letting guests munch their way with knife and fork through sea food, salad and entrée to dessert.

Before you begin, read through the list of layers—it serves as a shopping check list, too. Some of the salad fillings should be prepared in advance. You'll also want to have the bread all cut and ready.

Make a paper triangle pattern for the bread (three and three-fourths inches wide at the base and five and one-half inches high). Trim the crusts from all the bread and cut the loaves lengthwise into slices three-eighths inch thick. (If you use pre-sliced bread, your triangle will have to be smaller, of course.) Place your pattern on the slices and cut out forty-five triangles of white bread, eighteen of whole wheat and eighteen of pumpernickel. Keep the bread covered with waxed paper until you use it.

Now, here are the layers, reading from the top down. But remember—you'll work from the bottom (layer 17) up!

1. White bread with party trimming. For the whole sandwich, you need three large unsliced loaves.
2. Tuna salad: Drain and flake one can (about 7 oz.) of tuna. Combine with one tablespoon each minced onion and minced celery leaves, three tablespoons minced green pepper, one-eighth teaspoon garlic powder and salt and pepper to taste. Blend one-half teaspoon vinegar with four tablespoons mayonnaise and blend into tuna.
3. Pumpernickel bread. You need two large or three medium loaves, unsliced.
4. Bacon (fried crisp and drained), tomatoes (two, thinly sliced) and lettuce (about nine leaves).
5. White bread.
6. Egg salad: Hard-cook four eggs, mash with a fork and add three tablespoons chopped celery, two tablespoons chopped pimiento and salt and pepper to taste. Blend one-half teaspoon vinegar with three tablespoons salad dressing, then add to eggs and mix.
7. Whole-wheat bread. You need two large unsliced loaves.
8. Boiled ham (one-half pound, thinly sliced) and Russian dressing.

9. White bread.
10. Sliced turkey or chicken (one pound, thinly sliced), water cress and mayonnaise.
11. Pumpernickel bread.
12. American cheese (one pound, sliced) and mustard.
13. White bread. Now comes the dessert!
14. Cream cheese-pecan: Blend six ounces of softened cream cheese with enough milk or cream to spread smoothly. Stir in three tablespoons chopped pecans.
15. Whole-wheat bread.
16. Peanut butter (you need a medium-size jar) and two red-skinned apples, sliced thin but not peeled.
17. White bread. Isn't that "the end!"

When everything is prepared, arrange nine triangles of buttered white bread on a serving platter as if you were reassembling wedges of pie. Spread with peanut butter, top with thin red apple slices and cover with buttered whole-wheat triangles. The next layer is No. 14—and you continue right through the layers until you reach the top. For security, stick a long skewer through each of the wedges. Cover with foil or plastic wrap and refrigerate until party time. *Serves nine.*

CHECKERBREAD SANDWICH LOAF

Buy two sandwich loaves (one dark, one light) at a bakery. Have them machine-sliced from end to end into long, thin layers. To slice bread yourself, set toothpicks as a guide. After removal of the two long crusts, each loaf should have at least eight slices three-eighths inch thick, enough for two checkerbread loaves (1). *Each serves fifteen.*

You'll need these fillings:

Cheese Filling: Combine three cups finely grated Cheddar cheese with two sticks (one-half pound) softened butter or margarine.
Shrimp Filling: Combine one cup finely ground, cooked shrimp (or crab meat if you like) with three sticks (three-fourths pound) butter or margarine. Tint pale pink with a drop or two of red food coloring.
Chive Filling: Combine one-fourth cup minced chives with four sticks (one pound) of butter or margarine. Tint pale green with food color.

To assemble the loaf:

Stack bread this way: Two slices white, two slices dark, two more white— ending with two dark. Measure height of loaf; it should be about three inches (2). If you're making two loaves, stack second loaf now. (If you like, everything but the decorating may be done a day in advance, the loaves kept covered and refrigerated.)

Trim crusts from bread around the sides and ends of stacked loaf. Now measure width of loaf. This should be the same as the height—about three inches. If it is more, trim off excess.

Spread butter (three tablespoons) between top two dark slices of loaf; sandwich together and set aside. Butter next two white slices; sandwich together, set aside (3). Repeat—using three sticks softened butter or margarine in all.

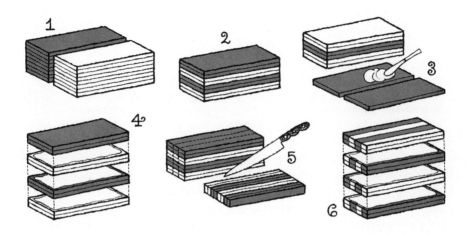

Add fillings: First spread one-third cup cheese filling on top of a double layer of white bread. Put double layer of dark bread on top; spread with one-third cup shrimp filling. Put double layer of white bread on this; spread with one-third cup chive filling (4). Top with remaining dark double layer. Wrap lightly; chill several hours or freeze until just firm. Meantime, fill second loaf.

Cut each loaf into four long equal slices. Use a sharp knife and cut through the stacked layers from end to end as shown (5). Since the loaf has been chilled, it will be easy to cut.

Restack into checkerbread: First spread one of the slices with a third-cup of filling. Now take a second slice and turn it—so the dark stripes on the second slice match up with the white stripes on the first slice (6). This is what makes the checkerbread effect. Repeat with other slices. Wrap well; chill again in refrigerator—overnight if desired.

Frost and decorate just before party time—an hour or two before at most. For frosting: combine three eight-ounce packages cream cheese (softened) with two teaspoons onion powder and two tablespoons milk.

When frosted, add flower garnish (below) and chill until ready to serve. Flowers: Make a tulip by notching a cherry tomato and trim it with green-pepper leaves. Use bits of carrot for daisy petals, currants for centers. Make the leaves from carrot tops. Corn kernels and bits of pimiento make another different flower. Press each flower into surface of cream cheese so they seem to grow from the base upward. At the base "plant" chive grass.

Though the following recipes involve no bread, they *are* hearty cold snacks and may be just what the party table needs for a touch of interest.

BLACK–EYED SUSAN

1 can (4½ oz.) deviled ham
1 teaspoon instant minced green
  onion
½ teaspoon Tabasco sauce

⅓ cup mayonnaise (about)
12 hard-cooked eggs
2 to 3 dozen pitted ripe olives
½ pimiento, cut into strips

Mix deviled ham, minced green onion, Tabasco and one tablespoon of mayonnaise in a bowl. Remove shells and slice eggs in half lengthwise. Remove yolks from eggs and set half aside. Place remaining twelve yolk halves in a small strainer. Sieve into ham mixture; blend together. Fill all egg whites with ham mixture (don't mound filling). Spread a thin layer of mayonnaise on top. Put filled egg halves close together on waxed paper and sieve remaining yolks over them. (Sieved yolks will stick to mayonnaise.) Chill until party time. To serve, arrange eggs in a circle. Fill olives with strips of pimiento, place in center to form the "black eye." *Makes two dozen.*

MEAT ROLL UPS

2 packages (3 oz. each) cream cheese,
  softened
3 tablespoons grated onion
1½ tablespoons prepared horse-radish
2 tablespoons minced black and green
  olives

1 lb. ready-to-serve meat: sliced
salami, pastrami, dried beef, ham
or bologna

Beat cream cheese until fluffy, then beat in onion, horse-radish and olives. Spread each slice of meat with cream cheese and roll up tightly. Skewer with toothpicks; chill in refrigerator at least two hours. At serving time, cut into one-inch slices. Arrange on platter lined with lettuce leaves. *Makes about fifty slices.*

Hot Sandwiches, Pizzas and Other Hot Snacks

*H*ERE are the hot snacks that you'll repeat and repeat—at lunch parties (even just-the-family parties) or as late-evening treats. Some of the recipes start with baker's bread or rolls, others use doughs you make yourself, some use no bread at all! The pizza recipes include both homemade and mix-made varieties.

DOUBLE–DATE SANDWICHES

(*Croque Monsieur and Croque Madame*)

By way of explanation, *croque* means something crisp in French—and a Croque Monsieur (or Madame) means something delicious—and French fried. Though the his and her fillings differ, both sandwiches start out and are finished the same way, like this:

16 thin slices white bread	4 eggs
2 cups (½ lb.) grated Swiss cheese	½ cup milk
½ cup heavy cream	¼ cup butter or margarine

Trim crusts from bread. Mix cheese and cream and spread this mixture on *all* bread slices, using two tablespoons per slice. Add a filling (page 326) to half the bread slices; top with remaining slices, cheese side down. Now beat eggs and milk with fork. Dip sandwiches into egg mixture, coating both sides. Heat butter until bubbling in a large skillet; brown sandwiches on both sides over moderate heat. (If an electric skillet, use just half the butter—and add more as you need it. Heat to 325°F.) Serve with knife and fork or cut into bite-size pieces. *Serves eight.*

Croque Monsieur filling: For four sandwiches, use four slices of boiled ham—one slice for each sandwich.

Croque Madame filling: For four sandwiches use six slices of bacon and one small can of sliced mushrooms. Drain mushrooms; sprinkle with juice of one lemon. Fry bacon over moderate heat. Drain on paper towel. Use about one tablespoon of mushrooms and a slice and a half of crisp bacon to fill each sandwich.

DIPWICH DAGWOOD

16 slices bacon
16 slices white bread
1 jar (5 oz.) cheese and bacon spread
1 can (12 oz.) luncheon meat
3 eggs
⅔ cup evaporated milk
1 tablespoon prepared mustard
2 teaspoons caraway seeds

Fry bacon over low heat until crisp, then drain on paper toweling. Meanwhile, arrange bread in sandwich pairs. Spread all the slices evenly with cheese spread. Cut luncheon meat into eight lengthwise slices. On half the bread slices, place a slice of luncheon meat and two pieces of bacon. Top with remaining bread, cheese side down. Beat together the eggs, evaporated milk, mustard and caraway seeds. Dip each sandwich in the mixture, turning to coat. Brown on both sides on sandwich grill or skillet in a little bubbling butter. *Serves eight.*

CHICKEN SOUP SANDWICH

½ lb. Cheddar cheese, grated
1 can condensed cream of chicken soup
1 teaspoon Worcestershire sauce
1 tablespoon instant minced onion
8 slices white bread

Combine cheese, soup, Worcestershire sauce and minced onion. Toast bread lightly on both sides. Spread each slice with cheese mixture. Broil five inches from heat for two minutes or until browned. Garnish with minced parsley if desired. *Serves four.*

TUNA TEASERS

1 can (7 oz.) tuna, drained and flaked
2 tablespoons pickle relish
¼ cup diced celery
¼ cup mayonnaise
1 tablespoon lemon juice
Salt and pepper to taste
4 slices whole-wheat bread
4 slices white bread
¼ lb. Cheddar cheese, grated
1 large ripe tomato

Combine tuna, pickle, celery, mayonnaise, lemon juice, salt and pepper in bowl. Mix, tossing lightly to blend. Toast whole-wheat bread and spread with tuna mixture. Toast white bread, butter it and cover tuna toast, buttered side down. Over the top slice of toast, sprinkle grated cheese. Cut tomato into four thick slices. Place one in the center of each cheese-topped sandwich. Grill in broiler under medium heat until cheese melts and is lightly browned. Garnish with lemon wedges, water cress and olives. *Serves four.*

APPLE DREAMS

16 slices (½ lb.) bacon
2 McIntosh apples
3 to 4 tablespoons lemon juice
8 slices white bread

Butter
Mayonnaise or salad dressing
8 slices (½ lb.) American process
  cheese

In advance, cook the bacon until slightly crisp. Wash and core the apples (don't peel) and cut crosswise into very thin slices. Dip in lemon juice to keep from turning brown. (Cover bacon and apples with waxed paper and refrigerate if desired.) Shortly before snack time, preheat the oven to 350°F. (moderate). Butter the bread and spread it with the mayonnaise or dressing; top with a cheese slice. Arrange three or four apple rings and a cross of two pieces of bacon on each Dream and bake fifteen minutes, or until cheese starts to melt. If you like crusty, browned Dreams, slip under the broiler a minute. Cut into halves or quarters. *Serves five.*

CRAB MEAT CHEESEBURGER

1 package (1 lb.) frozen Alaska
  crab meat
½ cup chopped green pepper
½ cup mayonnaise
2 teaspoons lemon juice
2 teaspoons prepared mustard
½ teaspoon grated onion

2 teaspoons pickle relish
½ teaspoon salt
⅛ teaspoon pepper
8 hamburger buns
⅓ cup butter or margarine
¾ cup (6 oz.) grated natural
  Cheddar cheese

Let crab meat thaw overnight in the refrigerator. When ready to use, drain crab meat, pick over (for tiny shell bits) and dice. Mix with green pepper. Combine mayonnaise, lemon juice, mustard, onion, relish, salt and pepper; fold into the crab mixture. Split buns and toast very lightly under broiler. Butter the cut sides, then place top halves of buns in slow oven to keep warm. Spread bottom half of each with a scant one-fourth cup of crab mixture, then sprinkle each with a heaping tablespoon of grated Cheddar. Broil slowly, five inches from source of heat, until cheese melts and is slightly browned. Cover with bun tops. For a delicious supper, surround each burger with potato chips, sliced tomatoes, lettuce and a sprig of water cress. *Serves eight.*

MUSHROOM MUNCHIES

½ cup (1 stick) butter or margarine
3½ cups finely chopped uncooked
  mushrooms (¾ lb.)
2 medium onions, peeled and minced
½ teaspoon salt

Dash of pepper
Dash of nutmeg
10 thin slices white bread
Melted butter
Paprika

Heat the butter in a large skillet. Add mushrooms and onions and cook until golden brown. Stir in salt, pepper and nutmeg. Remove from heat. Cut crusts from bread and spread mushroom mixture thinly over each slice. Roll each slice like a jelly roll and skewer with a toothpick. Place on cookie sheets. Brush tops of rolls with a little melted butter and sprinkle lightly with paprika. (If desired, refrigerate until serving time.) Broil until rolls are golden brown. *Serves five.*

HOT CHICKEN SANDWICH

2 tablespoons cooking oil
2 tablespoons minced onion
¼ cup chopped green pepper
3 tablespoons flour
1 can (8 oz.) tomato sauce
1 cup water
2 tablespoons lemon juice
2 teaspoons salt

¼ teaspoon pepper
2 tablespoons sugar
1 tablespoon prepared horse-radish
1 tablespoon prepared mustard
2 cups chopped cooked chicken
8 hamburger buns, split
Butter

Heat oil in a skillet. Add onion and pepper and cook gently five minutes. Blend in flour. Add tomato sauce and water gradually, stirring constantly. Bring to a boil, stirring. Add remaining ingredients except buns. Stir to blend; cover and simmer gently fifteen minutes. Meantime, spread hamburger buns with butter and warm in the oven. To serve, spoon chicken mixture over buns. *Serves eight.*

TALK-OF-THE-TOWN HAMBURGER

Place a large grilled hamburger on the bottom half of a buttered, toasted hamburger bun on a serving plate. Top with Hot Barbecue Gravy and over this spoon Horse-Radish Cheese Sauce (both on page 329). On the other half of bun, arrange a large lettuce leaf, a thick slice of tomato and a toothpick-speared pimiento-stuffed green olive. Serve with potato chips as a little lunch or a boy-size snack.

Hot Barbecue Gravy

Heat one can of beef or mushroom gravy with two tablespoons of bottled barbecue sauce.

Horse-Radish Cheese Sauce

Make one cup of homemade cheese sauce or use the kind that comes in a jar. Heat, and add one teaspoon prepared horse-radish.

CHEESER PLEASERS

½ lb. sharp Cheddar cheese
1 slice (¼-inch thick) sweet onion
1 slice uncooked bacon
½ green pepper, cored
2 teaspoons prepared mustard

2 tablespoons mayonnaise
6 English muffins
Sweet basil
Orégano

Use a meat chopper or a French knife to chop together the cheese, onion, bacon and green pepper. Blend with mustard and mayonnaise. Split English muffins. On each, place a generous teaspoonful of cheese mixture and spread to edges. Top each with a fleck of crumbled basil and orégano. If desired, the sandwiches may now be arranged on a broiler rack, covered and refrigerated. At party time, broil three to six inches from source of heat until lightly browned. Serve hot. Twelve halves *serve four to six.*

CURRIED BROILER SANDWICH

1 cup chopped pimiento-stuffed olives
½ cup thin sliced scallions (green onions)
1½ cups shredded American cheese
½ cup mayonnaise

½ teaspoon salt
½ teaspoon monosodium glutamate
¼ teaspoon curry powder
6 English muffins, halved

Mix olives, scallions, cheese, mayonnaise, salt, monosodium glutamate and curry. Toast the English muffins. Spread with cheese filling. Place under broiler until filling is heated and cheese melts. Use two muffin halves per serving—*serves six.*

CLOTHESPIN ROLLS

Make up a package of hot-roll mix. Let rise; knead; roll out into a twelve-by-sixteen-inch rectangle. Cut to make thirty strips, six inches long. Coil each around a greased clothespin, place on a greased baking sheet. Cover, let rise until doubled. Bake at 400°F. (hot) about fifteen minutes. Remove clothespins from rolls. Cool enough to handle, fill (from a pastry tube) with deviled ham or soft cheese spread. *Makes thirty snacks.*

PONCHO DAGWOOD SANDWICH

1 large loaf sour-dough French bread
   or 6 small hard rolls
1 pint or 1 package (6 oz.) soft
   process cheese
¾ lb. ground beef
½ teaspoon salt

1 cup sliced scallions (green onions)
1 small can chopped mushrooms, well
   drained
½ teaspoon crumbled orégano
1 cup tomato sauce
2 tablespoons catchup

Slice the bread or rolls lengthwise. Spread generously with the soft cheese, using it all. In a skillet, brown the ground beef until it is crumbly yet still moist, stirring with a fork. Stir in salt. Spoon this in even amounts over the halved bread or rolls. Top, in turn, with scallions, mushrooms and orégano, dividing carefully. Last add the tomato sauce mixed with catchup. If desired, cover and refrigerate or freeze at this point. Bake at 450°F. (very hot) twenty minutes or until bubbling. (If sandwich has been chilled, bake at 425°F. thirty minutes.) *Serves six generously.*

SAUERKRAUT BUNS

3 cups milk
½ cup warm (not hot) water
2 packages active dry yeast
8 cups sifted flour (about)

4 teaspoons salt
¼ cup melted shortening
4 tablespoons sugar

Scald milk and cool to lukewarm. Measure water into a mixing bowl. Add yeast and stir until dissolved. Stir in six cups of the flour. Let stand in a warm place two hours. Add salt, shortening, sugar, then beat in as much remaining flour as needed to make a dough. Turn out on a floured board; knead until smooth and satiny (about ten minutes). Let rise in a greased bowl, covered, in a warm place, free from drafts, until double in bulk. Punch down. Turn out again on floured board and toss until smooth. Divide dough into twenty-four pieces. Shape each into saucer-size patty. Place a large spoonful of Sauerkraut Hamburger Filling (below) on dough and pinch edges together to make a round bun. Put seam side down on a greased cookie sheet. Bake at 350°F. (moderate) until buns are browned, about forty minutes. Serve with butter. *Makes twenty-four.*

Sauerkraut Hamburger Filling

1 lb. ground beef chuck
2 onions, peeled and chopped

1 can (No. 2½) sauerkraut, drained

Cook beef over moderate heat until browned, adding onion during browning. Add drained sauerkraut and stir and cook over moderate heat five minutes. Cool.

LEBANESE LAMB ROLLS

First, make the yeast dough:

1 package active dry yeast	1 tablespoon sugar
1 cup warm (not hot) water	3 cups sifted flour
1 teaspoon salt	

Sprinkle yeast over water in a mixing bowl and stir to dissolve. Add salt and sugar. Add flour and beat well. Turn out on a floured board and knead about five minutes or until smooth and satiny. Place in greased bowl, cover and let rise in a warm place, free from drafts, until double in bulk. While the dough rises, make filling.

To make the filling:

2 lbs. lean boneless lamb	1 teaspoon cinnamon
2 onions, peeled and washed	Dash of pepper
2 tablespoons shortening	2 tablespoons lemon juice
1 package (3 oz.) cream cheese	½ teaspoon crumbled dried or
1 teaspoon salt	chopped fresh mint leaves

Cut the lamb into half-inch cubes. Chop onions fine. Heat shortening in a large skillet. Add lamb and onions and stir over moderate heat until nicely browned. In a separate bowl, soften cream cheese and blend remaining ingredients in well. Stir in cooked meat. Form dough into eighteen apricot-sized balls. Place these about five inches apart on greased cookie sheets. Let rise until doubled. Then, with palm of hand, flatten each dough ball into a pancake about one-fourth inch thick. Place about two tablespoons meat filling on each circle. Pull dough up around filling and pinch together at top. Bake at 375°F. (moderate) thirty to thirty-five minutes or until lightly browned. *Makes eighteen snack-sized rolls.*

HOT ZIGGITIES

First, make the filling:

1 lb. skinless frankfurters	1 egg, slightly beaten
2 tablespoons prepared mustard	

Run frankfurters through coarse blade of food chopper. Stir in mustard and egg and set aside.

To make the crust:

2 cups sifted flour
½ teaspoon salt
⅔ cup shortening

¼ cup catchup
3 tablespoons cold water

Sift flour and salt together into mixing bowl. Cut in shortening until particles are the size of small peas. Mix catchup with water and sprinkle over flour mixture, tossing lightly with fork. Roll out half the dough on a floured board to a twelve-by-nine-inch rectangle. Cut into four rectangles six by four and one-half inches. Repeat with other half of dough. Divide meat mixture equally on pastry rectangles. Fold over so that the four-and-one-half-inch edges are together. Seal. Place on an ungreased baking sheet. Bake at 425°F. (hot) fifteen to twenty minutes. Serve hot. *Makes eight good-size snacks.*

STAR BITES

2 cups sifted flour
3 teaspoons baking powder
1 teaspoon salt

⅓ cup shortening
⅔ cup light cream

Sift flour, baking powder and salt together into a mixing bowl. Cut in shortening with a pastry blender or two knives. Stir in cream. Form into a ball. Divide dough in half. Roll each half one-fourth inch thick. Cut into stars with a two-inch star cutter. Place half the stars in a nine-inch cake pan. Let them almost touch. Spread with Star Bite Filling (below). Top with remaining stars. Cover and refrigerate at this time if desired. At party time, bake at 450°F. (very hot) fifteen minutes. Invert on a cooling rack, put serving plate on top and turn right side up. *Makes snacks for ten.*

Star Bite Filling

1 tablespoon prepared mustard
1 tablespoon chili sauce

1 can (4½ oz.) deviled ham
1 teaspoon instant minced onion

Mix ingredients and use in the recipe above.

EMPANADAS

(*Spicy Meat Turnovers*)

First make the filling:

1 cup chopped onion
2 tablespoons chopped pimiento
1 lb. chopped beef or chicken, raw or cooked
½ cup chopped beef suet

1 jar (3 oz.) pimiento-stuffed olives
½ cup raisins
2 hard-cooked eggs
2 cups biscuit mix

Mix the onion, pimiento, beef and suet in a large skillet over moderate heat. Cook until meat is lightly browned and onions are tender, stirring constantly, about ten minutes. Set aside. Chop olives, raisins and eggs together coarsely.

Now make the pastry: make up biscuit mix, following package directions for rolled biscuits. Roll out on a floured board into very thin rectangles, twenty by fifteen inches. Cut into twelve squares, each five inches. Fill each square with a heaping tablespoon of meat mixture and a scant tea-spoonful of egg mixture. Fold square over filling, into a triangle shape. Crimp edges together. Bake at 350°F. (moderate) twenty-five minutes or until brown. Serve warm. *Makes twelve.*

PIGS IN BLANKETS

1 package (8 oz.) brown-and-serve pork sausage links	1 cup pancake mix
	2 tablespoons orange juice
¼ cup butter or margarine	½ teaspoon grated orange peel

Cut each sausage into thirds. Set aside. Melt butter in a large saucepan. Add pancake mix and stir until blended. Sprinkle orange juice and peel over surface and toss with fork until lightly blended. Roll out between two sheets of waxed paper to be one-eighth inch thick. Cut into strips one by two and one-half inches—you'll need as many strips as you have sausage bites. Wrap a pastry strip around each sausage bite, press to seal and skewer through seam with a toothpick. Place on a cookie sheet. (If you're making these in advance, cover them now and refrigerate until party time.) Then bake at 425°F. (hot) fifteen minutes. *Makes twenty-seven to thirty-six, depending on number of sausages in package.*

SAUSAGE–CORN BREAD BAKE

2 packages (8 oz. each) brown-and-serve pork sausage links	½ teaspoon salt
	2 teaspoons baking powder
2 cups corn meal	2 eggs
2 cups pancake mix	2 cups milk
½ cup sugar	½ cup melted butter

Brown sausages lightly in a large skillet. Set aside. Sift dry ingredients together into a large bowl. Add eggs, milk and butter. Beat to combine for about one minute—don't overbeat. Pour batter into a greased nine-by-thir-teen-inch pan. Arrange sausages over batter in rows about one inch apart and bake thirty to thirty-five minutes at 425°F. (hot) until lightly browned. Cut between sausages to make about twenty pieces. *Hearty eating for twelve.*

To do ahead: This dish may be completely baked in advance, then cooled, covered and refrigerated. At party time, reheat at 375°F. (moderate) for about fifteen minutes, cut and serve. Or if you prefer, make the batter, pour into pan, cover and refrigerate. Wrap and chill browned sausages. At party time, top batter with sausages as above and bake at 425°F. (hot) thirty-five minutes or until browned. Cut and serve hot.

ROLY-POLIES

1¼ cups milk	1 cup pancake mix
1 egg	2 tablespoons finely chopped onions
1 tablespoon cooking oil	or chives

If you like, make and fill these pancakes in advance of party time and refrigerate until needed, but extend the final baking time (below) five minutes. To begin, measure all ingredients into a shaker or bowl and shake or stir until just combined (batter should be somewhat lumpy). Pour batter, a small amount at a time, onto a lightly greased skillet. Bake over moderate heat until top is covered with bubbles. Turn and lightly brown remaining side. Continue to make fourteen medium-large pancakes or twenty-eight small ones. Lightly butter one side of each pancake; spread with a thin layer of filling—choose any of those given here. Make small pancakes into tiny envelopes (fold opposite edges to center, then fold in remaining edges). Roll larger pancakes jelly-roll style, then cut crosswise into inch-wide bites. Bake at 350°F. (moderate) ten minutes. *Enough to serve six generously.*

Cheese filling: Combine one-half cup shredded Cheddar cheese with one tablespoon mayonnaise or salad dressing and one-half teaspoon prepared mustard. Makes enough filling for about nine small pancakes.

Chicken filling: Combine one-fourth cup finely chopped cooked chicken, one-fourth teaspoon powdered thyme, one tablespoon mayonnaise or salad dressing and salt to taste. Makes enough for about eight small pancakes.

Ham-piccalilli filling: Place a thin slice of ham on a buttered pancake. Spread with mustard and small amount of finely chopped sweet mixed pickles.

Ham'n cheese filling: Lightly spread buttered pancake with softened cream cheese; top with a thin layer of deviled ham.

MEXICAN SHARE-A-DIP

1 can (15½ oz.) small tamales	1 cup grated sharp Cheddar cheese
1 can (15½ oz.) chili	1 large package large corn chips
½ cup catchup	

Remove the husks from tamales, then turn into a saucepan with sauce from the can. Coarsely chop and mash with wooden spoon while heating. Add chili and catchup, stirring to blend, and heat until bubbly. Pour into three or four cereal bowls. Top each bowlful with a mound of grated cheese. (Experienced share-dippers immediately use a corn chip to stir the cheese so it will melt.) Serve a bowlful to each couple, with a large plate of corn chips. *Serves six to eight.*

PERFECT PIZZA

First make the dough:

2 cups warm (not hot) water	2 teaspoons salt
2 packages active dry yeast	¼ cup olive oil
2 teaspoons sugar	7 cups sifted flour

Measure water into a bowl and sprinkle with yeast. Stir until dissolved. Stir in sugar, salt and olive oil. Add four cups of the sifted flour and beat until smooth. Then add as much of remaining flour as is needed to make a dough. Turn out on a floured board and knead until smooth and elastic. Place in a large greased bowl, then invert dough so it is greased all over. Cover and let rise in a warm place, free from drafts, until doubled in bulk (about forty-five minutes).

Now, the sauce and filling:

1⅓ cups (2 cans, 6 oz. each) tomato paste	1 lb. mozzarella cheese, sliced ⅛-inch thick
1 cup water	½ cup olive oil
2 teaspoons salt	½ cup grated Parmesan or Romano cheese
2 teaspoons crushed orégano	
¼ teaspoon pepper	

Mix together tomato paste, water, salt, orégano and pepper. Get remaining ingredients ready. When dough has risen, punch down by pushing fist into dough. Turn out on board. Divide into quarters. Form each into a ball and place on greased baking sheets or twelve-inch pizza pans. Press and gently pull with fingers into circle twelve inches in diameter and very thin, with edges about one-quarter inch thick. On each circle of dough arrange one-fourth of the mozzarella, one-fourth of the tomato mixture and two tablespoons each of olive oil and grated cheese. (Some people prefer to use sauce first, then mozzarella, etc.) Repeat to make four pizzas. Bake at 400°F. (hot) twenty-five minutes. *Makes four.*

Oblong pizzas: Pat out dough to a ten-by-fourteen-inch rectangle on cookie sheet. Use pizza cutter or knife to cut into squares when baked.

Hors d'oeuvres pizzas: Pat out dough to a ten-by-fourteen-inch rectangle. Lightly score diagonally in two directions to form diamonds. Cover with tomato sauce. Arrange toppings—cheese, anchovies, salami, etc., within scored lines to form a pattern. Bake, then cut with knife to form diamonds.

Pizza rounds: Pat out dough to even thickness. Cut out rounds with a three-inch cutter. Make a depression in each by pressing with the floured bottom of a glass. Fill each round with sauce, cheese, toppings and bake.

Other fillings: Instead of (or besides) the cheese, you can use: two small cans mushrooms, drained; one-half pound cooked or canned sweet Italian sausage, sliced; one medium-size onion, sliced, with one small can anchovy fillets; one-half pound uncooked cleaned small shrimp; one-half pound salami, thinly sliced; one-fourth pound prosciutto (Italian-style ham) or baked ham, thinly sliced.

Nine Tricks with a Box of Pizza Mix

Just to get you started on your own adventures, here are some delicious toppings for a box of pizza mix.

PIZZA TUNA

Make up packaged pizza mix according to directions. Before sprinkling on the cheese, drain a seven-ounce can of chunk-style tuna, saving the oil. Place the tuna on the pizza dough, sprinkle with cheese, then three tablespoons of the tuna oil. (If tuna is water-pack style, use olive oil.) Bake as package directs.

PIZZA SCAMPI

Place the contents of an eight-ounce package of frozen uncooked shrimp in a bowl. Cover with one cup bottled Italian dressing, two teaspoons parsley flakes and five peppercorns. Allow to marinate one hour at room temperature. Make up pizza, following package directions. After adding tomato sauce and cheese, top with drained shrimp, distributing them well. Bake as directed.

SWISS PIZZA

Place one pound of small link pork sausages in a skillet with surface barely covered with water. Cook, covered, five minutes. Remove cover, drain off water and fry, turning frequently, until golden brown; drain on paper towel. Make up pizza mix following package directions, topping with sauce and cheese. Arrange sausages over this, then sprinkle with one cup grated Swiss cheese. Bake as directed.

PIZZA STRUDEL

Make up dough from package of pizza mix and let rise as instructed. Then turn out on floured board and knead twenty times. Generously flour a kitchen towel. Place dough on towel and roll out very thin with a floured rolling pin. After rolling, dough should almost cover edges of towel. Brown one pound of bulk pork sausage over moderate heat, pouring off fat when necessary. Sprinkle the pizza sauce (from package) over dough within one inch of edge. Dot with browned sausage. If desired, sprinkle with cheese. Fold in long edges one inch on each side. Beginning at a narrow end, roll up dough with filling, like a jelly roll. Place on a cookie sheet. Bake at 400°F. (hot) twenty minutes. *Cut into sixteen slices and serve hot.*

HOLLY WREATH PIZZAS

Use packaged pizza mix and make it up into one big round pie or several small rounds. After baking, decorate with sliced pimiento-stuffed green olives around the edge, à la holly wreath.

TOWER OF PIZZAS

Make up pizza dough as package directs and let rise five minutes. Then shape into a roll twelve inches long. Have ready an electric frying pan with a cover. (For best results, the cover should be vented or left ajar.) Grease the cold fry pan liberally with shortening. Cut off one-inch sections from rolled dough. Shape into five-inch rounds at first with floured fingers, then finally in skillet with back of a wooden spoon, shaping edges upward slightly. Cover with pizza sauce and cheese. Turn heat to 325°F. and bake covered, with vent open, twenty minutes. Remaining pizzas will bake firm a little more quickly because skillet will be at a controlled temperature. Serve as they come from skillet or prepare beforehand so everyone can eat at once. To keep pizzas hot, place on baking sheet in a very slow (250°F.) oven. At serving time, stack on heated platter. *Makes twelve.*

PIZZA BURGERS

1 package pizza mix	1 teaspoon dry mustard
Water as package directs	¼ cup chopped onion
1½ lbs. ground beef chuck	½ cup chopped green pepper
½ cup cracker meal	1 egg
1½ teaspoons salt	⅔ cup (small can) evaporated milk
¼ teaspoon pepper	

Make up pizza dough following package directions. Dust hands in flour; mold dough into fourteen equal balls. Set on an oiled cookie sheet, cover with foil and put in a warm place to rise twenty-five minutes. Combine remaining ingredients; shape meat mixture into fourteen thin patties.

When dough has risen, shape into thin rounds four inches wide. Place on two oiled cookie sheets; top each with a burger. Spread some pizza-mix sauce on burgers (heat remaining sauce to pass with baked pizzas). Sprinkle with cheese and bake at 425°F. (hot) twenty-five minutes or until crusts are browned. *Makes fourteen.*

DO-AHEAD PIZZA

Use packaged pizza mix. Make up the dough not more than six hours before the party. Pat it out on greased pizza pans or cookie sheets. Cover each pan with greased foil or waxed paper. Stack one over the other and refrigerate. To serve, add sauce, cheese and topping and bake five minutes longer than package directs.

HAM AND OLIVE PIZZA

1 package pizza mix	1 clove garlic, minced
⅓ cup olive oil	1 can (12 oz.) chopped pressed ham
8 medium onions, peeled, washed and	or luncheon meat, cut into 40 thin
sliced	strips
1½ teaspoons salt	1 can (7 oz.) pitted ripe olives
¼ teaspoon pepper	

Open pizza mix. If it comes with separate tomato and cheese sauce, set these aside and use them for a platter of spaghetti another time. Make up the dough following package directions and, while it is rising, place olive oil in a large skillet or Dutch oven and heat. When hot but not smoking, add onions, salt, pepper and garlic. Sauté, stirring frequently, until onions become transparent and barely tender. Remove from heat. Press out pizza dough on greased twelve-by-fifteen-inch baking sheet or jelly roll pan or three nine-inch pie pans, following directions on box. Cover dough evenly with onions. Arrange ham strips on top in lattice design. Drain olives and center one in each square formed by the lattice. Bake at 400°F. (hot) thirty to thirty-five minutes until crust is golden. Cut into squares. *Serves six.*

QUICK, EASY LITTLE PIZZAS

1 can (8 oz.) refrigerator biscuits	Dash of orégano
1 can (6 oz.) tomato paste	1 roll (3 oz.) sharp Cheddar cheese
Dash of pepper	Grated Parmesan or Romano cheese

Set each biscuit on a cookie sheet. Mix tomato paste, pepper and orégano. Cut cheese into ten slices. Top each biscuit with a heaping teaspoonful of tomato mixture, add a cheese slice and sprinkle with Parmesan. Bake at 425°F. (hot) five minutes or until cheese bubbles and melts. *Makes ten tiny pizzas.*

For flatter pizzas: Oil cookie sheet and hands, and flatten each biscuit into a three-inch round. Top as desired, bake as above.

For Italian pizza-inas: Instead of Cheddar, use one-fourth pound mozzarella cheese, thinly sliced.

PIZZA ROLLS

1 lb. ground beef
⅔ cup tomato sauce
¾ teaspoon salt
¼ teaspoon garlic salt
¼ cup sliced stuffed olives

1 cup diced Muenster or mozzarella
    cheese
8 oblong hard rolls
Crumbled orégano

Cook meat in a skillet, stirring frequently, over moderate heat until browned. Add tomato sauce, salt, garlic salt, olives and cheese. Cut deep slits in the top of rolls. Fill with hamburger mixture. Sprinkle with orégano. Wrap in foil. Bake at 400°F. (hot) fifteen minutes, or on rack over hot coals for same time, turning often. *Makes eight.*

APPLES ON HORSEBACK

2 apples
6 strips bacon
1 large or 2 small green peppers

12 brown-and-serve pork sausages
12 small canned white onions
⅓ cup bottled French dressing

Cut each apple into six wedges. Core, but don't peel. Wrap each wedge in half a bacon strip. Cut green pepper to make twelve strips, each one by two inches. Cook in boiling water five minutes and drain. On each of twelve skewers, lace the following: bacon-wrapped apple wedge, pepper strip, brown-and-serve sausage, onion. Brush all with French dressing. Grill four inches from heat, rotating frequently, twelve minutes. *Four servings as a snack, three servings as a dinner dish.*

TEEN–TIME RABBIT

1 can (12 oz.) luncheon meat
2 small bottles ginger ale
1 package (8 oz.) process American
    cheese
2 teaspoons vinegar

1 teaspoon Worcestershire sauce
¼ teaspoon dry mustard
1 egg, lightly beaten
1 green pepper, chopped

Dice meat into one-half-inch cubes. Pour one bottle ginger ale over meat and let stand one hour; drain. Shred or grate cheese; place in top of double boiler and melt over boiling water. Add the vinegar, Worcestershire, dry mustard and three-fourths cup of the remaining ginger ale. Blend well. Add egg, stirring constantly until mixture thickens. Add meat and green pepper. Cover and keep warm over hot water until ready to serve. Serve over cooked rice, crisp cereal flakes, Chinese noodles or potato chips. *Serves four to six.*

FISH AND DIPS

1 package (8 oz.) frozen fish sticks   Chili Herb and Cream Dips (below)
1½ cups hot cooked shrimp, cleaned
   and shelled

Follow package directions to heat the fish sticks. Cut each one in two and arrange with hot drained shrimp on a serving plate or in a chafing dish. Serve to guests with food picks (spear a few so people get the idea) and a choice of dips. *Serves six.*

Chili Herb Dip

1 bottle (12 oz.) chili sauce   1 teaspoon Worcestershire sauce
¼ teaspoon tarragon   1 teaspoon instant minced onion

Combine ingredients in a saucepan. Heat to the boiling point; reduce to simmer and cook five minutes. Serve hot.

Cream Dip

1 jar (6 oz.) tartar sauce   1 teaspoon mustard
½ teaspoon onion salt

Combine ingredients and serve cold.

RUMAKI

(An Oriental Appetizer)

4 chicken livers   1 small bottle (3 oz.) soy sauce
12 canned water chestnuts   ¼ teaspoon ginger
6 scallions (green onions), chopped   ¼ teaspoon curry powder
12 slices bacon

Divide chicken livers into thirds. Roll each in flour and fold over a water chestnut. Divide scallions over bacon slices. Wrap each scallion-sprinkled bacon slice around liver and chestnut and fasten with a toothpick. Combine remaining ingredients. Pour over the rumaki and let stand

Add distinction to your party buffet with the Checkerbread Sandwich Loaf (page 322) ▶

one hour, turning occasionally. At party time, broil, turning frequently, seven minutes. If you have a tiny hibachi, your guests can complete the toasting over that. *Makes twelve.*

FANCY FRENCH FRIES

Serve them sizzling hot—as finger food. Fry them, broil them, pop them in the oven. Serve them hash-brown with scrambled eggs for a midnight breakfast after a dance. No matter how you serve them, you'll find frozen French fried potatoes easy to fix, economical—what more could you ask for? (Seconds, of course!) For dunking, pile hot fries on a platter to serve with chili or spicy hot catchup. To add flavor, "salt" potatoes with barbecue seasoning, curry powder or celery, onion or garlic salt. (Use half a teaspoon per nine-ounce package.)

To fix fries for a party, follow package directions. Or:

French fried—the traditional method: In a ten-inch skillet or pan, heat cooking oil one inch deep until bubbling hot but not smoking. Meanwhile, empty a package of frozen French fries onto paper toweling and wipe away frost (to prevent spattering). Fry potatoes just enough to brown and crisp them. Drain on toweling; salt, serve.

Pan fried: Heat two tablespoons cooking oil, shortening or butter in a ten-inch pan or electric skillet. Add French fries and cook (at moderate heat) until potatoes are defrosted, heated and browned. Turn potatoes with a pancake turner and salt generously during cooking.

Baked: Place a layer of frozen French fries in a baking dish; add two tablespoons butter. Bake at 350°F. (moderate) thirty minutes. Salt potatoes generously during baking; stir once or twice as butter melts.

A snack of crisp French fries with chili con carne makes a hearty treat after a date. Heat the canned chili to a simmering point, ladle it over hot fries arranged in a soup plate.

A dip that combines catchup with spicy extras adds a quick fancy touch to French fries. Mix one-fourth cup whipped salad dressing, one-half cup catchup, one-half teaspoon salt, one-eighth teaspoon pepper, a tablespoon each dried chives and prepared mustard.

A party's-over breakfast (after a dance) is a wonderful way to end an evening. A wonderful menu: scrambled eggs, hash-brown fries, coffee. To serve four, use two nine-ounce packages of French fries. Cut them into small pieces and season with salt, pepper and paprika. Add chopped onion according to judgment. Melt one-fourth cup butter in a skillet over moderate heat. Add potato mixture. Cook until brown, turning occasionally.

◀ *Popcorn fun! Spicy varieties (pages 311–312) and sweet (page 361).*

Filling Up the Cookie Jar

$\mathcal{M}$ost of the popular girls we know have one thing in common. In the kitchen, there's a cookie jar—and there's always something in it.

For after-school munching, brownies are favorites, and you'll find several ways to make them here. Runners-up are the fruit bars—boys seem to like their rich flavor. To keep bar cookies at their best, store them in their own pan, covered, at room temperature.

Drop cookies are almost as easy to make, and they can be made in just as many flavor combinations. They're always ready for informal parties too—just pile them up casually on platters. Store drop cookies in a cookie jar or a canister; use waxed paper to separate layers. A tight cover will keep them from becoming soggy or too dry.

The last group of cookies we've dubbed Party Cookies. They involve a little extra work, but the results are worth it—either in flavor or unusual appearance, or both. They're especially right for all-girl affairs when you want to show off your culinary skill and present something really different. Or you can make them for small-group parties when you're impressing a few friends and can lavish time on the details.

BAR COOKIES

Here is our best brownie recipe—amazingly tender and rich.

BROWNIES

1 package (6 oz.) semisweet chocolate
   pieces
3 tablespoons butter or margarine
¾ cup sugar

2 eggs
4 tablespoons flour
1 teaspoon vanilla
1 cup chopped walnuts

Melt semisweet chocolate pieces in a double boiler over hot, not boiling, water. In a mixing bowl, beat butter until soft, then add sugar gradually, creaming well. Beat eggs until light; add half the beaten eggs to the butter-sugar mixture and beat until very fluffy. Beat in remaining eggs. Add the melted chocolate, stirring to combine. Mix in flour, vanilla and nuts. Turn into a greased nine-inch square baking pan. Bake at 325°F. (slow) thirty to thirty-five minutes or until a toothpick comes out clean when inserted in center. Cool on wire rack; then cut into *sixteen squares*.

Like Toll House Cookies in flavor, but like easy-to-eat brownies in shape:

CHOCOLATE CANDY COOKIE CAKE

½ cup (1 stick) butter or margarine
1 cup brown sugar, firmly packed
2 eggs
¾ cup sifted flour
¼ teaspoon baking powder

½ teaspoon salt
½ teaspoon vanilla
1 package (6 oz.) semisweet
   chocolate pieces
½ cup chopped walnuts

Beat butter until light and creamy. (You can use an electric mixer right through this recipe except for the last "fold-in" step, or use a wooden spoon.) Add sugar gradually, beating until fluffy. Add one egg at a time, beating after each addition. Sift together flour, baking powder and salt. Add flour mixture and vanilla to egg mixture. Beat until smooth (with mixer at medium speed). Fold in semisweet chocolate pieces and walnuts. Pour into a greased eight-inch square pan. Bake at 350°F. (moderate) for about twenty-five minutes or until the cake is golden brown. Cool, then *cut to make sixteen little squares*.

Ever tried an applesauce brownie? Now's the time!

APPLESAUCE FUDGE SQUARES

2 squares (2 oz.) unsweetened
   chocolate
½ cup shortening
1 cup sugar
2 eggs, lightly beaten
⅔ cup canned applesauce

1 teaspoon vanilla
1 cup sifted flour
¼ teaspoon salt
½ teaspoon baking powder
¼ teaspoon baking soda
½ cup chopped walnuts (optional)

Melt chocolate and shortening over very low heat. Remove from heat and cool slightly. Add sugar, beaten eggs, applesauce and vanilla; mix well. Add the flour, salt, baking powder and soda; blend thoroughly. Stir in chopped walnuts if desired. Turn into a greased eight-inch square pan. Bake at 350°F. (moderate) thirty-five to forty minutes. Cool. *Cut into nine squares.*

Gild the lily! Top brownies with marshmallows, then frost with fudge!

MALLOW FUDGE SQUARES

3 tablespoons cocoa	1 cup sifted flour
½ cup boiling water	¾ teaspoon baking powder
¼ cup butter or margarine	¼ cup buttermilk
1 cup sugar	1 teaspoon vanilla
1 egg, lightly beaten	½ lb. marshmallows, cut in halves

Dissolve cocoa in boiling water; cool. Cream butter; stir in sugar a little at a time. Blend in egg. Add dissolved cocoa and mix thoroughly. Sift together the flour and baking powder; combine buttermilk and vanilla. To the creamed mixture, alternately add the dry and liquid ingredients, stirring after each addition. Turn into a lightly greased nine-by-twelve-inch pan. Bake twenty minutes at 350°F. (moderate). Remove from oven and cover cake completely with marshmallows. Return to oven and bake three to five minutes longer. Frost immediately with Fudge Frosting (below). *Makes twelve squares.*

Fudge Frosting

1 cup confectioners' sugar	3 tablespoons hot brewed coffee
2 tablespoons cocoa	2 tablespoons melted butter
Pinch of salt	½ teaspoon vanilla

Place all ingredients in a bowl; with a rotary beater, beat until smooth. (Mixture should be slightly runny, but if it is too runny, add more sugar.) Dribble over top of cake.

If you've never tasted the molasses-chocolate combination, here's a good excuse to try it. Directions include frosting in a musical mood for a record party.

CHOCOLATE BITE BARS

⅔ cup butter or margarine, softened	1½ cups sifted flour
½ cup sugar	2 packages (6 oz. each) semisweet
1 egg	chocolate pieces
¾ cup molasses	White White Frosting (1 recipe,
1½ teaspoons baking powder	page 227)
¾ teaspoon baking soda	

With a wooden spoon or an electric mixer, beat butter until light and fluffy. Gradually beat in sugar, then egg and molasses. Mix and sift baking powder, soda and flour into butter mixture and stir to blend. Stir in *one* package of semisweet chocolate pieces (save the second for decoration) and pour dough into a greased and floured thirteen-by-nine-by-two-inch pan. Bake at 350°F. (moderate) twenty-five minutes. Let cool in pan ten minutes, then turn out to cool one hour (right side up). Make up frosting and spread over cookie block. Let set. Cut block into three long strips and slice each strip into ten bars. To decorate, press the point of a semisweet piece into each bar to form a music note. Melt remaining pieces over hot (not boiling) water and press through a pastry tube to make the stem end of each note. *Makes thirty bars.*

Here's a very moist brownie with some extras—coconut and raisins.

CHOCOLATE FRUITIES

1 cup (2 sticks) butter or other shortening
4 squares (1 oz. each) unsweetened chocolate
2 cups sugar
4 eggs, well beaten
1 teaspoon vanilla

1¼ cups sifted flour
½ teaspoon salt
1 cup chopped nuts (preferably mixed walnuts, pecans and Brazil nuts)
1 cup flaked coconut
1 cup raisins

Melt butter and chocolate in top of double boiler. Remove from heat. Add sugar and mix well. Blend in eggs and vanilla, then flour and salt. Fold in nuts, coconut and raisins. Spread in a well-greased three-quart rectangular baking dish. Bake at 400°F. (hot) about twenty minutes or until top crust is firm. When cool, *cut into twenty-four squares.*

These cookies taste more like fruitcake than fruitcake! The recipe is from the Continent, and it deserves citizenship papers.

CONTINENTAL FRUIT BARS

1 cup dried currants
1 cup seedless raisins
1 cup chopped blanched almonds
1 cup chopped walnuts
1 cup dried apricots, washed, dried and chopped

1 cup raspberry or strawberry jam
2 eggs, beaten
1 teaspoon vanilla
2 cups sifted flour
1 teaspoon salt

Combine the ingredients in the order listed. Spread one-half inch deep in a greased shallow pan. (Use a twelve-by-fifteen-inch jelly roll pan or one pan ten-by-ten and one eight-by-eight.) Bake at 300°F. (slow) thirty-five minutes. Remove from oven. Cut in diamond shapes; return to oven five minutes to dry out edges. Remove from pan and cool on wire racks. *Makes about sixty bars.*

Butterscotch flavor, applesauce moistness—don't you want some, *now?*

APPLESAUCE BUTTERSCOTCH BROWNIES

½ cup butter or margarine
1 cup brown sugar, firmly packed
1 egg
⅓ cup cooked or canned applesauce
¼ teaspoon maple flavoring

1½ cups sifted flour
1 teaspoon baking powder
½ teaspoon salt
1 cup chopped walnuts

Melt the butter in a medium-size saucepan, then blend in brown sugar. Cool slightly, then beat in egg. Add applesauce and maple flavoring and mix thoroughly. Mix and sift together the flour, baking powder and salt; add to applesauce mixture. Last, stir in walnuts. Turn batter into greased eight-inch square pan. Bake at 350°F. (moderate) forty-five minutes. Cool. Cut into squares. *Makes about sixteen brownies.*

Cherry bars? Why not? To make a complete dessert, top with ice cream.

CHERRY BARS

4 cups sifted flour
¼ teaspoon salt
2 teaspoons baking soda
1 cup shortening

2 eggs, lightly beaten
1 cup sugar
1 cup commercial sour cream
Cherry Filling (below)

Sift flour, salt and baking soda into bowl. Add shortening and cut with pastry blender until mixture resembles coarse crumbs. Combine eggs, sugar and sour cream. Add to flour mixture and blend well. Chill about fifteen minutes. Save about one-fourth the mixture for topping. Roll out remaining dough to fit a sixteen-by-twelve-inch baking sheet. Transfer to sheet. Spread evenly with Cherry Filling. Crumble reserved mixture evenly over cherries. Bake at 350°F. (moderate) for thirty minutes. When cool, sprinkle with confectioners' sugar and cut into bars. *Makes twenty-four to thirty bars.*

Cherry Filling

2 cans (No. 2) pitted red sour
  cherries
1⅓ cups sugar

4 tablespoons cornstarch
2 tablespoons butter
½ teaspoon almond extract

Drain cherries, saving their liquid. Combine sugar and cornstarch in top of double boiler. Gradually stir in liquid. Cook over boiling water until thickened, stirring constantly. Remove from heat and stir in the reserved cherries, butter and almond extract.

These bar cookies are highly recommended for mailing, picnics and all other situations involving transportation.

ORANGE AND RAISIN SQUARES

1 large orange	2 cups sifted cake flour
1 cup raisins	1 teaspoon baking soda
½ cup butter or margarine	1 cup buttermilk
1 cup sugar	Orange Juice Topping (below)
2 eggs, lightly beaten	

Extract one-fourth cup of juice from orange and save for topping. Grind the orange (including rind) and raisins together. Set aside. Cream the butter and add sugar gradually, beating until light and fluffy. Stir in the beaten eggs. Sift flour and baking soda together. Add to the creamed mixture alternately with the buttermilk, beating well after each addition. Blend in ground orange rind and raisins. Turn into a greased eight-by-thirteen-inch pan. Bake at 350°F. (moderate) for fifty minutes. Remove cake from oven and brush with the Orange Juice Topping. Place under broiler for three minutes. Cool in pan about thirty minutes. Serve warm or cold, with whipped cream if desired. *Makes ten bars.*

Orange Juice Topping

Blend the one-fourth cup of orange juice with one-half cup of sugar.

Let your imagination run wild when you decorate these.

ARTY PARTY BARS

1 package (14 oz.) date-bar mix	½ cup chopped walnuts
¼ cup hot water	1 cup moist mincemeat
1 egg	

In a mixing bowl, combine the crumbly mixture and the date filling from the date-bar mix. Add hot water, egg, walnuts and mincemeat. Stir until well mixed. Spread in a greased pan thirteen by nine by two inches. Bake at 400°F. (hot) twenty to twenty-five minutes. Cool thoroughly. To decorate, use colored frosting in tubes or pressure cans. (Or mix up your own butter cream frosting in three or four different colors.) Make a "modern art" pattern of squiggles, overlapping several colors. Or arrange in a plaid of your own design. When frosting has set, cut into diamonds: first cut into lengthwise strips, then on the diagonal. *Makes four dozen.*

This cookie's special quality is its richness. You may choose it for your party best, but it is easy to make.

WALNUT BARS

½ cup (1 stick) butter or margarine
1 cup plus 2 tablespoons sifted flour,
    divided
2 eggs, well beaten
1½ cups firmly packed brown sugar
¼ teaspoon baking powder

Pinch of salt
1 teaspoon vanilla
½ cup flaked coconut
1 cup finely chopped walnuts
White White Frosting (page 227)

Melt butter over low heat; stir in one cup flour to make a paste. Press into an eight-inch square pan and brown lightly by placing in a moderate oven (350°F.) fifteen minutes. Remove from oven. Combine remaining two tablespoons flour with eggs, sugar, baking powder, salt, vanilla, coconut and nuts. Stir until blended. Spread evenly over browned dough. Cool. While still in the pan, frost the top with White White Frosting. Sprinkle additional chopped nuts over frosting. Cut into one-inch squares (it's very rich!). *Makes sixty-four.*

Read the recipe and you'll start imagining how good it is. Fun for a back-yard party.

CARAMEL COCONUT UPSIDE-DOWN BARS

Start by making a syrup for the bottom of the pan:

1½ cups brown sugar, firmly packed
2 tablespoons water

½ cup butter or margarine

Combine ingredients in a saucepan. Cook over low heat, stirring constantly until brown sugar dissolves. Set aside.

Now make the batter:

1¼ cups sifted flour
½ cup brown sugar
2 teaspoons baking powder
½ teaspoon salt
⅓ cup milk

¼ cup cooking oil
1 teaspoon vanilla
2 eggs
1 can (1¼ cups) flaked coconut

Sift the flour, brown sugar, baking powder and salt together into a mixing bowl. (Use a strainer for sifting, and press any stubborn lumps of brown sugar through with back of spoon.) Add milk, oil and vanilla to the flour mixture and beat until well combined. Add eggs one at a time, beating thoroughly after each one is added. Now grease a thirteen-by-nine-by-two-inch baking pan. Sprinkle bottom with coconut. Pour warm caramel syrup (above) over this and top with cake batter. Bake at 350°F. (moderate) twenty minutes or until cake springs back when lightly touched in center. Allow ten minutes to cool. Turn out. (If any topping sticks to pan, lift it off with spatula and pat it into place on top of cake.) *Cut into thirty bars.*

DROP COOKIES

A light, melt-in-your-mouth cookie, for parties or for the cookie jar.

PEANUT BUTTER CLOUDS

2 cups sifted flour	1 cup shortening
2 teaspoons baking soda	1 cup peanut butter
1 teaspoon salt	2 eggs, lightly beaten
1 cup granulated sugar	1 teaspoon vanilla
1 cup confectioners' sugar	

Sift flour, baking soda and salt together. Place both sugars, shortening and peanut butter in mixing bowl. With electric mixer or wooden spoon, beat until creamy and well combined. Beat in the eggs and vanilla. Gradually add the flour mixture, beating after each addition. (The batter will be very stiff.) Drop by teaspoonfuls onto a greased cookie sheet. Flatten each cookie with a floured fork. Bake at 350°F. (moderate) fifteen to twenty minutes. *Makes about six dozen.*

Perhaps you call them chocolate chip cookies—by either name, the recipe below is a national favorite.

TOLL HOUSE COOKIES

1 cup plus 2 tablespoons sifted flour	½ teaspoon vanilla
½ teaspoon baking soda	¼ teaspoon water
½ teaspoon salt	1 egg
½ cup butter or margarine	1 package (6 oz.) semisweet
6 tablespoons white sugar	chocolate pieces
6 tablespoons brown sugar	

Sift together flour, baking soda and salt. Cream butter until fluffy. Add white sugar and brown sugar, vanilla and water. Beat until combined. Beat in egg; add flour mixture. Mix well. Stir in semisweet pieces. Drop by half-teaspoonfuls on a greased cookie sheet. Bake at 375°F. (moderate) ten to twelve minutes. *Makes about four dozen.*

OATMEAL NUT TOLL HOUSE COOKIES

Use the recipe above, but reduce the flour to three-fourths cup. When you add the semisweet pieces, also add one-half cup chopped nuts and one cup uncooked rolled oats. Bake as above. *Makes fifty.*

Little boys love them, and so do big boys, including fathers.

RAISIN SUGAR COOKIES

4 cups sifted flour
1 teaspoon baking powder
1 teaspoon salt
1 cup (2 sticks) softened butter or margarine
2¼ cups sugar

2 eggs
1 cup sour milk (or one cup fresh milk with 1 tablespoon vinegar added)
1 teaspoon vanilla
2½ cups seedless raisins

Mix and sift flour, baking powder and salt and set aside. Beat butter until fluffy, then beat in sugar gradually. Add the eggs and beat until blended. Add the flour mixture alternately with sour milk, stirring after each addition. Stir in vanilla, then raisins. Drop by rounded teaspoonfuls three inches apart on greased cookie sheets. Bake at 375°F. (moderate) for fifteen minutes. *Makes five to six dozen cookies.*

For all who like cookies thin, crisp and tangy.

LEMON WAFERS

2½ cups sifted flour
¼ teaspoon baking soda
1 teaspoon salt
1 egg

1¼ cups sugar
2 teaspoons grated lemon peel
2 tablespoons lemon juice
¾ cup soft butter or margarine

Sift flour, soda and salt together and set aside. Beat egg with sugar. Stir in lemon peel and juice. Blend in the butter. Add half the flour mixture and beat well. Now add remaining flour and blend thoroughly. Chill three hours or overnight. Using a small amount of dough at a time and keeping remainder refrigerated, roll out to one-eighth-inch thickness on a well-floured board. Cut with a two-inch round cutter. Bake on an ungreased baking sheet at 400°F. (hot) six to eight minutes or until cookies have a crisp brown edge. Cool on racks. *Makes seven dozen.*

Put this recipe on your calendar, especially around the holiday season—it's the almondy-est!

SNOWCAP COOKIES

1 cup soft butter or margarine
⅓ cup sugar (and additional sugar to roll cookies)
1 cup blanched almonds, finely chopped

1 teaspoon almond flavoring
1⅔ cups sifted flour
¼ teaspoon salt
1 egg white, slightly beaten

Blend the butter with the sugar, then stir in almonds and almond flavoring. (Almonds may be chopped in a blender or a hand grater, or with a sharp French knife.) Add the flour and salt and work in, using a blending fork or clean hands. Chill dough. With hands, roll into one-inch balls. Dip into egg white, then roll in granulated sugar. Place on baking sheets. Bake at 325°F. (slow) twenty minutes or until delicately browned. Cool without removing from pans. *Makes about five dozen.*

PARTY COOKIES

Love peanut brittle? Try it in cookies! Crunchy good!

CHATTY CAKES

1 cup (2 sticks) butter or margarine
1½ cups finely rolled peanut brittle
1 tablespoon ice water

1 teaspoon vanilla
1½ cups sifted flour
Confectioners' sugar

Cream butter; add rolled peanut brittle. Mix well. Combine ice water and vanilla; add alternately with the flour, stirring after each addition. Roll out on a floured board to one-eighth-inch thickness. With a sharp knife, cut into small squares. Place on an ungreased cookie sheet and bake at 350°F. (moderate) ten to fifteen minutes. Remove from oven. While still hot, sift confectioners' sugar over top and bottom. *Makes two dozen cookies.*

A different cutting instrument yields an entirely different-looking cookie.

PEANUT CRINKLE COOKIES

½ cup butter or margarine
½ cup white sugar
½ cup brown sugar, firmly packed
½ cup smooth peanut butter
1 egg, slightly beaten

1 teaspoon vanilla
1½ cups sifted flour
½ teaspoon baking soda
½ teaspoon salt

Cream butter well; blend in both sugars and peanut butter. Stir in egg and vanilla. Sift flour, baking soda and salt together; add to creamed mixture. Blend well. Divide dough in half. Turn one half onto a lightly floured sheet of waxed paper and shape into a roll one and one-half inches in diameter and nine inches long. Repeat with second half of dough. Wrap tightly and refrigerate twelve hours or put in freezer two hours. Lightly butter two large cookie sheets. Use a lattice potato cutter to cut roll into thin slices. As you cut, turn roll half-over after each slice to make a waffle pattern. (This may sound complicated—but it just happens!) Bake on a cookie sheet at 375°F. (moderate) eight to ten minutes. Cool on a wire rack. *Makes about six dozen cookies.*

If you've ever wondered how people make the little rolled horns to be filled with whipped cream, here's one recipe. A bit tricky, but very pro-fessional-looking!

HONOLULU LULUS

½ cup light corn syrup
¼ cup butter or margarine
¼ cup shortening
⅔ cup brown sugar
1 cup sifted flour

¼ teaspoon salt
1 cup chopped walnuts
¾ cup flaked coconut
⅓ cup well-drained crushed pineapple

Combine corn syrup, butter, shortening and brown sugar in a saucepan. Cook, stirring often, until mixture comes to a full boil. Remove from heat at once. Blend in flour and salt. Fold in nuts. coconut, pineapple. Drop by teaspoonfuls three inches apart on greased baking sheets. Bake one sheet at a time at 325°F. (slow) ten to twelve minutes. Cookies should be shiny at edges and beginning to brown. Cool for just one minute or until slightly firm. With spatula, carefully lift cookies from baking sheet to cooling rack. If cookies begin to stick, return to oven to warm briefly. Roll into cone shapes the moment you remove from baking sheet and fill (when cool) with whipped cream. (Or skip the rolling—they're good just plain too.) *Makes sixty.*

PEANUT PEEK–THROUGHS

Make Peanut Crinkle Cookies (page 352). Use one or both of the fillings below to put them together sandwich style. Squeeze just enough to let some of the filling peek through the latticework.

Marshmallow Filling

Use one-half teaspoon marshmallow cream to fill each pair of cookies.

Chocolate Filling

½ cup semisweet chocolate pieces
1 tablespoon butter
2 tablespoons hot water

½ cup sifted confectioners' sugar
½ teaspoon vanilla

Melt chocolate pieces over hot, not boiling, water. Blend with butter, hot water and sugar. Add vanilla. Use one-half teaspoon filling for each pair of cookies. *Makes twenty Peek-Throughs.*

Mix, roll and bake six minutes—you'll be rewarded with a holiday sweet to serve at home or give to friends near and far away.

FRUITCAKE BONBONS

½ cup soft butter
¼ cup brown sugar, firmly packed
½ cup molasses
2 teaspoons vanilla
1½ cups sifted flour
1 teaspoon baking powder

1 teaspoon nutmeg
1 teaspoon cinnamon
½ teaspoon salt
2 cups raisins
1 lb. (2 cups) candied fruits and
     peels
1 can (8 oz.) walnuts

Cream butter with brown sugar. Stir in molasses and vanilla. Sift together flour, baking powder, nutmeg, cinnamon and salt. Blend into butter mixture. Using fine blade of meat grinder, grind together raisins, candied fruits and peels and nuts. Stir ground mixture into butter mixture. Roll with hands into one-inch balls. Flatten and press one of the following fillings into the center of each: three semisweet chocolate pieces; a half-date, a piece of walnut. Reshape balls around filling. Place on lightly greased cookie sheet and bake at 375°F. (moderate) for about six minutes or until bottom of bonbon is lightly golden. Cool on wire rack and roll in confectioners' or granulated sugar—to make snowballs. Or glaze and decorate tops of bonbons. *Makes about one hundred.*

How To Trim the Bonbons

First make the glaze: Use confectioners' sugar, adding just enough hot water to make a thin icing. (Consistency should be like medium cream sauce.) Spread smoothly over bonbons with a teaspoon.

For decoration use colored nonpareils, chocolate sprinkles, silver dragées, colored sugar, semisweet chocolate pieces and cinnamon dots. Sprinkle coconut on a sheet of waxed paper, add a few drops of food color, cover with waxed paper and rub back and forth until coconut is evenly tinted. For frosting trim, use the pressure-packed cake decorator frosting.

Delicious date sandwich cookies with a coconut filling—to go with tropical parties or stay-at-home dreams.

DATES AROUND THE CLOCK

¾ cup butter or margarine
1½ cups light brown sugar, firmly
   packed
2 eggs
1 cup flaked coconut
¾ cup uncooked rolled oats
½ cup finely chopped walnuts
½ cup chopped dates

5 drops lemon extract
3 tablespoons water
1 cup sifted flour
½ teaspoon baking soda
½ teaspoon salt
½ cup sifted confectioners' sugar
2 tablespoons butter or margarine
2 teaspoons vanilla

Cream the three-fourths cup of butter until fluffy, and gradually beat in sugar. Stir in, in order, eggs, coconut, rolled oats and walnuts, combining well. Reserve one cup of this mixture for filling. Combine dates with lemon extract and water and simmer over low heat until soft. Sift flour, baking soda and salt together and add with date mixture to larger amount of coconut mixture. Drop by small teaspoonfuls onto a cookie sheet and bake at 325°F. (slow) ten to twelve minutes or until firm. Combine confectioners' sugar, butter and vanilla and add reserved coconut mixture, beating until fluffy. Cool cookies. Ice half the cookies on bottom side, putting together sandwich style with remaining cookies. *Makes thirty-six sandwich cookies.*

These candy-cookies are quickly made from candy sticks and packaged fudge-mint refrigerator cookie dough.

PEPPERMINT SANDWICHES

1 roll (15½ oz.) refrigerator
   fudge-mint cookies
3 tablespoons instant powdered
   cream
3 tablespoons shortening

2 cups sifted confectioners' sugar
1 to 2 tablespoons hot water
1 cup crushed red-and-white
   peppermint candy

Place roll of cookie dough in freezer for thirty minutes. Then cut off one-third of roll and slice into five pieces; cut each into quarters. Now cut remaining two-thirds of roll into five thick slices; cut each into quarters. Arrange on an ungreased cookie sheet. Bake, following label directions, and cool on racks. This will produce twenty large and twenty smaller cookies. To make the filling, mix powdered cream thoroughly with shortening. Gradually beat in sugar. Add just enough hot water to ensure smooth spreading. Spread filling on bottom of each cookie, then sprinkle crushed peppermint atop the filling on the twenty larger cookies. (Be generous around rims.) Now cover with the smaller cookies, filled side down, to make *twenty sandwiches*.

Pretty as a Valentine, these. A real present—with heart!

VALENTINE CARD COOKIES

¾ cup butter or margarine
¾ cup dark brown sugar, firmly
   packed
1 egg
2 teaspoons vanilla
2 cups sifted flour

¼ teaspoon baking powder
½ teaspoon salt
Red and yellow food coloring
½ cup finely chopped walnuts
Confectioners' Frosting (below)

Measure butter, brown sugar, egg and vanilla into blender jar or bowl. Cream or blend at low speed until fluffy. Sift together flour, baking powder and salt. Add to creamed mixture and mix to form a moderately soft dough. Remove one-fourth of dough. Tint to light red, using about one drop of yellow food coloring for every four of red. On floured waxed paper, shape into a one-inch thick roll. Form this into a heart-shaped roll, wrap in waxed paper or foil and chill in freezer. (Lay one flat side against bottom of freezer.) Stir chopped nuts into remaining dough. Chill both doughs six hours or overnight. Roll out walnut dough on a fourteen-by-seventeen-inch cookie sheet (cover full area). With a second cookie sheet or some other straight edge, mark dough deeply into two-and-one-half-inch squares. Bake at 375°F. (moderate) twelve to fifteen minutes or until lightly browned. Cut thin slices from heart-shaped dough to make sixty hearts. Arrange these in sweetheart pairs on an ungreased cookie sheet. Bake at 375°F. eight minutes or until just beginning to brown. Cool. Make up Confectioners' Frosting (below). Use to frost all walnut squares completely. While frosting is damp, press a pair of hearts onto each square. *Makes thirty cookies.*

Confectioners' Frosting

Beat one egg white lightly with one teaspoon vanilla. Stir in enough confectioners' sugar (about two cups) for smooth spreading consistency.

When you want to cut cookies into special shapes, this is the recipe to use. The baked cookies don't crack easily, but still they are tender. The dough doesn't change shape much in its baking. In fact, you can hang these cookies from a mobile or from your Christmas tree without worry. Though our directions are for the yuletide, you can adapt them to other holiday occasions.

CHRISTMAS CUTOUT COOKIES

1 cup vegetable shortening	3½ cups sifted flour
1½ cups sugar	1 teaspoon baking powder
2 eggs, well beaten	½ teaspoon salt
1½ teaspoons vanilla	

Prepare this dough at least four hours before you plan to bake it. Beat the shortening until fluffy, then beat in sugar gradually. Blend in eggs and vanilla. Mix and sift together remaining ingredients. Blend into creamed mixture. Chill well. Roll out a portion of the dough to one-fourth-inch thickness right on a floured baking sheet. (Work with as much dough as will fit on the sheet.) Use floured cookie cutters. Or use paper patterns and cut around with sharp pointed knife. Remove the excess dough and set aside for rerolling. If cookies are to hang, make holes in suitable places with the round end of a pencil from which the eraser has been removed. *This amount makes eight very large cookies.* (If cookies are to be three inches in diameter or less, you may roll dough one-eighth inch thick and count on about thirty.)

To hang or mail Cutouts: Before frosting, cut a cardboard pattern to match the cookie. Cover the back of the cardboard with Christmas paper. Make holes to match those in the cookie. Attach cardboard to back of cookie with Sugar Glaze.

Sugar Glaze: Boil one cup light corn syrup for one minute, then cool until thickened.

Frosting

Cover the cookies with white or tinted frosting made as follows:

1½ cups sugar	2 egg whites
6 tablespoons water	1 teaspoon vanilla
1½ tablespoons light corn syrup	Food coloring as desired

Mix sugar, water and corn syrup in saucepan. Covering saucepan for first three minutes, boil slowly until it spins a seven-inch thread when dripped from the edge of a spoon (242°F. on a candy thermometer).

When syrup has cooked about fifteen minutes, beat egg whites with an electric beater or rotary beater until stiff enough to hold a point. (They must be ready the moment the syrup is, but shouldn't stand around too long before.) Pour the hot syrup in a thin stream very slowly into the beaten whites, beating constantly. Add vanilla and beat until frosting holds shape. Divide into bowls and tint desired colors with food coloring. This frosting will maintain its smooth spreadable consistency about one hour. If more than one color frosting is used on a cookie, leave a hairline-thin separation between colors.

To decorate: If your cookies will have features (example: Christmas angels) do not frost this area—instead paint on features using food coloring and a soft pointed brush. (Brown is the best shade—mix it from red with a touch of yellow and green.)

To trim: Perk up the paint work with sparkling ornaments, all edible. Look in the grocery store for white and colored sugars, cinnamon drops, silver shot, multicolored and chocolate sprinkles. In the variety store (or maybe at the penny candy counter) you'll find gumdrops (even prettier when sliced), multicolored sugar dots, tiny candy roses. At specialty grocery departments, look for marzipan fruits and vegetables, candied violets; at drugstores, for licorice lozenges and rock candy.

To string: Wait until frosting is thoroughly hardened. Then string with narrow ribbon and hang.

When you're having a party focused on games—from cards to Monopoly —these cookies will cheer even the losers.

VANILLA GAME COOKIES

4 cups sifted flour	2 eggs
½ teaspoon salt	½ teaspoon vanilla
3 teaspoons baking powder	½ teaspoon almond extract
⅔ cup soft butter or margarine	4 teaspoons milk
1½ cups sugar	

Sift together flour, salt and baking powder. In a large bowl, beat butter until fluffy (by hand or with electric mixer). Add sugar, eggs and flavorings. Beat until very light and fluffy. With a wooden spoon, stir in flour mixture alternately with milk. Shape dough into a ball; cut in half. Use as directed below.

Scrabble Squares: Use one-fourth of the dough. (That is, cut one half in half again.) Roll out on a lightly floured cookie sheet into a six-by-nine-inch rectangle. Cut, without separating, into one-inch squares. Bake at 400°F. (hot) seven to eight minutes or until golden. While cookies are hot, recut where marked. Separate; cool on racks. Decorate each square with a letter, using frosting-in-a-tube. *Makes fifty-four.*

Dice: Stack four Scrabble Squares, putting White Frosting (below) in between. Let dry. Frost top and sides. Add dots, copying real dice.

Poker Chips: Use one-fourth of dough. Roll out on a floured board one-eighth inch thick. Use a one-and-one-fourth-inch round cutter or a chili sauce bottle cap to cut tiny rounds. Bake on an ungreased cookie sheet at 400°F. (hot) six minutes. Cool on racks. Frost tops with White Frosting, some of which you have tinted to deep shades of blue and red. *Makes forty-eight.*

Playing Cards: Roll out half the dough into a ten-by-fourteen-inch rectangle. Use joker from a pack of cards as a pattern—cut around it with a sharp knife. Round corners of cards by pushing with fingers. Bake at 400°F. (hot) about seven minutes. Cool, then frost with White Frosting. Let dry. Then decorate: use prepared colored frostings (in a tube or a pressure can) and make designs similar to standard playing cards.

Chocolate Dominoes: Prepare the recipe for Vanilla Game Cookies, but when you add the flavorings, add four squares of unsweetened chocolate, melted and cooled, and increase the milk to four tablespoons. Divide dough in half. Roll out one piece on a floured board to form a nine-by-sixteen-inch rectangle. Use cover from a can of luncheon meat to cut sixteen rectangles. Make a neat dent across the center with a piece of cardboard. Repeat with remaining dough. Arrange on an ungreased cookie sheet and bake at 400°F. (hot) for seven minutes. Decorate with dots of White Frosting to look like dominoes. *Makes thirty-two.*

White Frosting: Beat one egg white until stiff but not dry. Gradually add one cup confectioners' sugar, beating until it forms firm peaks.

Here is a complicated cookie to make, but your time will be triply rewarded—with its taffy-flavored dough, delicious baked-in chocolate filling, and its party-dress appearance.

FUDGE CRISPS

First make the cookie dough:

2¼ cups sifted flour
½ teaspoon salt
½ teaspoon baking powder
½ cup butter or margarine

1¼ cups brown sugar, firmly packed
1 egg
1¼ teaspoons vanilla

Sift together flour, salt and baking powder and set aside. Cream butter until fluffy. Gradually beat in brown sugar. Beat in egg and vanilla. Now add the sifted dry ingredients and mix thoroughly. Turn onto waxed paper and chill well. Meantime, make filling.

To prepare chocolate filling and glaze:

1 package (6 oz.) semisweet
chocolate pieces
1 tablespoon butter or margarine
¾ cup sweetened condensed milk
1 tablespoon cocoa

½ teaspoon vanilla
1 tablespoon water
1 cup (3 oz. can) pecans, finely
chopped

Melt the chocolate pieces and butter over hot, not boiling, water. Stir until smooth and remove from heat. Blend in condensed milk, cocoa and vanilla. Put three tablespoons of this mixture in a custard cup. To it, add the water and blend. Set aside for glaze. To remaining filling, add chopped nuts. Cool both at room temperature.

To fill and bake:

Divide cookie dough in half. Roll half into an eight-by-fourteen-inch rectangle. Mark dough down the center of the fourteen-inch length. Spread one side with half the chocolate-nut filling. Fold over this the unspread half, then divide block to make two eight-by-seven-inch squares. Repeat with second half of dough. With spatula, lift onto waxed paper. Chill at least one hour. Transfer cookie blocks to foil-lined baking sheets. Bake at 375°F. (moderate) fifteen minutes. Let stand five minutes, cut in two, then at right angles into narrow strips. Before separating, drizzle glaze (in custard cup) over cookies. Cool well. *Makes about five dozen.*

Party Sweets

$\mathcal{S}$OME TASTES don't change and here's one: in spite of our modern consciousness of calories, teen-age boys still love fudge! These candies and sweet nibbles are good after-school snacks and nice party touches, too.

CANDY MAKING

To cook candy, use a large, fairly heavy straight-sided saucepan with a cover. A three- or four-quart size will be adequate for the average recipe.

To check doneness, use a candy thermometer plus the cold-water test. (See our candy box below.) Be sure the bulb of your thermometer is in the syrup but is not touching the bottom of the pan. For accuracy, bend down to read the thermometer—so that your eye is on the level of the temperature mark.

For beating or stirring, a wooden spoon (which is heatproof) is best. Follow recipe exactly: some candy must be stirred during the first few minutes to prevent burning; some must be covered for first three minutes

Kind of candy	Approximate Temperature	Cold Water Test
Fudge, penuche	238°F.	Can be shaped into *soft ball* which flattens out when released.
Caramels	244°F.	Forms *firm ball* which holds shape unless pressed.
Divinity, marshmallows	250°F.	Forms *hard ball* which holds shape even when pressed.
Butterscotch, taffies	272°F.	*Soft-crack* stage. Separates into threads which are hard, not brittle.
Brittles	300°F.	*Hard-crack* stage. Separates into hard, brittle threads.

to prevent graininess. (Note: Don't scrape pan when turning candy out; this will often cause graininess, too.) When the recipe calls for beating, always cool the candy to room temperature first.

For cold-water test, drop a little syrup from the tip of a spoon into a cup of fresh, cold water. (See tests, page 360.)

Make one basic syrup—turn it into any of the trio of sweets below.

THREE-WAY CANDY

2 cups sugar	1 cup water
⅔ cup light corn syrup	

Place ingredients in a saucepan and stir over low heat until dissolved. Cook without stirring to 272°F. (soft-crack stage). Use at once for:

Popcorn Balls: Have ready ten cups of popped corn tossed with two cups of salted peanuts. Add syrup (tinted with a half-teaspoon of food coloring); toss. With buttered fingers, *shape into sixteen two-inch balls.*

Lollipops: Before removing syrup from heat, add one teaspoon each lemon extract and green food coloring, or one teaspoon red food coloring and three-fourths teaspoon peppermint flavor. Drop syrup by tablespoons two inches apart onto greased pans. Press in wooden skewers for handles. Cool well; cover with plastic when dry. *Makes two dozen.*

Nugget Nuts: Have ready three cups of walnut meats. Flavor syrup with two teaspoons of vanilla or peppermint; stir in nuts. Pour out onto a cookie sheet. With a fork, quickly separate into nut-size pieces.

FABULOUS FUDGE

⅔ cup (small can) undiluted evaporated milk	½ teaspoon salt
1½ cups sugar	1 jumbo package (12 oz.) semisweet chocolate pieces
1 jar (8 to 10 oz.) marshmallow cream	1 teaspoon vanilla
¼ cup butter or margarine	½ cup coarsely chopped walnuts

Combine evaporated milk, sugar, marshmallow cream, butter and salt in a saucepan. Stir ingredients to blend slightly. Bring to a boil over moderate heat, stirring constantly. Continue to stir, and boil five minutes. (Mixture will brown lightly.) Remove from heat. Immediately add semisweet pieces and vanilla. Stir (*don't* beat) only until chocolate is thoroughly melted and mixture is shiny. Stir in nuts. Turn quickly into a buttered eight-inch square or nine-inch round pan, and swirl top. Chill. Cut into squares when firm. *Makes two pounds.*

How to make Fabulous Fudge fabulously yours:

Instead of using marshmallow cream, you can use thirty-two regular marsh-mallows or three cups of miniatures.

Instead of using walnuts, you can use pecans, salted peanuts, toasted, halved almonds, coarsely chopped Brazil nuts or broken black walnuts.

Or instead of using nuts, you can use one cup of seedless raisins or one cup of flaked coconut.

For very dark, chocolaty fudge, besides using the semisweet chocolate pieces, add one square of unsweetened chocolate, cut up, to the milk-sugar mixture before cooking.

For taffy-flavored chocolate fudge, use dark brown sugar instead of white.

CHOCOLATE NUTSY FUDGE

⅔ cup chocolate syrup
Evaporated milk

1 jar (10 oz.) chunk-style peanut butter
2 cups confectioners' sugar (about)

Measure chocolate syrup and add enough evaporated milk to bring liquid to three-fourths cup mark. Mix well with the other ingredients, working in as much sugar as possible. Form into two six-inch-long rolls, two inches in diameter. Wrap in waxed paper. Chill in refrigerator. Slice and serve for parties or whenever you are hungry for a bit of candy.

BRAZILIAN COFFEE CANDY

3 cups light brown sugar, firmly packed
1 cup strong coffee
2 tablespoons light corn syrup

2 tablespoons butter or margarine
1 teaspoon vanilla
1 cup chopped Brazil nuts

Place brown sugar, coffee and corn syrup in a saucepan. Cook, stirring constantly, to 238°F. on a candy thermometer, or until a little dropped into cold water forms a soft ball. Remove from heat. Add butter—do not stir. Cool until candy thermometer registers 110°F. or mixture feels lukewarm. Add vanilla. With an electric mixer or a wooden spoon, beat until mixture loses gloss and a small amount dropped from a spoon holds its shape. Stir in Brazil nuts and pour into a buttered eight-inch square pan. Cool. Cut in squares. *Makes one and one-third pounds.*

PRALINES

1 cup brown sugar, firmly packed
1 cup granulated sugar

2 cups pecan halves
½ cup evaporated milk

Combine all ingredients in a saucepan. Cook over medium heat, stirring constantly, until mixture reaches 238°F. on a candy thermometer or until a little dropped in cold water forms a soft ball. Remove from heat and cool to 110°F. Then beat with a wooden spoon until candy just begins to thicken. Drop quickly by wooden spoonfuls on a buttered cookie sheet to form thin patties about two and one-half inches in diameter. If mixture in saucepan hardens, stir in a little hot water. *Makes two dozen.*

CREAMY CHOCOLATE CLUSTERS

1 package (6 oz.) semisweet
   chocolate pieces
¼ cup light corn syrup

1 tablespoon water
1 cup miniature marshmallows, or
   regular size, cut up

Place chocolate pieces, corn syrup and water in top of a double boiler and melt over hot, not boiling, water. Remove from heat and cool ten minutes. Add marshmallows and mix gently until coated. Drop by teaspoonfuls onto waxed paper. Chill to harden. *Makes about three dozen.*

NOTE: Instead of marshmallows, you can use two cups of raisins or one and one-half cups of salted peanuts. In this case, there's no need to cool the chocolate after melting.

CHOC–TALK

2 cups light or dark raisins
½ cup salted peanuts

1 cup (6-oz. package) semisweet
   chocolate pieces

Mix together all ingredients, arrange in candy dishes and serve as nibble food throughout an evening. *Makes almost a quart.*

DREAMY BLIND DATES

40 dates
40 walnut halves
¼ cup butter or margarine
½ teaspoon vanilla
¾ cup brown sugar, firmly packed
1 egg, beaten

1¼ cups sifted flour
¼ teaspoon salt
¼ teaspoon baking soda
¼ teaspoon cream of tartar
¼ teaspoon nutmeg
¼ cup commercial sour cream

Pit the dates and fill each with a walnut half. Refrigerate while you prepare a cookie batter: Cream the butter with the vanilla and gradually blend in sugar. Stir in egg. Sift together flour, salt, soda, cream of tartar and nutmeg. Add to creamed mixture alternately with sour cream. When blended, drop three or four filled dates at a time into batter; coat well.

Lift onto a greased baking sheet. Bake at 400°F. (hot) ten minutes. *Makes forty.*

CHECKERS

¼ cup butter or margarine
1 tablespoon light molasses

1 cup light brown sugar, firmly packed
4 cups bite-size shredded rice cereal

Heat butter with molasses in a big heavy skillet over low heat until butter melts. Stir in brown sugar. Heat very slowly without stirring until mixture is all foam and doubles in volume. Then heat two more minutes. Add all the cereal. Stir to coat each piece. Spread out over a greased cookie sheet. Cool and break into pieces. *Makes five cups, snacks for ten.*

APRICOT SUGARPLUMS

1 lb. dried apricots, ground
2 cups sugar

1 large orange, ground (rind included)

Combine all ingredients. Stir and boil over moderate heat for nineteen minutes. Drop by spoonfuls onto waxed paper which has been sprinkled with additional granulated sugar. Sprinkle tops with granulated sugar and shape into rounds or half-apricot shapes. *Makes four dozen candies.*

COLA BALLS

1 cup vanilla wafer crumbs
1 cup finely chopped pecans
1 cup sifted confectioners' sugar
    plus ½ cup for rolling
2 tablespoons cocoa

¼ cup cola beverage or syrup
1½ tablespoons corn syrup
1 teaspoon black walnut or almond
    flavoring

Place wafer crumbs, pecans, the one cup of sugar and cocoa in large bowl. Mix cola (syrup, bought at your favorite fountain, will give a stronger flavor), corn syrup and flavoring. Pour into crumbs and work together. Form into walnut-size balls. Place the half-cup of sugar in a bowl and roll each ball in it. Store in a metal container with waxed paper between layers. These need not be refrigerated, but they may be frozen. *Makes twenty-four.*

DATE DREAMS

1 package (8 oz.) cream cheese,
    softened
¼ cup chopped dates

¼ cup pineapple preserves
Saltines or buttery round crackers

Place cream cheese in a bowl. Add dates and pineapple preserves and stir with a wooden spoon until well blended. Spread on crackers. Toast under broiler for one minute or until lightly tinged with brown. *Enough snacking for six.*

FORTUNE COOKIES

First type your fortunes (see suggestions below) on very light paper. Then cut the paper so that each fortune is on a strip four inches long and one-third inch high. You'll need thirty fortunes if you fill each cookie.

To make the cookies:

2 eggs	½ cup sifted flour
½ cup sugar	½ teaspoon salt
¼ cup cooking oil	¼ teaspoon ginger

Preheat an electric skillet or griddle to 300°F. (a lower heat than for pancakes). Brush it very lightly with cooking oil. (Reoil occasionally as you bake cookies.) In a small bowl with an electric mixer or a rotary beater, beat the eggs until light. Gradually beat in sugar, then oil. Fold in flour, salt and ginger gently but thoroughly. Drop by teaspoonfuls wide apart on preheated skillet or griddle, flattening with spoon into "pancakes" about two and one-half inches round. Drop batter for two cookies at a time, pausing several minutes before you begin the next two so they won't all be done at once. Otherwise you won't be able to keep up with the folding—which comes next. Bake the first side five minutes or until dry and very lightly browned. Loosen around edges, using a lifting motion. Carefully turn to bake the other side three minutes. Cookie should be soft. Remove baked cookies from skillet and shape immediately. Put fortune at center, bring edges together, barely touching, to form a cylinder. Now fold in half away from joined edges to make a bowknot shape. Cool on rack. *Makes about thirty cookies.*

Fortunes for Your Cookies

Your secret ambition may soon be realized, but don't trust all to luck.
An interesting stranger is coming into your life.
You will soon have humble honor of doing dishes. Not all fortune good, cooky!
Sudden wealth, not necessarily money, is headed your way.
Your heart line may soon become tangled, but there's a happy ending.
Some hidden capability is about to bring you good fortune.
Look for some unexpected money. You probably won't find it, but keep looking!
What you have been wishing for lately will soon come to pass.

POPCORN

Guide for perfect popping: Always test a few kernels first to see if they're fresh and to be sure the oil is hot enough for popping. If kernels spin around and explode, it's time to begin.

If nothing happens, heat the oil a bit longer and retest. To pop, corn must be very fresh. (Seal opened containers and refrigerate to keep moist.) To restore freshness, put a damp blotter in the container, seal and let stand twenty-four hours.

JUST PLAIN POPCORN

¼ cup cooking oil   ½ cup unpopped popcorn

Choose a large heavy kettle. Place it over medium-high heat and add cooking oil. When oil is very hot, test as indicated above. Next, add popcorn and stir with a long-handled spoon until kernels begin to pop. Cover immediately and shake kettle occasionally until popping stops. *Makes about three quarts.*

POPCORN SYRUP

½ cup sugar   ½ teaspoon salt
½ cup light corn syrup   Coloring and flavoring (see below)

When popcorn is popped, reduce the heat to medium and add Popcorn Syrup, made ready in advance. For this, combine sugar and corn syrup with salt. Add your choice of coloring and flavoring and pour over popcorn. Stir for three minutes to coat popcorn well, then turn out onto a large sheet of foil. Spread evenly and let stand to harden a bit. While still warm, form into balls. Or let cool thoroughly and break into nibble-size pieces.

Cherry-O: Add one-half teaspoon almond extract and five drops red food coloring to the Popcorn Syrup. Pour over popcorn and stir as directed. Add one cup chopped candied cherries; mix and turn out.

Chocolate: Add one teaspoon vanilla to Popcorn Syrup. Pour over popcorn, stir; cool as above. With a vegetable peeler, make shavings from two small bars of semisweet chocolate. Add to popcorn and toss.

Pistachio: Add one-half teaspoon almond extract and six drops green food coloring to the Popcorn Syrup. Pour over popcorn; add one-half cup chopped pistachio nuts.

Lemonella: Add one-half teaspoon lemon extract and five to six drops yellow food coloring to the Popcorn Syrup.

Orange Pop: Add one-half teaspoon orange extract, three drops each of yellow and red food coloring to Popcorn Syrup.

Peppermint Dandy: Add one-half teaspoon peppermint extract to the Popcorn Syrup. Pour over popcorn. Mix in one-half cup crushed peppermint candy; toss.

Caramel-Nut: Use one-half cup dark corn syrup instead of light when you make the Popcorn Syrup. Pour over popcorn. Mix in one cup salted peanuts.

You've heard of chips and dips, of course, but have you tried cookies for dipping? The dips are sweet (as frosting, for instance), the service is informal, the fun comes in mix-matching and crazy combinations.

COOKIES AND DIPS

First, buy some plain non-crumbly cookies like vanilla, coconut or oatmeal and a few toppings (chopped nuts, coconut, sprinkles). Add salty crackers to your list too; you can't believe how good they taste with sweet dips! For twelve, choose three dips. Add another flavor for every three couples more. Leftovers can be used for topping cake slices. Make the dips ahead if you like and store in the refrigerator in pretty dishes, all ready to put on a Lazy Susan or a buffet at party time.

Chocolate Fudge Dip

1 package creamy fudge frosting mix	¾ cup commercial sour cream
Soft butter (as called for on package)	½ teaspon rum extract (optional)

Place frosting mix in small bowl of electric mixer or a mixing bowl. Add butter, sour cream and extract. Beat at low speed until blended, then beat at medium speed until smooth and glossy. Turn into a serving bowl; chill. Let soften thirty minutes at room temperature before serving time. Here are some variations:

Caramel Dip: Substitute caramel frosting mix for chocolate; add butter and sour cream, but omit the rum extract.

Orange Dip: Substitute creamy white frosting mix for chocolate. Use butter called for on package; reduce sour cream to one-third cup and add one-third cup orange juice concentrate. Use yellow and red food color to tint the mix to desired shade of orange.

Lemon Dip: Prepare as for orange dip, substituting lemon juice for orange juice concentrate. Tint yellow.

Raspberry Dip

1 package (8 oz.) cream cheese   ½ cup raspberry preserves

Let cream cheese stand at room temperature until soft. Blend with preserves and pour into serving dish. Refrigerate. Let soften at room temperature thirty minutes before serving.

Variations: Any strong-flavored preserves may be substituted for raspberry, such as strawberry, pineapple, cherry, blackberry or black raspberry. If preserves are not stiff, add only one-third cup, then check consistency for dipping. If too stiff, add more preserves; check again.

Applesauce Dip

1 container (8 oz.) vanilla yogurt   ½ teaspoon cinnamon
½ cup applesauce or appleberry sauce   ¼ teaspoon nutmeg
2 tablespoons brown sugar   ¼ teaspoon allspice

Combine yogurt and applesauce in a serving bowl. Mix the sugar and spices together; stir into yogurt mixture. Refrigerate until serving time.

Variations: Use preserves in place of applesauce; omit spices, sugar.

Honey Butter Fluff

½ cup butter   ¾ cup honey

Beat butter until fluffy with wooden spoon or electric mixer. Add honey gradually; beat mixture until well combined. Serve at room temperature.

Barbecues and Picnics

$\mathcal{I}$N MANY WAYS, parties outdoors are the best kind. No longer bound by four walls, you can plan larger parties and expect them to be more relaxed. Especially if there's a barbecue involved, you'll find a new crew of willing hands—those experts, the boys.

But it takes a smart girl to make a boy look like an expert. It means setting the stage carefully so that the right equipment is at hand, completing the preliminary steps of food preparation with care and imagination, and providing guests with a comfortable and colorful spot to relax in while they enjoy their meal.

Picnics—those that don't involve a charcoal fire—are usually planned by girls. But if you're clever, you'll find that a man is absolutely indispensable to your plans. He can help you pick the site, carry the heavy bundles, put up the picnic table and clean up the area later. Party tip: all the boys have more fun when a boy shares responsibility for entertainment.

A BARBECUE IN THE BACK YARD

What could be more fun, almost any summer night, than a barbecue? It's exciting to cook out, and everything tastes simply wonderful. The perfect place to hold a barbecue is right in your own back yard. You have all the freedom of outdoors and all the conveniences of home, too. Beverages and salads can cool in your refrigerator, along with an ice cream dessert for a surprise later on. Your kitchen range is handy to heat soups and vegetables while the outdoor grill is free for the main course: barbecued what-you-will. And (we hate to mention it, but it *could* happen) if it rains, you just move the party temporarily indoors.

To barbecue, by the way, means to grill slowly over an open fire, often simultaneously drenching the food with a sauce. Most people use charcoal to build the fire, and the flavor created by charcoal smoke is the flavor generally associated with good barbecued meat.

On this page, you'll find the basic directions for handling the simplest types of charcoal grills. Your back yard equipment may include (lucky you!) a stone or brick fireplace. If so, get your father to show you how to use it, and practice on the family a time or two until you really understand it. Or you may have a rolling barbecue cart with a large cooking area and movable grids and perhaps a rotisserie. Follow the manufacturer's directions for using it and, once again, practice!

A few words of wisdom: Place a portable grill away from strong drafts—breezes on the fire cause flames instead of the desired slow, steady heat. Build the fire early, especially if there's a thick steak on the menu. The thicker the meat, the longer it will take to cook, so the deeper the bed of white-hot charcoal must be. Provide the barbecue chef with a huge apron (the sillier the better), asbestos mitts and long-handled tools—spatula, forks, tongs and knife according to the meat you choose.

RULES FOR CHARCOAL FIRES

Equipment: The basics are a firepan to hold up the charcoal and a stand or support for the grill which holds the food. Good grills provide for some adjustment of grill height. For a good fire, there must always be air space between coals and grill (1). If you have only a grill, you can balance it on four stones of equal height and lay the coals on the ground. Building a fire: Crumple a good bit of newspaper and light it, then add

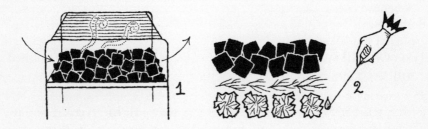

tinder (wood shavings or small sticks). When the tinder is burning well, add the charcoal. (2). Short cut: use charcoal starter, available in liquid and solid forms, instead of paper and tinder. For faster, hotter cooking, line the firepan with foil.

Heat test: To determine heat of fire, hold your hand over the grill, count off seconds. You can hold your hand three seconds over a hot fire, six seconds over a low fire. Coals must be at least glowing red for cooking. When coals become gray-white, the fire is at its hottest.

Cooking tips: Quick grills like franks need only a one-inch charcoal bed and can be cooked low over the fire. Thicker meats need a deeper coal bed— to last through longer cooking time; such meat should be five inches from fire or it will char before it is done.

To control flames: Use a light sprinkling of water so meat will not brown too quickly. To prevent flames: trim fat from meat carefully before grilling.

Test for doneness: Slit the meat with a sharp knife to check the inside color. Don't be fooled because the outside looks done; the inside may still be uncooked.

BARBECUED FRANKS

Simplest item on the barbecue roster is the frankfurter. Almost everybody likes it and you can give it the glamour treatment in a number of ways. Since franks grill in about one minute per side, you'll want to have all the accompaniments ready before the sausages go on the fire. Then offer your guests a choice:

New Orleans Po' Boy: Two grilled hot dogs between halves of individual French bread (hero loaf), smothered with Pepper Relish (page 163).

Coney Island Red Hot: Cooked (to be authentic, in water) frank with hot sauerkraut, mustard and garlic dill pickles.

Philadelphia Frankfurter: Grilled hot dog served with hot German Potato Salad (page 149).

Arkansas Cheese Wiener: Frankfurter split and filled with a strip of American cheese, then grilled.

Boston Bean-Topped Wiener: Grilled frank on a grilled roll with a topping of hot baked beans.

Texas Chili Chihuahua: Grilled frank under a blanket of chili, garnished with sweet onion slices and grated cheese.

FRANK–LY FABULOUS PARTY HOT DOGS

8 large frankfurters
1½ cups grated Cheddar cheese
2 tablespoons minced onion
4 tablespoons prepared mustard, divided

3 cups biscuit mix
1½ teaspoons chili powder
⅔ cup milk

Simmer the franks in water five minutes. Remove and split lengthwise, leaving a hinge. Combine cheese, minced onion and two tablespoons of the mustard. Stuff franks with this mixture. Now make "blankets" for the franks. Combine biscuit mix, remaining two tablespoons mustard and chili powder. Add milk and stir until barely blended. On a floured board, roll out into a twelve-inch square. Cut into eight strips. Spiral-wrap strips around stuffed franks, pinching ends to secure. Place (with space between) in a two-piece grill basket. Cook, turning often, four inches from coals, about ten minutes or until brown. *Makes eight.*

PRONTO PUPS

1 cup biscuit mix
1 egg
¾ cup milk (about)

2 lbs. skinless frankfurters
Cooking oil for frying

Measure biscuit mix into a medium-size bowl. Beat the egg in a one-cup glass measure, then add enough milk to fill to the one-cup mark. Stir into biscuit mix, and stir just enough to moisten ingredients. Add franks and turn to coat well. Heat one-half inch of oil to the bubbling point. Drop in the well-coated franks, one by one, turning almost at once and continuing to turn until brown on all sides. Drain on absorbent paper. Serve on a grilled roll with grated cheese. *Makes sixteen to twenty Pronto Pups.*

CHARCOAL-GRILLED HAMBURGERS

For each person, allow one-third to one-half pound of chopped beef, chuck or round steak. For ten, these are the proportions:

4 lbs. ground beef
4 teaspoons salt

2 teaspoons monosodium glutamate
½ teaspoon pepper

Combine the ingredients, shape into twenty patties and store, separated by squares of waxed paper, in the refrigerator until barbecue time. Place in wire hamburger broiler or on broiling grid and cook over hot coals about four minutes per side or until brown outside and pink inside.

CHARCOAL-GRILLED STEAK

Boneless steaks give two or three good servings per pound. Cuts with bones may call for one pound per person. You can use top quality chuck or round steak for barbecuing if you pretreat it with meat tenderizer according to label directions. Whatever kind of steak you buy, get it thick —one and one-half to two inches at least. Remove from refrigerator one hour before grilling. Trim away excess fat. Gash edges to prevent curling.

Grill three to five inches from coals (the thicker the steak, the farther away), turning once and seasoning with salt and pepper. Cooking time for steak varies, but a one-and-one-half-inch steak usually needs at least ten minutes per side. To check doneness, make a gash near the bone at least halfway through and note color of meat.

CHARCOAL–GRILLED CHICKEN

Buy broiler-fryers, two to two and one-half pounds each, and have the butcher cut them into quarters and break the hip, knee and wing joints so the chicken will lie flat. You'll need three chickens for ten persons. Wipe each bird clean and brush with a barbecue sauce or melted butter, flavored with lemon juice. Sprinkle with monosodium glutamate, if desired, concentrating on areas without skin. (Use about one-half teaspoon per quarter.) Cook over glowing coals about twenty-five minutes, turning frequently and basting with more sauce until meat is well browned and cuts easily.

For a delicious all-around barbecue basting mixture, see Tomato Barbecue Sauce, page 121.

CHARCOAL CHICKEN EN PAPILLOTE

4 whole chicken breasts, or 2 cut-up fryers	Salt, pepper, butter and aluminum foil

Have chicken breasts split and place each piece on a large square of heavy-duty foil. Salt and pepper the chicken, and place a tablespoonful of butter on each piece. Bring up sides of foil into a double drugstore fold (see page 38). Turn over ends of foil twice for a tight seal. Place on charcoal grill over a deep bed of coals and bake, turning every now and then, for one hour. Serve the chicken in its foil to give each eater all the buttery-good juices. *Ample for five good appetites.*

HAM AND BEEF TERIYAKI

2½ lbs. round steak, one inch thick	1 can beef consommé
2½ lbs. precooked ham steak	½ cup soy sauce
1 can lemonade concentrate, undiluted	½ cup chopped onion
	1 clove garlic, minced

Begin making the Teriyaki the night before or the day of the party. Cut round steak into long strips, one-fourth inch wide. Cut ham into one-inch cubes. Combine lemonade concentrate, consommé, soy sauce, onion and garlic in a large bowl. Add cut-up meat and refrigerate several hours or overnight. On long hibachi skewers, thread meat alternately, beginning with one end of a beef strip, then a ham cube, then the other end of the beef strip. Place two of these groupings on each skewer. Broil over hot coals or under broiler for about five minutes on each side or until beef is browned. *Serve immediately on the hibachi skewers to eight people.*

NOTE: Marinade may be thickened and served as a hot gravy. First strain the marinade. Then combine two tablespoons flour with two tablespoons cold water. Add to strained marinade. Heat and stir until thick. Serve.

Don't overlook Dixie-Deviled Chicken—it travels cold to a picnic, may be reheated on a grill. See page 76.

CHICKEN AND SHRIMP SHOYU

4 whole chicken breasts
½ cup shoyu (Japanese soy sauce)
⅓ cup pineapple juice
2 tablespoons sugar

¼ teaspoon garlic powder
1 lb. shelled, deveined uncooked shrimp

Start preparing the Shoyu on the afternoon of your party. Remove skin from chicken breasts, then remove meat from the bones. Cut into bite-size pieces. Combine remaining ingredients in a bowl. Add chicken and shrimp; marinate for several hours. When ready to cook, place chicken and shrimp in a broiler basket. Broil over hot coals for about ten minutes, turning over once, or broil in range broiler. *Serves eight.*

CHARCOAL–GRILLED SHRIMP, SCAMPI STYLE

5 packages (12 oz. each) frozen shrimp or 3½ lbs. fresh shrimp
½ lb. butter or 1 cup olive oil

2 cloves garlic, minced
2½ teaspoons salt
½ teaspoon pepper

Thaw frozen shrimp. Cut shells down center back and peel off. Melt butter (or heat olive oil) and add garlic, salt and pepper. Simmer five minutes. Pour this over peeled shrimp and let stand, covered, in refrigerator one hour. Thread on skewers or place in a hamburger grill basket and grill two minutes to a side or just until pink. *Serves ten.*

To barbecue rock lobster tails, see page 108.

CAMPER'S CORN

There are two good ways to cook corn on a charcoal fire, the first rich and buttery, the second, a weight-watcher's delight.

Remove husks from corn. Lay each ear on a square of foil. Spread corn with about one and one-half teaspoons butter, then salt to taste. Bring up sides of foil snugly around length of ear and seal in double drug-store fold (see page 38). Fold up one end twice to make a tight seal. Into hole at other end, pour two tablespoons (one standard coffee measure) of water. Then tightly seal this end. Repeat until all ears are packaged. To grill, place over a deep bed of glowing coals and bake about twelve minutes on one side. Turn and grill twelve minutes more. Sample for doneness and continue cooking six minutes more if necessary. *Or:* for each ear of corn, dampen a piece of paper towel. Wrap it around husked ear, then wrap again in heavy-duty foil, sealing as above. Grill as in first method. Paper towel keeps corn moist and juicy and is discarded when corn is served.

CHARCOAL-GRILLED FRENCH FRIES

Frozen French fries are easy to heat over a barbecue fire. The quickest way is to spread them in a single layer on a sheet of heavy-duty foil placed on a grill over hot coals. Heat twenty minutes, turning occasionally. Or you can make a long flat packet of heavy-duty foil and, using asbestos mitts, turn the whole packet from time to time. A portable popcorn popper will also hold the French fries—and you can even add a bit of butter and salt before cooking. In any case, provide plenty. *You can count on one regular-size package to serve only two boys, though perhaps four girls.*

PICNIC STUFFED TOMATOES

16 small tomatoes (plum or pear size)
1 lb. cottage cheese
¼ cup mayonnaise or salad dressing
¼ cup chopped scallions

½ teaspoon salt
Pepper to taste
1 tablespoon vinegar

Wash tomatoes. Cut out green stems and core. Remove a half-inch slice from each top and set aside. Use a teaspoon to scoop out tomato seeds and loose pulp, making a cavity in center. Turn upside down to drain. Mix remaining ingredients. Pack a heaping tablespoonful of this mixture into each cavity. Replace tops and set upright in a disposable pan; wrap the whole thing in foil. Chill. Carry to the picnic in an insulated container or wrapped in several layers of newspaper. *Makes sixteen.*

APPLE JUICE COOLER

2 bottles (1 quart each) apple juice
1 bottle (1 pint) cranberry juice
cocktail

1 can (6 oz.) frozen orange juice
concentrate
2 trays ice cubes
2 lemons, thinly sliced

Use a four- to five-quart insulated jug. Cool it by filling with very cold water, letting it stand awhile, then draining well. Now, mix in it the above ingredients; cover and carry to picnic site. *Makes sixteen one-cup servings.*

DREAM BOATS

Heavy-duty aluminum foil
Vanilla wafers
Any flavor jam

Semisweet chocolate pieces
Miniature marshmallows

First make little foil boats: For each, tear off a six-inch piece of foil; fold in half for extra strength. Turn up the longer sides one inch—to make the sides of the boat. At each short end pinch foil in gathers, to form bow and stern; secure with a fold so the two ends of the boat won't come undone.

To fill the boats: Stack five wafers, spreading each layer with jam. Put stack on its side into boat. Separate layers a bit; sprinkle chocolate and marshmallows between.

Heat the filled boats over a low fire on the grill or range until chocolate and marshmallows soften, about ten minutes. Eat with forks.

CANCAN SHORTCAKES

1 can (7 oz.) chocolate nut roll or
date nut roll

1 can (1 lb.) peach or pear halves
1 can (5½ oz.) chocolate sauce

Remove the chocolate roll from can and cut into eight slices. Place one or two pieces of drained fruit on each slice and top with sauce. *Yield: eight happy people.*

PICNIC QUICKNICS: BARBECUED SANDWICHES

Here's a different kind of sandwich to grill on your charcoal stove or under the broiler. For a back-yard picnic, make sandwiches in advance, wrap in heavy-duty foil and refrigerate until party time. For beach picnics, pack sandwiches cold in insulated bags for toting.

To make barbecued sandwiches: Tear off a fourteen-inch piece of foil, put a buttered slice of bread—buttered side *down*—on foil. Add filling (see below), top with a buttered slice of bread—buttered side *up*. Bring two ends of foil together, make two folds: turn other edges under to seal. Place over hot coals, grill each side seven minutes. In a broiler, grill each side ten minutes, three inches from the heat source.

Pickle Dilly Filling: sliced liverwurst, crisp crumbled bacon, chopped onion, dill pickle slices, a little mayonnaise.

Peanut-Bacon Filling: peanut butter, plenty of crisp bacon bits, a light spreading of prepared mustard or mayonnaise.

Walnut Surprise Filling: equal portions of chopped ripe olives and chopped walnuts, mixed with softened cream cheese.

Beef Barbecue Filling: canned corned beef hash and tartar sauce. Add salt to taste.

Chicken-Almond Filling: canned sliced chicken sprinkled with toasted slivered almonds, chopped pimiento, soy sauce.

Mexicali Filling: undiluted black bean soup, minced onion and crumbled bacon (or minced salami). Add a light spreading of salad dressing and salt to taste.

Burger Italiano Filling: a little deviled ham topped with sliced mozzarella cheese, spicy catchup, sliced green olives and a pinch of orégano.

THREE SPUR-OF-THE-MOMENT PICNICS

If you believe that the best parties are the ones that just happen, this section is for you. One party meal you buy nearly all of on the way (of course, you'll have the gear packed in advance); one you snatch from the pantry shelf and get ready with the help of a can opener; and one you freeze now, grill later.

With the aid of these menus, you can plan a party that is dependent on something besides your own decision to go. For instance, kite-flying—it has to be done when the wind is right. Or a party which waits until that special boy comes home on leave. Or the day the blossoms are best in a nearby park or orchard. Plan ahead and you're ready to take off on a moment's notice!

DELICATESSEN-PLUS MENU

Can't-Wait-for-Lunch Chowder
Grilled Franks with Chili Beans
Hot Dog Relish
Potato Salad   Coleslaw
Tiny Tomatoes
Fresh Fruit   Cookies   Soft Drinks

Keep this shopping list (for eight) handy:

2 cans condensed mushroom soup	3 lbs. coleslaw
1 can condensed tomato soup	2 lbs. tiny tomatoes
1 can condensed cream of celery soup	3 lbs. frankfurters
1 quart milk	4 packages frankfurter rolls
1 jar hot dog relish	1 box assorted cookies
1 bottle chili sauce	Fresh fruit in season
2 cans smoky beans in tomato sauce	4 packs (6 bottles each)
5 lbs. potato salad	chilled soft drinks

Also, collect this picnic gear in one spot:

1 vacuum jug	1 can opener
1 portable grill or cooker	1 bottle opener
2 unbreakable salad bowls	Tongs or forks to handle franks
2 serving spoons	1 paring knife
Paper plates, cups and napkins	1 pot for chili beans
(twice as many as you think you need)	1 stirring spoon
Plastic forks and spoons	

Before you leave for the picnic, make the soup:

CAN'T–WAIT–FOR–LUNCH CHOWDER

2 cans condensed mushroom soup	1 can condensed celery soup
1 can condensed tomato soup	1 quart milk

Blend soups and milk together in a large pan. Heat, stirring now and then, until steaming. Meanwhile, fill vacuum jug with very hot water; let stand three minutes. Empty out water; fill with soup. *Serves eight.*

All the remaining foods can be bought on the way to the picnic. At eating time, put the boys in charge of the grill, the girls in charge of setting the table and arranging the salads. The girls can also mix the chili beans, to heat at the side of the grill.

CHILI BEANS

2 cans (1 lb. each) smoky beans in tomato sauce	½ cup chili sauce

At the picnic site, combine beans and chili sauce in a saucepan. Heat and ladle over franks on rolls or use as a side dish. *Enough to sauce sixteen franks.*

CAN-DO PICNIC

Chilled Cocktail Vegetable Juice
Tunaburgers
Sweet Mixed Pickles
Canned Apricots and Cherries
Cookies

Almost everything goes right from the jar or can to serving cups or plates, but the main dish you put together at the picnic:

TUNABURGERS

3 cans (7 oz. each) tuna
2 cans condensed mushroom soup
2 cans (1 lb. each) peas

8 hamburger buns
1 can (3½ oz.) French fried onion rings

Drain oil from tuna into a skillet; stir in undiluted soup and liquid from the peas. Heat; add tuna and peas. Heat through. Meantime, split and toast buns. Spoon tuna mixture over buns; top with onions. *Serves eight.*

FREEZE NOW—HEAT LATER

Barbecued Chicken
Hobo Bundle
Parker House Rolls
Soft Drinks   **No-Bake Fudgies**

Keep the chicken, vegetables and dessert all ready in the freezer. Pick up the rolls and soft drinks on your way. A real banquet!

BARBECUED CHICKEN

4 lbs. chicken legs
1 can (9 oz.) crushed pineapple
½ cup soy sauce
½ cup vinegar

½ cup cooking oil
2 teaspoons monosodium glutamate
¾ teaspoon ginger
1 teaspoon sugar

Rinse chicken and pat dry. Combine remaining ingredients in a nine-by-thirteen-inch baking pan. Add chicken legs; let stand thirty minutes. Turn legs and bake at 350°F. (moderate) for thirty minutes. Cool, then wrap pan in foil or plastic wrap and freeze. On the day of your party, remove pan from freezer three to five hours before cooking. At the picnic, place on a slow fire with grate of grill set about six inches from heat. Turn chicken and baste occasionally with pineapple mixture in the pan. Cook half an hour or till meat is tender when pierced with a fork. *Serves eight.*

HOBO BUNDLE

1 package (10 oz.) frozen peas
1 package (10 oz.) frozen corn
1 jar (3½ oz.) tiny pickled onions, drained, or 1 tablespoon instant minced onion

2 tablespoons butter
Salt and pepper

Break up frozen peas and corn and mound on a large square of heavy-duty foil. Add onions, dot with butter and sprinkle generously with salt and pepper. Twist foil corners together tightly—like a hobo bundle—and freeze until the day of your party. Allow three hours for defrosting. Place bundle on hot grill. Cook twenty-five minutes, remove from grill and gently open top of bundle. (It's steamy—watch out!) Give vegetables a stir. *Serves eight.*

NO–BAKE FUDGIES

2 packages (6 oz. each) semisweet chocolate pieces
1 cup undiluted evaporated milk
2 cups marshmallows

4 cups vanilla wafer crumbs (2 boxes, 7¼ oz. each)
1 jar (4 oz.) candied fruit, finely diced (about ½ cup)
½ cup pecan halves

Combine one package semisweet chocolate with milk in a medium-size saucepan. Place on low heat to melt chocolate, stirring all the while. Add marshmallows, stir until melted. Remove from heat; gradually stir in wafer crumbs and fruit. (Mixture will be stiff.) Press into a greased seven-by-eleven-inch pan. Melt second package of chocolate over hot (not boiling) water; spread over wafer-chocolate mix. Mark into two dozen squares with a toothpick; place a pecan half in each. Wrap pan in foil and freeze. Allow two hours to defrost; cut and serve. *Makes twenty-four.*

Giant Recipes for

Giant Groups

$\mathcal{I}$S IT YOUR TURN to cook wholesale style? If you have landed on the refreshment committee for the school dance, or if you've simply become carried away with the idea of a great big party at home, this chapter will make your work easier.

These recipes are planned for a minimum of twelve (to double or triple if you like) up to the quantities for eighty and one hundred. They're pre-planned to take the guesswork out of amounts to use for each portion. In addition, they recognize the fact that you do not have a complete restaurant kitchen in your home.

The recipes fall into four general categories: main dishes; desserts and cookies; sandwiches and other snacks; punches.

The first four recipes (plus Peaches-and-Cream Pie on page 390) add up to a banquet for eighty—perhaps the number of girls in your graduating class, or the number expected at a club supper.

You probably can't (at least you shouldn't try to!) prepare a dinner for eighty all by yourself, but you *can* do it with the help of just seven other girls: Two of you to make the chicken and barbecue sauce, one each to work on the salad and corn casserole, one to make the biscuits and three to make the pies.

Let each girl be responsible for shopping for her own ingredients. Most of the dishes travel well; they can be made at home, carried to the party spot and reheated there. The biscuits are the one exception, for of course, they taste best when freshly baked and should therefore be finished in the ovens at the club, school or wherever.

BARBECUED CHICKEN FOR EIGHTY

1 cup (1½ oz.) instant minced onion
1 cup water
5 cups chopped green pepper (5 medium-size peppers)
½ cup shortening
3 cups vinegar
3 cups brown sugar, firmly packed
1 No. 10 can tomato purée (3 quarts)
6 tablespoons salt
¾ cup prepared mustard
¾ teaspoon cayenne pepper
1 tablespoon ground cloves
2 tablespoons ground allspice
2 tablespoons chili powder
1 teaspoon garlic powder
3 tablespoons celery salt
1 quart water
60 lbs. chickens, quartered (24 broiler-fryers)
6 tablespoons salt and 4 teaspoons pepper to sprinkle on chickens

Add onion to the water and let stand for a few minutes. Add green pepper and mix. Heat shortening until bubbling. Add vegetables and cook until barely tender, about six minutes. Add all the remaining ingredients except the chicken and its salt and pepper. Let the mixture simmer over low heat ten minutes, stirring occasionally. Remove from heat. Wash the chicken and drain on absorbent paper. Sprinkle with salt and pepper. Place in roasting pans skin side down. Cover with the barbecue sauce. Cover pans and bake at 350°F. (moderate) forty-five minutes. Remove the covers. Turn the chicken and baste with the sauce in the pan. Bake without cover forty-five minutes more, basting frequently. *Serve chicken with the sauce from the pan to eighty.*

BAKED CORN AND TOMATOES FOR EIGHTY

10 cans cream-style corn (No. 2) or 2 No. 10 cans
2 No. 10 cans tomatoes
4 tablespoons salt
1 tablespoon pepper
4 tablespoons sugar
4 quarts (2½ lbs.) soft bread cubes
3 cups (1½ lbs.) butter or margarine, melted

Combine corn, tomatoes, salt, pepper and sugar. Pour into two greased roasting pans, each seventeen by twenty-six inches. Mix bread cubes with butter. Spread over corn-tomato mixture. Bake at 325°F. (slow) forty minutes or until bread cubes are crusty brown. *Makes eighty portions of a heaping half-cup each.*

DROP BISCUITS FOR EIGHTY

6 quarts (6 lbs.) sifted flour
¾ cup baking powder
2 tablespoons salt
1 quart (1¾ lbs.) shortening
3 quarts milk

Sift the dry ingredients together; then cut in shortening, using a pastry blender or two knives, until the mixture resembles coarse corn meal. Gradually stir in milk to form a very heavy batter. (Batter may be refrigerated one hour or more before baking.) Drop mixture by tablespoonfuls two inches apart on lightly greased cookie sheets. Bake at 450°F. (very hot) about twelve minutes or until browned. *Makes 160 biscuits; serves eighty.*

GREEN BEAN AND ONION SALAD FOR EIGHTY

2 No. 10 cans green beans
½ cup instant minced onion
¾ cup liquid drained from beans
1½ cups cooking oil
1 cup vinegar

½ cup sugar
½ teaspoon garlic powder
2 teaspoons salt
1 teaspoon monosodium glutamate

Drain the beans, saving the liquid. To the minced onion, add the three-fourths cup liquid. Let stand five minutes. Add to the beans, tossing to mix. Combine remaining ingredients, blending well, and pour over the beans, tossing gently. Chill before serving. Place one-fourth cup portions on crisp lettuce leaves. *Serves eighty.*

ESCALLOPED CHICKEN, SOUTHERN STYLE

1 chicken (4 to 5 lbs.)
1 cup butter or margarine (about),
  divided
¾ cup sifted flour
6 eggs, well beaten
2 tablespoons minced onion

3 to 4 cups soft bread crumbs
½ teaspoon celery salt
1 teaspoon salt
¼ teaspoon sage
⅛ teaspoon pepper
Fine dry bread crumbs

Place whole, cleaned chicken in deep kettle. Cover with boiling water; simmer until tender, twenty to thirty minutes per pound. Cool. Remove meat from bones, leaving it in large pieces. Melt one-half cup of the butter over low heat; blend in flour; gradually stir in six cups of the stock the chicken cooked in. Cook, stirring constantly until thickened, about five minutes. Add eggs and cook two minutes longer, stirring constantly. Remove from heat; cool. To make dressing: Melt six tablespoons of butter over low heat; add onion and sauté until transparent, but not browned. Combine with bread crumbs and seasonings and turn into a shallow greased pan (twelve by thirteen by one and one-half inches). Arrange layer of chicken on top. Pour stock-egg mixture over all. Sprinkle top with additional crumbs. Bake at 350°F. (moderate) forty-five to sixty minutes or until mixture is heated through and crumbs browned. *Serves twelve to fifteen.* To serve twenty-four, make two pans, doubling each ingredient.

PONCHO SQUARES

5 lbs. ground beef chuck
6 tablespoons chili powder
1 tablespoon salt
2 teaspoons orégano
2 teaspoons monosodium glutamate
2 bay leaves, crumbled
3 cloves garlic, minced
2 quarts beef broth
2 cups sifted flour
4 teaspoons sugar

4 tablespoons (¼ cup) baking
  powder
½ teaspoon salt
4 cups yellow corn meal
8 eggs, beaten
3 cups milk
¾ cup melted butter or margarine
3 cups grated sharp Cheddar cheese
1 cup minced green onions

Preheat two large skillets. Add meat and brown until well done, scrambling with fork. Transfer into large kettle (at least five-quart size). Sprinkle with chili powder, the tablespoon of salt, orégano, monosodium glutamate, bay leaves and garlic. Add beef broth and stir to blend. Simmer, uncovered, forty minutes, at which time liquid will be reduced to about one cup. Meantime, sift flour, sugar, baking powder and the half-teaspoon of salt into a large mixing bowl. Stir in corn meal. Add eggs, milk and melted butter. Stir lightly until blended. Stir in cheese and onions. Spread meat mixture evenly over bottoms of two nine-by-thirteen-inch baking pans. Spread corn meal mixture evenly over the meat in each pan. Bake at 400°F. (hot) ten minutes. Reduce heat to 325°F. (slow) and bake thirty minutes longer until firm and golden brown. Cut each pan into twelve squares (three by four inches). Remove squares with spatula to serving dishes. (If you are serving fewer than twenty-four, cover seconds with foil and keep warm in oven, reducing heat to 200°F. *Serves twenty-four.*

SPAGHETTI AND MEAT BALLS FOR TWENTY

To make the sauce:

¼ cup olive oil
1½ cups chopped onions
2 cloves garlic, minced
3 cans condensed tomato soup,
  undiluted
2 cans (1 lb. 14 oz. each) tomatoes

3 cans (6 oz. each) tomato paste
3 teaspoons salt
½ teaspoon black pepper
1 teaspoon orégano
¼ cup chopped parsley

Pour olive oil in a large saucepan or kettle. Add onions and garlic and cook over low heat until transparent. Add remaining ingredients. Simmer, stirring occasionally, for one hour and fifteen minutes, or until proper sauce consistency is reached. Meantime, make the meat balls. When they are browned, add to the simmered sauce and continue to cook slowly twenty minutes. Now, if desired, cover and refrigerate—up to two days. At party time, reheat and serve with hot spaghetti to twenty.

To make the meat balls:

3 lbs. chopped beef chuck	1 teaspoon black pepper
4 eggs, slightly beaten	2 teaspoons salt
3 onions, grated	1 teaspoon nutmeg
1 cup fine dry bread crumbs	1 teaspoon grated lemon peel
1 cup water	¼ cup shortening for browning

Break up chopped chuck and place in a large bowl. Add remaining ingredients and stir gently with a fork until blended. Shape into small Ping-pong-size balls. Melt shortening in a large skillet and brown meat balls on all sides. Add to sauce and proceed as above.

To cook spaghetti:

You will need a total of three gallons of water for three pounds of spaghetti. Start heating water (in one or two pots) about an hour before dinner. When water is boiling, add spaghetti and three tablespoons salt. Cook twelve minutes, or until barely tender. Drain in a colander. Serve with meat balls and sauce. *Enough for twenty*.

PENTAGON SHRIMP

1 cup cooking oil	8 oz. blanched, toasted almonds,
2 cups sliced green pepper	finely chopped (1⅔ cups)
5 cups sliced onion	1 teaspoon thyme
2 cups diced celery	1 teaspoon curry powder
1 cup chopped celery leaves	1 teaspoon salt
½ cup chopped parsley	1 teaspoon pepper
2 cans (No. 2½) tomatoes (about	1 teaspoon cayenne pepper
7 cups)	3 large bay leaves
1 cup chili sauce	5 lbs. shrimp, cooked, shelled and
1 cup seedless raisins	deveined

Heat oil in a large skillet or roasting pan. Add green pepper, onion, diced celery and celery leaves. Cook over low heat until onion is transparent but not browned. Add remaining ingredients with the exception of the shrimp. Simmer gently one hour, stirring once or twice to prevent sticking. Add the prepared shrimp and heat through, about thirty minutes. Serve over hot, buttered rice. *Serves twenty*.

NOTE: Sauce may be made early in the day and stored in the refrigerator to blend flavors. The shrimp is added forty minutes before serving and the sauce heated through. If you wish, you can make sauce days in advance and store it in the freezer. The shrimp may be cooked, cleaned and frozen, too. Then thaw, combine and heat through.

First, make the basic sauce—two weeks ahead, if you can store it in the freezer, two days ahead if it is to be kept in the refrigerator:

THREE–WAY CURRY FOR A CROWD

3 large apples, peeled, cored and
   quartered
2 large onions, peeled, washed and
   quartered
1 cup (2 sticks) butter or margarine
4 tablespoons cornstarch
4 tablespoons flour

3 tablespoons curry powder
3 teaspoons monosodium glutamate
3 tablespoons salt
1¼ teaspoons paprika
3 large cans and 1 small can
   evaporated milk
2 quarts water

Run apples and onions through a food grinder, using the fine blade. Heat butter in large (gallon-size) Dutch oven or saucepan. Add onions and apples and cook gently until tender and translucent, twenty to thirty minutes. In a little bowl combine cornstarch, flour, curry powder, monosodium glutamate, salt and paprika. Sprinkle over onion mixture and blend. Slowly stir in evaporated milk, then water. Gradually bring to simmering point. Cook over low heat thirty minutes, stirring often. *Makes three quarts.*

To turn your basic sauce into a triple treat, use it for the three different curries which follow. Serve each of them with hot, fluffy rice made according to package directions or those on pages 138-139. Use enough (about four cups regular rice) to yield twelve cups when cooked.

Curried turkey: Heat together one quart curry sauce and two cups diced cooked turkey. Use equal parts white and dark meat. *Serves eight.*

Curried shrimp: Heat together one quart sauce and one pound cooked cleaned shrimp. Prepare these as follows: Bring two quarts of water to boil. Add shrimp (still in shells) and cook just until tender, about seven minutes if shrimp are still frozen, four minutes for fresh or thawed shrimp. To clean, peel off shell around body, starting at inner curvature; then slip off tail shell. Cut down center of back and lift out sand vein. If shrimp are large, keep just a few whole for garnish and cut up remainder into thirds. *Serves eight.*

Curried eggs: Heat together one quart curry sauce with eight whole, shelled, hard-cooked eggs. *Serves eight.*

For curry condiments, refer to page 84.

DESSERTS

At some giant parties, guests will have their desserts sitting down, with all the convenience a fork implies. At others (for instance, the school dance) you'll need a dessert which can be eaten in the hand. Here are recipes for both kinds; choose one that fits your situation.

CHOCOLATE NESSELRODE DELIGHT

1½ cups finely rolled chocolate-
 cookie crumbs
⅓ cup melted butter
1 envelope unflavored gelatine
⅔ cup sugar, divided
⅛ teaspoon salt
3 eggs, separated

1¼ cups milk
¼ cup quick chocolate-flavored drink
 mix
2 teaspoons rum flavoring
1 cup heavy cream
1 package (6 oz.) semisweet
 chocolate pieces, chilled

Combine chocolate-cookie crumbs and butter. Spread evenly in a greased nine-by-thirteen-inch baking pan. Bake for about eight minutes at 375°F. (moderate). Set aside to cool. Combine gelatine, one-third cup of the sugar and the salt in the top of a double boiler (off the heat). Beat the egg yolks, milk and quick chocolate mix together. Stir into gelatine mixture. Cook over boiling water, stirring constantly, until gelatine is dissolved (about five minutes). Remove from heat and stir in rum flavoring. Chill in refrigerator, stirring occasionally, until mixture mounds when dropped from a spoon. While gelatine sets, put aside one-fourth cup chocolate pieces for garnish. Chop the remaining pieces fine with a French knife or chopper in a wooden bowl. When gelatine has begun to mound, beat with a rotary beater until smooth. Whip the cream until soft peaks form, then fold in. Beat egg whites until stiff but not dry. Gradually beat in remaining one-third cup sugar. Fold into gelatine-cream mixture along with the chopped chocolate pieces. Pour mixture over baked crumb crust and refrigerate for several hours or overnight. At party time, cut into two-inch squares. Garnish top of each square with a rosette of pressure-packed whipped cream, centered with a single chocolate morsel. *Makes twenty-four squares.*

QUICK SHERBET SUNDAE

½ gallon plus 1 pint lime sherbet

4 packages (10 oz. each) frozen
 raspberries, thawed

Scoop lime sherbet into pretty champagne or sherbet glasses. Then pour about one-fourth cup thawed raspberries with syrup over each serving. If you have a freezer, you can speed up your last-minute party preparations by making the sherbet balls the night before. Set scoops of sherbet on a foil-covered baking sheet (or in foil-lined ice cube trays). Freeze until serving time. Drop into glasses, top with thawed raspberries. *Serves eighteen.*

CHERRY CRUMBLE

First, make the Crumble crust and topping:

1½ cups butter or margarine	2 teaspoons baking soda
2 cups brown sugar, firmly packed	2 teaspoons cinnamon
2 teaspoons vanilla	2½ cups quick-cooking rolled oats
3 cups sifted flour	2 cups chopped flaked coconut
2 teaspoons salt	

Beat butter until fluffy and gradually beat in brown sugar, then vanilla. Sift together flour, salt, baking soda and cinnamon. Stir into butter mixture, then add oats and blend to make a crumb mixture. Fold in the coconut. Press two and one-half cups of crumb mixture into each of two nine-by-thirteen-inch baking pans. Set aside.

Now, for the magic cherry "cheesecake" filling:

2 cans (15 oz. each) sweetened condensed milk	4 cups (2 cans) cherry pie filling
½ teaspoon salt	½ teaspoon cinnamon
1 cup lemon juice	2 tablespoons cornstarch
2 tablespoons grated lemon peel	2 tablespoons cold water
4 eggs, slightly beaten	¼ teaspoon almond extract

Mix condensed milk, salt, lemon juice and peel, and stir until thickened. Blend in the eggs. Pour cherry pie filling into a saucepan. Combine cinnamon, cornstarch and water and stir into pie filling. Cook over low heat until clear and thickened. Stir in extract, removing from heat. Pour half of milk-lemon mixture into each pan. Top with half of cherry mixture, spreading evenly. Top each pan with two cups of remaining crumbs. Bake at 350°F. (moderate) for forty-five minutes. Cool in pan. Cut each panful into twelve squares. Serve warm or cold. *Serves twenty-four.*

LIFE PRESERVERS AND PORTHOLE COOKIES

3½ cups sifted flour	1½ cups sugar
1 teaspoon baking powder	2 eggs, well beaten
½ teaspoon salt	1½ teaspoons vanilla
1 cup (2 sticks) butter or margarine	White Frosting (page 389)

Combine flour, baking powder and salt and sift together. Cream butter. Gradually add sugar, beating until fluffy. Add eggs and vanilla. Blend thoroughly. Stir in dry ingredients and mix thoroughly. Chill several hours or overnight. Roll out about a third of the dough very thin on a lightly floured board. Use a doughnut cutter to make Life Preservers—save centers to make Portholes. Repeat with remaining dough. Bake on lightly greased cookie sheets at 400°F. (hot) for six to ten minutes or until lightly browned. *Makes about six dozen.*

For fifty guests, you'll need two batches, or 144 cookies. Make ahead and freeze in moistureproof containers if desired.

For extra emphasis, decorate cookies with White Frosting. Make small dots around edge of portholes. Decorate Life Preservers by outlining stripes at four points around the rim.

White Frosting: Beat one egg white until stiff. Gradually add one cup sifted confectioners' sugar and a pinch of salt, beating until stiff.

COCONUT PASTRY BOATS

2 cups sifted flour
1 teaspoon salt
2/3 cup vegetable shortening
1 1/3 cups fine grated coconut
5 tablespoons cold water
1 can (No. 2) pineapple tidbits, drained

2 cans (11 oz. each) mandarin oranges, drained
1 lb. green seedless grapes
1 jar (8 oz.) maraschino cherries
1 jar (1 lb.) pineapple preserves

Sift flour and salt into a mixing bowl. Cut in shortening with a pastry blender until it looks like coarse corn meal. Add coconut and mix well. Add water and stir with a fork until mixture clings together. Divide dough into thirds. Roll out each third between two pieces of waxed paper until less than one-eighth inch thick. Cut into two-by-three-inch rectangles. Gently fold each rectangle in half, bringing longer sides together. Pinch open edges together *only* at the two ends. Transfer to cookie sheet with fold at bottom. The pinched ends are the fore and aft ends of the boat. Broaden bottom of boat by pressing pastry from inside. Bake eight to ten minutes at 375°F. (moderate) until lightly browned. Cool. If you are waiting until the next day to fill the boats, wrap and store them. To fill with fruit: Arrange one well-drained piece of pineapple, a mandarin orange section and one grape in each boat. For color, add a maraschino cherry to some boats. Slowly bring preserves to a boil. Cool slightly, then spoon a little bit over each of the boats to glaze fruits. *Makes fifty.*

PEACHES–AND–CREAM PIE

10 pastry shells, each ten inches,
  baked and cooled
3⅓ cups sugar
2½ cups sifted flour
5 teaspoons salt
5 teaspoons ground nutmeg

7½ quarts drained canned cling peach
  slices (use 13 No. 2½ cans or 4
  No. 10 cans)
10 cans (14½ oz. each) evaporated
  milk (1 gallon plus ⅔ cup)

After pastry shells are baked, in a large bowl combine sugar, flour, salt and nutmeg. Sprinkle two tablespoons of mixture over bottom of each pastry shell. (Save remainder.) Half-fill the shells with drained cling peach slices, using about three cups per pie. Gradually blend the evaporated milk into the remaining sugar-flour mixture. Pour one and three-fourths cups over each peach-filled pie. Bake at 375°F. (moderate) forty-five minutes or until mixture turns a light golden color. Cool at least one hour before serving. (NOTE: If oven space is limited, pour evaporated milk mixture only over those pies which are ready to bake. Keep unbaked ingredients cold.) *Makes ten pies, ten inches each, or eighty portions.*

GOLD RUSH TURNOVERS

4 cups seedless raisins
4 cups pitted prunes
1 cup walnut meats
4 cups sugar
¾ cup finely crushed saltines (24
  crackers)

½ cup grated orange peel
½ cup orange juice
¼ cup butter or margarine
8 egg yolks
13 sticks (6½ packages, 10 oz. each)
  piecrust mix

Using an electric blender or a sharp knife, chop the raisins, prunes and walnuts separately. Combine in a large mixing bowl with all the remaining ingredients except the piecrust mix. Set aside. Follow package directions for combining piecrust mix, rolling each stick into a ball. Roll out each ball into rectangle one-eighth inch thick. Cut rectangle (rerolling scraps when necessary) into eight four-inch squares. After you have prepared twenty-four squares, fill: On each pastry square, center one scant tablespoon of filling; moisten edges. Fold each into a triangle, sealing tightly with tines of floured fork. Place on cookie sheets. If desired, brush tops with lightly beaten egg white and sprinkle lightly with granulated sugar. Bake at 450°F. (hot) twelve to fifteen minutes or until browned. Cool on racks. Repeat with remaining dough and filling. *Makes about 105 boy-sized turnovers.*

SNACKS

When the occasion calls for sandwiches or "something light," turn to this section. Here are cold sandwiches you can make ahead (some can be frozen). There are hot snacks here too, all planned to eliminate guesswork.

SHORT CUTS TO SANDWICH MAKING

Whenever sandwiches are prepared in advance, be sure they are kept covered and refrigerated until served.

Let butter or margarine soften at room temperature before you begin so it will spread easily and quickly. Whipped butter or margarine is also easy to spread and is lower in cost and lower in calories.

Make just one kind of sandwich at a time to speed production.

Line up the bread slices in sandwich pairs.

Butter all bread slices first, working assembly-line style. Then add filling: use a quarter-cup measure (long-handled is best) or a small ice cream scoop when using salad fillings. Cover with top slices. Cut.

To save time when you have a lot of sandwiches to wrap, arrange them in layers on a tray. Put foil, waxed paper or plastic film between layers. Cover all with foil, plastic or two layers of waxed paper.

BUY-LINE GUIDE TO QUANTITY

To make two dozen sandwiches, you'll need:

Bread: three loaves of one and one-fourth pound each if slices are regular thickness; two one-pound loaves if thinly sliced.

Butter or margarine: one-half pound.

Ready-to-eat meats: four pounds. (Salami, liverwurst, bologna, etc.)

Packaged pre-sliced cheese: one and one-half pounds.

Cream cheese: five packages, eight ounces each.

Jelly: one quart (thirty-two ounces).

Dressings: one pint of mayonnaise or whipped salad dressing
two jars of mustard
three bottles of catchup.

CHICKEN SALAD SANDWICH FILLING

½ cup mayonnaise
2 tablespoons lemon juice
1 cup minced celery
⅓ cup minced onion
¼ cup chopped olives

1 teaspoon salt
¼ teaspoon pepper
6 cans (5 oz. each) boned chicken, or
  1 quart diced chicken meat
6 hard-cooked eggs, chopped

Blend ingredients thoroughly, adding chicken and eggs last and tossing them in lightly. Keep cold. Use three tablespoons (a scant quarter-cup) filling per sandwich. *Enough for twenty-four sandwiches.*

TUNA SCHOONERS

8 cans (7 oz. each) tuna, drained and flaked
16 hard-cooked eggs, chopped
1 cup chopped celery
4 jars (4 oz. each) pimientos, chopped
2 packages (10 oz. each) frozen peas, cooked one minute, drained and cooled
½ cup minced onion
2 tablespoons salt
1 teaspoon pepper
1 pint mayonnaise or salad dressing
½ cup vinegar
100 small finger rolls or round butter rolls

Choose a large mixing bowl and into it measure tuna, eggs, celery, pimiento, peas and onion. Toss to blend. In a separate bowl, mix salt, pepper, mayonnaise and vinegar until blended. Add to the tuna mixture and toss to mix well. Refrigerate, covered. Slice the tops from the rolls and hollow out part of the soft interior. Fill each scooped-out roll with two tablespoons (one standard coffee measure) of the tuna-egg filling. (The crumbs may be used for croutons, breading or bread puddings.) Replace tops. Cover with plastic film or foil and refrigerate until serving time. *Makes 100.*

SALMON–CREAM CHEESE TREATS

2 cans (1 lb. each) salmon
3 packages (8 oz. each) cream cheese, softened
2 tablespoons chopped chives
4 loaves whole-wheat bread

Drain salmon and remove any bits of bone. Place softened cream cheese in large bowl of electric mixer and beat until light and fluffy. Add salmon and chopped chives. Beat at low speed until combined. Use a No. 24 scoop or a very scant one-fourth-cup measure of filling for each sandwich. Stack three filled sandwiches together. Trim off crusts. Cut through from point to point in both directions to cut each large sandwich into four small triangles. Wrap in plastic wrap, foil or freezer paper. Seal with freezer tape. Freeze until party day. Allow four to six hours for defrosting. Unwrap when packages are soft to the touch and you are ready to serve them. *Makes 140 finger-size party sandwiches.*

HAM HANDIES

3 jars (12 oz. each) smooth peanut
  butter
1 lb. margarine or butter, softened
6 cups coarsely ground cooked ham
  (about 2 lbs.)

1 jar (16 oz.) pickle relish, drained
6 loaves square pumpernickel or dark
  rye bread

Blend peanut butter and margarine in large bowl of mixer. Add ham and pickle relish; combine at low speed. Prepare sandwiches as directed in Salmon-Cream Cheese Treat recipe (page 392), but cut each into six rectangles. Freeze and defrost as above. *Makes 210 bite-size sandwiches.*

TROPICAL CHICKEN SANDWICHES

4 jars (6½ oz. each) boned chicken
  or 4½ cups cooked diced chicken
2 cans (5 oz. each) water chestnuts,
  drained
1 can (1 cup) blanched almonds

2 cans (No. 2) crushed pineapple,
  drained
2 teaspoons salt
4 loaves firm white bread

Dice chicken, chop the drained water chestnuts fine and combine. Place almonds in jar of electric blender and blend until as fine as corn meal. (Or use a rotary hand grater.) Add to chicken and water chestnuts. Stir in pineapple and salt. Blend well. Fill and trim seventy slices of bread as in Salmon-Cream Cheese Treat recipe (page 392). Cut each sandwich into four squares. Wrap and freeze as directed for salmon sandwiches. *Makes 140 tiny sandwiches.*

SWISS CHALET SANDWICHES

2 lbs. bacon (1¼ cups after frying
  and chopping)
2 lbs. Swiss cheese
1 cup heavy cream
2 tablespoons Worcestershire sauce
1 teaspoon salt

2 teaspoons monosodium glutamate
48 slices white bread
12 eggs
2 cups milk
1 teaspoon sugar

Fry the bacon until it's very crisp, then drain on absorbent paper and chop fine. Grate cheese into a large bowl. Add bacon. Combine cream, Worcestershire, salt and monosodium glutamate. Pour sauce over cheese mixture and lightly toss with a fork until well combined. Taste and correct seasoning accordingly. Spread about one-fourth cup of the mixture on each of twenty-four slices of bread. Top with remaining slices. Beat eggs, then beat in the milk and sugar. Dip and drench each sandwich in the egg-milk mixture. Fry on a well-greased griddle on both sides until golden. *Makes twenty-four sandwiches.*

Serving suggestions: Accompany these melt-in-your-mouth sandwiches with a crisp green salad, coleslaw, sweet pickle chips or lettuce leaves.

Advance preparation: The cheese mixture may be refrigerated overnight. Keep covered. Sandwiches may be prefilled, then at serving time dipped in egg and fried. Sandwiches may also be made one hour before serving time and kept (uncovered) in a warm oven. They may be served with a fork or cut into quarters so they can be easily managed by hand.

SOUPER BURGERS

4 lbs. ground beef round	2 teaspoons salt
1 quart celery, chopped (about 1 lb.)	2 tablespoons mustard
2 cups chopped onion	5 cans condensed tomato soup
2 teaspoons chili powder	24 hard rolls or hamburger buns

Heat a lightly greased skillet over moderate heat, add chopped beef, celery and onion. (If skillet is small, divide ingredients equally into two fryings.) Stir lightly over low heat until browned. Add chili powder, salt, mustard and tomato soup. Cook, stirring often, until celery is tender, about fifteen minutes. Meantime, split and toast the rolls. Ladle one-fourth cup of the mixture over bottoms of buns, add top halves. *Serves twenty-four.*

PIZZA PUPS

¾ cup cooking oil	1½ teaspoons orégano
2 teaspoons minced garlic	1 teaspoon chopped parsley
1 can (46 oz.) tomato juice	24 frankfurters
1½ teaspoons salt	24 frankfurter rolls
¾ teaspoon pepper	3 cups grated mozzarella cheese

Heat oil in a large saucepan. Add garlic and stir over low heat until lightly browned. Add tomato juice, salt, pepper, orégano and parsley. Cook (without cover) about twenty-five minutes or until thickened, stirring occasionally. During last five minutes, simmer franks in water to cover. Split frankfurter rolls lengthwise and open. Arrange on broiler pan. Cut franks lengthwise, almost through. Arrange on rolls. Top each with two tablespoons tomato sauce, letting some run down sides. Sprinkle each with two tablespoons grated mozzarella cheese. Place under broiler until cheese melts and is slightly browned. *Makes two dozen.*

HAMBURGERS FOR A CROWD

4 lbs. ground beef chuck	½ teaspoon pepper
2 teaspoons seasoned meat tenderizer	2 tablespoons water
2 tablespoons Worcestershire sauce	½ cup prepared mustard
2 teaspoons salt	½ cup (1 stick) soft butter

Combine all ingredients (except butter) lightly with fork. Pat out and divide into twenty portions. Shape each into a patty. Spread both surfaces with mustard. Stack with squares of waxed paper between patties and refrigerate at once; keep refrigerated until ready to cook. At party time, get ready a tray of trimmings—crisp lettuce leaves, sweet onion rings, catchup, mustard, pickle relish. Slice and butter twenty hamburger rolls. Warm them for eight minutes in a 400°F. (hot) oven. Meantime, cook hamburgers two to three minutes per side on a greased griddle or on a broiling rack three inches from heat source. Serve on buns, letting guests add their own trimmings. *Makes twenty*—boys will undoubtedly eat two!

PUNCHES FOR A LARGE CROWD

Making punch for forty people involves a few problems. Keeping things cold, for example. If your refrigerator is full of giant cans of fruit juices, where do you chill the sandwiches?

For that reason, you'll find many of the recipes which follow are not really "ready" until they're in the punch bowl. Often, you'll mix some of the ingredients first, then mix in another ingredient as you fill the punch bowl. If your party is to be at home, get a friend to lend refrigerator space to help with the chilling. If it's to be at school, you may be able to use space in the refrigerators of the cafeteria kitchen or the home economics department. But *do* plan for really cold punch—punch at its best!

PINK–APPLE PUNCH

4 to 8 lemons, sliced very thin	16 bottles (7 oz. each) chilled lemon-
3 jars (1 lb. each) maraschino cherries	lime carbonated beverage
8 quarts chilled apple juice	Red food coloring

First make lemon and cherry ice cubes: cut from outside to center of each lemon slice, twist slice to make a spiral and wedge one in each section of ice cube tray. Drain cherries (saving the syrup for punch) and drop a cherry in the center of each section of another tray. Prepare as many trays as you have time and storage space for. Fill trays with water. Freeze until firm. At the prom, you can supplement with plain cubes. To make the punch: Combine apple juice, lemon-lime and cherry syrup. If punch bowl holds less than four gallons, mix half at a time. Add a few drops of food coloring until desired shade of red is reached. Add lemon and cherry ice cubes and serve immediately. *Three gallons or enough for fifty.*

LIME SHERBET PUNCH

4 quarts lime sherbet
¾ cup lemon juice
1½ cups honey
3 cans (46 oz. each) pineapple juice

4½ quarts orange juice (6 cans, 6 oz. each, frozen orange juice reconstituted)
3 large bottles club soda
2 limes, sliced

Pack sherbet into two eight-cup ring molds. Freeze in coldest part of freezer until ready to serve. Have other ingredients chilled. Combine lemon juice and honey; stir into pineapple juice and orange juice. Pour half of this into punch bowl. Just before serving, fizz with one and one-half quarts of soda. Unmold sherbet onto cookie sheet and slip into center of punch. Garnish with lime slices. When bowl is empty, add rest of punch. *Makes three gallons or enough for fifty.*

NOTE: If desired, instead of molding sherbet, put a small scoop into each paper punch cup; freeze. At serving time, fill cups with fruit juice mixture.

MOCK CHAMPAGNE

5 packages (10 oz. each) frozen whole strawberries, defrosted
10 cans (6 oz. each) pink lemonade concentrate, defrosted

10 bottles (28 oz. each) ginger ale
Mint leaves, chilled, for garnish

Defrost strawberries, reserving syrup. Combine with pink lemonade. Add ginger ale. (If punch bowl is small, use only half of lemonade and ginger ale at a time.) Add ice; garnish with mint. *Makes three gallons, enough for fifty.*

JEWEL PUNCH

First make the jewel ice cubes:

2 cans (6 oz. each) frozen orange juice concentrate
7½ cups water (about), divided
Food colorings

2 cans (1 pint 2 oz. each) grapefruit juice
1 can (46 oz.) tropical fruit punch

Empty eight ice cube trays. Mix frozen orange juice with two and one-half cups water and a little red food coloring. Pour into two ice cube trays. Freeze. Mix grapefruit juice with a little yellow food coloring. Freeze in two trays. Mix a little red food coloring with tropical fruit punch and freeze in two trays. Measure two and one-third cups water and add to that enough blue food coloring to make a medium shade of blue. Pour into ice cube tray and freeze. Repeat, using green food coloring. If the party is to be at school, tote jewel cubes in insulated bags to the school freezer.

Mix the punch at party time:

6 cans (6 oz. each) frozen lemonade concentrate

6 cans (6 oz. each) frozen grapefruit juice concentrate

6 bottles (28 oz. each) club soda

12 bottles (28 oz. each) lemon-lime carbonated beverage (or 48 bottles, 7 oz. each)

The ideal punch bowl for this recipe holds twenty quarts. If yours is smaller, prepare one-half or one-third of the recipe at a time. Combine juices at party time. Add half of each color of frozen ice cubes to juices —these will tint and flavor punch. Add remaining cubes as needed. *Makes 135 servings, five ounces each, or enough for fifty guests.*

SUCCESS PUNCH

1 dozen lemons
3 oranges
2½ cups sugar
4 cups water

3 cans (46 oz. each) pineapple-grapefruit juice drink
9 bottles (7 oz. each) lemon-lime carbonated beverage

Cut lemons and oranges into wedges and place in a saucepan over moderate heat. Mash fruit while bringing it to the boiling point; press out all the juices from pulp. Remove from heat, add sugar and water. Stir until dissolved. Strain; chill. Combine with chilled pineapple-grapefruit drink and lemon-lime and pour over a block of ice in a punch bowl. *Makes two gallons, about forty punch cup servings.*

ROSY PINK PUNCH

2 cans (46 oz. each) tropical fruit punch

8 bottles (7 oz. each) lemon-lime carbonated beverage
2 tablespoons rose water

Chill the beverages thoroughly before mixing. Pour the fruit punch into a large party bowl. Add lemon-lime and rose water; stir. Add ice cubes. Float real rose petals on top of punch just before serving. *Makes about thirty-six servings, four ounces each.*

NOTE: Rose water may be purchased at your drugstore.

PUNCH ON THE ROCKS

5 quarts cranberry juice cocktail
20 whole cloves
3 sticks cinnamon (or about 6
   inches), broken

2 teaspoons grated lemon peel
2 teaspoons grated orange peel
¼ cup lemon juice
3 quarts apple juice

Heat the cranberry juice. Add spices. When cool, remove spices. Add other ingredients and chill. For garnish, use orange and lemon slices ("pink" their edges with kitchen shears). Stud slices with cloves. *Makes two gallons: serves twenty.*

ICED TEA PUNCH

First make a pretty decoration for the punch:

1 pint fresh strawberries, hulled and
   washed

2 oranges, sliced thin
Water

Remove cube divider from two ice trays. In one place the strawberries, in the other the oranges. Add enough water to cover fruit, not float it. Chill until frozen. Add enough water to fill tray completely. Freeze again. At party time, dip trays briefly in hot water to unmold ice and place in punch bowl.

Now for the punch. You'll need:

2 cups boiling water
⅓ cup instant tea or 15 tea bags
2 teaspoons nutmeg
⅔ cup superfine sugar
3 cups cold water

6 cups apricot nectar
1½ cups lemon juice
1 bottle (28 oz.) ginger ale
2 bottles (28 oz. each) strawberry or
   raspberry soda

Combine boiling water with instant tea or tea bags. (Stir tea bags occasionally and let steep four minutes, uncovered.) Add nutmeg and sugar and stir. Add cold water, apricot nectar and lemon juice. Stir, then chill. When ready to serve, pour over fruit-ice blocks in punch bowl. Stir in ginger ale and fruit soda. *Makes about fifty servings, four ounces each.*

HOT FRUIT SIZZLE

4 quarts apple cider or apple juice
1 quart cranberry juice cocktail
Peel of two oranges
2 packages (12 oz. each) mixed dried
   fruit

6 sticks (two inches each) cinnamon
2 teaspoons whole cloves
1 teaspoon whole allspice
12 whole cardamoms
2 cups honey

Combine all ingredients in a large saucepan or kettle. Bring to a boil, reduce heat and simmer for twenty minutes or until dried fruit is very soft. Strain into a heatproof punch bowl and serve warm. (Fruit may be puréed in blender and used as a dessert sauce.) *Makes about thirty-two servings, five ounces each.*

For Flaming Toppers: Soak sugar cubes in lemon extract. Place on lemon slices and float on punch. Ignite cubes.

STRAWBERRY FROSTED—PARTY SIZE

2 quarts vanilla ice cream
3 quarts milk

1 box (½ lb.) quick strawberry-flavored drink mix

Spoon ice cream into the large bowl of an electric mixer. Add strawberry mix. Turn mixer to low speed and slowly pour one quart of milk into bowl while mixer is on low, being careful not to spatter. When ice cream is melted and thoroughly combined with milk, pour into a large punch bowl while mixer is on low, being careful not to spatter. When ice cream combine. Serve with a punch ladle into tall glasses or paper cups. *Makes about twenty servings, eight ounces each.*

26

Prom Planner's Guide

$\mathcal{T}$HE RULES FOR PLANNING a good prom are the same as for planning a good party—it's the size of the party that's different. And that means committees instead of one hostess, a hall instead of a rumpus room, and a budget which at first glance looks like a lifetime clothes allowance.

No matter what your position on the prom committee, remember that cooperation and organization are the two key words. Work with your chairman with enthusiasm and dependability. Or if you're the chairman, work with your committee members to build enthusiasm and a determination for excellence. It takes a big team pulling together to make a prom sensational, but here are some general guidelines.

Where will it take place? It's important to determine this first. Schools, clubs, restaurants and halls all have special values—and usually special drawbacks, too. Visit and select well in advance; be sure to find out the price, whether the place serves food, whether they will let you bring in food, what decorations you may use, what hours you must observe.

What music will you use? If it's a band, audition several and ascertain prices. Find out how long their "breaks" are and plan for extra entertainment (professional or student amateur) if it seems indicated.

What will you serve? Perhaps nothing if guests will be able to purchase their own refreshments easily. The most popular prom menu includes sandwiches, punch and cookies. But you may decide to prepare or buy a complete meal and combine a banquet and dance in one evening.

What will your theme be? Further on in this chapter, you'll find suggestions for two dances, each with the theme fully carried out in decorations. An exciting theme, especially one which hasn't been used in your school often, attracts more people to the dance, makes it more memorable. Executing a theme will take research at the public library or among friends, but it's worth the effort.

SOME THEME IDEAS

Under the Sea (or Neptune's Garden): Construct a clamshell for the bandstand, use crepe paper and aluminum foil for rippling water effect, trim with fish, octopus, shells.

Japanese Garden: Set the bandstand in a temple, have arching bridges, parasols, Mount Fujiyama, a rising sun.

King Arthur's Court: Decorate walls with cutouts of battlements and towers, as if you were within a medieval castle. A cutout cardboard herald blowing his trumpet might greet the guests. Let coats of arms, a suit of armor made of molded aluminum foil accent different areas.

Lollipop Hop: Create a candyland in gumdrop colors. Use man-size lollipops, candy-cane signposts (to Marshmallow Township and Chocolate Sauce Springs), a paper backdrop to be the Mountain of Whipped Cream (topped with a maraschino cherry) and strings of real gumdrops to trim the refreshment table.

Old South Garden: Backdrop for the orchestra is a painting of a plantation mansion. Enclose the bandstand in white railing and shrubs. Extra touches—trees hung with crepe paper Spanish moss, a trellis trimmed with roses, real or paper.

Evening in Paris: The Eiffel Tower, cut from cardboard, is on the wall behind the band, and the refreshment area looks like a Paris street café. Waitresses, dressed like midinettes, serve guests punch. Travel posters, a sidewalk show of reproductions of old masters decorate other walls.

Venetian Night: The bandstand becomes the embarkation dock with two- or three-dimensional gondolas tied to it. (Make them from wooden boxes, covered with black cardboard to give the gondola shape—guests can have their pictures taken there.) Around the walls, more painted gondolas float through moonlit canals. Guttered candles in wine bottles add interest to the refreshment table.

Over the Rainbow: If your committee includes carpenters, your rainbow can be three-dimensional and really dominate the dance floor. (Make and decorate it in sections for easy storage; assemble as early as possible on prom day.) Or make it a painted rainbow with a three-dimensional pot of gold (gold-foil covered chocolates) at the end of it. Other decorations: puffy white clouds, bluebirds, butterflies.

Holiday in Mexico: Prickly cactus plants and desert sands line the walls but the bandstand is a hacienda, and the musicians wear serapes. A gigantic piñata hangs from the ceiling—breaking it and collecting its nonbreakable favors will be a high point of the evening.

One more thought: If you'd like to go all out on decorations, try to find another school (close, but not too close) whose prom is on a different night and see if you can share major costs by using the same decorations.

What will go on at the prom? Some ideas: group sings; door-prize draw-ings; crowning "royalty" (this has good advance publicity possibilities, especially if you have a contest); floor shows which fit the theme of the dance. Additional fun: announcing couples on a loud-speaker as they arrive; having everyone's picture taken.

Who are the best committee workers? If it's your job to choose them, include someone from every clique in your class. You need leadership, but you need know-how, too. It takes a boy with an eye for art and a flair for carpentry to head up a crack decorating committee—assisted perhaps by a girl who is clever with her hands to produce the buttons and bows. Don't be afraid to involve lots of people—you're more apt to have an outstanding attendance record if everyone is working for a dance's success.

How many meetings should there be? Enough, but not too many! Heads of committees should meet every two weeks, beginning three to five months before the prom. Each chairman should have definite and dif-ferent responsibilities—each one should count backward from Prom Day to determine how many hours it will take to get the job done and plan schedules accordingly. There should be at least two meetings of the entire prom organization—one at the beginning, for members to get to know one another, and one a few days before the prom to coordinate last-minute problems and whip up that final spark of all-out enthusiasm.

Will you have favors? At senior proms, the favor is often a school symbol such as a key ring charm, a pin or a ring. But even more fun are tiny whatnots that reflect the theme of the dance. Tiny Eiffel Towers, Japa-nese parasols, masks, paper *leis*, chopsticks have all been used with suc-cess. Dance cards, prettily decorated, are treasured forever, especially if the card is well filled in!

Have you reviewed your budget? If the financing for your dance is coming from ticket sales, the head of the ticket committee and the treasurer may be having some anxious moments. Make sure that the cost of favors and refreshments planned won't exceed a certain percentage of the ticket's price, and that the costs for music and decorations will be paid for by the attendance you can logically expect. If you aren't careful to do that, someone (your class?) might wind up out of pocket. On the other hand, if the dance is a wild success, you'll have the great pleasure of deciding what to do with all the money earned.

In some schools, money for the dance comes from a fixed treasury—collected from class dues, sales, etc. The treasurer must then allocate to each committee a certain budget, and it's the chairman's job to see that her committee stays within it. When money is low, willing hands can save the day. Though it takes more work on the part of each committee member to operate with little money, results are often more spectacular and creative than those that come the easy route, by way of purchase.

Now, for the two proms-in-detail:

BON VOYAGE PROM

It's the most festive night aboard ship you can imagine. Your gym or dance hall has been transformed to the main cabin of a luxury liner. Fringes of red, white and blue crepe paper festoon the ceiling. Ship's flags dip out below them. Guests enter by coming down a red-carpeted gangplank. The walls seem rimmed with portholes and through each porthole can be seen a travel poster of a faraway place. The bandstand is below a crow's nest, silhouetted against a sky dotted with sea gulls. The buffet table, which holds shipshape cookies and punch, is sparked with two fat potted pompons and at its center is a cardboard ship's model. On each table is a wee baggage cart holding favors. The catch-phrase is "Welcome aboard!"

FRINGED CEILING STREAMERS

To find out how many streamers you would need, we gave our decorations a trial run in a basketball court (ninety-four feet by fifty feet). In the center of the room was a ring which dropped down from the ceiling to working height. We attached one end of the fringed streamers to this. The other ends were attached at five-foot intervals to a wire which went all around the room about nine feet from the floor. We found we needed a minimum of one thousand feet of streamers—in lengths varying from twenty-four to fifty feet. You make the streamers in seven-and-one-half-foot lengths, then join them together (more about this later).

First collect what you will need: packages (twenty inches wide) of red, white and blue flameproof crepe paper; rolls of white crepe paper streamers; parcel-post twine; a stapling gun; cellophane tape; scissors or a paper cutter. All ready?

Cut each package of white paper in half as in (1); cut each package of red and blue into thirds as in (2). While paper is *folded*, fringe narrow end as shown. Fringe the white every half inch, eight inches deep; fringe the red and blue every half inch, about four and a half inches deep. Now roll out seven and one-half feet of white paper streamer. Lay a piece of red fringe alongside as in (3). Then move fringe so it overlaps streamer a half inch; staple together every four inches. A half inch above, staple white fringe in place. Lay twine along the stapled seam (4), leaving an extra six inches of twine at each end; staple twine in place. (After you get the feel of it, you can staple fringe and twine in one step.) Half an inch above the white fringe staple the blue (5) in place. Next step (6) is to fold the blue fringe neatly up, then the white, then the red.

To store, roll fringe loosely.

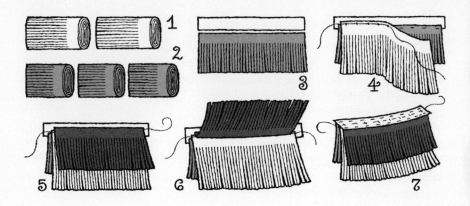

When ready to hang, unroll and join the pieces by tying the ends of twine together in neat, close square knots. Use tape to join paper portion of fringe so that it looks like one long streamer, as in (7). When hung, it will show all blue and white as you dance in one direction—all red and white from the opposite direction.

Potted Pompons

Make these for the buffet table from two seven-and-one-half-foot fringed streamers like those for the ceiling (above). Roll each streamer tightly, stapling at every turn, and fan out the fringe. Insert a dowel stick into the stapled end of each pompon; tape in place. Wrap the stick in red crepe paper and tape on two leaves. Plant in a flowerpot filled with sand; stand on the buffet.

Bon Voyage Ship

The ship stands between two pompon plants on the buffet table. Have an artistic model-maker on your decorating committee build ship of heavy matte paper. Fill stacks with crepe paper fringe (rolled as for pompons) and add crepe paper waves.

Ship's Flags

Cut the flags from red, white and blue stiff paper. Leave most of them plain, but decorate some with red and blue paint in nautical designs. Punch holes at two corners of each flag and tie them (as shown) on rope or clothesline. You will need four pieces of rope, each about sixty-two feet long. When flags are all tied on the ropes, store them neatly in a box. On prom day, suspend them from gym corners to the center ring (they should hang lower than the fringed streamers).

Walls

To decorate the walls and make portholes, you'll need: long rolls of white paper (about six feet wide); black paint; travel posters of faraway places. Unroll paper and draw a porthole every ten feet. Draw hole eighteen inches in diameter; draw a circle around it that's twenty-one inches in diameter. Paint both circles—adding black "rivets" between them—then paint the half-open porthole doors. Cut travel posters to size; paste inside. Reroll paper, store till the prom; then staple onto tall stanchions around the gym.

Gangplank

Hunt in the school storeroom for a ramp and borrow or rent a red carpet to cover it. For the posts to hold rope railing, use wooden two-by-two's. Drill a small hole in each (for the rope); cover the posts with crepe paper and nail to the ramp. Use clothesline for rope. Make life preservers from white matte stock paper and fasten them to both rope and ramp. Use red, white and blue crepe paper streamers (two inches wide) to form a curtain over the door.

Bandstand

Make the rail around the bandstand as you did for the gangplank. Trim the bottom with red, white and blue crepe paper fringe. On a paper background, draw puffy clouds. Make the crow's nest from red matte stock. In advance, you can cut sea gull shapes from white matte stock. On prom day, fold wings lightly for a life-like appearance, then hang the gulls from the ceiling on light strings. Staple crow's nest to a tall stanchion, or use it to disguise the basketball hoop.

Refreshment Table

Cover the table with a white cloth trimmed with festoons of blue crepe paper pinned in place. To make the "champagne bucket," use a washtub; line the inside with heavy-duty foil; spray-paint outside of tub white. When dry, paint on wide red stripes.

CHAMPAGNE BOTTLES

Get a sample bottle of each soft drink you'll be serving and plenty of aluminum foil. For each bottle, tear off a twelve-inch square of foil. Hold center over top of bottle. Smooth and shape foil downward to mold exactly over bottle. Smooth foil at bottom of bottle but *don't* tuck under bottle. Trim neck with colored sticky tape and notary seal. Slip bottle out, mold another cover over it; repeat. You can nest covers together to store. On prom night, slip bottles inside covers, chill in champagne bucket. Remove cap (including its foil cover) with a bottle opener.

BAGGAGE TRUCKS

Use these to decorate individual tables. Use cardboard for the base and wheels, blue pencils or dowels wrapped in crepe paper for the poles. Trim the cart with tape, crepe paper fringe and tiny paper pennants. Place on the cart a doll-size suitcase from the dime store for each person at the table. The suitcases can hold—or be!—favors.

ON PROM DAY

Appoint at least ten boys and ten girls to set up the prepared decorations. Start early and bring your lunch—time flies!

HAWAIIAN HOP

It must be Paradise—the *gym* never looked like this! Behind the band-stand, which is surrounded with colorful spears, float gaily colored paper tropical fish. What used to be the basketball hoop has become a tall palm tree complete with orange and gold balloon coconuts. In front of it is a Hawaiian canoe surrounded with baby palm trees—here guests are having their pictures taken.

Refreshments are being served in a hut roofed with palm leaves. There's a cardboard volcano filled with sandwiches—over it erupt popcorn balls. Beside it is a mirror lagoon, surrounded with corn meal sand. On the lagoon float Coconut Pastry Boats, fruit filled. Tiny clothespin Hawaiians stand guard. The punch is served from a war drum and the paper cups mimic war masks.

It's going to be a marvelous evening! Here's how it happens:

For advance work: appoint an assembly crew to collect materials (card-board, bamboo poles, balloons, etc.) and an art committee to make the foil wall decorations, decorate the paper cups, cut out the palm leaves and dress the clothespin Hawaiians.

On the day of the dance: have at least eight boys and eight girls on hand to set up decorations.

THE REFRESHMENT HUT

Clothespin Hawaiians: Glue on tiny scrap-fabric *muumuus*, add pipe-cleaner arms, *leis*. Dress men in *lava-lavas*, use straw spears.

Tiny palm trees: Use brown pipe-cleaner trunks. Cut crepe paper leaves; glue onto pipe-cleaner center veins; twist ends onto trunk.

Lagoon: Use a dressing table mirror and surround with corn meal sand.

Foil mask, shield, fish: Outline on cardboard, cut out with razor knife. Decorate with foil gift wrap, using rubber cement to glue the foil.

Volcano: Tape empty coffee can to center of a large round platter. Now take a one-foot-wide strip of corrugated cardboard, tape one end to coffee can, bring other end of strip around in a funnel shape; tape firmly in place. With a razor knife, cut jagged peaks. Tape eight-inch-wide cardboard strip around platter; cut peaks. Make a bed for sandwiches with crumpled tissue paper. Add yellow and orange cellophane "flames." Suspend caramel popcorn balls on wire from canopy overhead; add bits of popcorn popping away from surface with toothpicks.

Palm leaf canopy for hut: Use large sheets of construction paper in two shades of green for leaves. Outline leaves (make about two feet long), cut out with a razor knife; fringe edges. Tie bamboo poles firmly to table legs; tack or tie clothesline on top of poles; staple leaves to clothesline.

Cover table with green burlap, slashing bottom. Trim table with about twelve paper *leis* from the dime store. Add carnations between the *leis*. Make these of accordion-pleated facial tissue colored with lipstick at edges. Pin to burlap.

Mask cups: Spread out cup handles, then tape foil around cup; fringe the foil. Use rubber cement to add foil mouth, other facial features to handles. Or add colored paper faces.

War drum punch bowl: Cover a large kettle with copper-toned foil gift wrap. Cut scalloped pieces of cardboard to fit around top and bottom of kettle. Punch holes in cardboard and run string through holes to give a laced drum effect. For drumsticks, use one short, scrubbed bamboo pole, one ladle. Cover ends with orange cloth, first padding ends to achieve drumstick look.

HAWAIIAN CANOE SETTING

Basketball palm tree: Beg a large cardboard linoleum tube from your local dealer. Fringe the edge of a twelve-inch-wide length of burlap; wind around tube and staple in place. Secure tube to basketball hoop; tape on orange and gold sprayed balloons. Make three-foot-long palm leaves (see palm leaf canopy, page 407) and tack to top of the cardboard tube.

Canoe: Cover a long wooden box with colored burlap. Cut the pointed ends of the boat from cardboard; cover with burlap; staple the ends together, then staple to box. Trim with leis, paper flowers.

Cut waves from heavy blue paper.

Plant little bamboo palm trees in buckets of sand; trim them the same as the basketball palm tree above.

Island Paradise Bandstand

Cover stand with burlap, slash the bottom. Nail bamboo poles to stand; add foil spear points. Tape foil fish (see under refreshment hut) onto wall and poles; drape with fish net.

INDEX

Index

4 0 9